MAIN STREET ON THE MIDDLE BORDER

Lewis Atherton was born in Bosworth, Missouri, and studied at the University of Oklahoma and the University of Missouri. He is the author of *The Pioneer Merchant in Mid-America*, *The Southern Country Store 1800-1860*, and *The Cattle Kings*, as well as numerous articles in historical journals. He is at present Professor of History at the University of Missouri, Columbia.

MAIN STREET
on the
Middle Border

By Lewis Atherton

Quadrangle/The New York Times Book Co.

THIRD PRINTING, 1975

MAIN STREET ON THE MIDDLE BORDER. © 1954 by
Indiana University Press. This book was originally published
in 1954 by Indiana University Press, Bloomington, and is
here reprinted by arrangement.

First QUADRANGLE PAPERBACK edition published 1966
by Quadrangle/The New York Times Book Co., 10 East 53
Street, New York, N.Y. 10022. Manufactured in the United
States of America.

ISBN: 0-8129-6043-2

Dedicated to:

THE D. N. CAULK FURNITURE AND MUSIC STORE
1916-1919
of BOSWORTH, MISSOURI

and

THE C. A. DAVIS GROCERY COMPANY 1921-1942
of BOSWORTH, MISSOURI

ACKNOWLEDGMENTS

Permission to use quoted material has been kindly granted by the publishers and agents noted. *The American Magazine*, "This is My America," Margaret Weymouth Jackson, February, 1933; *The American Mercury*, "Mid-Western Nights' Entertainment," Marquis W. Childs, October, 1928; Appleton-Century-Crofts, Inc., *Full Harvest*, Dora Aydelotte, copyright, 1939, D. Appleton-Century Co., Inc.; *The Atlantic Monthly*, "The Country Store," Charles M. Harger, January, 1905; *One Man's Life*, by Herbert Quick, copyright, 1925, 1953, used by special permission of the publishers, The Bobbs-Merrill Company, Inc.; *The Invisible Woman*, by Herbert Quick, copyright, 1924, 1952, used by special permission of the publishers, The Bobbs-Merrill Company, Inc.; Brandt & Brandt, *The Magnificent Ambersons*, published by Doubleday & Company, Inc., copyright, 1918, 1946 by Booth Tarkington, and *Morally We Roll Along*, published by Little, Brown & Company, copyright, 1938, by Gay MacLaren Backman; City Bank of Portage, Portage, Wisconsin, *Friendship Village Love Stories*, Zona Gale; *Collier's*, "The Caller from Collier's—What the Folks are Thinking About in Oskaloosa, Iowa," June 2, 1923, and "At the County Fair," Arthur Ruhl, August 16, 1913, and "The Old Home Town Fights to Live," Alfred H. Sinks, July 2, 1949; Coward-McCann, *Village Year: A Sac Prairie Journal*, August Derleth, 1941, reprinted by Stanton & Lee, Sauk City, Wisc., 1948; Dodd, Mead & Company, *Plain People*, Ed Howe, copyright, 1929, by Edgar Watson Howe, and *The Story of a Country Town*, Ed Howe, copyright, 1917, 1927, by Edgar Watson Howe; Doubleday & Company, *Sons of the Puritans*, Don Marquis, 1939; General Federation of Women's Clubs, *History of the General Federation of Women's Clubs*, Mary Wood, 1912; Harper and Brothers, *Autobiography*, Mark Twain, 1924, and *The Gilded Age*, Twain & Warner, 1915; House Beautiful Magazine, "A Village Street—Before and After," April, 1910; *Iowa Journal of History and Politics*, "The Evolution of the Agricultural Fair in the Northwest," Earle D. Ross, July, 1926; *Journal of Economic History*, "American Historian and the Business Elite," William Miller, November, 1949; *Kansas Historical Quarterly*,

viii   ACKNOWLEDGMENTS

"Eastern Kansas in 1869-1870," Paul H. Giddens, November, 1940; Alfred A.
Knopf, Inc., *Youth and the Bright Medusa,* Willa Cather, 1920; *Ladies' Home
Journal,* "Our Jazz-Spotted Middle West," John R. McMahon, February, 1922;
McGraw-Hill Book Company, Inc., *Rural Social Trends,* Bruner & Kolb, 1933;
The Macmillan Company, *Autobiography,* William Allen White, 1946, and
The American Commonwealth, James Bryce, 1891, and *A Son of the Middle
Border, Back-Trailers from the Middle Border, Rose of Dutcher's Coolly,
Afternoon Neighbors,* and *Daughter of the Middle Border,* Hamlin Garland;
W. W. Norton and Company, *Chosen Valley,* Margaret Snyder; *North Dakota
Historical Quarterly,* "The Great Dakota Boom," Harold E. Briggs, January,
1930; Harold Ober Associates, *Memoirs,* Sherwood Anderson, published by
Harcourt Brace in 1942; Oxford University Press, *Democracy in America,*
Alexis de Tocqueville (ed., Henry Steele Commager), 1947; The Ronald Press
Company, *The Course of American Democratic Thought,* Ralph H. Gabriel,
1940; *The Rotarian,* "Rotary is Thirty Years Old," Paul H. Harris, February,
1935; Scott, Foresman and Company, *People and Progress,* "Highwater in
Arkansas," Charles J. Finger; Charles Scribner's Sons, *The Circuit Rider,*
Edward Eggleston, 1902; *Survey Graphic,* "Want a Factory?" Dale Kramer,
August, 1940; The Viking Press, Inc., *Winesburg, Ohio,* Sherwood Ander-
son, 1949.

• Contents

❖ Introduction

AMERICANS EVERYWHERE think of country towns as museum pieces. They argue that Main Street has not only lost population, but also the hope, daring, and orginality necessary to fight back. They point to vacant store buildings and sagging, unpainted houses, to numerous old people vegetating in village homes, and to boys and girls anxiously looking forward to the time when they can join the rush to the cities. Even towns whose service clubs post signs proclaiming "The Friendliest, Biggest Little City in the Middle West," mock themselves with the futility of their claims. In confidential moments their businessmen admit that things are "dead" locally, and that nearby cities have prospered at their expense.

To offset these distressing opinions, villagers need to discover that country towns have more people today than in 1900, and that smaller villages possess farm loyalty, their greatest asset, more than ever before. And even "live wires," intent on escaping to the city, love the pleasures of village life.

Why then the defeatist attitude? Why do residents and non-residents alike think that country towns are finished? To know why is to know the basic hopes and convictions of country towns, and, in many ways, the hopes and convictions of America as well. Spawned by an agricultural frontier, where idealism, optimism, materialism, and an abiding faith in progress were strangely intermingled, every country town expected to become an enormous city of fabulous wealth. Every town believed and still believes in "progress," but progress in terms of *growth* in numbers and real-estate prices. Every town believed and still believes in the "cult of the immediately useful and the practical." Every town sought and still seeks unobtainable goals, and perhaps even false goals. The result has been disillusionment and lethargy.

To understand small towns one needs to know their hopes and philosophies. One needs also to ponder alternatives which men and women as diverse as Mark Twain and Zona Gale, Edgar Lee Masters and William Allen White offer in stories and autobiographies growing out of their own village childhoods. And, of course, one should know the pleasure and pain of day-to-day village life. When Sherwood Anderson accused Sinclair Lewis of having missed the boyhood pleasure of kissing his girl goodnight, with her father standing just inside the porch door, and the excitement of the home run which defeated a rival town, he recognized how important so-called trifles can be in shaping one's reaction to village ways.

This book is a cultural and economic history of midwestern country towns from 1865 to 1950. The Middle Border, as I have defined it, consists of Ohio, Indiana, Illinois, Missouri, Michigan, Minnesota, Wisconsin, and Iowa and the eastern farming fringe of Kansas, Nebraska, and the Dakotas. Studies of American regionalism by Howard W. Odum and others as early as the 1930's described this area as a unit on the basis of various measurements. I have defined the term "country town" and its synonyms in terms of functions. If a town has been primarily a service center for farmers it has been included, although in general my examination has been limited to places of less than 5,000 population. I have also tried to deal primarily with towns outside the range of "standard metropolitan districts," as they are defined by the 1950 census, because other studies have shown that such towns differ from those located within the orbit of cities. It is not always possible to structure historical studies perfectly. Rockville, Indiana, which is mentioned frequently in the following pages, has been greatly influenced by neighboring cities, and Greencastle, Indiana, to which reference is made in its earlier years, is certainly no longer a country town if it ever belonged in that classification. My only excuse for lapses from the general scheme of selection and handling of material rests on paucity of records and an awareness on my part of the dangers involved in such departures.

I am indebted to the University of Missouri Research Council for a Summer Research Professorship in 1948 and for additional subsequent grants to facilitate my efforts. A Newberry Library Fellowship in Midwestern Studies and sabbatical leave from the University of Missouri enabled me to spend the academic year 1950-51 on the project. As one scholar who likes "to go it alone" in an era of group research, I am deeply appreciative of the help extended to me by my own university and by foundations. Dr. Stanley Pargellis, Librarian of the Newberry Library, and Mr. Fred D. Wieck, formerly of the Newberry Library, kindly read my first draft and suggested improvements in style. To both I wish to express my appreciation. To Mrs. Judith Buress, formerly secretary of the history department of the University of Missouri, I am indebted for typing drafts of my manuscript.

As to sources, I have tried to read all the reminiscences, autobiographies, and novels depicting the region and period of which I am writing. I think I have seen virtually all of the magazine articles and scholarly studies on my subject. I have spot-checked at least one country newspaper in each of the eight states wholly included in my region of study and I have used nothing from newspaper sources which was not confirmed in more than one paper. Location of manuscripts cited in the book is given in the first footnote reference to them. Newspaper files were used in the following libraries: Iowa State Department of History and Archives, Des Moines; State Historical Society of Wisconsin, Madison; Burton Historical Collection, Detroit Public Library; Indiana State Library and Historical Society, Indianapolis; Illinois State Library, Springfield; Minnesota Historical Society, Minneapolis; State Historical Society of Missouri, Columbia; Historical and Philosophical Society of Ohio, Cincinnati; and The Ohio State Archaeological and Historical Society, Columbus.

I have tried to avoid making this another "I remember" story by eliminating my own personal experiences in midwestern country towns and oral traditions of my family going back to the Civil War and before in Ohio and Missouri. Nonetheless, my own interest in research has been determined by family background and I have also felt more competent to judge the records and experiences of others when my own family has participated in so many of the same things. I was born in Bosworth, Missouri, in 1905, and moved at the age of six with my family to my grandfather's farm in Carroll county. I attended high school in the county-seat town of Carrollton, six miles away. Fourth of July celebrations, Christmas programs, county fairs, Chautauquas, where I heard "Cyclone" Davis and other headliners of the day, funerals, weddings, and all the other social activities of rural and village life were open to me as a youngster.

Two of my brothers-in-law operated stores in Bosworth, Missouri, for a period of years, which provided still another contact with life in the country town. One brother-in-law, D. N. Caulk, sold Kimball pianos and Columbia graphonolas as well as furniture. On vacation trips to Bosworth I spent many pleasant afternoons pumping music rolls on player pianos, listening to "Uncle Josh" or Hawaiian records, and watching demonstrations of musical instruments. Another brother-in-law, C. A. Davis, operated a grocery store for many years. He and his wife frequently sang at country funerals, and farmers visited for long hours in his store. When business activity reached a peak on Saturday nights I sometimes candled eggs in the back of the building or filled vinegar and kerosene jugs and cans. On quieter days, I listened to conversation around the single stove which warmed the whole store. From this brother-in-law and his friends I heard story after story about the history of Bosworth and competing communities. In his own experiences, he exemplified the adaptability of the small-town merchant. When one customer complained of an aching tooth, he sterilized a pair of pliers in a pan of hot water on top of his stove and then extracted the offending molar. An elderly farmer who heard of the operation asked for similar attention. Just as my brother-in-law was ready to use the pliers, the old gentleman terminated a budding career as a dentist for him by remarking, "Art, I sure do appreciate this. My heart just won't stand climbing them stairs to the dentist's office."

After my father's death, my mother joined the circle of elderly people in Bosworth and I came to know their interests and activities from first-hand observation and participation. In returning to my home town at vacation periods and in hearing conversation in my brother-in-law's store and elsewhere, the whole pattern of my own family's life took on new meaning. I also taught for a year in high school in a midwestern country town and served on the faculty of a private boarding school in a county seat town for another six. All this alone did not qualify me to speak as an authority. The following pages contain the experiences and thoughts of other towns and other families than my own. But I have been impressed by how much this parallels what my own family and I saw and experienced in our own midwestern community.

LEWIS ATHERTON

University of Missouri

MAIN STREET ON THE MIDDLE BORDER

I ❈ Early Days on the Middle Border

FOUNDATIONS

THE HISTORY of the Middle Border has been largely the history of its towns. Even today, when automobiles have greatly reduced the necessity for decentralized trade centers, villages a few miles apart speckle the midwestern countryside. Their bleary, naked street lights seem constantly in view at night from the streamliner's window, and they are found hugging the sides of country roads, no matter what bypath the tourist may take.

Their location and growth depended on a combination of factors, some as old as recorded history, others as new as the agricultural frontier itself. Farmers on foot, or with horses and oxen, had to shop within a radius of six to twelve miles in order to return home to care for livestock before nightfall. Slow and primitive transportation thus required the presence of market towns every few miles. The first store in such a village was likely to contain a post office to serve farmers who had to ride once or twice a week for mail—rural free delivery was still in the future. Farmers also rode horseback with a bag of grain across the withers of their mounts to obtain corn meal from the gristmills that dotted the countryside. Here, too, opportunities for retail trade often resulted in the founding of a store, and perhaps of a blacksmith shop to repair or to rebuild the limited and precious farm equipment of the early days. Such opportunities encouraged the establishment of villages at close intervals, and became the basis for survival when flush frontier days of town promotion had passed.

It would be a mistake, however, to assume that midwestern country towns were born of reasoned conviction. Settlement proceeded at a rapid pace. When the Black Hawk purchase opened Iowa to farmers in 1832, a frantic rush of settlers replaced trappers and fur traders. By the outbreak of the Civil War the state was one-third settled; by 1890, its free lands were gone. Such rapid occupation of rich, western lands encouraged dreams of great cities, extravagant speculation in town real estate, and the creation of country villages in excessive numbers. Many towns advanced no farther than the planning stage; others grew feverishly, only to join the long list of ghost towns when new rivals, changes in transportation, or unexpected complications blighted them. Heroic struggles of small groups of settlers against wilderness and Indians have stimulated the imagination of historians and novelists. Although the death struggle of midwestern country towns was on the whole more prosaic, they, too, battled to survive in an atmosphere which spawned them in reckless and fickle optimism.

Perhaps such a development was inevitable. The early settlers wanted neighbors, churches, and schools, and they were correct in believing that a growing population would foster these. Every effort was made to attract people and to sell them a town lot or a farm.

As early as 1852 the state of Wisconsin established a Commissioner of Immigration in New York City to promote settlement. Thousands of pamphlets describing Wisconsin's resources and opportunities were printed in German, Norwegian, and Dutch. Five thousand of these were sent to Europe and twenty thousand more were distributed on vessels, in taverns, and directly to immigrants in the port of New York. In 1853 Wisconsin appointed another agent to advertise the state among Americans. In one year he travelled over 42,000 miles, visited every important city in the northern states and eastern Canada, and nearly every village in New York and New England. Wisconsin notices were placed in over 900 newspapers. Although Wisconsin abandoned promotional efforts in 1855, she resumed them with renewed vigor in 1867, when other midwestern states were beginning to adopt similar programs.

State agencies contributed to the speculative mania which characterized the town frontier. A Wisconsin pamphlet in 1867 described the state as healthy, fertile, well-watered, well-wooded, and rapidly growing; farmers owned their own land and honest labor always provided a living; land was cheap, property was constantly increasing in value, and every man had a voice in government. In such phrases the Middle West courted immigration. By the 1890's attention was shifting toward preventing newer areas from "exploiting" settlers away from much of the Middle West, but the frontier stretching beyond—in the Dakotas, for example—continued into the twentieth century to boast of unlimited opportunities.[1]

Railroads also had a stake in promoting immigration. Though eastern lines profited from transporting European immigrants to new western homes,[2] midwestern railroads were still more involved. Some had received grants of public land to aid construction and wanted to convert their holdings to cash. Moreover, since all were inclined to build ahead of settlement, they had to foster immigration if they wanted passengers and freight.

Unlike the states, railroads often were directly involved in town-site speculation. When the Illinois Central Railroad received the first federal land grant in 1850, it decided to establish stations approximately every ten miles along its tracks. An amendment to the charter in 1851 forbidding the corporation to lay out towns on or near its line made necessary the creation of another organization to achieve the same end and to reserve all profits for the promoters. A station site would be quietly located on government land along the road, which was then purchased by an agent of the group at low prices since it was not publicly known that a depot would be established.

Construction of freight and passenger stations brought a swarm of tradesmen and mechanics to purchase lots. The Chicago branch best illustrates the rapid development of country towns through such means. Prior to 1850 only three settlements existed along this route. Twenty years later, twenty-eight cities and towns of sufficient size to be reported in the census had developed around the stations on the Illinois Central, thirteen of which had been laid out by the railroad associates. Manteno's rapid growth was typical of all. In October, 1854, Manteno had no houses. By the next June, sixteen had been built and a considerable freight and passenger traffic had developed. Grain elevators, gristmills, lumberyards, stores and hotels brought population needed to service the agricultural hinterland. By 1860 the town had 861 people; by 1870 it had grown to 1,681.

The Illinois Central used a standardized plan for all villages. Streets running east and west were named after trees; those running north and south were numbered. Prices of blocks and lots were determined by distance from the center of town and from the station. The historian of the Illinois Central's colonization activities estimates that it made over a half million dollars from its town-site business.[3]

Later roads pursued much the same basic pattern as the Illinois Central. In many instances, the Northern Pacific retained full ownership of town sites and used its own land department to sell lots, but in some cases it kept only a half-interest and let private parties handle sales. Much of the drab monotony of prairie towns comes from the uniform plan of buildings originally mapped out in a railroad office. The box-like station, the grain elevator, the water tank, and the inevitable Main Street were a part of virtually all.[4] And always, of course, the very nature of such promotion contributed to the speculative mania of the western town frontier.

Wealthy promoters from older states and land corporations also contributed to the speculative nature of town development. Since their operations were more limited than those of states and railroad companies, their plans could more easily be adjusted to unusual local conditions. All were inclined, however, to seek railroad connections for their newly plotted town sites and to subsidize a few business establishments. In 1871 Edwin Clark offered to give a free right-of-way and the choice of a third of the town lots in his new town of Melrose, Minnesota, to the St. Paul and Pacific Railroad in return for a passenger and freight depot and a guarantee that no other station would be established within six miles.[5]

Solomon G. Comstock of Moorhead, Minnesota, operated in much the same way. He lived near the Dakota frontier, served as agent in obtaining the right-of-way for the St. Paul, Minneapolis and Manitoba Railroad, and represented the Northern Pacific in a case involving indemnity lands—all of which provided opportunities for land speculation. In 1883 he and a partner incorporated the Northwest Land Company to sell land in Minnesota and in the territories of Dakota and Montana. Comstock offered to donate town lots to newspaper publishers, blacksmiths, and other businessmen who would agree to erect buildings.[6] After a few business establishments had been obtained through such means, a promoter could advertise his town as a going concern.

A constantly changing variety of technological and transportation factors stimulated booms on new frontiers. Dakota territory underwent such a boom between 1879 and 1886. From the establishment of its first land office until June 30, 1880, a period of eighteen years, the number of pre-emptions and claims filed was only 44,122; but from the taking of the census of 1880 to December 31, 1881, less than nineteen months, 16,718 claims were entered. Population increased from 135,177 in 1880 to about 330,000 in 1883. Rising real-estate prices in other states and a cycle of increased rainfall locally made Dakota land more attractive.[7] Introduction of hard spring wheat and the roller-milling process seemed to promise increased prosperity for Dakota settlers. Railroad extensions into Dakota territory, accompanied by the usual railroad, private, and governmental promotion of colonization, increased the appeal of this new frontier to farmers.

Since the opening of new frontiers was advertised widely in midwestern country newspapers year after year, existing towns had trouble in attracting settlers. Asa C. Call arrived on the site of Algona, Iowa, in 1854 with the intention of investing in western lands. Typically American, Call had travelled widely to investigate real-estate opportunities before he selected Algona as his home and erected the first house. He was born in Ohio, lived in New York and Indiana for a time, and had spent four years in California.[8] Though Call made a fortune from Iowa real estate, he and other Algona citizens spent several anxious years before they were sure that their town would survive. Indian depredations as late as 1861, a grasshopper plague, and inadequate transportation injured Algona's prospects. In 1867, at the end of thirteen years of effort, Algona had only four hundred people.

Newspaper editors were quick to defend their home communities, especially so when there was a danger of losing inhabitants to other places. In the spring of 1867 the Algona editor pointed out that local thermometer readings for the past winter had been honestly reported to the Smithsonian Institution and suggested that other frontier towns had been less than honest in describing their weather conditions. He claimed to have information from people who "knew" that the past winter in Wisconsin, Illinois, Missouri, and Kansas had been very severe. Farmers moving to those places in quest of an earlier spring would be severely disappointed. In July, 1867, he published an article headed "Not Satisfied with Missouri," in which a local man who had moved to Missouri and had "seen the elephant" explained why Algona was superior. The editor said that the article would "show" the few remaining "impatients."[9] Here was an infant community in the heart of good farming land already feeling the pangs of competition from newer frontiers.

Ten years later, in 1877, Algona had grown considerably, but the local editor still worried about competition from Eldorados on beyond. A small advertisement in the Algona paper by the Texas Immigration Agent in St. Louis, offering to send pamphlets, maps, and circulars to prospective immigrants, and perhaps some local expression of interest in Texas, led the editor to publish a report on the Southwest. He included comments from an "unhappy" Iowan, now in Texas, to the effect that grasshoppers were worse in Texas than they had ever been in Iowa. The state lacked good water. Moreover, in Texas parlance, a free country was synonymous with free whiskey and licentiousness generally. Texas women used tobacco in all forms, even snuff.[10]

Advertisements of new frontiers continued to appear no matter how much criticism they aroused among defenders of older communities.[11] A six-inch advertisement by the land department of the Northern Pacific Railroad in the Algona paper in 1896 illustrates the appeal of new frontiers. It was headed "Your Wife Wants a Home." Why, ran the argument, should a man pay three dollars an acre yearly rent when for a cost of $2.50 to $4.00 an acre, payable over a ten-year period, he could own good land outright? Settlers could choose from level land, rolling prairie, or timber. Dingley, Cook and Company, an Algona real-estate firm, had arranged to accompany customers on trips to the new country.[12]

Advertising campaigns continued into the twentieth century in spite of rapid settlement. In 1908 the Pacific Coast extension of the Chicago, Milwaukee and St. Paul Railroad advertised eight free pamphlets on land in the Dakotas, Montana, Idaho, and Washington. One pamphlet explained how to obtain government homesteads free. The railroad was running Homeseekers' Excursions at special low fares for those "interested in success and future independence."[13] Local real-estate agents also began to promote excursion trips to places that had been somewhat neglected in the first rush of settlement. Hull, Yowell and Company of Gallatin, Missouri, in 1908 and 1909 sponsored a series of full-page advertisements describing real-estate opportunities in Coffey County, Kansas. These emphasized what "chumps" local citizens had been for failing to invest more heavily in Gallatin lands, which had increased greatly in value over the past ten to twenty years. But there was no need to be a "chump" twice; the same opportunity now existed in Kansas for anyone sufficiently alert to grasp it.[14] Moreover, virgin frontiers still beckoned to those who sought free land. The Hastings, Michigan, paper in 1910 contained a large advertisement, sponsored by the Canadian government, promising to send on request a free pamphlet labelled "Last Best West." Canada was offering homesteads of 160 acres and an additional 160 could be pre-empted at three dollars an acre. Many farmers, according to the advertisement, had paid for their land out of the first crop.[15]

Though common stock and oil wells now rival real-estate speculation, they have not replaced it, partly because so many generations of Americans pinned their hopes for wealth on rising land values. Whether they won or lost, their activity gave meaning to the phrase "doing a land-office business." Frenzied speculation, often with little consideration for truth or honesty, gave point to Mark Twain's satirical novel, *The Gilded Age*. Twain depicted the promoter, Colonel Beriah Sellers, whose enthusiasm for western lands and railroads blinded him to the difficulties involved and the shoddy methods employed in achieving his ends. The Colonel expressed his optimism in a letter to relatives and friends, urging them to join him in the Middle West:

Come right along to Missouri! Don't wait and worry about a good price, but sell out for whatever you can get, and come along, or you might be too late. Throw away your traps, if necessary, and come empty-handed. You'll never regret it. It's the grandest country—the loveliest land—the purest atmosphere—I can't describe it; no pen can do it justice. And it's filling up every day—

people coming from everywhere. I've got the biggest scheme on earth—and I'll take you in; I'll take in every friend I've got that's ever stood by me, for there's enough for all, and to spare. Mum's the word—don't whisper—keep yourself to yourself. You'll see! Come!—rush!—hurry!—don't wait for anything! [16]

There was the story of Stone's Landing, which became the City of Napoleon—on paper! And the surveyor of the railroad, which had everything but the rails and the iron horse, who could sight from the top of one divide to the top of another and strike "plumb" every town site and big plantation within twenty or thirty miles of his route. In his own language, he "just went booming." Like the Colonel, he was inclined to magnify the virtues of the countryside. In his estimation, if Columbus River, alias Goose Run, could be "widened, and deepened, and straightened, and made long enough, it would be one of the finest rivers in the Western country." [17]

Rootless, new and raw, booming and optimistic, the human tide swept across the Middle West. It took courage to remain behind when reports of fabulous developments on the frontier drifted back to older, settled communities. In the late 1860's the Franklin, Pennsylvania, *Venango Spectator* furnished subscribers complete information on the drilling of the first oil well some twenty miles away and the subsequent excitement along Oil Creek. Despite the sensational nature of these events, they failed to monopolize the columns of the *Spectator*, which frequently printed letters from persons who were either visiting or settling beyond the Mississippi. Letters about Colorado, Minnesota, Nebraska, Iowa, Kansas, and other western places emphasized the old theme of land and town-site speculation.

A letter written by "R" from Girard in Crawford County, Kansas, appeared on May 13, 1870. Girard, said the writer, had ceased to be a railroad terminus since track had now been laid to the state line at Baxter Springs, forty miles south. Gamblers, streetwalkers, the floating population, and mushroom business houses had also moved on but Girard still had 900 people. In "R's" opinion, western towns of 500 to 1,000 people would do as much business as eastern places of 4,000 to 8,000. Land prices locally were constantly rising and would be from 50 to 100 per cent higher in a year. Bitter contests were now under way among rival towns to determine which would obtain the county court house, and all the advantages of serving as the seat of local government. "R" had frequently been asked about the principal limitations of the region, but could think of nothing which it lacked.

In a second letter, published on May 27, 1870, "R" described the excitement at Baxter Springs over the arrival of the Missouri River, Fort Scott and Gulf Railroad. At the moment, Baxter Springs was a real boom town. Although the people had forgotten to build churches, they had a nice brewery and over fifty saloons. At one of these "R" counted twenty tables, all occupied by men playing cards for the drinks, which were served by "polite lady waiters." A raised platform containing a piano and several musicians stood in one corner. In another, a healthy looking chap wearing a plug hat and diamond studs was dealing faro to as many gamblers as could crowd around his table. But all this was only temporary:

The trade of Baxter is already large and is rapidly increasing. Considerable government freighting is done from this point and before long the Texas cattle trade, already large, will be immense. Valuable lead mines have been discovered near the place . . . and the time is not far distant when the magnificent water power of the Spring river will turn many a shaft and spindle. I think I do not exaggerate when I say that in two years Baxter Springs will be the metropolis of southern Kansas.[18]

The same feverish spirit marked the birth of towns on the Dakota frontier in the early eighties. The editor of the *Devils Lake Democrat* on December 11, 1884, said:

Two years ago the number of inhabitants in Ramsey county did not exceed twenty, and today the county takes rank with the best in the Territory. Devils Lake, eighteen months old, is a city of 1,000 people with a city government, fire department, a United States land office, and with substantial brick places of business and handsome residences, while the surrounding prairies are dotted with shacks and substantial farm buildings.

Every town expected to become the county seat. In several counties official records were captured by violence with that in mind. Many towns also hoped to become the capital of the future state. Towns grew rapidly, but they disappeared as quickly. A gazetteer for 1881 dismissed Huron, which rapidly became an important town, with a few lines, but devoted thirty lines to describing Jamesville in Yankton county, which soon disappeared.[19]

When James Bryce visited America in the 1880's, the town frontier centered in Dakota and beyond. Bryce quickly recognized the spirit of optimism and boom which had accompanied town-site speculation from the beginning. He was present in 1883 when the youthful town of Bismarck laid the cornerstone of what it hoped would soon become the state capitol. The building was located on the top of a hill in the brown and dusty prairie, almost a mile from the city limits. Bryce thought that the surrounding land had been reserved for a public park but was told that it would be needed for future population. This capitol burned in 1930, and when rebuilt as a nineteen-story skyscraper, it was placed nearer the city. Realism had prevailed at last. In Bryce's day, excessive optimism was commonplace, as another comment of his indicated:

Many a place has lived upon its "boom" until it found something more solid to live on; and to a stranger who asked in a small Far Western town how such a city could keep up four newspapers, it was well answered that it took four newspapers to keep up such a city.[20]

Bryce decided that America's rapid settlement had encouraged all citizens to become speculators. In his estimation, American life was comparable to that of a squirrel in his revolving cage, never still even when it did not seem to change.[21]

LOST GENERATIONS

THE INFLUENCE of this boom-or-bust philosophy, this constant starting over, this eternal looking to the future, this concern with material accomplishments is most clearly revealed in terms of individual families and individual towns, even though the process affected no two towns or families in exactly the same way. Hamlin Garland's family shows the impact as well as any, and Garland himself has obligingly provided a virtually complete record of its experiences and thoughts in six volumes of family biography. As a clannish folk, the Garlands lacked the extroverted love of fellow man and innate zest for life which made William Allen White's father happy on the midwestern frontier. The gnawing ambitions and frustrations of the Garland family illuminate, however, both the dreams and the limitations of midwestern small-town and country culture.

Garland's earliest recollections go back to his childhood home in a little Wisconsin coulee near the village of Onalaska where his grandparents and other relatives lived. As a lumber town, Onalaska had the usual number of saloons and deeds of violence, but Garland was more impressed by the school which he attended. His family lived comfortably and had no need to join the westward migration, except for a pioneering streak in his father's character, accentuated perhaps by the fact that his parents before him had migrated to Wisconsin. The Garlands loved music. On request, Hamlin's mother would sing of the debate between husband and wife concerning the advantages of frontier life. Hamlin's father sympathized with the husband's urge to seek wealth in new surroundings:

> Away to Colorado a journey I'll go,
> For to double my fortune as other men do,
> *While here I must labor each day in the field*
> *And the winter consumes all the summer doth yield.*

But Mrs. Garland agreed with the wife's opinion of such ambitions:

> Dear husband, I've noticed with a sorrowful heart
> That you long have neglected your plow and your cart,
> Your horses, sheep, cattle at random do run,
> And your new Sunday jacket goes every day on.
> *Oh, stay on your farm and you'll suffer no loss,*
> *For the stone that keeps rolling will gather no moss.*

Such advice displeased the Garlands. A more buoyant refrain became the marching song of three generations of the family as it moved west:

> Then o'er the hills in legions, boys,
> Fair freedom's star
> Points to the sunset regions, boys,
> Ha, ha, ha-ha! [22]

Before long the Garlands were living in a log house on a farm two miles west of Hesper, Iowa. Even this was temporary. A visiting Englishman, who wanted to try wilderness farming, offered more than Garland had paid for the land, and a deal was soon made. The father now travelled for several weeks in southern Minnesota and northern Iowa looking for a new location. His choice was a quarter section of land in Mitchell County, Iowa, near the town of Osage.

Here the family moved into a new home built of pine lumber, with three rooms below and a garret above. Garland remembered it as standing naked on the sod, as devoid of grace as a dry goods box—the beginning of his dislike for frame houses. As time went on, he returned again and again to the theme of wooden houses, ephemeral things, whereas stone represented permanence. Although seemingly unaware of deeper meanings in his preferences, he was beginning to express his resentment against the constant change and the rootless nature of his family life.

Within a short time the family was farming 300 acres of land, owned a herd of cattle and many hogs, and had become leaders in the local community. Garland's mother and sister now asked for a "best room," an organ, and an ingrain carpet, and all wanted a spring wagon, the first fruits of prosperity on the Iowa farm frontier. In the middle 1870's the Garlands moved to Osage so the father could serve as elevator manager for the local Grange organization. Town and country life were much the same. Although the Garlands noticed the greater ease, comfort and sociability of village life, they adjusted easily and quickly to its tempo. They took several cows and a span of horses with them to Osage. Tilling the large garden connected with their home at the edge of town and work on the Garland farm during the summer months kept Hamlin thoroughly familiar with agricultural ways.

Although Mrs. Garland and the children liked Osage, it was only an interlude in the family's long migration. In 1877 they returned to the farm. Chinch bugs soon began to injure the Iowa wheat crop, and farmers had to turn to general farming. The Dakota boom was under way, however, and Hamlin's father could not resist moving there in the early 1880's. The family was already beginning to break up. An uncle had located in the Missouri valley, another had gone to Georgia, and one grandfather and his daughters now lived in western Minnesota. When Garland's parents made the Dakota move, he and a younger brother began to develop a life of their own—Hamlin in the direction of a literary career and the brother as an actor.

In furthering these ambitions, the brothers moved eastward even while the parents were settling still farther west on the agricultural frontier. Hamlin was to spend six years reading, studying, and teaching in a Boston school of expression before he made a return visit to the West.

Garland's literary career grew directly out of his childhood experiences. His best books described agricultural life on the Middle Border frontier, and he later supplemented his income by lectures on the same subject. Garland deeply loved his parents and relatives, but their rootless migrations and dispersals to new frontiers deprived him of any sense of a real family home. They were literally wanderers in the Middle Border, a part of it only in the same ephemeral sense that multitudes of others belonged to the new states being created. The resulting civilization was new not only because much land remained unsettled until late in the nineteenth century; constant moving prevented many people from taking hold of even the limited sense of stability possible for those who remained in one spot. Osage, Iowa, was an infant community in comparison with villages in the East; for the Garlands it was only an episode in a long migration. Interpreters of American life like to speak of its newness in terms of time elapsed since the arrival of settlers at Jamestown. But America was never more than ten years old to people like the Garlands who wandered over the whole of the country without putting down roots anywhere.

Even those who remained in one locality felt the pressure of the constant stream of transients that flowed around them. Small towns acquired their old families rapidly—people who had lived there for a whole generation! And even they were affected by the technological revolution which constantly battered and reshaped their community. Like the Garlands, they saw their children choose careers differing from their own, thus lessening the sense of stability and continuity which all societies crave.

Hamlin Garland wanted his parents to have a family home, partly, perhaps, to satisfy his own needs. Moderate literary success enabled him to visit his father's Dakota homestead with that in mind. The barren, treeless surroundings and his mother's precarious health convinced him that he must act immediately if he expected to achieve his dream. But first a visit to California, a trip which appealed to his father's urge to move westward. While age had halted him in Dakota, a brother had moved from Iowa to Dakota, to Montana, and on to California. As a boy, Hamlin had admired the giant physique of this uncle and, like his parents, was greatly shocked at the aged and broken man, now working as a day laborer, whom they met on their California visit. Here was proof of the wife's lament in the ballad: *"For the stone that keeps rolling will gather no moss."*

His parents could now appreciate the charm of the two-story frame cottage nestling on a four-acre plot of rich, level ground at West Salem, Wisconsin, which Garland purchased as a family home. His description of this revealed Garland's own nostalgia for his youth, for a permanent family home. The house was sheltered on the south by three enormous maples, and the front gate opened on a double row of New England elms whose branches almost arched over the wide village street. Grape vines, asparagus beds, plums, raspberries and other fruiting shrubs appealed to his mother who had lived so long on sun-baked plains. To his parents, "The leafy village, so green, so muddy, so lush with grass, seemed the perfection of restful security. The chuckle of robins on the lawns, the songs of catbirds in the plum trees and the whistle of larks in the pasture appealed to them as parts of a familiar sweet and homely hymn." [23] From the west windows the family could look out on the wooded hills where Hamlin had played as a boy. Lilac, syringa and snowball, and beds of old-fashioned flowers revived memories of other days. Perhaps now this son of the Middle Border who had pondered its history and was to chronicle its pioneer years could sink family roots where his father had failed.

His marriage to Zulime Taft, sister of the famous Chicago sculptor, Lorado Taft, and herself a former Paris art student, only encouraged his dream, for her own childhood involved memories of a small Kansas town. Garland met her after he moved to Chicago in 1893—following nine happy years in Boston and New York—in order to live near his parents at West Salem.

The dream was too shallow-rooted to survive. For all its rural beauty, West Salem could not give Garland the peace and stability which he craved. The fault was partly his. He cut himself off from the life of the village, except for the friends of his parents, only to discover that he lived with a dying generation. Moreover, his own rootless childhood made him a wanderer in spite of his craving for permanence and stability. West Salem, too, was at fault. Garland never fully understood why the village meant little to him apart from his parents, but his visits to England at a later date should have enlightened him. There he found stone buildings, centuries old, symbolizing England's past. The clammy mustiness of these palled on him during a second English visit, since they were only distantly connected with his own cultural heritage. Garland never mentioned visits to old landmarks in West Salem. Even midwestern preachers defined progress in terms of bigness, newness, and change—more members and a new church building. If they could add a hundred people to the congregation and build a new church, God was sure to call them to larger and more remunerative fields. As a result, the Garlands, typifying the lost generations of the Middle West, found no church where they could worship in surroundings hallowed by memories of their parents.

The death of Garland's mother made him restless and left his father a bewildered old man. The latter, too, was looking for stability in his declining years. Hamlin took him back to visit Osage, Iowa, but both were astounded at how few people they knew, although they had been gone thirty years. Most of his father's friends were dead or had moved. The few remaining groped for a sense of permanence in their brief visit with this companion of former years. And again, the Garlands found no churches or other landmarks to ease the ache of human frailty.

At the age of fifty-four Garland took his own family to New York. Because the change symbolized the failure of his dreams, Garland tried to justify the move in various ways. After all, he was only following the back trail of other men of letters. Howells and John Hay had begun it; Eggleston, Twain and Harte had followed. The move would put him in touch with publishers and his literary market. The West had never paid or published him, and he needed to be near his fellow writers. But he still felt guilty. By the

1920's he was accusing himself of spiritual degeneration because he could not endure the thought of living in a small town or an inland city. At times he added up the advantages of city life, only to burst out:

No! I am not *entirely* content. Deep down in my consciousness is a feeling of guilt, a sense of disloyalty to my ancestors, which renders me uneasy. It may be that this is only a survival of the mental habit of my boyhood, a tribute to my father and his self-reliant generation.[24]

Garland was excusing and condoning his desertion of the Middle West in a comment concerning the whole American people: "We hardly know our need, but that need we know." [25] In other passages he clearly stated the rootless nature of midwestern (and even American) culture and the impact of technology which made it difficult for country towns to develop a sense of continuity:

Our new and hustling cities, our barbed-wire lanes, our monotonous towns and villages create an aching hunger for the age-worn, the vine-clad, the storied. Eager to escape newness, ugliness and uniformity, we go to Italy, to France, to England, but the life we find there is, after all, alien and remote, whereas in a house like those of Old Deerfield we feel ourselves in the immediate presence of our forebears. In seeking the places where poetry still lingers, where something exists which is distinguished and our own, we are paying tribute to those who were trailmakers in another and earlier fashion.[26]

And again:

My own life is not yet a long life but I have seen more of change in certain directions than all the men from Julius Caesar to Abraham Lincoln. I have seen the reaping hook develop into the combined reaper and thresher, the oxteam give way to the automobile, the telegraph to the radio, and the balloon to the flying ship. I have witnessed the installation of electric light, the coming of concrete highways, and the establishment of airmail. Television is certain to arrive tomorrow.[27]

Garland apparently decided that a sense of continuity could not be found in midwestern culture. In his estimation, contentment with an inland American town could arise only from lack of knowledge, resignation born of need, or "deep philosophy."

Life at West Salem had disillusioned him. The villagers were progressive. New ideas appealed to them and they liked fads. When the mail-order houses told them that brass beds were more sanitary, more modern and shinier than the beautiful wooden beds in which their parents had conceived them, they tossed away their old furniture. They wanted nothing to do with outmoded ideas. Consequently, they were surprised when Garland decided to build a rough brick fireplace inside his home. Did he expect to heat the house by that means, and wouldn't it be expensive to do so? To them fireplaces, if remembered at all, recalled cold and drafty rooms. Garland discovered that the art of building fireplaces had been lost. The first carpenter consulted had never done such work; the second had helped put in one hard-coal wall pocket; and the third had seen fireplaces in Norway but remembered little of their construction. Finally, the local plasterer agreed to try, and with Garland's help succeeded in completing the work.

Unable to develop a feel for West Salem life, Garland chose to escape. The home at West Salem was sold and another was purchased in the Catskills to avoid the summer heat of New York City. He and his family travelled abroad. Ironically, in his declining years, he moved to the Valhalla of prosperous Midwesterners, California, where he built a "Monterey Colonial casa" for a home. What an ending for a man who had devoted his life to writing and lecturing about the pioneers of the Middle Border!

Rootless to the end, Garland accepted a hodge-podge of ideas and opinions from various sources—middle western, eastern, American, European. He felt most at home among the "blond, blue-eyed people" of England and disliked to see Jewish and Slavic faces among marching American soldiers in England during World War I. He proclaimed himself an intellectual aristocrat, with no faith in a "democratic

art." He thrilled over a moonlight visit to (
with an Indian Maharajah, and carefully o
tesies due such royalty. He was ashame
when only one member of the English d
University of Wisconsin wore a dinner ja
for him when he received an honorary de
Ida Tarbell could send him away deeply ir
calm, clear, authoritative nature of her co
ciple of order and stability, he liked her
sense of grandeur and order being broug
chief citizen, Benito Mussolini, with his "[
veltian pervasiveness." Still, George Berna
ment at his interest in royalty could mak
able, and the condition of the English lowe
him.

A common interest in early midwestern l
ship with Henry Ford. Ford undoubtedly
Garland's debasement in his presence aro:
less conflict of wealth versus humanism w
plague the Middle West:

We talked as we walked, easily and without the slightest failure
to understand each other, so alike are his origin and mine. His
life on the farm, his schooling in a district schoolhouse, and the
position of his parents among his neighbors are very like my own.
There our likeness ends. He is a colossal genius, I am merely an
industrious writer of obscure books; and yet he did not appear to
despise me for my failure to make money.[28]

EARLY TOWNS

ROOTLESS, new and raw, the Middle Border neglected
cultural values and devoted little time to reflective thinking.
The founders of Algona, Iowa—which was representative of
the many new agricultural towns on the farming frontier
—by necessity or otherwise, concerned themselves almost
wholly with material things. The first formal organization in
Kossuth County, Iowa, of which Algona became the county
seat, was a claim club in 1855, established to protect its

members in possession of 320 acres of real estate until the national government legalized pre-emption. Asa Call erected a block house at Algona in 1855 and platted out the new town in readiness to sell lots to other early arrivals. He left a block for the court house, another for a park, and a third for a college.

Promoters could select government land, borrow money to enter it, and before the end of a year sell out at a large profit.[29] Call and his associates rapidly exploited the promotional possibilities but even they were taken by surprise when rival promoters organized the nearby town of Irvington, with the intention of making it the county seat. Every vote was needed when the plot was discovered on election eve in 1855. One man, Jacob Cummins, who had started for Cedar Falls, was overtaken many miles away and rushed back to vote for Algona. By such heroic measures the county seat was saved and Call himself was chosen to the county board with the title of judge.

Asa Call continued to occupy a key position for many years among the small group that dominated the village. Every country town had an inner circle whose own personal interests were so tightly interwoven with those of the community at large that one cannot determine where self-interest ended and public spirit began. Sometimes by necessity, often by choice, their moves were cloaked in secrecy.

Ambrose Call arrived in Algona shortly after his brother, Asa, and naturally became a part of the governing inner circle. Although a practical businessman, he devoted some attention to literary and artistic matters. In 1861 he started the Algona *Pioneer Press* to advertise the local community, and to profit from publishing delinquent tax lists of Kossuth and adjoining counties which had no newspapers. The venture prospered, even though readers received the paper free. In 1892 he built the Call Opera House and later still recorded his reminiscences for the use of county historians. When he died in 1908, he was president of the First National Bank and owned 2,000 acres of Iowa land.

Asa Call concentrated more directly on business. Real-estate additions to Algona in 1871, 1882, 1883, 1895 and 1896 bore the family name. When the county historian, writing early in the twentieth century, commented, "Throw a stone into any crowd and you will be sure of hitting a real estate agent," [30] he recognized the chief source of midwestern speculative wealth. In 1857, Call and others organized the McGregor Railroad Company to promote better transportation for Algona, and incidentally to boom real-estate prices. Although this venture failed, the Calls continued to agitate for railroads. They contributed several town lots and 400 acres of land to help obtain the first line that entered Algona.

In 1862 Asa Call represented the county board in efforts to obtain swamp and overflow lands to which the county was entitled by act of Congress. Call received for his services one-fourth of all lands recovered. As lawyer, claim agent and real-estate broker, he bought and sold lands, located warrant, scrip and homestead lands, and handled payment of taxes and other business for people owning property in western states.[31] A newspaper report in January, 1877, revealed the extent of his wealth and influence. During the past year 44,000 acres of new land involving 270 farms had been sold locally, of which 8,000 acres in eighty farms had come from Judge Call's private holdings. Call had also rented out 1,100 milk cows at nominal rates to encourage dairying and to offset the heavy emphasis currently being given to wheat production.[32]

Algona, Iowa, benefited greatly from the presence of the Reverend Chauncey Taylor, who became active in local affairs almost immediately upon his arrival in 1856. Born in Vermont in 1805 and university trained, Taylor gained experience as a Congregational minister in eastern states. He dreamed of establishing a church and school on the western prairies, an ambition which the Home Missionary Society helped him realize at the age of fifty.

Taylor was responsible for many of the early Algona community improvements. He sponsored the erection of a town hall in 1856 to serve as church, school and social center. This hall ultimately became the local Congregational Church over which Taylor presided for sixteen years. He established the first reading club and conducted the first singing school. Indeed, for many years he was the only musical instructor in Algona. He served as the first county superintendent of schools in 1859 and was re-elected for several terms. The creation of a local college, scarcely more than an academy, owed much to his efforts. As one county historian suggested, he was in great measure the father of most of the county's religious interests.

As Kossuth County superintendent of schools, Taylor fostered religion and sobriety. He expected his teachers to exemplify "good moral character." To do this, they must avoid Sabbath breaking, profanity, card playing, chess, and dancing. In his estimation, parents would forgive a teacher who was not strictly religious, if pure morality was taught, but Kossuth County obviously placed a premium on fundamentalism and sobriety. Taylor himself favored Bible reading and religious exercises in the schools, especially when children voluntarily participated.[33]

Though Taylor's moral and religious convictions may seem unnecessarily narrow and hidebound today, they were liberal in terms of the more rugged code expounded by circuit-riding Methodist preachers. And even the circuit riders have not lacked for defenders. Edward Eggleston praised their work in his novel *The Circuit Rider,* when he commented: "Methodism was to the West all that Puritanism was to New England. Both of them are sublime when considered historically; neither of them were very agreeable to live with, maybe."[34] The wild drinking and associated evils which some critics have traced to western revivalistic outbursts may after all have been the antecedents which created the revivals and not the results. Like the circuit riders, Taylor was laboring on a new and raw frontier in which an impeccable standard of morality and faith was needed if order and stability were to prevail.

Since even the simplest social graces easily could be lost on the frontier, Taylor encouraged early Algona settlers to practice them. The "Rev. C. Taylor and lady" were among the thirty ladies and gentlemen who spent a social evening at the home of Judge Call and his wife during the Christmas season of 1866. According to the local paper, such meetings were decidedly beneficial because they afforded opportunities for improvement in the young, gave social enjoyment to the middle-aged and old, and cemented a bond of union that lasted for life. On one occasion the Taylor home was the scene of a social party. Dinner was served at seven, followed by social conversation until the hour of departure at ten. In reporting still another party, at which the Reverend Mr. Taylor asked the blessing, the local editor commented: "The Algonians have a way of passing the winter evenings, that strikes us as being pleasant and profitable. Better by far than spending their evenings at saloons and billiard tables." [35]

Here was the crux of the matter: A clean shirt, a dinner served with some attention to manners, and the necessity of manufacturing conversation apart from the routine of the business day helped to restore a sense of civilization to inhabitants of frontier towns. Only by conscious effort could they husband the cultural graces.

Unlike other Algona leaders, Taylor failed to acquire wealth, but he perhaps found satisfaction in less material things. At least, he escaped the censure and fear aroused by business leaders whose intentions at times were said to conflict with community welfare. Wealthy and influential men were not criticized lightly by formal agencies of public opinion because of their very power to strike back. Common citizens might grumble at high-handed acts or impugn the motives behind the program of a local capitalist but criticism broke into the open only when such a man overstepped the recognized limits of his power. Although Judge Asa C. Call contributed to the establishment of a college at Algona, his desire to locate it in a section of town favorable to his own real-estate investments was said to have hastened its failure.[36] In 1886, the local paper openly criticized Call for feuding with the American Emigrant Company over 20,000 acres of swamp land, originally deeded to him by Kossuth County. In fighting his own battle, he was said to have jeopardized titles to 120,000 acres of other land, including part of Algona, thus making it necessary for owners to spend considerable money on litigation.[37]

Other frontier towns developed much like Algona. The first white settler in Fillmore County, Minnesota, arrived in 1851. The towns of Chatfield, Elliota and Carimona were laid out in 1854; Fillmore and still another Carimona followed in 1855. Twenty-four villages were platted in Fillmore County before the state was admitted to the Union in 1858.[38] The establishment of a United States land office in Chatfield made it a boom town, and the streets swarmed with real-estate speculators. Even the Panic of 1857 did not destroy enthusiasm for town sites and land entries on this new frontier. An advertising pamphlet of 1857, describing opportunities in Fillmore County, opened with a poetic invocation:

> To the West, to the West, to the land of the Free,
>   Where mighty Missouri rolls down to the Sea,
> Where a man is a man, if he's willing to toil,
>   And the poorest may gather the fruits of the soil.[39]

Among the arrivals in 1856 was Jason Easton of New York, who had formed a partnership with an eastern congressman to speculate in Minnesota real estate. Under the name "Gilbert and Easton, Land Agents" Easton began the financial operations which, according to the Chatfield paper, made him Minnesota's first millionaire. He loaned money on land and cashed drafts on eastern banks in gold for an 8 per cent commission. The Root River Bank, which he established shortly after his arrival, obtained fabulous interest rates on its loans. Easton platted Winnebago City and owned that town when the United States land office moved there in 1861. According to the historian of Chatfield, a generation after his death the legend remained that no one in Chatfield beyond his own family considered him a friend.

The mingled fear, distrust, and respect with which citizens regarded the small circle of leaders in frontier towns became evident when someone was accused of being their hench-man. Newspaper editors and politicians were especially sen-sitive to such accusations and reacted promptly. In 1867 the Algona editor vigorously denied that Judge Call owned part of the paper, was its "real editor," or did any writing for it.[40] In 1886 the opponents of Captain Ober's candidacy for a county office circulated the rumor that he was "Jason Easton's man." In trying to rebut the charge, the Chatfield editor called the rumor a "silly story" with the intent of de-feating Ober. According to the editor, Easton probably was unaware of Ober's candidacy,[41] a comment of doubtful valid-ity since Easton was greatly interested in politics.

Leaders of European group settlements in the Middle West naturally were also highly influential. In 1873 a Dutch minister visited communities established by his countrymen in Iowa, Minnesota and Wisconsin. In spite of his overall im-pression of uniformity and monotony in towns and land-scape, he pointed out differences between the Dutch towns of Holland, Michigan, and Pella, Iowa. Varying soil condi-tions accounted for part of the difference, but the personali-ties of the original leaders were evident. Holland, Michigan, for instance, still displayed the zeal for church and school which had characterized its leaders.[42]

Rapid changes in early years have blurred surviving ac-counts of the founding of midwestern country towns. Old settlers remembered the first house in town and then bogged down in recalling the rapidity and variety of growth. Only ideas changed slowly enough to permit some order in re-counting them. Within seven years after the first white settler entered Fillmore County, Minnesota, Chatfield had four dry goods and grocery stores, three grocery and pro-visions stores, eleven real-estate dealers, five lawyers, three doctors, three civil engineers, two hotels, a watchmaker, a stove and tinware shop, a boot and shoe shop, a livery stable, and a Masonic lodge. Episcopal, Baptist, Methodist, and Presbyterian churches and two newspapers had been started. A flour mill, three sawmills, a furniture factory and a brick-yard completed the picture at the moment, but the town seethed with anticipations of even more rapid growth. Chat-field had been the county seat for a period of two years, but had lost out temporarily to Carimona in 1855, and then per-manently to Preston in 1856. Loss of the county seat perhaps accounted for Chatfield's business district developing along one Main Street instead of centering around a square occu-pied by a court house or municipal building.

Country towns often started from nothing more than a tavern or a log-cabin store. Promoters enticed other business establishments with offers of free lots. In highly successful towns, stores clustered on the four sides of the square until necessity forced businessmen to locate on side streets. More often, and especially if the dream of becoming a county seat failed, the central square became a park with a bandstand, or an unsightly weed patch and dumping ground, and the disappointed town straggled off along a Main Street as if to hide from its former ambitions.

Dust or mud, a scattering of rude buildings with hitching posts in front, a stock of general merchandise, perhaps a blacksmith shop and a doctor's house—these were the inden-tifying marks most likely to catch the visitor's eye as he entered from the prairie or timber which pressed in on infant towns from all sides. A Swedish visitor to Rush City, fifty-five miles directly north of St. Paul, in the early 1870's was astounded at its crudeness. The streets contained knee-deep water holes which trapped the traveller when he tried to avoid getting stuck in the mire. Occasionally, one had to fight off an angry sow which had appropriated the drier parts of a thoroughfare for herself and her family. Tree stumps two or two-and-a-half feet high dotted all the streets.[43] Although prairie towns had no stumps, residents waded in dust over their boot tops in dry weather and pried their wagons out of mudholes on Main Street when the rains came.

Immigrants driving ox teams hitched to covered wagons, with a crate of chickens tied on behind, and with children of the family herding the family livestock close behind the wagon as they passed through, were common sights in pioneer towns. Customers came from miles away. Within a few years, however, remarkable changes would occur. When Simeon Harding homesteaded 160 acres of land in Minnesota in 1854 he was within two-and-a-half miles of Springer's Tavern at St. Charles, but had to visit Winona thirty miles away for his mail and groceries. Within ten years he had moved to St. Charles, then a going town, and could make the trip to Winona on the railroad in three hours.[44] Ox teams and loneliness were transients on the town frontier.

New and raw, pioneer towns made no pretense to physical beauty and gave no thought to the devastation which they inflicted on the countryside. Even the Iowa prairies, which impressed some travellers as bleak and monotonous, possessed a clean and appealing freshness in their virgin state. Hamlin Garland returned to his father's Iowa farm with renewed perception of nature's beauties after the family's brief sojourn in the village of Osage. Spring was likely to arrive suddenly after a long and depressing winter. At the close of a warm March day Garland could hear pulsing down through the golden haze of sunset the mellow boom, boom, boom of prairie cock. Within a few days the whole horizon would ring with a sunrise symphony of exultant song. The booming of the roosters and the answering calls of hens came from all sides as the mating dance of prairie chickens reached its floodtide, a symphony made all the sweeter by the slender wistful piping of the prairie lark.[45]

The autobiography of Herbert Quick, Iowa lawyer and novelist, shows the appeal which that virgin land made to still another of its early inhabitants. Speaking of the brooks in Iowa when he was a boy and before farming got under way, he said:

I close my eyes now and see it as vividly as if I had seen it only yesterday. In my native part of it the hills were merely gentle undulations but a few feet high, and the slopes were long and gradual. Between the watersheds and at distances of two or three miles from one another were little clear brooks with banks of black sod, their waters flowing on floors of bright-colored glacial pebbles, their expansions little pools covered with the pads of the yellow pond lily or lotus. These streams could be stepped across almost anywhere. They were beautiful little brooks, so clear, so overarched with tall grasses and willows, so plaided with the colors of the pebbles in the sun, so dark and mysterious in the shade; with secret pockets under the soddy banks for the shiners, pumpkin seeds, dace, chubs and other small fish which populated the pure waters.

Quick was no sentimentalist who thought that all beauty lay in the past. He could recognize beauty wherever found:

There is nothing more beautiful in its way than a well-cultivated Iowa cornfield, with its deep green rows of maize slanting in the breeze; or a field of oats of a still morning, with its nodding heads jeweled with dew; or a green pasture, with its grazing herd; but they have displaced something the beauty of which will never return, and may be recalled to memory as a rare and beautiful thing in a gallery of pictures in the Land of Nevermore; and not without a touch of sadness, in spite of the inevitability of its passing.[46]

Unfortunately, settlers with Herbert Quick's perceptive eye were a decided minority among early arrivals on the midwestern frontier. In the late 1830's a French visitor to America, Alexis de Tocqueville, offered a discriminating judgment that was still applicable in Quick's generation and for years to come:

I readily admit that Americans have no poets; I cannot allow that they have no poetic ideas. In Europe the people talk a great deal of the wilds of America, but the Americans themselves never think about them: they are insensible to the wonders of inanimate Nature, and they may be said not to perceive the mighty forests which surround them till they fall beneath the hatchet. Their eyes are fixed upon another sight: the American people views its own march across these wilds—drying swamps, turning the course of rivers, peopling solitudes, and subduing Nature. This magnificent image of themselves does not meet the gaze of the Americans at intervals only; it may be said to haunt every one of them in his least as well as in his most important actions, and to be always flitting before his mind.[47]

This poetic dream of subduing a new land filled the minds of townsmen as they went about their daily work. In their blind preoccupation they exterminated the deer almost overnight by clubbing them to death in the heavy winter snows, rapidly decimated the seemingly inexhaustible flocks of pigeons, and polluted the streams with offal from their slaughterhouses.

Fertile land and concentrated effort rapidly transformed the face of nature. Country towns quickly developed to the point where they could offer a surprising variety of services. The legacy of the foundation period and the continued impact of technology were also evident in the number of ghost towns which fell prey to an attack almost as destructive as that which changed the face of nature. By actual count, Iowa alone, for example, had 2,205 abandoned places—towns, villages, hamlets and country post offices—to record the conflict for town supremacy in less than a hundred years.[48] Such an appalling mortality indicates that necessity as well as inclination may have furthered the continuation of a boom philosophy beyond the founding years. The law of town survival on the Middle Border demanded constant alertness to competition from rival centers and to technological change.

2 ❖ The Horse is King

CARRIAGE, DRAY, AND WAGON

VILLAGE LIFE moved at the pace of horse-drawn transportation. Tourist homes, tourist courts, garages, filling stations, and stores selling automobile accessories lay in the future. There were no concrete curbs, and parking meters were nonexistent; and small-town workmen would have been baffled at the idea of painting parking lines in streets consisting of dust or mud.

The presence of horses was evident everywhere. Droppings in the streets and town stables attracted swarms of flies, and narrow-rimmed wheels of wagons and buggies cut gaping ruts during rainy seasons. Hitching posts, connected with iron chains, surrounded the village square. Until business growth necessitated removal of hitching lots to the edge of business districts, farmers tied their teams around the courthouse square, let down check reins to ease the tired necks of their horses, and walked across the street to do their trading. Thirsty farm teams quickened their step when they approached town pumps and watering troughs, which also doubled as fire-fighting equipment.

Horses were sentient beings, capable of affection, and an unwritten code censured their abuse. In cold and rainy weather farmers paid the modest fee necessary to stable their teams in commercially operated feed barns and livery stables. The occasional drunk who forgot his team was roughly criticized by the village paper after some citizen had removed them late at night to a livery barn for food and shelter.[1]

Even within the town itself business and social life depended on horse-drawn transportation. Most citizens had horse-and-carriage barns at the rear of their homes to shelter driving equipment. Commercial drays hauled freight to and from the depot, did heavy moving for local citizens, and made daily deliveries for stores unable to afford their own private wagons. Most stores, however, owned single-horse, spring wagons, with business advertisements painted on the sides, which made morning and afternoon deliveries to residential areas. Younger clerks enjoyed driving these conveyances at speeds beyond the limits of safety demanded by elderly residents of the town. Local hotel hacks, pulled sometimes by as many as four horses, rushed back and forth from depots at speeds supposed to impress travellers with their efficiency. By loading sample trunks of travelling salesmen smartly and with dispatch, sounding their horns sharply, and dashing off before a rival hack could clear the depot platform, drivers scored a point in favor of the establishment which they represented.[2] Peddling carts, ice wagons, and sprinkler carts moved more sedately, much to the pleasure of children who begged fruit and small chunks of ice or played in the streams of water being sprayed on dusty streets.[3]

Livery stables served those who could not afford to own rigs or who had temporary and unusual demands. Young people courted and eloped with livery stable teams, and circus agents drove them leisurely round the countryside to post bills. Drummers employed drivers and rigs to haul their sample trunks on two- and three-day side trips to hamlets lacking railroad connections. Picnics, celebrations and fairs in nearby towns, baseball trips, sleighing in winter, funerals —all these and more called for livery-stable teams.

A good bay trotter and a fine buggy appealed to the young

man of the 1870's much as the convertible does to his great-grandson. At the peak of its development, a truly fine buggy was an expensive item. Polished and varnished ash shafts, rubber-tired wheels with shiny brass inner rims, brass lamps decorated with large glass rubies, and patent-leather dashboards pleased the eye. Even the harness had its charms—gleaming tan leather with brass fittings, rainbow-colored celluloid baubles, and ruby rosettes.[4] The current generation will never know the thrill of spending $1.75 on a horse and buggy for an afternoon and evening of dating. The carriage with its fast team, yellow fly nets, linen lap robe, and beribboned whip lifted the spirit of the young blade as he drove up and down Main Street with one foot hanging over the body bed and a cigar at an angle in his mouth. Loafers shouted at him and received the expected quip in reply, commented on his extravagance, and wondered at his destination. A touch of the whip and he was on his way. With one horse pacing and the other trotting, he passed the fragrant slaughterhouse at the edge of town and on to the meeting with his best girl.[5]

Men loved a fast horse and a reputation for permitting no rival to pass. To curb this passion, town ordinances provided fines for careless and reckless driving. Gallatin's charter of 1857 specifically authorized punishment for "furious riding of any horse or animal" within the limits of this Missouri city.[6] In spite of such laws, citizens still complained about fast driving. One report on Colon, Michigan, in 1879 said that the most reckless kind of driving occurred daily on Main Street.[7] The Croswell, Michigan, paper in 1897 reported an incident which showed how severely a proud man could be tempted when a rival driver tried to pass. "Landlord" Wagg of the local Franklin hotel had driven over to the neighboring town of Lexington on the preceding Tuesday to buy some goods. At the edge of Lexington, Gus Swackhammer managed to pass Wagg by running his horse, and the two raced on into town. They were stopped by a man spading thistles at the side of the road who proved to be the city marshal. Landlord Wagg was fined two dollars for travelling more than six miles an hour within the city limits, but Swackhammer, who lived in Lexington, was still fighting the charge. In his anger, he had refused to let the marshal ride downtown with him when accosted, and had also refused to plead guilty.[8]

Horses could be a nuisance in many ways. In 1876 the Monroe, Wisconsin, editor warned his readers that city ordinances prohibited the riding of horses on sidewalks, even though it was a temptation to do so in muddy times.[9] When a citizen of Chillicothe, Illinois, in 1875 spoke of Saturday as a lively day, with vacant lots filled with teams, and then added that he thought he was on Broadway in New York City until he saw "George" and his dogs, he expressed in a lighter vein the problem of congestion and the greater danger of accidents on Saturdays.[10] Occasional runaways added zest for spectators if not for the unfortunate individuals involved. A team belonging to a Mr. Bumpus took fright on State Street in Algona, Iowa, in 1877 and dashed around the corner of Thorington Street, breaking the wagon tongue, the whiffletrees, and creating general havoc. Citizens got inside so quickly during the fracas that the town took on a Sunday air of desertion within a matter of seconds.[11]

Constant activity at private and railroad stockyards in country towns also emphasized the importance of horse-drawn transportation. Produce and livestock had to be concentrated at local shipping points because they could not be moved great distances over muddy and unimproved roads in wagons pulled by horses. Small-town elevators and stockyards thus handled an enormous volume of agricultural produce. During 1878, J. J. Wilson's private yards at Algona, Iowa, shipped almost 350 cars of hogs, wheat, and oats, and several more of minor produce. In return, he received 388 carloads of lumber and coal. From the adjoining new depot stockyards 817 cars departed during the same year with wheat, corn, oats, flax, cattle, hogs, butter, and cheese.

Wagons converged on Algona from all directions during

weeks when as many as fifty carloads of cattle and hogs left for Milwaukee. Their drivers ate a noon meal at the local hotel and bought family supplies in Algona stores. Livery stables, blacksmith shops, harness shops, and feed barns benefited from their presence. In commenting on business during 1878 the Algona editor said that State Street occasionally had been filled with teams and loaded wagons four and five abreast. At times the line had stretched from the elevator and cattle yards at the depot to the City Hotel, a distance of nearly a mile.[12] Dust and mud, bawling cattle and squealing hogs, horses and men, the plank platform of the Fairbanks scales, loading chutes, and lines of box- and cattle-cars on sidings—all have been challenged by the trucks which now travel midwestern highways. But in the 1870's horses and country towns were equally necessary to assemble agricultural produce for market and to supply country homes with merchandise.

As a focal point in the age of horse-drawn transportation, the livery stable had a form, a personality, and an odor as distinctive as that of its twentieth-century successor, the garage and automobile showroom. Brick construction, feed chutes connected directly with the hayloft, and running water in stalls and washrooms marked the more pretentious establishments. Most, however, were large, boxlike structures of graying unpainted wood, with oversized doors to permit carriages to enter the central ramp. A few had signs in front, perhaps a horse's head with crossed whips carved in wood, but, as a rule, the only decorations were tin advertising strips of patent remedies for horseflesh nailed at random to exterior walls. All stables had the same mingled smell of horse urine and manure, harness oil, feed and cured hay.

A small office near the door contained a battered desk, a pot-bellied stove, a few chairs, a cot, and a lantern hanging on a wooden peg for the use of an attendant who was on duty twenty-four hours a day to wait on customers and to guard against the constant threat of fire. A slate on the wall near the office or just within listed the names of horses out on trips and rental charges. So far as possible, customers were held accountable for abusing horses by furious driving, for turning rubber-tired conveyances so short as to fray the rubber against the buggy bed, for failing to feed horses on long trips, and for other injurious acts. Some stables posted slogans to encourage better care of equipment:

> Whip Light,
> Drive Slow.
> Pay Cash
> Before You Go.

and all gave careful instructions to new patrons.

Well-equipped livery stables possessed a surprising variety of vehicles. Fancy buggies and curved sleighs were rented out for single dates; fringed surreys served for double-dating and more prosaic family trips. Carryalls, with seats along the sides and entrance steps in the rear, were used on special occasions—for Sunday School picnics, to carry visiting ball teams to hotel and the playing field, to take elderly ladies to the cemetery on Memorial Day, and in Autumn to taxi passengers to the fair grounds. Light spring wagons hauled drummers and their sample trunks on visits to country stores and hamlets. Of more somber mien were the hearses, with black enclosed sides and oval windows, fringe and plumes, and elaborate box lights. Hearses decorated in white were preferred for children's funerals. Perhaps one or more of the local doctors kept a team and glass-enclosed coupe at the livery stable. Hotel hacks, the town watering cart, and vegetable wagons added to the variety of conveyances parked along the walls.

Stalls were to the rear, from which horses were led up cleated ramps to the main floor for hitching. A second-floor loft over the stables facilitated the forking down of hay used for feed. Harness for each animal hung on wooden pegs at the front of his stall. Somewhere in the building was the washroom where buggies were washed and wheels were greased. Curry combs, hair clippers, sponges, axle grease, harness soap, and pitchforks were scattered through the building at points most convenient for their use.[13]

Louis Bromfield's home town had three livery barns, each more or less specialized in nature. Painter's Stables occupied an alley lined with sycamore trees, and was a great center for gossip, primarily because it supplied cabs for weddings and funerals. If a murder was committed, all the gruesome details could be learned at Painter's; if the son of a church deacon was arrested in the Railroad Hotel with a waitress and gave a false name, loafers at the stable knew it immediately. Wilmerding's Ten Cent Barn was only a block from the courthouse. Built with huge sawn beams and standing four floors high, it had wide sweeping ramps that permitted teams to go directly to the top. On Saturdays, market days, and in bad weather it was filled with country teams, and groups of farmers gathered in front to discuss politics and the weather with local politicians. A third establishment, "Grimses," held a horse fair twice a month, a sale attended by farmers and buyers from a distance. There, a high roof sheltered a vast open space, littered with tanbark, in which a constant procession of stallions, mares and geldings, Percherons and Clydes, Morgans and hacks, and trotting horses passed under the auctioneer's hammer.[14]

The livery barn was universally condemned by pious mothers who rated it only slightly above the town saloons. Its robust life shocked those refined people who spoke of bulls as "gentleman cows."[15] Unlike twentieth-century automobile dealers, who move in country-club circles, livery stable owners generally ignored high society. Addicted to slouchy attire, sometimes noted for profanity, they were numbered among the few local men of property who avoided religious activities and booster movements. Since the usual explanations—stinginess, a choleric disposition, or free-thinking religious principles—did not apply in their case, they puzzled even their own contemporaries. For these mothers, however, it was enough that they were hard to understand and did not practice the finer points of accepted social conduct. The livery stable also served as a loafing place, especially for those most addicted to betting on horse races. Checkers and playing cards were often in evidence, and liquor was tolerated within limits. Most horrible of all, stallions were offered at service as long as public opinion would tolerate it, usually only until mothers of impressionable boys learned of the presence of "gentleman horses" within the city limits.

It was distinctly a man's world and hence a fascinating one for small boys. Such diverse interpreters of midwestern life as Louis Bromfield, Sherwood Anderson, and William Allen White have all paid tribute to the attractions and the educative force of the livery stables which they knew as boys. As a youth Anderson worked for a time in the livery stable at Clyde, Ohio. His services consisted of currying horses, hauling out manure, washing buggies, and sleeping at night on a cot in the office to wait on late customers. Loafers initiated Anderson into the mysteries of heavy drunkenness and nausea by giving him a half-glass of whiskey under the guise of beer. As a man, White chortled at the memory of his and other mothers' insistence on the removal of a stallion from a livery stable in his home town of Eldorado, Kansas, thinking that the small boys did not know the facts of life! While working on the Eldorado paper in his teens, White discovered that one of the livery stables on Main Street doubled as a liquor joint. There, on a hot day, one could fish out bottles of beer from a tub of ice covered with a gunny sack in a rank-smelling box stall, or obtain bottles of whiskey stashed away in the manger and leave his payment in a feed box. Bromfield belligerently defended the livery barn's influence. In his opinion, small boys who learned of sex in such places gained a more wholesome attitude than those who listened to whispered stories in YMCA locker rooms.[16]

Probably no other loafing place in town provided so fine a setting for tall stories, and there the town liars competed for supremacy. They told of working for the contractor who built Niagara Falls, of ice worms ruining a whole summer's supply of ice, and of the half-believable hoop snake. Stories of Civil War exploits appealed to an audience composed in large part of veterans, who could relish the ludicrous overtones:

Still another told of coming on the battle field of Gettysburg on a gunboat in a driving snow storm. It was the morning of the third day of the battle. He had been drinking gun powder in his whiskey to make him brave, and he performed such feats of daring and valor that General Meade, with tears in his eyes, shook his hand and said, "Abel, I won't forget this." [17]

Youngsters found additional attractions. Horseshoe nails could be bent into rings; old bottles and junk lying around the premises were collected and sold. And when the "Tom shows" (*Uncle Tom's Cabin*) came to town the trained dogs which would chill the local audience by baying on Eliza's trail generally were housed at one of the local livery stables.

Nineteenth-century midwestern civilization was obviously geared to the strength and limitations of horse-drawn transportation. The horse accounted for the carriage sheds and barns in residential sections, for livery and feed barns, for stockyards, harness shops, and blacksmith shops, for the many small carriage factories in country towns, for hitch racks, town pumps, and watering troughs. Cemeteries and schools were laid out with horse-drawn transportation in mind. The horse played a major part in determining trade areas, and his potentialities helped determine nineteenth-century recreational patterns.

Other forces began to play an increasingly important part in shaping midwestern life in the years immediately following the Civil War. Technological and managerial revolutions exerted more and more influence. Railroads were already bringing goods from distant points to be exchanged for crops and livestock, and agencies of short-range communication, like the telephone and trolley line, and then the truck and automobile, would soon appear. Tremendous change generated by them would destroy many small-town crafts, and country towns would suffer from wildly fluctuating trade areas. Greater specialization and a higher standard of living would accompany a declining independence from the outside world. But, for the moment, these were the very characteristics—a low standard of living, relative lack of specialization, and freedom from outside control—which set the country town apart from its twentieth-century successor.

People did things for themselves or did without far more than is either possible or necessary today. They lacked hospitals, funeral homes, florist shops, dry-cleaning-and-pressing establishments, beauty shops, country clubs, plumbers, waterworks, telephones, electric lights, ten-cent stores, commercial laundries, radio and television shops.

Small-town business felt little external control. Though manufacturers and wholesalers were beginning to advertise directly to consumers the unique virtues of their own special packaged, branded and trade-marked wares, which finally would compel retailers to stock such items, general stores still carried coffee and calico, not a variety of packaged or labelled brands. Storekeepers were relatively free to select their own stock; their customers in turn needed judgment of quality and price in order to spend their money wisely. Officials at the court house were still county and local officials only; and local banks enjoyed a measure of independence unknown in federal reserve and deposit-insurance days.

Even the homes of the period were relatively independent. Storms and blizzards might isolate country towns, and even individual families, without seriously affecting their mode of living. Coal oil lamps, a supply of cordwood in the back yard, meat in the smokehouse, fruits and preserves in the cellar, a cow for milk in the barn—here was food, light and warmth which continued to function when neighbors and the outside world were cut off.

Americans thrill to this saga of independence as their own lives daily become more interdependent. They envy their ancestors, those artisans and storekeepers who rose early in the morning to milk their cows and slop their pigs in order to have their individually owned shops and stores open for early customers. But, as in all Edens, there were serpents. Town ordinances show that conditions were not idyllic. Gallatin, Missouri, in 1873, instructed city authorities to order the removal of "every hog-pen, slaughter house, privy, mud hole, stable . . . in a stinking or unhealthy condition." [18] It was easy to order drastic action, but enforcement in specific cases was another matter because no citizen in a closely-knit community wanted to issue a complaint.

Artisans flourished in the relatively isolated and unspecialized economy. Blacksmiths were able and willing to build wagons and plows; harness shops both made and sold harness; shoemakers and tailors turned leather and cloth into finished goods. The revolutions in transportation, manufacturing, and management ruined such business. Gunsmiths, wagon makers, coopers, millers, tanners, and cigarmakers are gone from the country towns where they were well known in the 1870's. Other artisans have survived by changing to new occupations—from tinsmiths to plumbers, for instance, or most commonly by abandoning all manufacturing in favor of service and repair. The shoe repair man on Main Street today is thus a lineal descendant of the craftsman who actually produced shoes in the 1870's.

THE GENERAL STORE

BUSINESS DISTRICTS made little pretense to beauty. They generally contained one or more brick buildings, sometimes two or three stories high. Upper floors often served as lodge halls, opera houses, or offices for professional men. An occasional building had gingerbread decorations at the top of the first story or at the eaves, but most were plainly finished. Most stores, and virtually all the shops of artisans, were single story, wooden buildings. Their pointed roofs were often concealed behind rectangular wooden fronts, which made them appear larger. Before the era of concrete sidewalks and hard-surfaced streets, walks often varied in elevation. Wooden platforms on a level with wagon beds and buggies extended from the front doors of many stores to enable farmers to cramp their wheels and unload families and produce without lifting or inconvenience. No one seems to have objected to the resulting two or three steps up or down which pedestrians had to take as they walked along Main Street.

General stores were much alike. In good weather, racks of brooms, seed potatoes, and other seasonal items were set outside on the front platforms, but merchandise in the narrow windows flanking the front door remained unchanged for long periods. More emphasis seems to have been placed on illustrating the range of stock than on style, price, or other competitive possibilities. Since both sides of the interior first floor were lined with shelving, stores were invariably dark and gloomy places, with ventilation so poor that the distinctive and not unpleasant odor which identified them became evident immediately on one's entrance. It was possible to identify the distinctive smells of molasses, vinegar, damp cellar floors, fish, cheese, freshly ground coffee, rope, rubber boots, dress goods in bolts, leather goods, or kerosene, depending on one's location, but the mingled odors permeated the whole of the store.

In the center and toward the rear stood a pot-bellied stove —the sole source of heat—with an enormous extension of pipe to the roof above or to the side wall. A pan of ashes in front for a spittoon and a circle of chairs encouraged the interminable conversations of loafers who have been described by so many novelists and local colorists. A yellow bench, the gift of some shoe company, rested near a glass showcase toward the front of the store. It was popular with the women, who hesitated to approach the group of loafers surrounding the stove. A small elevated platform, enclosed with heavy knit wire, contained a high desk and a stool. There, close to the stove and the conversation, the storekeeper worked on his books and orders during the evening when business was slack. Groceries were located along one side of the store, with hardware items toward the rear. Shelves on the other side contained dry goods and clothing, and boxes of shoes. Gauntlet gloves, fly swatters, stocking caps, mufflers, milk pails, and cooking vessels were suspended overhead on strings of wire.

General stores were cluttered with piles of merchandise and space was at a premium. Sales at a general store in Philadelphia, Indiana, on one Saturday in 1873 included eggs, tablecloths, calico, flour, lard, tacks, blankets, muslin, batting, shoes, socks, sugar, crackers, cheese, coffee, thread, cigars, collars, spices, screws, castor oil, shawls, axle grease, matches, and fish.[19]

The dank cellar, reached by a trap door at the rear of the store, was most cluttered of all. It contained barrels of syrup, turpentine, kerosene, and molasses. Stocks of rope, crocks of butter taken in trade, wood-encased cheeses, hams hanging from rafters, empty boxes, barrels, crates, and excelsior were stored in the cellar. All helped to make excellent runs for enormous rats, which were trapped and tossed into the alley at the rear.

Some of the larger stores used a second story to house surplus stock and as a salesroom for carpets, rugs, oilcloth and wallpaper. In some cases the second story extended beyond the main floor in the rear, and connected with the haymows of a horse barn to form an overhead feed room, which permitted farmers to drive beneath and load or unload by means of a hand-operated elevator. Stores so equipped could buy feed and flour in carload lots, one of the early means of cutting costs of distribution.

Most merchandise arrived in bulk, which accounted for the presence of numerous bins, kegs, and barrels. Behind the grocery counters were built-in bins containing tea, coffee, dried peaches, dried peas, beans, rice, corn meal, prunes, dried apples, and oatmeal. Smaller receptacles held cinnamon, cloves, allspice, nutmeg, salt, and pepper. Gunpowder tea came in large foreign-looking cans, lined with lead. Tipped forward in front of the counters were open tubs or kegs, more or less covered with their original lids, containing butter, pickles, mackerel, and fine-cut chewing tobacco. Toward the rear stood the cracker barrel, and still farther back were barrels of vinegar, kerosene, and molasses. Here the cans and jugs of farmers were filled and then stoppered with corn cobs or cork. Here, too, clerks fished out eggs from buckets partially filled with oats, a cheap and convenient method of preventing breakage on the trip to town.

Only a few mechanical devices aided clerks in waiting on customers. Circular cheeses often were mounted on rotating platforms equipped with hinged cleavers to slice out wedges according to rough estimates of customers' orders. A covering of cheesecloth gave some protection from flies, and progressive merchants even covered the whole with a circular wire net, which could be lifted off when slicing cheese. A red coffee mill with two large balance wheels and an enormous scoop beneath stood near the end of the grocery counter to accommodate those farmers who were beginning to have their coffee ground before leaving the store instead of troubling with their own small home grinders. Here, too, was the plug tobacco, long, brown, fruity-smelling strips, which could be cut at conveniently marked lengths by a hinged blade.

Canned goods were relatively new in the 1860's and also of more dubious quality than the rows of home-canned produce which graced most cellars in village and country homes. Merchants were beginning to push the sale of the commercial product, however. J. L. Mohler's store at Lacon, Illinois, in 1865 advertised one thousand cans of peaches at $4.50 a dozen. Canned pears, pineapples, tomatoes, damson plums, blackberries, and whortleberries were also available at his store. In addition to advertising his canned goods, Mohler gave the local editor a generous sample of the stock, and received the usual compliment in return. According to the paper, the commercially canned fruit was "unequalled for freshness and flavor," and Mohler was said to be selling as many as 200 cans a day.[20]

Tin-covered glass canisters on shelves near the front of

the grocery side contained stick candy—wintergreen pinks, peppermint stripes, and plain. Conical chocolates, filled with an almost insoluble fondant, licorice strips, which enabled youngsters to ape tobacco-chewing habits of their elders, and long sticks of white, heavily sugared chewing gum of the consistency of wax were favorites. As the range and quantity of candy increased, storekeepers began to display it in glass-enclosed cases or under a cover of cheese cloth.

Counters on the opposite side of the store were kept bare, if possible, for unrolling and measuring bolts of calico, muslin, and silk. Circular stools fastened to the floor in front of counters enabled women to sit down while examining dry goods. Spool cases with many narrow drawers containing thread by size appeared before the turn of the century. Hats, caps, bolt goods, ready-to-wear, jewelry, and shoes competed for space. Millinery departments were operated by general stores in many towns but naturally tended to gravitate to firms specializing in dry goods and even to separate buildings of their own.[21]

The old general store opened its doors as early as five in the morning and its lights went out at night after most of the villagers had gone to bed. On Saturday afternoon, and on Saturday night as roads improved, bedlam reigned as clerks rushed madly about to wait on country trade. But on Sunday morning they could sleep late, at least until eight or nine o'clock, when some customer who had failed to complete his trading the night before or who had left something behind asked them to open up for a few minutes.

The physical structure and the stock of general stores emphasized existing standards. Relative lack of specialization was evident in the range of goods carried. Cured and pickled meats, dried fruits and vegetables, and oatmeal cereal were the basis of a limited diet. After a long season of such monotonous diet, supplemented by fruits canned in heavy syrup and preserves from their own cellars, citizens looked forward to the first mess of spring greens, and "thinned their blood" by doses of sulphur and molasses. Housewives picked out the bugs from bulk oats before soaking the cereal overnight in preparation for breakfast. Crackers from open barrels were soggy, stale, and dirty. In the absence of recognized grades of calico and silk, colors ran and garments shrank at the first washing until they could not be worn. By twentieth-century standards, stores of the 1870's were dirty, unsanitary places, offering a limited range of quality in merchandise, and with no assurance that prices paid would guarantee colors, durability, or fit.

Conversely, modern stores have lost the easy social life that went along with trading in the old days. Though stocks of goods were limited, they were more than adequate when every home in town kept a garden for summer vegetables, when every housewife canned fruits for winter use, and every husband stocked his cellar with vegetables and apples in season. The sloping doors which gave entrance through the mound of dirt covering the family cellar made excellent slides for youngsters; to older members of the family they were a symbol of security. Cow barns, pigpens, smokehouses, and chicken houses were standard equipment in country towns. Scraps from the table might pass for garbage in the language of city youngsters, but the village boy, like his country cousin, knew such things as "slop" which was destined to go directly from the kitchen to waiting pigs and chickens.

Farmers were even more self-sufficient than townsmen. Itinerant shoemakers and tailors went from farm-to-farm among Norwegian settlers in Wisconsin in the 1860's to turn homemade fabrics and leather into clothing, which was used until completely worn out. Coffee was mixed with chicory to make it go farther; flour was ground from wheat raised on the farm. Since coal oil was expensive, homemade candles served families for lighting except on company occasions. Tableware was carved from wood. These settlers were acquiring land of their own and looked forward to the increasing prosperity which rapidly came their way.[22] In the interval, they bought as little as possible from storekeepers, a habit that tended to linger even after they were financially able to expand their purchases.

"SALESMANLIKE PUSILLANIMITY?"

THORSTEIN VEBLEN's FAMILY belonged to the mass movement of people that settled the American Midwest. Though others of his generation found satisfaction in rapidly expanding material standards of wealth, Veblen gained fame as economist and philosopher for his original and devastating dissection of American life. One of his essays was built around the theme that the "country town of the American farming region is the perfect flower of self-help and cupidity." As an unfriendly critic, Veblen outlined a number of adverse criticisms of small-town economy. If proved in their entirety, they would show the small town to have been virtually a parasite, feeding on the life blood of farmers. If examined one by one, they measure the adequacy of country towns in meeting basic economic needs.

Veblen accused country towns of trying to monopolize the farmer's trade and of exploiting him whenever possible. Needless duplication of overhead and personnel led to exorbitant prices. In groceries and banking, where Veblen thought monopoly was most complete, top price levels often were reached, but they had to be somewhat lower in the conduct of ordinary trade. In the latter, the dominant tone was "circumspection" or "salesmanlike pusillanimity." Veblen also accused merchants of being "aggressively and truculently" conservative. They contributed only to causes that pandered to local sentiment and then advertised their charities as a means of attracting trade. Lastly, in Veblen's opinion, farmers and townsmen co-operated only to boom local real estate; otherwise, relations were generally hostile.[23]

There can be little doubt that country merchants liked the idea of trade monopolies. The constant hammering of technological, transportation, and managerial innovations on existing trade areas made monopoly all the more appealing. A visiting Englishman commented on the intensity with which American towns hated one another—hate as intense as that which once prevailed between Athens and Thebes or between Pisa and Florence.[24] When Tiffin, Ohio, bested its rival, Mansfield, in 1869 in a contest to obtain a new railroad, the editor of the Tiffin paper jibed at Mansfield's aspirations, attributing the slowness with which it had moved to its "ponderous" size. After all, was not Mansfield the largest city in the Union in the estimation of its inhabitants? [25] Monroe, Wisconsin, became greatly excited on a Saturday in 1869 when a Milwaukee auction firm dared to display a stock of goods on the west side of the square and to hire the local band as a means of attracting customers. Much noise and competition immediately developed. Readers of the Monroe paper were told that Morris Roth was on his way to Milwaukee and that Ed Morris was leaving for Chicago, both to purchase goods comparable to those being offered by the intruder. Once stocked with such shoddy merchandise, according to the implication of the report, they would put the Milwaukee auction firm out of business locally.[26]

Actually, country towns never achieved a monopoly. The railroad itself, although devoted primarily to long-distance transportation, enabled villagers along its route to shop in cities. As early as 1865, residents of Lacon, Illinois, were being urged to visit Putnam's Clothing Emporium in Chicago, a hundred miles away. According to an advertisement, Putnam's had the largest stock and was the oldest established clothing house in Chicago. Their large turnover enabled them to sell a fine suit of clothes at a saving sufficient to cover the round-trip fare from Lacon.[27] Putnam's advertisement was somewhat unique only in its attempt to explain the economies involved in shopping trips to larger cities. By the 1860's and 1870's country newspapers often carried advertising from city stores.[28]

Local newspapers solicited advertising from stores in competing cities and towns, and complimented them as freely as they did local men in news-column "plugs" concerning "elegant" stocks, "progressive" business methods, and "bargain" rates. On September 7, 1865, the Gallatin, Missouri, editor devoted a whole column to praising St. Joseph business houses which had recently advertised in his paper. The editor felt sure that local citizens would not visit St. Joseph for small purchases since Gallatin retailers carried "extensive" stocks. No! He was speaking only to three classes of people: citizens who went to St. Joseph to buy items not available locally; Gallatin retailers who relied on the St. Joseph wholesale market; and wealthy farmers who laid in major supplies twice a year.[29] St. Joseph was fifty miles from Gallatin, and part of the trip involved stagecoach travel. Nonetheless, St. Joseph businessmen advertised dry goods, clothing, farm machinery, groceries, books, musical instruments, drugs, saddles, furniture, and hardware in the Gallatin paper, all of which could be obtained at retail locally.

Local papers also contained a large volume of advertising from nearby towns of comparable or smaller size. In some cases, small-town merchants had to advertise elsewhere because no newspaper existed locally. Nonetheless, many advertisements challenged comparisons. When Jesse Drake of La Rose advertised his general store in the Lacon, Illinois, paper in 1875 he invited customers to examine his prices and then concluded: "Here we are. Business is business. If you want bargains we can furnish them."[30] Many farmers could easily visit both Lacon and La Rose. Although Lacon had more stores and better facilities, general stores in La Rose still were able to compete for a share of the business.

In view of such evidence, Veblen exaggerated the existence of trade monopolies. Horse-drawn transportation seriously limited the farmer's range of trading, but the very duplication of stores and towns, of which Veblen also complained, enabled customers to select their goods from at least two or three trading centers. Though farmers visited towns in their immediate vicinity for minor purchases, they were inclined to make real trading expeditions once or twice a year. In the interval, they had fingered the merchandise on display in various general stores and had pondered advertisements from other villages.

Hamlin Garland's family visited Osage, Iowa, in the early 1870's to purchase school clothing. Unlike today, when women do most of the family shopping, trading was a family affair in the 1870's, with the father carrying the pocketbook and making final decisions. Though the Garlands used a lumber wagon for the Osage trip, two spring seats cushioned them somewhat against the jolts of rough country roads. After a summer on an isolated farm, children felt awkward and shy in a city of 1,200 people. The youngest clung to his father's trousers and the small daughter held her mother's hand. Hamlin and another sister stumbled over nail kegs and dodged whiffletrees in their concentration on jars of pink and white candy, books, and buckskin mittens. Odors of salt codfish, spices, calico, kerosene, apples, and gingersnaps assailed their nostrils. Each soon carried a candy marble in his cheek, like a chipmunk carries a nut.

Merchant and family quickly settled down to the ritual of trading. Hamlin and his brother stood like sturdy hitching posts while the storekeeper fitted them with cotton-plush caps. Footwear came next. High-topped cavalry boots were all but universal, a survival from the recent war. Hamlin selected a pair with red tops, with a golden moon in the center, but his brother preferred blue tops decorated with a golden flag. Even the father's insistence that the boots must fit loosely so the boys would not outgrow them failed to lessen their joy in the new footwear. They liked the oily new smell and the absence of copper toes, which most commonly were found on little boys' boots. School books were last— McGuffey's reader, Ray's arithmetic, Mitchell's geography, and then slates, the frames of which would soon bear names or initials of their owners.[31]

Farm diaries reveal rural trade patterns best of all. Fred Downer kept a diary of his life in Milan township, DeKalb County, Illinois, some three miles from the village of Lee, from 1873 to 1891. His family obtained mail and many business services in Lee, and, in the dead of winter, they occasionally had to shovel snow to go even that far. Their Uncle Eb owned one of the stores and they felt at home on the village streets. Corn, hogs, chickens, and oats were sold at Lee. In 1887 and 1888 Fred Downer made almost daily trips to deliver milk. Lee also offered some social competition to their own township schoolhouse and church.

But the village exercised no monopoly on their purchases. Trips to Sycamore, the county seat, to pay taxes and attend court naturally resulted in purchases of merchandise. Even more important was Rochelle, where the family bought lamps, a buggy and a wagon, washing machines, overcoats costing twenty dollars, and suits at thirty-seven. They relied on Rochelle doctors and dentists and lived there for a time during the winter months so the children could attend school. The presence of an aunt at Aurora made it convenient for occasional visits to the dentist and for the purchase of a cookstove. Bed springs, mattresses, and a sofa were bought at Cornton. Visits to larger cities at a distance occurred over the years. "Pa and Ma" attended the Chicago Exposition in 1877, and the diarist bought his mother a fifty-dollar fur-lined cape while visiting the same city in 1885.[32]

As substantial farmers, the Downers maintained a standard of living somewhat above the prevailing level. The better-quality clothing and professional services available in larger country towns naturally appealed to them. Rank-and-file farmers, like the Garlands, found general stores in smaller places more adequate for their needs. For all classes, however, a choice among stores, and even among villages and towns, was available in the age of horse-drawn transportation. Veblen's charge that merchants priced goods on the basis of obtaining all that the traffic would bear loses force in view of this competitive situation. Studies of the purchasing power of farm crops in terms of merchandise indicate that in general the farmer's position improved in the second half of the nineteenth century.[33] In other words, a bushel or a pound of the farmer's product with the passage of the years obtained more clothing, shoes and groceries. Declining manufacturing costs and more economical retailing contributed to that end.

Cumbersome merchandising methods rather than conspiracy among merchants were primarily responsible for the "high" prices charged by country stores in the 1870's. A few storekeepers visited eastern cities or large western wholesale centers like Chicago and St. Louis to select merchandise twice a year,[34] but many relied almost wholly on travelling salesmen or written orders.[35] In 1873, Goetsch and Borchardt, who owned a general store at Watertown, Wisconsin, ordered dry goods by mail from three different houses, and hats, groceries, yarn, and crockery from others. At least twenty-five different wholesalers were patronized during the year. Goods came on order from Chicago, Boston, New York City, and St. Louis, and from Milwaukee, Monroe, and Oshkosh within the state. Goetsch and Borchardt bought in small quantities. Reduced to its simplest terms, their business consisted primarily of placing orders for their customers. An order to Troy, New York, for shirt fronts costing $5.95 indicated the petty nature of their business.[36]

Travelling salesmen regularly visited village stores with sample trunks of merchandise. Genial and ingratiating, they often became close friends of the storekeepers to whom they sold. Merchants were inclined to reserve orders for their favorite salesmen, who, in turn, often shielded them by failing to report financial difficulties to wholesale houses.[37] In some cases, friendship became more important than quality and price in determining the source of goods on a merchant's shelf.

Most storekeepers started out as clerks for older merchants, and were inclined to perpetuate the methods which they learned. Pre-Civil War ways still prevailed in the 1870's. Heavy advertising twice a year, with advertisements remaining unchanged for long periods,[38] and semiannual clearance sales[39] were common, as in the earlier period. Storekeepers still liked the ante-bellum practice of not mentioning specific prices. Advertisements like that of Ball and Young in the Monroe, Wisconsin, paper in 1869 offering four-and-a-half pounds of coffee or ten pounds of brown sugar for a dollar were not uncommon, since groceries were more standardized than other merchandise and price advertising had a greater meaning. But J. B. Treat of the same town expressed a common attitude concerning prices of dry goods and clothing when he said: "We consider it a humbug to advertise prices; we will do that at our counter, and will always sell good goods, and sell cheap!" [40] "Low prices" and "Good goods at fair bargains" marked the common limits of price advertising on dry goods and clothing for several years to come. Merchants had no liking for price wars, it is true; but salesmen and customers alike knew how meaningless advertised prices could be when standardization, grading, and other uniform qualities of modern-day brand goods had not yet invaded the merchandising world to any great extent.

Revolutionary changes were brewing in the 1870's, but, for the time being, old methods were dominant. Storekeepers seldom mentioned brand goods in their own advertising and continued to buy where they pleased. Wholesale orders arrived in driblets, and most stores were satisfied to turn their stock twice a year. All were inclined to respect the farmer's view that monthly bills reflected on a man's honesty. Farmers, in turn, complained about high prices but liked the convenience of nearby stores. They expected village merchants to credit them for a year, and looked forward to Saturday visiting in their favorite stores. None realized how swiftly and how thoroughly the rising tide of revolutions in transportation, manufacturing, and management was going to challenge current practices.

Veblen's charge that storekeepers endorsed prevailing social and moral standards to obtain trade has been repeated by others. According to one interpreter, storekeepers knew that customers liked to hear them say that politics corrupted men. They also gained favor by refusing to criticize the value of churches and schools and by signing local-option petitions. Constant debate and discussion in their stores enabled them to sense the slightest shift in prevailing ideas. Of all the listeners to debates on familiar themes, they were least likely to be taken by surprise. When a local disaster revived a favorite argument of the relative destructiveness of fire versus water, storekeepers were prepared to hear some contestant rout an adversary with the scornful rejoinder, "You can squanch fire but you can't squanch water." [41] After all, the same debate and the same arguments had been heard in their stores after every fire in the town's history. Even novelists and local colorists have found it difficult to make the merchant anything but a passive character. Milliners, travelling salesmen, town characters, local professional men, even the local grave digger, have all provided more scope for individual interpretation. The storekeeper, the most average man in an average town, was a poor literary hero.

Perhaps, however, merchants supported prevailing ways because they believed in them and not from "salesmanlike pusillanimity." Daniel M. Storer kept store for forty years, most of the time in Shakopee, Minnesota. His diary shows that he liked and believed in the small-town code. He was miserable in St. Paul, where he moved temporarily in an attempt to better himself financially. When his friends in Shakopee presented him with a goldheaded cane on his twenty-fifth wedding anniversary, he was so choked with emotion that he had to ask a friend to deliver his speech of thanks. After his little granddaughter, Edna, sang at a Methodist festival in the GAR Hall, he confided to his diary that "She done first rate." He played the fife in Decoration Day parades, fiddled for an Episcopalian dance, and was active in the local band. Lodge affairs, funerals, socials, and community festivals all appealed to him. Farm women who won prizes on canned goods displayed from a booth in front of his store during the local street fair were no prouder over their successes than was he in making them possible. As a small-towner, he was more interested in the names and family connections of the young ladies who served cocoa in his

store on Saturday afternoons than he was in the manufacturers who used that means to popularize new brand
names.[42] The social and intellectual code of Shakopee seemed
as right and natural to him as did food and sleep. "Salesmanlike pusillanimity" scarcely explains a man like Daniel Storer.

BARBERSHOP, SALOON, AND HOTEL

WHILE LIVERY STABLES and general stores best characterized country towns of the 1870's, many other economic
agencies existed. Dry-goods stores, lumber and fuel yards,
hardware and implement shops were common.

Barbershops, with candy-striped poles, kept the same long
hours as general stores. They were open Sunday, weekdays,
and evenings to provide the country boy's first haircut for a
quarter and ten-cent shaves for men. As time passed, these
"tonsorial parlors" took on something of their modern ele-
gance. By the 1890's, many had bathrooms in the rear, where
in the winter season for twenty-five cents one could obtain
soap and towel and a bath. Barber chairs were made of high-
toned wood and velours, with a wheel in the back for tilting.
Water pitchers and basins, the finest of barber tools, steriliz-
ing bowls, stacks of towels, razor papers, hair boxes, mirrors,
stocked cigar cases, spittoons, clothes poles, comfortable
chairs, and the titillating pages of the *Police Gazette* were
standard equipment.

Located in basement rooms or in small individual buildings, often with a billiard hall nearby, the barbershop was a
man's world, and ladies hurried by to escape the ogling and
raucous laughter so evident through the flimsy façade. Cigar
smoke, sweet tart scent of bay rum, and stench of lavishly
applied tonic greeted visitors as they opened the door and
prepared to match wits and stories with their cronies. A mug
rack or cabinet along the wall contained the rows of privately owned shaving mugs of regular customers. Each was
engraved with an appropriate symbol of the owner's occupation, the only coat of arms which democracy permitted.
Farmers liked engravings of their favorite horses or perhaps

a sheaf of wheat. Trades, lodges, nicknames, and homes provided appropriate symbols for those living in town.[43]

Saloons prospered except when local option temporarily closed them down and compelled their customers to patronize local drugstores or neighboring towns. In heavily Protestant communities, where Christians claimed to be "teetotalers," saloons attracted only those intending to get dead drunk. They were violent places, shoved off to some side street called "Battle Row," if the wishes of respectable people prevailed. Their very numbers, however, made it difficult to exclude them from main streets. Marble Hall Saloon at Gallatin, Missouri, illustrates their evil reputation. About five o'clock on an August afternoon in 1865 Gallatin was terrorized by Seaman Miller. After a drinking bout and a quarrel in the Marble Hall Saloon, he rushed to his home at the edge of town and obtained a double-barreled gun loaded with buckshot. Thus armed, and in a drunken rage, he rode back and forth in front of the saloon, threatening murder until he was shot down after all efforts to calm him had failed. The preceding June another man had been killed in a quarrel over a gambling game in a shed adjoining the Marble Hall Saloon. Such incidents caused the local editor to condemn all saloons and to suggest that they be closed down before troops returned home from the Civil War.[44]

In some communities, notably those with a German element, saloons had a better reputation. They were informal clubs where men gathered for social drinking. A nickel glass of beer entitled patrons to help themselves at the free-lunch buffet to pickled pigs' feet, slices of roasts and other cold meats, hard-boiled eggs, stacks of rye and white sliced bread, cheese, and condiments. An ornately mirrored wall pictured the numerous bottles of whiskey standing on shelves behind long, highly polished counters. Side walls contained paintings of famous race horses and prize fighters and, perhaps, also one or more portraits of voluptuous and scantily attired women. One novelist has his two central characters, village boys, approach the counter for their first glass of beer with considerable surprise at the revealing lines of such a picture. When one asks the other if he has ever seen anything like that before, he can only reply: "Nope, not since I was weaned." [45]

Small towns had drugstore soda fountains and ice cream parlors before the Civil War. Ice cream had long been a delicacy, and sodas, sundaes, and even malted milks were favorites by the 1890's. [46] Most ice cream parlors maintained the highest standards of decorum. Charley Simmons opened a suite of "elegant ice cream rooms" at Monroe, Wisconsin, in 1869, where he served his own special product. One room upstairs was reserved for ladies, or for ladies and their escorts, if any were timid about sitting at tables in the nicely furnished and pleasant room below, which was open to all. [47] A few towns experimented with combination ice cream saloons and temperance billiard parlors, [48] but ice cream and billiards were never compatible. On the other hand, ice cream parlors were popular throughout the year, and especially so when summer arrived. During a heat wave at Centreville, Michigan, in June, 1888, Jack Hampson's place was the most crowded spot in town. "The continuous rattle of the popular milkshake" could be heard at Jack's all day long. [49]

Even hamlets were likely to have hotels because of the leisurely moving pace of travel. Some village hotels were two and three stories tall, with long porches, chairs and settees, where guests cooled off on drowsy summer evenings and lazily watched the parade of strolling villagers. Livery-stable advertisements above the registration desk in the main office called attention to facilities available for side trips. Sample room for drummers, perhaps a "saloon parlor" with piano, and a dining room were common. Guests often ate at a single, long table, staffed by waitresses who had acquired a breezy familiarity from the constant joshing of travelling salesmen. Many hotels charged farmers thirty-five cents and drummers fifty for the same noon meal, and no one seemed to object. On the second floor were the guest rooms, furnished with bed, chairs, pitcher and basin, and a chamber pot. Even the best establishments could not wholly eliminate the discomforts of chilly rooms and smoky coal-oil lamps, and a guest's displeasure when a domestic rapped on doors early in the morning to announce a pitcher of hot water.

Local villagers saw only the glamorous side. The constant coming and going of theatrical troupes, travelling salesmen, visiting baseball teams, and women milliners from Chicago, the presence of a Negro porter—perhaps the only member of his race in town—and the hotel hack with its gaily painted sides appealed to townsmen who craved variety. Even Ed Howe, who stimulated a vogue for realism in his novel on small-town life, as a young man had a glorious time boarding in the Maysville, Missouri, hotel while working on the local paper. The hotel had a comfortable office, as Ed remembered it, a piano in the parlor, and travelling salesmen daily telling new jokes at the dinner table. Ed entertained them with piano music after the meal and gave his own humorous sketch of a church meeting, and they in turn punned that here was the place where "one got bored [board] for nothing." [50]

In larger towns, capable of supporting two or more hotels, the lesser drummers and house-to-house canvassers, who enlarged photographs of loved ones, made crayon portraits, or sold cooking utensils and stereopticon slides, could register at cheap, second-rate establishments. Faded wallpaper, frayed carpets, and poor food were more likely to be found in such hotels, and the night clerk met local trains with a lantern instead of sending a hack.[51]

ARTISANSHIP

LOCAL TAILORS still made most of the better quality suits and took more than ordinary pride in their knowledge of styles and craftsmanship.[52] Photographers and marble cutters fancied themselves even more as the real artists among local craftsmen. Feazel and Clark of Lacon, Illinois, in 1865, proclaimed their ability to "execute likenesses from infant days to silver-haired age."[53] The Gallatin, Missouri, Marble Yard in 1873 reminded local citizens that nothing compensated mankind more richly than the time and money spent on sepulchres for departed friends. In suggesting suitable carvings, the marble yard accurately predicted the appearance of more expensive monuments in midwestern cemeteries for years to come:

The language of the heart is eloquently expressed by the figures of the lamb, the guardian angel, the rose bud, and half blown flower broken from the parent stem and fallen to the earth: also the lilly [lily] seperated [sic] from its stalk, . . . the broken shaft, the anchor, the shield, the wreath of oak and ivy, and wreath of flowers and cross and crown, and many other beautiful emblems appropriate and significant symbols, speaking the language of affection, regret and hope from living and loving hearts.[54]

Artisans as a whole, however, were rapidly turning to the retailing of manufactured products. Silver and goldsmiths were settling down to keeping jewelry stores, their earlier craftsmanship now finding an outlet in repairing watches and fitting eyeglasses.[55] Perhaps most interesting of all was the change from carpentering and cabinetmaking to the building of coffins, and the resulting historical connection between furniture and undertaking which still survives in small midwestern towns. In 1867, Kimble, Sherfy and Company of Greencastle, Indiana, carried, in addition to furniture, a full stock of coffins and metallic burial cases. They had only recently accepted the local agency for Dr. Chamberlain's celebrated embalming process.[56] More common in the 1860's, however, were advertisements like that of Charles Cummings of Centreville, Michigan, who sold furniture and "cabinet ware," and repaired furniture. Cummings kept on hand a large stock of coffins, which he could trim and furnish on short order to suit individual tastes. He accepted lumber of all kinds in payment at his shop.[57]

Carpenters served both as architect and builder in erecting new homes. On the fringes of the highly skilled trades were men who engaged in seasonal work like papering and painting. Some of them were expert in "graining" woodwork to bring out the natural colors.[58] As a rule, they came from the ranks of day laborers or from those who had failed in more remunerative occupations.[59] Small-town tanneries were rapidly disappearing by the 1860's, but the leather crafts were still represented by harness makers and shoemakers. Many of the latter were already combining the sale of factory-made shoes with custom-order work,[60] and some had shifted completely over to selling factory-made shoes. Cigar "factories," employing two or three workmen under a master craftsman, were common until the turn of the century. Most of them also retailed cigars. Wooden Indians standing near the doorway were a silent reminder that cigars could be had at wholesale and retail.[61]

Slaughterhouses at the edge of villages provided local butcher shops with fresh meat, which was cut for retail sale on circular slabs of wood standing on sawdust-covered floors.[62] By the turn of the century, slaughterhouses were going the way of the old market house, which had provided an outlet for vegetables and meats from surrounding farms. By the 1870's market houses remained in only a few of the older towns.[63]

Many villages had woolen mills and gristmills. A Trenton, Missouri, woolen mill in 1873 advertised in papers of neighboring towns that people wishing to have wool spun or made into cloth could leave fleeces at certain stores which acted as agents. Most such factories turned out cloth, yarns and woolen rolls, and many accepted raw wool in payment.[64] Farmers could bring wool and wheat in the spring and summer months to factory and flour mill, and draw out cloth and flour later in the year, thus reducing cash expenditures.

In spite of mutual interdependence of town and countryside, some evidence supports Veblen's charge of ill will between the two. More commonly, passive indifference marked the relationship, but this could flare into active conflict when farm crops were selling at sub-normal prices. The Grange movement of the late 1860's and early 1870's, with its emphasis on improving the farmer's social life and eliminating middlemen's profits wherever possible, had its greatest strength in the Middle West. While this movement was injured by destruction of farm co-operatives in the Panic of 1873, and declined as farm prices improved, farmers continued to believe that middlemen as a whole received too large a return.

Country newspaper editors were always embarrassed when farmers and merchants fell out. Although businessmen paid for advertising, farmers provided the equally vital subscription lists. When a conflict developed, editors generally resorted to diplomacy. In the spring of 1874, the central council of the Putnam County, Indiana, Grange debated whether to purchase all merchandise from one source as a means of obtaining lower prices. Some Grange members also wanted to build a local implement factory, with the idea of producing cheaper farm machinery. The county editor at Greencastle watched with considerable anxiety, and local merchants must have been disturbed by the rising tide of discontent. Within a short time, however, the paper published an editorial complimenting the local Grange for refusing to concentrate its purchases. This, said the paper, would have ruined local merchants and stimulated monopolies. In the editor's opinion, "We are one people, with a common brotherhood, and when we disable one member we endanger the whole body." But he could enthusiastically endorse the building of a local implement factory, as this harmonized with the universal craving of all country towns for industry.[65]

The Grange and subsequent farm organizations undoubtedly showed village businessmen that farmers were not defenseless against exorbitant charges. On the other hand, as long as prices remained fair, there was little to fear. Hamlin Garland's father was disappointed while managing the Grange elevator at Osage, Iowa, because farmers sold to private elevators whenever they could obtain even slightly better prices.[66] And Grange stores seldom improved on business methods followed by independent merchants. A Grange store at Oshkosh, Wisconsin, in the 1880's bought calico and gingham in quantity; but separate orders for two milk pitchers, seven ladies' corsets, four hair nets, three linen handkerchiefs, a dozen corncob pipes, one tin funnel, and so on, offered no competitive threat to other Oshkosh stores.[67]

As a rule, village businessmen were satisfied to let farmers work out their social life around their own township schools and churches. Since the village already possessed the farmer's trade, it concentrated organized efforts on attracting industry in hopes of equalling the tremendous increase in numbers, wealth, and real-estate prices occurring in American industrial cities.

Aspirations to become city people made villagers conscious that they were almost as rural as the farmers who thronged local streets on Saturday afternoons, and they were inclined to look askance at country ways. An Indiana writer of the 1870's pictured the loafers in the little declining village of Colfax as making sport of country people,[68] and country boys and girls walked the streets of such places conscious of the assumed superiority of local inhabitants.[69] The very similarity of culture in countryside and town, and the ease with which individuals moved back and forth, bred ill will rather than wholesome farm-village relations.

Within a few years, revolutions in transportation, manufacturing, and management threatened the control of farm trade by country towns. For the moment, they had a chance to establish cultural, social, and economic ties with the countryside which would have served as powerful allies in the trying days ahead. But, like Hamlin Garland, they tried to escape. They wanted to become great industrial cities and to cut themselves off from their rural heritage.

3 ✻ Ethics, Folklore, and Morality on the Middle Border

CHURCH, SCHOOL, AND HOME

BETWEEN 1850 and 1900 Americans bought one hundred million copies of William Holmes McGuffey's school readers.[1] Though well received virtually everywhere, they appealed particularly to the Middle Border. As an apostle of religion, morality, and education, McGuffey wanted to bolster midwestern civilization against the dangers inherent in pioneering new frontiers. Since his Readers were directed to a supposedly classless society, they were all-inclusive in their appeal, and from them came a set of principles which remained unchallenged in the minds of common people until the turn of the century.

McGuffey worried so much about frontier dangers that he overlooked the revolutionary changes in transportation, manufacturing, and management which were then taking place. The 1857 revision of his Readers, which most Midwesterners studied, barely mentioned steamboats, and railroads received no attention at all. Pupils learned about horse-drawn transportation, about merchant rather than manufacturer, about artisan in place of factory laborer, of the outdoors, of birds and farm animals, of gossipy barbers, of Longfellow's "Village Blacksmith," and of town pumps, watering troughs, and village greens:

> Then contented with my State,
> Let me envy not the great;
> Since true pleasures may be seen,
> On a cheerful village green.[2]

Moreover, children learned that village and country life surpassed that in cities. As a rule, McGuffey simply ignored urban ways or used them as examples of corruption. The story, "Mysterious Stranger," described the unhappiness of a man from another planet when he learned that city pleasures in our world were accompanied with the penalty of death. Still another story told of "Old Tom Smith," the drunkard, whose downfall came from city life. Through a clerkship in a city store, he became acquainted with bad company. Instead of spending his evenings reading, he went to theatres, balls, and suppers. Drinking and card playing followed next, and soon thereafter his saintly mother had to pay large gambling debts for him. Although his mother and wife grieved themselves to death over his city vices, nothing could stop his drinking. The story ended with reception of the news that he had received a ten-year prison sentence for stealing.[3] Village boys often misbehaved in McGuffey's stories but they seldom fell prey to major vices.

McGuffey's emphasis on rural and village life pleased an agrarian age. His environmental picture squared with physical facts, and people knew just enough of the outside world to share his doubts about cities. His Readers thus gained strength by applying the eternal verities to a simple culture, uncomplicated by urban and industrial problems. This very strength, however, became a source of weakness as village and farm gave way to city and factory.

McGuffey ideals retreated slowly. Rural America believed in a classless society, which helped enforce still other pressures toward conformity. In the 1830's Tocqueville commented on the tyranny of the majority in making Americans conform to a common pattern. Although disagreeing with Tocqueville's analysis, James Bryce said much the same in the 1880's. According to him, American public opinion was not stated along class lines; it applied to all. In Bryce's estimation, Americans believed that common sense resided in the minds of the majority, with a consequent "fatalism of the multitude" evident in much of American life. Ed Howe commented that city people would behave better if they knew one another as well as did villagers who heard gossip about their sins on the way home from committing them,[4] thus implying that conformity was even greater in small towns.

Perhaps also an emphasis on the immediately useful and the practical contributed to the survival of current moral values. An Iowa lawyer who spent his youth in a small town commented that most pioneers were of the earth, earthy. They knew practical things—weather, rains, common plants and animals, good livestock. But they were not philosophers.[5] Whatever the explanation, small-town beliefs changed slowly, and this characteristic gave village life an impression of stability and permanence.

The God-centered, small-town code emphasized man's immortality. School and home both paid obeisance to God's plan and God's laws, for everything fell within His master plan. From McGuffey's Readers the pupil learned that Jesus was above Plato, Socrates, and all the philosophers, for He was a God.[6] Evidences of His power and wisdom existed on every hand. McGuffey proved this with simple stories. Washington's father, for instance, secretly planted seeds in a design which spelled out George's name when they sprouted. Although George was surprised, he refused to accept his father's suggestion that chance explained the phenomenon. His father now admitted that he had planted the seeds to teach George a lesson, and urged the boy to look around him at God's planning on every hand. And thus, said McGuffey, driving home his point as usual, from that day George never doubted the existence of a God who was the creator and owner of all things.[7]

Even the problem of evil in a universe governed by divine law was explained to school boys through simple stories. Everything happened for the best and every object had a purpose in the great plan of things. When one of two boys caught in a thunderstorm remarked that he hated the evil lightning, the other explained that lightning was necessary to purify the air of bad vapors, a greater good thus offsetting a lesser evil.[8] Understanding would always clarify the appearance of evil. An observant boy asked his father to help him cut down thorn bushes and thistles which were snagging wool from the sides of passing sheep. Since parents in McGuffey's Readers were always wiser than children, the boy profited by taking his father's advice to wait until morning. In doing so, he discovered that birds used the wool to build their nests, and that God indeed was wise and good and had made everything for the best.[9]

A former resident of Hillsboro, Iowa, described the operation of this philosophy in his childhood days. Belief in God was universal. People wondered why certain things occurred, chiefly the deaths of children and very good people, but no one doubted God's existence and His fatherly care. If a death occurred, the Lord willed it. The Lord sent afflictions to punish sin and disbelief. The Lord could be prevailed upon to help His people out of difficulties. If the corn needed rain, the churches set a day of prayer. If success accompanied this, it had been the proper thing to do; if intercession failed, the people had not prayed with sufficient faith. The heavenly books were balanced daily by an omniscient bookkeeper who recorded every act. The idea of universal and impersonal law was displeasing. These people wisely turned to something warmer, something more directly personal in which man played the central part. He participated in a drama which included sky and earth, which began with Adam, and which would end only when the heavens were rolled up as a scroll.[10]

McGuffey taught that society depended on religion. Christianity was conducive to national prosperity. It raised the poor from want, brought rich and poor together on a common level for an hour of prayer, and promoted good order and harmony. Self-respect and elevation of character, softness and civility of manners came from religious teaching. Christianity strengthened the family circle as a source of instruction, comfort, and happiness.[11] Moreover,

If you can induce a community to doubt the genuineness and authenticity of the Scriptures; to question the reality and obligations of religion; to hesitate, undeciding, whether there be any such thing as virtue or vice; whether there be an eternal state of retribution beyond the grave; or whether there exists any such being as God, you have broken down the barriers of moral virtue, and hoisted the floodgates of immorality and crime.[12]

Insofar as school books are concerned, small-town Mid-America now reads of miracles of science. God, church, and even human death are generally ignored. Separation of church and state and a desire to shield children from morbid thoughts help explain this marked change. Perhaps, however, it would not have occurred had science not become the god of so many people, for gods are too important to be omitted in formal education of the young.

In the second half of the nineteenth century grade schools commonly opened the day with brief devotional exercises. Lessons also had a religious slant. McGuffey's *First Reader* pictured a little girl kneeling in prayer and asking God to protect her from sin.[13] A poem in the *Second Reader* stressed the blessings of immortality:

A little child who loves to pray,
And read his Bible too,
Shall rise above the sky one day,
And sing as angels do;
Shall live in Heaven, that world above,
Where all is joy, and peace, and love.[14]

These simple stories and poems in public-school readers document the tremendous shift in faith between the nineteenth and twentieth centuries, from a man-centered and God-centered universe on the one hand to an impersonal and science-centered universe on the other.

McGuffey also stressed the need for public schools. "We

must educate!" Literary as well as religious institutions must keep pace with the headlong rush of western settlement. If the Middle Border expected to preserve republican institutions and universal suffrage, both *head* and *heart* must be trained.[15] McGuffey thus urged pupils to feverish activity:

> Haste thee, school boy, haste away,
> While thy youth is bright and gay;
> Seek the place with knowledge blest;
> It will guide to endless rest;
> Haste thee, school boy, haste away,
> While thy youth is bright and gay.[16]

Newspapers expressed the same ideas.[17] Parents supposedly could do nothing finer for their children than to educate them.[18] Although children often attended school only irregularly and quit at an early age, and less than half the adult population were formal church members,[19] citizens generally believed that churches and schools made communities "decent places" in which to live.[20] Even real-estate promotion— the most absorbing interest of all—stressed the presence of churches and schools as selling points.

McGuffey ranked family life with church and school as a third major conservator of ideals. Families were like a bundle of twigs; the strength of all far surpassed that of the individual:

> We are all here!
> Father, Mother,
> Sister, Brother,
> All who hold each other dear.[21]

McGuffey stressed love of brother and sister in a nature poem which Theodore Roosevelt later was to criticize for its ignorance of birds:

> Birds in their little nests agree;
> And 'tis a shameful sight,
> When children of one family
> Fall out, and chide, and fight.[22]

Idealization of motherhood and the mother's central position in family life was a frequent theme. One poem referred to the mother's voice:

> It always makes me happy, too,
> To hear its gentle tone;
> I know it is the voice of love
> From a heart that is my own.[23]

Mutual interdependence was illustrated in simple stories. In one, grandfather sat in his easy chair before the fire, smoking his pipe. The family dog reclined nearby, and grandmother was busy at her spinning wheel. A granddaughter sat on the man's knee. As he thought about the death of the child's mother, tears rolled down his cheeks. Although the innocent child had not yet realized her loss, she was already repaying her grandparents for their care by catching the flies which buzzed around grandpa's head.[24]

McGuffey stressed complete obedience to parental direction and parental ideals in return for the love and care lavished on younger members of the family. The poem "Casabianca" told of a boy burning to death on the deck of a naval vessel in obedience to his father's order to await his return, which was prevented by the father's death during the naval battle then under way. While such Spartan obedience may seem unduly severe to modern-day parents, it obviously was better to die than to suffer the intense remorse of a daughter who returned to her mother's grave in the village cemetery thirteen years after the funeral. Grief overwhelmed her at the memory of how unwillingly she had brought a glass of water at her mother's request the night of the latter's death. True, she had planned to ask forgiveness the following morning, but her mother was then cold in death.[25] "Meddlesome Matty" received her just deserts in McGuffey's stories, as did a group of curious boys who applied to a rich old squire's advertisement for a youth to wait on him at table. To test the applicants, he filled his reception room with appealing items. The first boy could not resist eating a luscious-appearing cherry, only to find it filled with cayenne pepper, and others received equally just rewards for their curiosity. The one applicant who sat in the room for twenty minutes without yielding to temptation got the job, and ultimately a legacy from the rich old squire.[26] Obedience paid off in many ways in McGuffey's stories, as the disobedient little fish learned after being pulled from the water on a hook:

> And as he faint and fainter grew,
> With hollow voice he cried,
> Dear mother, had I minded you,
> I need not thus have died.[27]

At company dinners, McGuffey-trained parents made children eat at the second table and also expected them to be seen and not heard. Elders were always addressed as "Mr." and "Mrs." by properly reared children. At the same time, parents wanted their offspring to have every advantage of religion and education, if they really had taken the McGuffey lessons to heart.

CULTURAL PATTERNS

CHURCH, SCHOOL, AND HOME thus furnished education for *heart* and *mind,* a process which involved the teaching of an extensive code of morality. Without doubt, this fitted best the needs and desires of a pious, church-going, middle-class society. For such people, the McGuffey code was both adequate and right. In their estimation, it underlay decent society in this world and salvation in the next. Midwestern ideals did not come solely from this one middle-class group, however. Although it dominated education and fought hard to enforce its convictions, it was never able to establish conformity on the part of all citizens.

At least four additional sources competed with and modified the dominant middle-class code. The first can be loosely identified as upper class in nature, although its ramifications

were broader than simple class structure. Virtually everywhere on the Middle Border were families which held substantial or respectable places in society without bowing to
the McGuffey code. Episcopalians like Benjamin F. Mackall
of Moorhead, Minnesota, and Daniel M. Storer of Shakopee,
Minnesota, danced and played cards and ignored the gloomy
restrictions which dominated so many of their contemporaries.[28] Even good Presbyterians and Methodists who read
more than church and secular newspapers often slighted
McGuffey's code. In 1865 Helen Clift Shroyer of New Castle,
Indiana, and her friends played euchre and seven-up without the slightest sense of guilt; and she and her fiancé accompanied others to a dance in a neighboring town which
lasted so late that they reached home at five in the morning.
Her wedding trip included visits to the Chicago theatre.
Oyster suppers, cards, dances, popcorn parties, visits to ice
cream parlors, and Sunday afternoon buggy rides appealed
to her. She dodged funerals if at all possible and ignored
many of the common commercial entertainments. The "Mysterious Man," a sleight-of-hand performer, was passed by on
the grounds that she was too tired to attend, a lame excuse
for one of her energy. She was critical of a temperance lecture which she made herself attend, and was bored in
Brother Norris' Sunday School class because she thought he
could not teach "worth a cent." The Sunday reading of the
Atlantic Monthly, which she and her husband enjoyed, may
have taken the bloom from Brother Norris' penetrating remarks on the scriptures.[29] The families of Edgar Lee Masters
and Thomas Hart Benton were neither pious nor active
church members, and both taught their children a set of
standards which deviated from McGuffey's code. Zona
Gale's father, a self-educated railroad engineer, taught her
that the spirit of man is God, and that no other God exists.
From him she obtained other convictions, like pacifism,
which ran counter to dominant middle-class beliefs.[30] Such
families generally dared not flaunt their heresies in the face
of local society, especially since they relied on local people

for their livelihood, but they did maintain a measure of individuality.

Catholics represented still another departure from the
dominant code. In their views on education, Sabbath recreation, and intoxicants, they clashed with middle-class
Protestant sentiments. Although McGuffey opposed religious
intolerance, anti-Catholic feeling existed in midwestern
country towns. Don Marquis, himself the product of a small
Illinois town, pictures this in his novel, *Sons of the Puritans.*
Aunt Matilda, guardian of the dominant small-town code,
becomes alarmed when she learns that a Catholic has been
entertaining village youngsters with stories. She suspects him
of showing them beads, speaking in Latin, and even of exhibiting idols, with an invitation to fall down and worship
them. Aunt Matilda belongs to the group that circulates
rumors about collections of firearms in Catholic churches.[31]
Bromfield's novel, *The Farm,* in large measure the story of
his family's life in Ohio, recounts the anti-Catholic sentiment
which a youngster in his family heard in livery stables, police
stations, and other gathering places. Copies of a paper, *The
Menace,* containing vivid accounts of rapes committed by
Catholic priests and of illegitimate children born to Catholic
nuns, passed from hand to hand. Secret passages supposedly
connected homes of priests with neighboring convents so
they could visit nuns at their convenience.[32] An occasional
minister condemned Catholicism from the pulpit. In a
Thanksgiving Day sermon in 1869 at Centreville, Michigan,
a Methodist preacher boasted that infidel France and Catholic Mexico had been incapable of reaching the same high
civilization then prevalent in Protestant America. Three generations locally, he said, had been sufficient to stamp out
Romanism in family life.[33] Similarly, a Baptist preacher preparing for a revival meeting at Gallatin, Missouri, in 1893,
claimed that Protestants modelled themselves on Christ
while Catholics worshipped lesser figures.[34]

Although many immigrants were Catholics, it is well to
note that still another cultural influence in small towns came

from foreign immigration. Immigrants could not know all the shadings of the dominant, moralistic code followed by middle-class Protestants. A considerable number of German Lutherans and Catholics at Monroe, Wisconsin, in the late 1860's and early 1870's, organized a local Turnverein and carried on an active social program in Turner's Hall. Masked balls, beer drinking, and uniformed acrobatic groups of young Germans performing on the bars and trapeze conflicted with local ideas of proper behavior. People got along, to the credit of all groups, but "Christians" sniffed nonetheless. In December, 1869, the Monroe editor reported that the Turners had decided to close their bar on Sunday nights in favor of a "Lyceum Concert." Older and wiser heads had persuaded the younger people to make the change. Perhaps a Turner's idea of God was different from that of a "genuine" Christian, said the editor. If the Turners thought God liked conviviality, a good glass of lager beer, or even a comic song, the community might indulge them so long as they closed their bar on Sunday.[35]

Lastly, every community had a group of inhabitants who simply ignored the middle-class code of respectability and religious observance. They drank and fought and caroused and "cussed," or they hunted on Sunday, shunned the churches, and pursued their simple pleasures without yielding to community pressure to lead a "better" life. Here, then, was the cultural pattern—a dominant middle-class Protestant group given to religion and stern morality; an upper-class group of "respectable" people who failed to see any necessary connection between pleasure and sin; Catholics; foreigners; and a "lower" class, which ignored the dominant code except perhaps for temporary allegiance following revival meetings. In spite of latent antagonisms, villagers lived close together and could not avoid influencing one another. It was a rare boy indeed who grew to manhood solely as the product of one cultural layer.

Outstanding interpreters of small-town culture have recognized this diversity of beliefs. Americans chuckle at the exploits of Huckleberry Finn, son of the town drunkard, who was free to swear, smoke, swim and go barefooted, and who ran away from riches when they came his way simply because he refused to conform to local standards of respectability. Mark Twain grew up in small midwestern towns and he knew from experience the conflicting cultural patterns within such communities. When Van Wyck Brooks later wrote *The Ordeal of Mark Twain*,[36] in which he presented Mark as wanting to rebel against a sex-warped and barren culture, he ignored the many cultural differences illustrated in Twain's own small-town characters. Bernard De Voto has pointed out the dangerous oversimplification in Brooks' thesis and the many strands running through midwestern culture.[37] In the so-called "battle of the village" which novelists fought in the early twentieth century, some, like Zona Gale, emphasized sweetness and light, and others, like Sinclair Lewis, concentrated on the drab and monotonous aspects of town life. In such novels, emphasis became distortion instead of insight, and they inevitably fell below the level of realism which Twain achieved.

MIDDLE-CLASS IDEALS

THE DOMINANT, middle-class code of McGuffey and his followers held that life was a serious business. In selections like Longfellow's "Psalm of Life" readers were urged to make the most of their opportunities:

> Tell me not in mournful numbers,
> Life is but an empty dream!
>
> .   .   .   .
>
> Life is real! Life is earnest!
>
> .   .   .   .
>
> Footprints on the sands of time.
>
> .   .   .   .
>
> Let us, then, be up and doing,
>   With a heart for any fate;
> Still achieving, still pursuing,
>   Learn to labor and to wait.[38]

Even the ancients were cited to the same effect. Hercules turned away from the siren called "Pleasure" to follow a maiden whose path to happiness involved both pain and labor.[39] In this selection, and others like "Hugh Idle and Mr. Toil," [40] McGuffey stressed the virtues of labor. Youngsters who took him seriously could not indulge in leisurely enjoyment of wealth later on without a sense of guilt. Moreover, perseverance was highly recommended:

> Once or twice though you should fail,
>   Try, Try, Again;
> If you would at last prevail,
>   Try, Try, Again;
> If we strive, 'tis no disgrace,
> Though we may not win the race;
> What should you do in that case?
>   Try, Try, Again.[41]

Truth, honesty, and courage belonged to the cluster of desirable traits. Washington's father so loved truth that nailing George in a coffin and following him to the grave would have been less painful than hearing a lie from the boy's lips. When George cut down the cherry tree, he manfully told his father "I can't tell a *lie*, father. You know I can't tell a *lie*." And his father in turn joyfully cried, "Come to my arms, my dearest boy. . . ." Common people could be equally noble. Susan's widowed mother made the family living by taking in washing, and Susan helped by making deliveries. On one occasion, Farmer Thompson gave her two bills in payment by mistake. She was severely tempted. The additional money would mean a new coat for mother, and little sister could have the old one to wear to Sunday School. Little brother could have a new pair of shoes. In spite of such desperate need, Susan corrected the mistake, and, sobbing with anguish, refused a shilling's reward on the grounds that she did not want to be paid for honesty. In this case, she received only a lightened heart, but McGuffey's heroines usually gained financially as well. McGuffey also stressed courage, even at the risk of ridicule. A boy who snowballed the schoolhouse to avoid the taunts of others, when he knew the act was wrong, was pictured as lacking in true courage.[42]

Contentment, modesty, and kindness were praised. One story told of Jupiter permitting unhappy people to exchange burdens with others. One man discarded his modesty instead of his ignorance; another his memory rather than his crimes. An old man threw off his gout in favor of a male heir, only to obtain an undutiful son discarded by an angry father. All begged Jupiter to restore their old afflictions. Patience stood by as they resumed their old troubles and automatically reduced their loads by a third. The moral was plain, according to McGuffey. One should never repine over his own problems or envy another, since no man could rightly judge his neighbor's misfortune.[43] A beauty who tossed her glove into a ring with lions to prove her lover's devotion, only to have him throw it in her face after regaining it, showed the silliness of vanity.[44] A poem about Mary's lamb demonstrated the rewards for kindness to animals. When it followed her to school one day, and the children marvelled at its affection, the teacher commented:

> And you each gentle animal
> To you, for life may bind,
> And make it follow at your call,
> If you are always *kind*.[45]

Greed, revenge, and selfishness toward others were castigated in stories which made plain the moral involved. "The Tricky Boy," for instance, was mean and given to teasing others. When a tired little girl asked help in shifting a jug of milk to her head in order to rest her weary arms, he purposely let it fall to the ground and break. He thought it was fun to see her cry until he slipped on the ground, made slick by the spilled milk, and was laid up for three months with a broken leg.[46]

While McGuffey's code has been ridiculed for its emphasis on material rewards for virtue and unremitting labor—and a hasty reading of his stories may seem to bear this out—he offered a nicely balanced philosophy in which life's purpose and rewards transcended material gains. In his own life and in his Readers, McGuffey preached against the foolishness of material ambition alone, to which so many of his pupils turned:

> Praise—when the ear has grown too dull to hear;
> Gold—when the senses it should please are dead;
> Wreaths—when the hair they cover has grown gray,
> Fame—when the heart it should have thrill'd is numb.[47]

Newspapers and preachers supported McGuffey's scheme of values. In 1870, the Centreville, Michigan, paper published a letter addressed to "My Dear Obadiah," urging young men to attend church, to act and dress modestly, to be ambitious, and to abhor drinking, smoking, and chewing. A companion letter to "My Dear Dorinda" encouraged girls to be sober and thoughtful in preparation for marriage and motherhood. Many were interested only in clothes, and their vocabulary was studded with vapid expressions like, "I thought I should die," "O my," "What are you going to wear," "O ain't that pretty," "Now you're real mean," "You think you're smart, don't you," and "Well I don't care, there now." The writer asked what such girls could do in the kitchen or sick room.[48] A Chatfield, Minnesota, sermon on the "Fast Young Man" in 1896 pictured various types—"the Dude," "the Softie," "the Lazy," "the Dissipate." Young men, said the preacher, should adopt habits of personal cleanliness, avoid bad company, retire early at night, and practice modesty.[49]

Protestant pulpit and press also generally supported McGuffey's views on Sabbath observance. At Monroe, Wisconsin, in 1896, the local Presbyterian preacher asked bicycle riders to discontinue the practice of visiting neighboring towns in groups on Sunday. Another local preacher used the bicycle problem as a springboard for discussing the relation of Sabbath observance to morals as a whole. Granting that times had changed and that the Sabbath was made for man, he insisted that people still must square their actions with their consciences. In developing this theme, he offered a number of observations paralleling McGuffey's ideals. Gambling at church affairs was as evil as gambling in saloons. Card playing wasted time that could be better employed. A man should feel just as free to encircle the waist of his neighbor's wife in a round dance as he would on the way home from prayer meeting. And there was no more harm in a bicycle "spin" on Sunday than in a drive with horse and carriage; less, as a matter of fact, if the horse was tired. People winked at bigger sins on weekdays, liquor drinking for example.[50]

McGuffey firmly believed in private property and in its blessings to society. He quoted Blackstone to prove that necessity begat property and recourse was had to civil society to insure it. Private property had enabled a part of society to provide subsistence for all. It had insured leisure to cultivate the mind, invent useful arts, and to promote science. Simple stories again drove home the lesson. Although a little chimney sweep wanted more than anything else a beautiful, tune-playing watch which he saw in a lady's boudoir, he did not touch it because of his aversion to stealing. Fortunately for him, the lady saw him resist the temptation and took him as her ward. Education and success naturally followed. If he had stolen the watch, said McGuffey, he would have gone to jail. One could not steal the smallest thing without sin, and children should remember that God's eye saw all that transpired.[51]

McGuffey also recognized an obligation of the rich to aid the unfortunate. "Grateful Julian" set the standard. Beyond old rags for clothing and a straw pallet, he possessed nothing but a rabbit which he dearly loved. When he fell ill, a rich and good man took him in and cured his sickness. In return, Julian wished to present the rabbit to his benefactor, an act which so touched the latter that he sent the boy to school. Julian naturally grew up into a bright and honest lad.[52] Moreover, people were expected to give according to their means, as illustrated in a poem called "The Philosopher's Scales":

> A long row of alms-houses, amply endow'd
> By a well-esteem'd Pharisee, busy and proud,
> Next loaded one scale; while the other was prest
> By those mites the poor widow dropp'd into the chest;
> Up flew the endowment, not weighing an ounce,
> And down, down the farthing-worth came with a bounce.[53]

Apart from illness and misfortune, no man needed to be poor. As one McGuffey story put the matter, all could find employment and there was no place for idlers and vagrants. Of course, one should be frugal, as the famous story of the string-saving boy proved, and labor was essential to success:

> Shall birds, and bees, and ants, be wise,
> While I my moments waste?
> O let me with the morning rise,
> And to my duty haste.[54]

Henry, the orphan boy, illustrated the fruits of rugged individualism. In need of a new grammar book, he shoveled snow to earn the price, thus proving "Where There's a Will, There is a Way." [55]

Newspapers elaborated the same theme. In 1867 the editor of the Algona, Iowa, paper replied sharply to a letter from a local citizen who objected to raising money for foreign missions when Algona had poor and destitute families of its own. The editor doubted if any Algonans were too poor to deny themselves at least one luxury, like owning a worthless cur, smoking or chewing at a cost of twenty-five to fifty dollars a year, or the inordinate use of tea or coffee. A man had recently told a local storekeeper a pitiful tale of hard times and no job, and had been given a sack of flour on credit. Having obtained this, he immediately produced twenty-five cents in cash to buy tobacco. With that style of poverty the editor had no sympathy. Furthermore, he had no sympathy with thievery, since any healthy man could "earn a living in this land of plenty." [56]

Preachers and newspaper editors agreed with McGuffey that individuals could rise in the world through their own efforts. A Centreville, Michigan, preacher in 1869 affirmed that his community had no rich, no poor, no ignorant citizens save as each individual's own vice or virtue, own energy or indolence had made him so.[57] When former Senator John J. Ingalls of Kansas expressed similar sentiments in 1893, the editor of the Gallatin, Missouri, paper devoted virtually a whole column to summarizing his remarks. According to Ingalls, all men were self-made; even chance and circumstance were made by men and not the other way round. He who was born poor was fortunate. Future leaders of thought, business, and society would not come from the gilded youth of 1893 but from ambitious sons of farmers and laborers.[58]

Near the turn of the century, Markham's famous poem, "The Man with the Hoe," disturbed defenders of the old order because it seemingly condemned the economic system for injuring the common man. Businessmen offered prizes for poetical rebuttals, and William Jennings Bryan lectured on the implications of the poem. Small-town Mid-America was also disturbed. A "goodly contingent" of Brookfield, Missouri, businessmen gathered at the local Congregational church in the fall of 1899 to hear the pastor discuss the poem. According to him, the idea that the hoe could debase mankind was utterly un-American, degenerate, and unpatriotic. The man with the hoe was the man with opportunity; one needed only to keep an eye on the individual who refused to grasp its handle. Our mightiest leaders had been the products of lives of toil with the hoe, axe, crucible, mallet, and saw.[59]

According to McGuffey, the inferior animals made no mistakes and no improvements; man made both.[60] People were inclined to agree, although they accepted progress as so natural as to need no proof or analysis. And, of course, American standards were the measuring sticks. When John E. Young summarized world events in his diary at the close of 1868, he concluded that China was making rapid progress toward civilization and political greatness. American influence was given as the reason. Political revolution in Japan, moreover, gave hope that civilization and human progress would find a lodgment there. Even Abyssinia had been compelled to bow before the prowess of English civilization and Christianity.[61]

Progress was most generally interpreted as growth in material things. When the historian of Kossuth County, Iowa, came to the subject of progress, he followed a very common pattern in telling the story in terms of *growth*—growth of population, of property values, of roads, of the butter and cream industry.[62] Although the editor of a Kossuth County paper was inclined to agree with such measurements, he expressed some doubts in an article published in 1896. After pointing out the great growth in population, fine homes, wealth, and railroads in the short interval since Algona's first New Year's celebration in 1859, he raised the question of whether people locally were any happier. How much, he asked, had such externals added to the zest for life of those pioneers still present? [63] Even town boosters could be sentimental about the good old days, but sentiment was not allowed to interfere with the constant itch for bigness, growth, and numbers—in short, with progress.

MAJOR AND MINOR SINS

MC GUFFEY also introduced his young readers to the major moralistic theme of the dominant, middle-class group, the dangers of liquor and its associated evils. In a story called "Touch Not—Taste Not—Handle Not" he described the terrible economic, physical, and moral consequences of drinking. Still other stories told of "intemperate husbands," who abused their first-born sons and brought their wives to a sorrowful death, and of the "venomous worm" which was more deadly than the rattlesnake or the copperhead. In an account filled with suspense, McGuffey described this terrible creature which bit only the human race, and then identified it as the *"Worm of the Still."* [64] Gambling was also bad, for it grew on one at an insatiable rate and ultimately led to other evils, such as drinking, cheating, and murder.[65] While not condemned outright, dancing obviously found hospitable allies in liquor and cards, and the serious-minded-and-aspiring youngster was taught to avoid all three.

This cluster of moral convictions fascinated later novelists like Don Marquis, who pictured the saloon and church as concrete symbols of the age-old conflict of light and darkness, of evil and good. Church and saloon offered escape and refuge.[66] The swinging doors of a saloon gave sanctuary from too much virtue; the double portals of a church opened avenues to goodness. Neither church nor saloon could win total victory in the eternal struggle of good versus evil.

The Middle West was not unique in supporting both church and saloon. McGuffey himself came from a moralistic, middle-class background farther to the East, and only through his fear that savagery would destroy civilization on the Middle Border frontier did he express sentiments peculiar to that area. Although the battle of church-versus-saloon perhaps was more intense on the Middle Border, the struggle itself was nationwide.

The conflict left no room for halfway measures on either side. Men generally drank to excess or were teetotalers. In this battle of extremes drunkenness often led to disaster. The warden of the Indiana state prison in 1859 reported that 446 of the 556 inmates had been addicted to drink.[67] Newspapers and diarists constantly referred to tragedies resulting from intoxication. John E. Young of the little town of Athens, Illinois, recorded the death of a local physician in 1893 from an overdose of morphine following a drunken spree; the serious injury to a local citizen, who fell off the railroad cars while on a "tare" in Springfield on the Fourth of July in 1894; the loss of an arm by "old man Hess," who fell under a train at the local depot while on a Christmas drunk in 1895; and drunken antics at local saloons during the Christmas season of 1896.[68] Such widespread evidence fired the opponents of liquor to greater efforts in behalf of total prohibition, and this in turn encouraged still heavier drinking by those who dared to transgress.

Dancing, cards, and smoking also continued in spite of moral opposition. William Allen White's father and mother occasionally played euchre and seven-up, but when White caught his son doing the same with other boys in the hay-mow, he set up a table on the front porch and made them play in full view of citizens passing on the street. That was sufficient to cure his son of the habit for years to come.[69] Chewing and smoking by men were tolerated within limits, but many thought of them as dirty, expensive, and conducive to still greater evils. An exchange item labelled "Boys Beware" in a Michigan paper in 1869 warned youngsters against chewing tobacco, smoking cigars, drinking, and playing cards or billiards. Such habits cost money, led to stealing, and were filthy in nature.[70]

Cigarettes increased greatly in popularity near the turn of the century. Youngsters liked the early cigarette brands like Duke's Cameo and Sweet Caporals. Each packet of the latter contained a picture of an "opera star" dressed in tights, of which Lillian Russell was the favorite. Smokers who preferred Sweet Caporals could assemble a whole collection of twenty-four near-to-nude beauties.[71] In the 1890's papers began to publish material from the National Cigarette Association explaining the evil effects of smoking. According to Dr. David Starr Jordan, president of Stanford University, boys who smoked cigarettes were like wormy apples and very few ever got to college. While other boys pushed ahead, they had need of the undertaker and the sexton. Still, said Dr. Jordan, philosophically, this speeded up the race for the survival of the fittest.[72] One country paper in 1893 mentioned a cigarette "fiend" who, on his way to the World's Fair, missed his train in Brookfield while trying to purchase a nickel's worth of "coffin nails." [73]

The word "sex" was too horrible a thing for McGuffey to bandy about. Others might frighten pubescent youngsters with the dire consequences of "impure thoughts," but Mc-

Guffey seemingly preferred to believe that Christian children would concentrate on school books and their duties to parents. McGuffey said that marriage and a family gave men the necessary stimulus to succeed, and that marriage and motherhood constituted the natural and most honored vocation for women.[74]

This attitude harmonized nicely with prevailing opinion on the Middle Border. Since all women were expected to marry, spinsters had no place in society. They could work as domestics for others or live with more fortunate married relatives, but no woman was supposed to have become an "old maid" by choice.[75] If no husband was available, a woman could save her pride by pretending that her lover had died on the eve of their marriage and that she had been unable thereafter to think of caring for another man. Idealized love appealed to that sentimental age, partially because it helped conceal the grim practicality surrounding so much of the marriage relationship.

Although circumscribed, the wife's position was important. She prided herself on being a good cook and housekeeper. Company dinners with lavish quantities of food demonstrated her ability as a cook and her husband's success as a "good provider." While guests crammed themselves with food, she bustled about the table to see that all were properly served, and not until the last guest had finished did she permit herself to eat. As an angel of mercy to neighbors in distress and an avenging instrument of gossip, she maintained her family's influence in society and church affairs. She was economical of her husband's worldly goods, condemned the vanities of rouge and the sin of cigarettes, and got her washing on the line at an early hour on Monday morning. Most of all, she sought "advantages" for her children, and operated as a matchmaker in behalf of her marriageable daughters. In carrying out these functions she personified the traits of the successful middle-class housewife.

Marriage itself involved a combination of Rabelaisian humor and prudery. The Christmas season rivalled June for weddings, perhaps because routine activities slackened between Christmas and New Year's. Charivaris, infares, and joshing often marked the occasion. When William Allen White's parents returned from their honeymoon, they found that every chamber pot in their home had been gaily decorated by friends in honor of the occasion. Similarly, the editor of the Gallatin, Missouri, paper honored the marriage of a respectable couple in 1865 with the comment that he was glad to see them obeying the Apostle Paul's injunction that it was better to marry than to burn.[76]

In marriage, as in most aspects of life, the puritanical streak was uppermost. When Tocqueville visited America in the 1830's he was surprised to see how freely unchaperoned young girls went places with men. In his opinion, this very freedom explained in part why American women made excellent wives in a practical sense. At the same time, he felt sure that mothers had to warn girls of the dangers in unrestricted association with men, and he wondered if this did not invigorate judgment at the expense of imagination.[77] A midwestern paper put the matter more bluntly in 1898 in a story headed "Where is Papa?" In this case, an unfortunate girl had been deserted by her lover, and the editor urged mothers to warn their daughters against the falsity of men's promises. Girls should be told that shame could not be covered up no matter how long one lived or how good one became in later life. A woman's entire life could not atone for such a sin.[78]

Mothers apparently needed little urging to instruct their daughters in matters vital to maintaining their purity before marriage. Unfortunately, advice and information seems to have gone no further. Young girls and old maids were excluded from matronly discussions of delicate matters. In watching their elders at home and in society, girls must have concluded that virtue and prudery were synonymous. Married people in small towns carefully avoided any appearance of undue interest in the opposite sex. Social intercourse was stilted and formal, and men and women sat apart at social gatherings to prevent any threat of gossip. Parents avoided displays of affection toward one another in front of their children, and widowed people waited at least a year to re-marry in order to escape community censure.

"Sex-warped" attitudes were common enough on the Middle Border. Both Sherwood Anderson and Edgar Lee Masters were obsessed with sex. Both engaged in a series of tawdry sexual alliances, and both had trouble living a normal married life. Although few others wrote equally frank autobiographies, these men were not unique. Still other Midwesterners, seemingly repelled by the sexual crudity which they observed, turned to an impossibly idealized love. The tragedy played out in Ed Howe's *Story of a Country Town* rests basically on Jo Erring's ridiculous and impossible ideal-ization of the gentle and innocent Mateel. Howe's own boy-hood was marred by his father's desertion of the family for another woman, and Howe's own marriage in later years came to grief. Idealized love and sex-obsession alike owed something to the puritanical code which permeated much of the Middle Border. But before one joins with Van Wyck Brooks in calling this culture "sex-warped," he must explain the happy marriages which are spelled out in the writings and autobiographies of other men like Garland, Quick and White. Midwestern culture was complex, composed of sev-eral layers, and out of this came markedly different men.

THE W.C.T.U. CRUSADE AGAINST SEX AND LIQUOR

PROTESTANT CHURCHES and auxiliaries like the W.C. T.U. led the fight against the cluster of moral evils con-demned by the middle-class code. The ledger of the Baptist church of Attica, Indiana, for 1870-1901 shows the extent to which some religious groups supervised their members. In the seven years preceding 1877, the hand of fellowship was withdrawn from twenty-two members of the Attica church. A few were restored to good standing, but most remained permanently outside the pale. On October 31,

1871, three charges were preferred against Sister Laura Martin for dancing, breaking promises, and unfaithfulness.[79] In Attica, as elsewhere, one could be "churched" for offenses ranging from failure to attend worship regularly to moral delinquency.

Since the W.C.T.U. cut across church lines and also led the fight against the chief symbol of evil, the local saloon, its activities illustrated most spectacularly the moral crusade. Organizations of men opposed to liquor antedated the Civil War, but never achieved the fame of those pious, psalm-singing Christian women who dared to enter saloons during the W.C.T.U. crusade.

The Woman's Crusade began in Hillsboro, Ohio, in 1874, where a band of women, led by a daughter of a former Ohio governor, after prayer and reading of the 146th Psalm—which became known as the crusade psalm—went daily for several months to pray and sing in local saloons. Washington Court House, Ohio, however, first witnessed the closing of all saloons by such action. After morning prayer at a local church, women marched to the saloons to chant their message. Other women and men continued to pray at the church, and a bell rang constantly to announce that the crusade was in motion. On the second day, all saloons were barred to the women but they knelt in snow on pavement outside the doors to pray. One saloon keeper, unable to resist their appeal, gave them his liquor stock to destroy. Within eight days all eleven local saloons had closed down.

The movement now swept rapidly over the Middle West. Though victory was in the air, within six months the initial impulse had waned. Within another year, Washington Court House had more saloons than ever before. Formal organization of the W.C.T.U. in 1874, however, and the selection of Frances E. Willard as president in 1879 led to 44,000 paid members in 1880 and a rapid increase in the years following.[80] Red Ribbon clubs for men, children's organizations, strolling temperance lecturers, and annual fights in city elections over high-versus-low-license-fees for saloons dramatized the fight of church-versus-saloon constantly to the turn of the century.

The Woman's Christian Temperance Union at Thorntown, Indiana, was very active in the 1880's. In the front of their record book some faithful member pasted the eight stanzas of the "Battle Hymn of the Crusade," set to the tune of the "Battle Hymn of the Republic," and with the same chorus:

> On the plains for bloodless battle, they are gathered true
> and strong—
> All the hero-hearted women who have wept in silence
> long
> At the terrible oncoming of this raven-winged wrong.
> Now God is leading on.
>
> Chorus: Glory, glory, hallelujah, etc.
>
> They have rallied forth to conquer, and will never beat
> retreat
> While the banner of the rum-fiend is still flaunted on
> the street,
> And his hellish snares are waiting for the all unwary
> feet,
> For God will lead them on.
>
> .   .   .   .
>
> They have looked to law's enforcement for the help that
> never came;
>
> .   .   .   .
>
> They are working, weeping, praying, in their weakness,
> side by side
>
> .   .   .   .
>
> Oh, the beauty and the blessing when the curse is swept
> away
>
> .   .   .   .
>
> Then the desert and the wilderness shall blossom with
> the flowers
> Of industry and plenty, in this blessed land of ours,
> And the grace of God unstinted shall come down in
> gentle showers,
> For God is leading on.

The dominant, middle-class code emphasized "social purity," which meant fundamentally that youngsters and adults should avoid thinking about their own bodies, and most certainly about those of the opposite sex. Boys who wondered about sex found themselves automatically convicted of violating "social purity" and subject to the terrible consequences said to follow. A clipping in the Thorntown W.C. T.U. minute book led to a number of local discussions on the subject. The clipping called attention to a widely circulated paper which advertised for subscribers in the temperance and religious press. One issue of this paper contained nineteen advertisements to "weak men." Obviously, according to the clipping, nineteen establishments, and many more, obtained enough business to pay them to advertise widely. W.C.T.U. mothers were told that their "loved sons" were quietly "sowing the seeds" from which "charlatans would reap a rich harvest on the morrow." Since Christian youth did not realize the damage caused by impure thoughts, mothers were urged to display the necessary moral courage to warn them. Boys as young as six years of age needed this advice. The clipping recommended a specific book as helpful because it listed the results of evil thoughts and offered suggestions on how to control them. It gave examples of no impure act occurring to self or others, and yet of evil thoughts alone leading to marked nervous disorder.

And why not? Country newspapers contained numerous advertisements of remedies for "impure thoughts," which scared ignorant and conscience-stricken boys out of their wits by suggesting that if they hurried to reply they could be cured without "use of the knife." Such advertisements did not decline in numbers until the 1880's, and after that travelling doctors kept alive the theme.[81]

The impact of misinformation must have been a lifelong source of worry to some men. For ten cents boys could obtain a postal card from Dr. E. C. Abbey of Buffalo, New York, on *The Sexual System and Its Derangements* which told them of the terrible consequences of thinking about girls and promised additional information on request concerning the causes of nervous and sexual debility, languor, tiresome feelings, forgetfulness, gloomy forebodings, lack of energy, despondency, unfitness for business, unsociability, cowardice, bashfulness, irritable temper, lack of confidence, unfixedness of purpose, broken sleep, trembling, dizziness, staggering, soft muscles, weak back, pasty skin, hollow eyes, blunted senses, eruptions, scanty beard, and a thousand other symptoms which made life miserable and ushered in epilepsy, palsy, idiocy, insanity, nervousness, and other diseases.[82] And all this could happen to a boy simply because he thought about sex!

Fortunately, many youngsters were protected by well-balanced parents. Herbert Quick, Iowa novelist and lawyer, came in contact with vicious filth and ignorant sex knowledge as a boy in Iowa towns without injury. As he put it:

This ability to walk in a sort of fiery furnace without much scorching of the garments—I won't say with none—was possible for me because of the inflexible moral rectitude of my parents, and the atmosphere of fundamental righteousness in which we were bathed at home. On the surface, at least, it was not a religious atmosphere, though we all felt a basis of religion in the characters of our parents. We never had any religious family services, never had the blessing asked at the table, and none of us were ever baptized until such as chose to do so became church communicants in later life—which never took place with me. It was rather an indwelling spirit of integrity in the family, a conclusive presumption that the way marked out for us to follow was not the way for any reasons of mere conformity to the rest of the world.[83]

But a boy whose mother was overly enthusiastic on the subject of "social purity" had a rough time listening to her exhortations and those of the Dr. Abbeys.

The Thorntown W.C.T.U. also agitated against the use of tobacco. One clipping in their minute book reported that six hundred million dollars annually went for tobacco in the

United States but only five-and-a-half million to foreign missions. Some eighty diseases and 80,000 deaths annually supposedly resulted from the use of tobacco. In order to prevent sales to minors, the Thorntown women maintained constant vigilance, and also encouraged local doctors and teachers to write to Congress in behalf of restrictive legislation.

Their activities extended to any local problem involving reform or relief of mankind. They urged the county to remove orphans from the poor farm and to build a county orphanage. They provided funds to send a local prostitute and dope addict to a sanitarium for treatment, and encouraged another citizen to submit to the "bichloride of gold" cure for a social disease. Members visited with the sick and prayed and sang with them. Destitute citizens received clothing and food from the organization.

Always, however, the moral-religious theme remained uppermost, with the saloon as the major enemy. Women installed brackets in local saloons to hold temperance tracts, raised money for the national organization, opposed the opening of additional local saloons, and sponsored oratorical contests to propagandize for the cause.

The Demorest oratorical contests were popular for many years. In these, younger members of W.C.T.U. auxiliaries presented readings favoring total prohibition. The national organization provided contest books, and schools of expression in nearby cities occasionally sent teachers to coach the speakers. Six to eight young ladies would "read" first for a silver medal. The winner could then compete with other first-round winners for the gold, grand-gold, diamond, and grand-diamond awards, given in that order for those who chose to continue until they reached the top.[84]

On July 24, 1890, the Thorntown W.C.T.U. staged one of its most successful contests. Promptly at eight that evening the presiding officer opened the program by asking everyone to join in singing "All Hail the Power of Jesus' Name." A second member of the organization then gave "an impressive and energizing prayer," and a third read the thirteenth chapter of Corinthians. After explaining the nature of the contest, the chairman introduced the first elocutionist, and the program proceeded as follows:

Edith L. Crist, "Prohibition, the Hope of Our Country."
Song by mixed quartette, "Sleeping on Guard."
Daisy Wetherall, "The Rumseller's Legal Rights."
Quartette, "Lift the Temperance Banner High."
Anne McDowell, "Not Dead Nor Dying."
Pearl Brookie, "The Cry of Today."
Duet, "A Child's Pleading." (Tender enough, said the report, to soften the drunkard's heart for whom it was intended.)
Stella Ridenour, "The New Declaration of Independence."
Quartette, "Save the Boy." (Miss Emma Campbell took the solo part, said the report, and as the voices came in on the chorus one could hear a pin fall.)
Norah Reber, "An Honest Rumseller's Advertisement."

While the judges retired to determine the winner, the audience sang "The Light of Truth is Breaking," and then came a recitation by a little girl. This and other medal contests sponsored by the Thorntown chapter attracted enthusiastic audiences.

Some twenty women constituted the core of the Thorntown chapter. Deeply religious in outlook, they opened their meetings with prayers and gospel favorites of the day—"Rescue the Perishing," "Let the Lower Lights be Burning," "What a Friend We Have in Jesus," "I Love to Tell the Story," "Work for the Night is Coming," "Nearer My God to Thee," and others. Although they sought advice from their husbands in handling the more scandalous problems, they were courageous enough to invade local saloons. Most of them were frugal by necessity, the raising of eighteen cents to purchase a broom being an order of business, and granting the chairman the privilege of spending a dollar before approval by the chapter a daring financial innovation. Some citizens undoubtedly thought of them as meddlesome busybodies, and they were not without social pretensions. On one occasion they voted their thanks to two members for providing a "faithful domestic" to wait on table.[85] But they were capable of rising at four in the morning to can cherries for the cause, devoutly believed in their mission, and supported some programs which even a more worldly twentieth century still endorses. In the W.C.T.U. crusade McGuffey's middle-class ideals reached a peak of expression.

UNCO-OPERATIVE SINNERS

MC GUFFEY and his followers liked to speak of the simple virtues of the village green. A rigorous moral code, closely knit communities in which sinners could easily be exposed, and devoted guardians like the W.C.T.U. supposedly created an ideal environment in which to rear the young. All this, however, ignores a large body of contrary evidence which reduces much of the bucolic theme of rural and small-town purity to the status of folklore. Less than half of the people maintained church membership.[86] Many unaffiliated individuals, like the Quick family, were respectable citizens, but virtually every community also had ne'er-do-wells or submarginal families who lived by intermittent day labor. Transient day laborers, bums, and wandering horse traders also invaded small towns at various periods of the year. Boys and girls engaged freely in unsupervised play at school and in outbuildings of family homes. Actually, the environment was both good and bad, as a large body of evidence clearly indicates.

The autobiographies and other published works of Floyd Dell, Edgar Lee Masters and Sherwood Anderson describe an appalling amount of moral laxity in small towns. A series of slovenly hired girls in his parents' home introduced Masters to sex at an early age. Moreover, the two "Shetland Ponies," as they were widely known, who provided gossip in Sherwood Anderson's boyhood town, had rivals in virtually every midwestern village. One was the daughter of a ne'er-do-well who travelled about exhibiting a stuffed whale, and the other had a drunken tailor for a father. One of them became interested in Sherwood, and asked her confederate to bring him to a rendezvous in the recesses of a rail fence at the edge of town. She had hung her little white pants on a rail and was enticing Sherwood to intimacy at the moment when a barrage of stones was thrown by a young man who, learning of the rendezvous, had followed the couple. Sherwood immediately took off in a wild flight of dismay, yelling as he ran, "Get your pants, Lily. Get your pants, Lily." [87]

Small-town oral tradition contains similar episodes, differing only in details, and the writings of well-balanced, moral men confirm the pattern. William Allen White early acquired a knowledge of basic Anglo-Saxon four-letter words which were scribbled on sidewalks and school toilets. One summer day he and his friends discovered a covered wagon in a wooded camping place near town where strange girls were meeting local men: in his words, "And the knowledge of good and evil came to us, even as to the Pair in the Garden." On another occasion he and his friends discovered the Sunday School Superintendent and a visiting teacher in the woods cooling their toes in the water and rapidly returning to nature. When the boys yelled from a concealed vantage point, the couple rushed hurriedly away. The youngsters were even more astonished, however, when the Superintendent returned to the spot with his wife. Only later in life did White understand the purpose in this. It prevented a divorce when the story circulated in town since the wife naturally believed that she was the woman in question. White's father permitted him to sell cigars and listen to stories by travelling salesmen in the family hotel. As he saw it, there was little to teach a youngster who

had grown up in a pioneer town around the slaughterhouse and in the livery stable, who had roamed through the romantic woods where the peripatetic strumpets made their camps, who had picked up his sex education from Saxon words chalked on sidewalks and barns, who had taken his Rabelaisian poetry from the walls of backhouses, and who had seen saloons spew out their back door their indigestible drunkards, swarming with flies, to furnish amusement and devilment for the entertainment of little boys, as it was in the beginning of civilization.[88]

Anderson and Masters succumbed to the erotic appeal of such influences; White and Quick continued to place girls on a pedestal and to honor chastity in womankind. White knew a boy from an Ohio boarding school with quite a different point of view, and Quick discerned more immediately than did his elders the purpose behind the very embarrassing but seemingly innocent questioning carried on by a young hellion in his own home town who had served a period in a reform school. According to Quick,

Rural simplicity was supposed to make for a virtuous life. We had this delusion in our family. I have often wondered what city boy ever had more evil associates than did I out there on the prairie. . . . The simple innocence of the Deserted Village was absent. . . . I went with these boys, played with them, and knew them for what they were; but so far as I can see I took little harm from them. They seemed to be mere phenomena, like the weather, interesting but nothing to imitate.[89]

"Social purity" of *thought* was only a myth everywhere on the Middle Border; in practice it varied from individual to individual.

Prudery and frankness went hand in hand. There is truth in the legend that refined women spoke of "lower extremities," while the less refined used the word "limbs," and only those of no standing spoke of "legs." On the other hand, an advertisement of Velpeau's French Female Pills in the Monroe, Wisconsin, paper in 1869 would not be accepted today by village editors. According to the descriptive material, the pills had been kept off the American market until recently because of the ease with which they caused abortion. Pregnant married ladies were warned to avoid them because they invariably caused a miscarriage. Customers could obtain them by mail in packages sealed against the eyes of the curious and they were guaranteed to be entirely safe to take.[90]

Undesirable transients and a rough local element caused trouble everywhere. Itinerant field hands were especially bothersome during the harvest season. Hamlin Garland had to deal with them while operating his father's farm near Osage, Iowa, in the 1870's. They reminded him of a flight of unclean birds. To these former soldiers, errant sons of poor farmers, and unsuccessful mechanics from older states a "girl" was the most desired thing in the world, to be enjoyed without remorse. They furnished local boys with smutty information from South Clark Street in Chicago and the river front in St. Louis. On rainy days and Saturday nights they fought and caroused with local riffraff in country towns. In Garland's words:

Saturday night in town! How it all comes back to me! I am a timid visitor in the little frontier village. It is sunset. A whiskey-crazed farmhand is walking bare footed up and down the middle of the road defying the world.—From a corner of the street I watch with tense interest another lithe, pock-marked bully menacing with cat-like action a cowering young farmer in a long linen coat. The crowd jeers at him for his cowardice—a burst of shouting is heard. A trampling follows and forth from the door of a saloon bulges a throng of drunken, steaming, reeling, cursing ruffians followed by brave Jim McCarty, the city marshal, with an offender under each hand. . . .

We are on the way home. Only two of my crew are with me. The others are roaring from one drinking place to another, having a "good time." The air is soothingly clean and sweet after the tumult and the reek of the town.[91]

When a heavy Sunday-night rain stopped harvesting on a Monday in 1876 near Chatfield, Minnesota, nine fights occurred, and hands were "drunk, fighting, raising h–l generally." Some Chatfield residents had participated, and the local paper warned them that order would be maintained, even if it meant a policeman on every corner.[92] Garland's description of such men and their activities applied widely over the Middle West except for a shortage of "brave" Jim

McCartys. Constables generally lacked his fortitude and strength, and when a town started boiling over they often failed to meet the crisis.

Nor was the problem limited simply to the harvest season. During one week in December, 1879, the marshal at Mendon, Michigan, accommodated twenty-eight tramps overnight in the village lockup, a part of the immense army, according to a local citizen, which was willing to live by begging and petty thievery.[93] In September, 1897, Centreville, Michigan, had a number of hoboes on its streets daily. They were described as umbrella menders, chimney sweeps, tinkers, and the blind, deaf, lame, lazy, and crazy. The local editor warned that while they seemed harmless, they usually were "whiskey suckers," and would bear watching. Housewives were warned not to leave their washing on the line unguarded.[94]

Local rowdies seem to have been awed only slightly by the better classes. At Athens, Illinois, in the 1890's, the rougher element stole ice cream intended for church socials and slashed harness on teams tied to hitching racks at local churches. At times, officers were called out to handle rough individuals intent on disrupting revival services. A local group of gamblers and petty thieves engaged in a gun fight with the city marshal and tortured an individual in his isolated home in hopes of learning where his money was hidden.[95]

The activities of this class can be traced in the newspaper files of any midwestern town. Though Gallatin, Missouri, was very proud of its city park in the 1890's, ladies stayed away to avoid the vulgar and profane language being used by male loafers. On Saturday nights, when the "Honey Creekers" tried to "take the town," women remained at home as no section of the business district was immune. At times, the local editor lectured readers on the low respect shown for law and order. According to him, an especially brutal murder aroused only mild resentment. Howling mobs of men and boys surrounded the town marshal in an effort to keep him from taking reluctant drunks to the calaboose. Crap-shooting games and "young blades" intent on injuring school property added to the problem of law enforcement. When "smart" boys pelted a disorderly house near the Windsor hotel one of the women returned the insult with gun fire. Although she left town before arrests could be made, two remaining "soiled doves" had to be brought into court before they would agree to depart. Travelling "crap sharks" had no trouble locating gamblers in Gallatin and neighboring towns.[96]

Twentieth-century cities surpass country towns in crimes against property, but they differ little in crimes of violence. Murder, rape, and manslaughter are sufficiently common in smaller communities to deny them any claim to special purity,[97] and small-town newspaper records indicate that such communities never were better in curbing crimes of violence.[98]

EQUALITY IN A CLASSLESS SOCIETY

THE AMERICAN DREAM of democracy, equality, and material prosperity for the common man naturally appealed to residents of the Middle Border during its formative years. The optimism of new communities arose from the belief that settlers could improve their status in life. McGuffey taught that this had already happened in older American states. America had also proved that the masses of mankind were capable of rising to a level of self-respect and competence sufficiently high to justify self-government.[99]

Equalitarian beliefs were based on faith rather than reasoned conviction. According to McGuffey, the great leveller, death, marked the essential equality of all mankind:

> Here the vassal and the king
> Side by side, lie withering:
> Here the sword and scepter rust:
> "Earth to earth, and dust to dust!" [100]

While the Middle West believed that man was capable of improving himself in this world, it did not bother to define the word "equality." People seemed to assume that, normally, western society offered complete equality of opportunity, although the power of concentrated wealth was occasionally condemned. On the other hand, equality of ability seems never to have been affirmed or denied by major agencies like the church and school. While McGuffey's Readers remained silent on the problem of equality of ability, his unpublished, four-volume work on mental philosophy said that every community had some people who would do best on easy tasks and at low wages.[101] But McGuffey must have realized that the rank-and-file would never read such a treatise.

On the surface, midwestern faith in a classless society at the very time when people also used the phrase "living across the tracks" seemingly could exist only through a failure to probe the meaning of equality. Many modern students believe that country towns have a class structure, some going so far as to set up three classes with three grades within each. Such writers, however, have concentrated on classes existing at the moment without sufficient attention as to how social status has been achieved. Viewed historically, barriers to crossing the tracks and joining the more respectable elements in local society were sufficiently flexible to help explain why individuals held seemingly incompatible views on equality. Moreover, class lines were based on only a limited number of barriers, and less-favored citizens could mingle freely with fellow townsmen in most community activities.

Perhaps this explains why novels of small-town life generally have been inclined to stress relationships between individuals and the community as a whole rather than as between classes. An occasional novel, like Dorothy Canfield Fisher's *The Squirrel-Cage*, has dealt with discontented, ambitious wives, motivated by class ambitions. In this novel, the judge's wife finds it worth while to encourage her friends to employ class terminology—"maids" for "girls" or "hired help," "laundress" for "washwoman," and "coachman" or "gardener" for "hired hand." [102] Nonetheless, most creative writing on the small town has stressed the pressures of society in the broad sense of the term. In doing this, novelists can scarcely be accused of falling prey to the folklore of a classless society, for almost to a man they have recognized the existence of classes in country towns. But society at large and not class has burdened or lightened the lives of their characters.

Foreign visitors to America naturally were curious about a country which proclaimed the democratic common man when the old world still frankly recognized class lines. In the 1830's Alexis de Tocqueville said that Americans preferred equality to liberty.[103] Fifty years later, Lord Bryce thought he saw less jealousy of greatness and less desire to hold society to a common level than in Tocqueville's time, but, in the West especially, Americans still resented any manifestation of social superiority. According to Bryce, America permitted no rank of an external or recognized stamp; no man was entitled to think himself better than another or to ask for special privilege; precedence was given only to a few public officials and to the aged.[104] And yet, Bryce agreed with Tocqueville that classes existed in America. Both of these observers quickly recognized the unpopularity of class lines, the unwillingness of individuals to acknowledge their own social inferiority, and the existence of classes in spite of all beliefs to the contrary.

Midwestern writers and professional men who grew up in nineteenth-century country towns gained the same impression. William Dean Howells' mother introduced him to class distinctions in the small, pre-Civil War Ohio towns where he lived as a boy. Youngsters took part in May Day parades according to their social position, and a mechanic's daughter was at a disadvantage when competing with the child of a professional man.[105] Mark Twain knew of the existence of class lines as a Missouri boy in the 1830's:

And there were grades of society—people of good family, people of unclassified family, people of no family. Everybody knew everybody, and was affable to everybody, and nobody put on any visible airs; yet the class lines were quite clearly drawn and the familiar social life of each class was restricted to that class. It was a little democracy which was full of liberty, equality, and Fourth of July, and sincerely so, too; yet you perceived that the aristocratic taint was there. It was there, and nobody found fault with the fact, or ever stopped to reflect that its presence was an inconsistency. . . . My mother, with her large nature and liberal sympathies, was not intended for an aristocrat, yet through her breeding she was one. Few people knew it, perhaps, for it was an instinct, I think, rather than a principle. So its outward manifestation was likely to be accidental, not intentional, and also not frequent. But I knew of that weak spot.[106]

Much the same attitude prevailed in post-Civil War years. The "better people" dared not speak openly of their superiority, but children of professional men and of the wealthy were indirectly made aware of their importance. At Neosho, Missouri, Thomas Hart Benton's father, like his hero, Thomas Jefferson, had certain reservations about gentility and honorable company. Benton's sense of breeding, propriety, and conduct encouraged his children to adopt an intangible social line, drawn not so much on conduct as on general attitude.[107] William Allen White's mother made him class conscious, and even his father opposed certain kinds of work. Although he wanted Will to learn the value of labor, he sent the boy home with a reprimand for blacking boots on Main Street. Edgar Lee Masters' parents reacted much the same way during his boyhood in Illinois towns. His father disliked many of the ideas held by the respectable elements and was always ready to defend the underdog at law, but he was ashamed to have his own son carry coal for a local justice of the peace and earn money by delivering newspapers.[108]

Newspapers recognized classes indirectly by the contrasting manner in which they reported club dances and the hoedowns open to all, and by occasional levity or severity in reporting on happenings in poorer sections of a village, such as "Slab Town" in Chatfield, Minnesota.[109]

But such hurdles were far from being class lines in the old sense of open and insurmountable barriers. Although William Allen White's little coterie of boyhood companions thought of themselves as local "society," White later frankly recognized the confused and individualistic way in which members were chosen:

We accepted a Jew. We rejected a rich lumber dealer's girl. We took farmers' sons and daughters, even the saloonkeeper's boy and girl; children whose parents our parents rejected. But here and there we drew the line. Why and how, I do not know. I only know that our class lines were not set by money, but they were set. And we thought we were somebodies—this Trundle Bed Trash—and swished our little tails in school with something like social arrogance.[110]

Obviously, people crossed such "class lines" in less than a single generation. Ed Howe, who rose to prominence by his own efforts, felt no burden of social inferiority in the towns where he lived as a youngster, although he found class barriers more pronounced in cities:

One thing I immediately noticed at St. Joe I have noticed all my life: poor people get along better in little towns than in large ones. In the little towns I had known everybody, and lived about as well as anybody, but in St. Joe I was compelled to go to a printer's boarding house, an unsatisfactory place not at all like the comfortable places I had lived in [in] Gallatin and Maysville. Besides, in St. Joe I could know the principal people only by sight, whereas in Maysville I knew the merchants, bankers, county officials, and the judge of the court to speak to, and attended picnics where the best families were represented.[111]

The qualifications for social distinction could be acquired too easily to have great significance. Though long and respectable residence helped, one generation made families "old settlers" on the rapidly shifting town frontier. Occupation made a difference, but doctors needed only a few short lecture courses and lawyers only a few months of study in some local office in order to practice. Wealth, while helpful to one's social position, was neither essential nor impossible to attain on new frontiers. As elsewhere, education, breeding, and manners helped. In a new society, however, codes of polite behavior were so simple as to require no great ingenuity on the part of ambitious individuals. Churches and lodges were open to all respectable people, and most social life centered in them. Ambitious and capable families moved up rapidly in country towns, and a hardened social stratification seemed evident only if one observed such a community as a static thing and not historically. At any one time, a small inner group of people based on varying combinations of wealth, length of residence, occupation, and breeding stood at the top. God-fearing, middle-class people devoted to church and lodge formed still another layer. And, always, a lower class of common day laborers, generally indifferent to dominant ideals, could be distinguished. Like sex, these divisions were not discussed openly. Ideals of a classless society and social purity ranked too high in the small-town code to permit open doubts.

FOLKLORE AND SUPERSTITION

FOLKLORE and superstition found expression in many of the common, everyday aspects of life. In pre-Civil War villages, where William Dean Howells lived as a boy, people believed that warts came from playing with toads; that one could charm warts away; and that if one killed a toad, the family cow would give bloody milk. "Hoop snakes" were thought to be able to sink their poisonous horned tails in victims by putting their tails in their mouths and rolling toward the object of their attack. Snakes charmed birds and could charm people. If one killed a snake early in the day, its tail lived until sundown.[112] Newspapers made weather forecasts on the basis of conditions on Ground-hog Day, although many did so in a jocular vein. Many people wore foul-smelling asafetida in little bags around their necks to ward off illness. Mad stones, capable of extracting the poison from bites by rabid animals, were thought to exist, and some individuals were supposed to possess the power to check bleeding by mysterious rites passed from one generation to another. Effects of the moon on planting and the care of animals were laid out in calendars for the benefit of farmers. Midwestern culture carried these and many other beliefs of a similar nature into the twentieth century as a part of its intellectual baggage.

AMERICA'S WORLD MISSION

THE MC GUFFEY ERA followed a set of principles in foreign affairs which still find expression in midwestern thinking. McGuffey eulogized the patriotism of Washington and others, and quoted liberal excerpts from the speeches of Lord Chatham, who was opposed to England's fighting the Revolutionary War. Young Americans must have thrilled to Chatham's statement that if he were an American he would never lay down his arms, and that Spain could no longer boast of pre-eminence in barbarity since England had turned the Indians loose on her fellow Protestants in America.[113] McGuffey left the impression that America was wholly right in the Revolutionary War and that she whipped John Bull virtually alone. The Readers also stressed the glorious death of patriots in defense of liberty. The poem, "Make Way for Liberty," told of Arnold Winkelried's heroic sacrifice in gathering to his body the spears of an Austrian phalanx in order to save Swiss freedom:

> 'Make way for Liberty!' he cried:
> Then ran with arms extended wide,
> As if his dearest friends to clasp;
> Ten spears he swept within his grasp:
> 'Make way for Liberty!' he cried,
> Their keen points met from side to side;
> He bowed among them like a tree,
> And thus made way for Liberty.[114]

On the other hand, McGuffey printed many excerpts condemning the horrors and evils of war, "Things by their Right Names," "The Dying Soldier," and "Somebody's Darling" being representative examples.[115] Perhaps the most famous of all was the poem "How Big was Alexander, Pa?" questioning the worth-whileness of conquerors:

> How big was Alexander, Pa
> That people called him Great?
>
> Did killing people make him great?
> Then why was Abdel Young,
> Who killed his neighbor, training day,
> Put into jail and hung?
> I never heard them call him great.
>
> Then they that kill and they that praise,
> The Gospel do not mind.
> You know, my child, the Bible says
> That you must always do
> To other people, as you wish
> To have them do to you.
>
> But, Pa, did Alexander wish
> That some strong man would come
> And burn his house, and kill him, too
> And do as he had done? [116]

McGuffey encouraged people to believe that America had a mission to show the world the way to a better society; that America had fought only for freedom; that war was evil; and that international conflicts pitted "good" nations against "bad" nations in contests of liberty against despotism. McGuffey mentioned nothing of power politics or that America had relied on despotic France and Spain for aid in winning her freedom and her place in the world. Boys who read McGuffey found pacifism attractive, but appeals based on "liberty," "freedom," and a world remodelled on American principles exerted even a stronger pull.

One historian of American culture has suggested the ob-

vious relation of this "mission of America" theme to Wood-
row Wilson's war message on the eve of our entry into World
War I. In a way, it was an appeal to take up the quest for the
Holy Grail:

In his demand that the world be made safe for democracy he assumed the role of prophet of the American democratic faith. He
reminded the people of its great doctrines: the doctrine of the
moral order, the philosophy of progress, the doctrine of the free
individual, and the doctrine of the mission of America to carry
democracy to the world. He called upon his people to fight not
simply to maintain the rights and the honor of the nation but to
achieve a world victory for the national democratic religion.[117]

In these words, Wilson touched the core of conviction of
those Midwesterners who had been nurtured on the McGuffey Readers and the dominant moral code of the late nineteenth century. They closed their eyes to the presence of
despotisms fighting on our side and ignored the realities of
power politics. As a war of liberty-versus-autocracy it fitted
the McGuffey code and could join the folklore of a classless
society and social purity in the cluster of ideals dear to the
midwestern heart.

4 ❖ Where Your Treasure Is . . .

THE IMMEDIATELY USEFUL AND THE PRACTICAL

Edgar lee masters' *Spoon River Anthology*, which appeared in 1914, severely indicted midwestern country towns for their spiritual and cultural poverty. Since Masters grew up in that part of Illinois from which Abraham Lincoln rose to greatness, his attack struck at the very roots of the legendary goodness of village life. But Masters appealed only to a limited circle of readers. Six years later, Sinclair Lewis published his famous novel, *Main Street*, which succeeded in reaching a large audience. Almost overnight Gopher Prairie and Carol Kennicott came to symbolize sterile towns and despondent heroines who found it impossible to change village cultural patterns for the better. Didactic and simply written, *Main Street* penetrated the consciousness of even the obtuse, and thus joined with *Spoon River* in completing an indictment which now influenced all classes of Americans.

Earlier realists, such as Mark Twain, Edward Eggleston, and Ed Howe had described the limitations of small-town culture, thus depriving Masters and Lewis of any claim to fatherhood in creating the realistic vogue. *Spoon River* and *Main Street* were timely books because they marked the peak of disillusionment with small towns. Americans were ready for them, even if only to scoff and jeer at their conclusions. For generations Americans had at least pretended co believe that log cabins surpassed mansions in producing statesmen, that farms and country towns were the breeding grounds of future leaders in the arts and professions, and that pastoral pursuits contributed to virtue, the "good life," and happiness. Masters and Lewis challenged these assumptions, and thus served a new age of industry, urbanization, and revolution by weakening the convictions which had justified an agricultural America for so long. Carol Kennicott might deplore the boosters of Gopher Prairie who wished to make it a replica of the Twin Cities, but she found release from the aridity of Gopher Prairie life in urban centers. Similarly, Masters left the melancholy surroundings of the Spoon River country for Chicago's vibrant life.

During the 1920's Main Street and the farm were even more thoroughly debunked. Although defenders rallied to the cause, and later depressions and wars revived a nostalgia for the past, American ideals had been too firmly altered to permit complete acceptance once again of the old cluster of idealistic convictions concerning rural life. It now became more evident that cities always had been the nurseries of intellectual and artistic advancement. An occasional village like Concord, Massachusetts, or Taos, New Mexico, had won attention through its scholars and artists, but Main Street as a whole had never been exceptionally attractive to such people. Critics, moreover, began to feel that midwestern country towns would remain primarily consumers of arts, and that cities must provide the necessary training and leadership.

This was far more realistic than the pattern of thinking which it replaced. Creative artists had fled from small towns all over America since well before the Civil War. Their reasons for doing so came partially from Main Street's anti-intellectualism, but, most of all, from conditions which neither they nor country towns could control.

In fairness, it must be recognized that Americans as a whole, and not villagers alone, have slighted artistic and intellectual fields. When Alexis de Tocqueville published his famous work *Democracy in America* in the 1830's he concluded that few civilized nations were as lacking in great artists, fine poets, and celebrated writers as was America. In explanation, he suggested that while Americans were a very old and a very enlightened people, coming as they did from European backgrounds, they found a new and physically rich empire which won their attention. In subduing this bountiful land, Americans became eager for knowledge of the practical applications of arts and sciences, but were willing to leave theoretical study to England and Europe. In Tocqueville's judgment, Americans would also have developed theoretical study had they been unable to rely on England and Europe. Relying on the European theoretical background, Americans became consumers of arts and sciences rather than creative workers.[1] In other words, the practical and the immediately useful became the norm in early American civilization.

William Holmes McGuffey confirmed this emphasis on the immediately useful and the practical on new frontiers. In a sketch called "The Colonists," which appeared in his *Fourth Reader*, the leader of a new colony interviews applicants who wish to accompany him. He quickly accepts farmers, millers, carpenters, blacksmiths, masons, brickmakers, shoemakers, tailors, barbers, and doctors, for all are "useful" occupations. He also welcomes a schoolteacher because the colonists must not grow up in ignorance. A silversmith almost fails to qualify, however, until he explains that he will be "useful" in making clocks and watches. Lawyers, soldiers, and dancing masters are excluded as parasites, and a gentleman is smugly dismissed from the group with the statement that the honor of his company is not needed.[2] Here, in brief compass, McGuffey placed his stamp of approval on the immediately useful; obviously, no dreamer or theorizer could hope for admission to this band, and if he sneaked in under false pretenses he was likely to be a most unhappy man.

This selective process of migration actually operated in

the Middle West. In 1856 Shelby County, Iowa, had 126 inhabitants. Of these, eighty-eight were farmers, seventeen were laborers, and four were blacksmiths. The remaining eleven consisted of carpenter, stone mason, tailor, shoemaker, surveyor, wheelwright, wool carder, lumberman, doctor, preacher and teacher.[3] In every case, the immediately useful and the practical dominated, for even churches and schools were justified on the grounds that they buttressed law and order.

This emphasis on immediate, practical utilitarianism was defended on every new frontier as a means to an end. Many slighted intellectual and artistic matters for the moment on the grounds that America would thus more quickly acquire necessary wealth and leisure to cultivate the arts. Indulged in too long, this attitude could make wealth an end in itself, and everything that could not be justified on grounds of immediate utility would lose value. Thirty years after Algona, Iowa, was established the local editor endorsed a proposed tax levy to erect a court-house monument in honor of the Civil War dead. Apparently sensing the degree of opposition, he remarked that expenses for material necessities were always heavy in a "new" country, and this seems to have been the excuse for defeating the increase in taxes.[4] Although Algona had made remarkable gains in population and wealth during the thirty-year period, she was still excusing herself for emphasizing the immediately useful and the practical by pleading the necessities of a new civilization.

Some thoughtful Americans saw the danger in relying on *time* alone to solve our artistic poverty. One commentator writing in 1857 pointed out that two hundred and fifty years had passed since the founding of Jamestown without America creating its own architectural styles. In his opinion, imported architectural ideas, however good, were not American. Revolutionary changes had kept American culture young, and, as yet, Americans lacked the ability to think in terms of permanent family homes. They changed houses like clothing, and with the same pleasure of having new and fresh garments. Salability and show determined the selection of architectural forms. As Americans earned more money, they wanted new and larger houses, moved to town, or had to change locations because new highways ruined their dwelling sites. In a new and unsettled country, where young people set out for new lands and new fields of work, the family house was only a temporary abode, and was built accordingly.[5] In short, American culture needed *effort* and *stability* as well as *time* to flower.

Three generations later, Thomas Hart Benton, one of the Middle West's most distinguished artists, in his autobiography, *An Artist in America,* stressed anew the Tocqueville theme of American addiction to the immediately useful and the practical. Like so many other artists, he escaped from his midwestern, country-town environment as soon as possible by way of Chicago to Paris and then to New York City, and returned to the Middle West only after gaining recognition as a successful painter. Increasing maturity, and first-hand acquaintance with markedly different cultures, enabled Benton to evaluate the cult of the immediately useful and the practical more sharply than most critics.

On lecture tours, Benton had explained that artists drifted to cities because of greater opportunities to make a living, but later on he admitted that economics played only a minor part in drawing him to Chicago in 1907. Fundamentally, he was bothered by the cult of the immediately useful and the practical which still dominated country towns. He had an uneasy feeling in respectable society which, he said, would be recognized by every artist who came from families devoted to law, politics, or business, in which shrewd connivance and acute attention to a course of action were emphasized.

In Benton's home town of Neosho, Missouri, citizens had ideas of purpose and use, and held that artists were impractical dreamers. The prevailing short-range philosophy of action crushed all interest in the simple nature of things. Unwilling to blame this state of mind on pioneer psychology,

Benton claimed that artistic impulses had been vitiated by a parvenu spirit during the exploitative period following the Civil War. Aesthetic values could not survive when the particular pragmatism of the parvenu was socially dominant. Benton realized that the cult of the immediately useful and the practical was reinforced anew by technological and managerial change which kept people from achieving a sense of stability and depth.

Even well-educated people disliked to see their children turn to artistic careers. Benton's father, a prominent lawyer and politician who served as United States Attorney under Cleveland and later as congressman from Missouri, knew the classics and the world at large but suspected all artists. He was disturbed over his son's addiction to drawing and lectured him on the evils of such lazy habits.[6] Edgar Lee Masters also had trouble with his father. A successful lawyer and politician, the elder Masters refused to accept many of the middle-class convictions of Illinois country towns where he lived, but he agreed with his neighbors on the immediately useful and the practical. In order to curb his son's interest in writing and his seemingly indiscriminate and voracious appetite for literature, Masters agreed to finance college work for Edgar only if he would abandon his literary aspirations and buckle down to preparation for a legal career.[7]

William Allen White's father employed milder methods. A doctor, merchant, and real-estate dealer himself, he belonged to the governing class in his own community, and his wife was an ex-schoolteacher. They wanted their only son to have every advantage. On his tenth birthday they presented him with an expensive Mason and Hamlin cabinet organ, distinguished by an ornate chromo of an autumn field as a centerpiece. They were also happy to pay for music lessons. When Will participated in impromptu musical affairs or earned two or three dollars by calling and fiddling at country dances, they were pleased at his social accomplishments. But when serious practicing on his part indicated possibilities of a musical career, that was a different matter! His father pointed out to him the example of a local "whiskey-soaked failure" who gave fiddling lessons and played for dances, and urged his son to turn to a more suitable occupation.[8]

Even though cities also believed in the immediately useful and the practical, they contained cultural and artistic islands which provided encouragement and training for young artists. Country boys could find other artists with similar ambitions in Chicago and New York and could wall themselves in against the cult of the immediately useful and the practical. They could talk with other exiles, obtain advanced professional training, and visit publishers and other outlets for their work.[9]

Selective migration in the beginning, a period of struggle on all new frontiers, and then a constant hammering by technological, transportation, and managerial revolutions provided a poor environment for the arts and professions in their higher forms. Main Street, Mid-America, simply repeated and reinforced a national characteristic in its addiction to the immediately useful and the practical. Benton found that Chicago and Neosho endorsed the same shrewd practicality. Even the young men who went to Chicago to study art generally planned to be illustrators for great magazines after they had finished sowing a few wild oats of rebellion.

Benton also learned that country towns had something to offer mature artists. Though Paris and New York provided new experiences and new ideas, his immediate circle of artists cultivated romantic and esoteric notions. Many wished to create an American art, but had made a fatal mistake in insulating themselves against their American environment.[10] Native themes demanded contact with native sources, and permanent withdrawal from the heart of America made it very difficult for artists to achieve a high measure of fidelity.

SUPPORTING THEMES

THE CULT of the immediately useful and the practical had several corollaries. One of these held that every art and profession must justify itself financially. Lawyers, doctors and bankers did very well financially, and were envied members of the community. Teachers, preachers, and the other arts and professions did less well, and suffered accordingly.

Willa Cather's short story, "The Sculptor's Funeral," illustrates a voluminous literature describing small-town esteem of financial success in determining prestige. In this brief sketch, several residents are sitting up with the corpse of a famous but poor sculptor, who has been returned to his Kansas village home for burial. They enjoy themselves thoroughly in listening to one another recall foolish and impractical incidents from the sculptor's boyhood. Finally, the local lawyer, who has turned to drink to dull his distaste for local society, and who knows something of the sculptor's greatness, turns on the others and accuses them of drumming nothing but money and knavery into the ears of the younger generation. The bankers may pride themselves on being able to "buy" the local town if they wish, but they know that the sculptor would not give a tinker's damn for their banks and their cattle farms. In an angered peroration the lawyer concludes, "Now that we've fought and lied and sweated and stolen, and hated as only the disappointed strugglers in a bitter, dead little Western town know how to do, what have we got to show for it? . . . the drivel he's been hearing here tonight is the only tribute any truly great man could have from such a lot of sick, side-tracked, burnt-dog, land-poor sharks as the here-present financiers of Sand City—upon which town may God have mercy!" [11]

A second corollary held that "artistic matters" should be left to females. James Bryce commented on this in the 1880's. Especially in the West, he said, more girls than boys went through the secondary schools, and women played a relatively greater part in shaping literary tastes than they did in Europe. Bryce suggested three explanations: easy access to education, recognition of equality among the sexes, and the greater leisure available to women.[12] A former mayor and businessman of Red Wing, Minnesota, speaking in the twentieth century, put the matter more aptly when he commented that art had nothing to do with the realities of life and should be left to women. The men were too busy! [13]

Sentimental unreality permeated artistic and intellectual life because of the poor balance of interest as between the sexes and the futility of trying to accomplish more when men themselves considered art unworthy of serious attention. White's mother wept when he gave up his music, and women generally wanted their children to have "advantages." Dora Aydelotte's novel, *Full Harvest,* presents the problem in terms of a mother who persuades her husband to move to town so that the children can enjoy the "advantages" of what is really a prairie village. These consist of more schooling for the boys, and lessons in painting and music for the daughter. Although doubtful of artistic "advantages," the father secretly prides himself on being a sufficiently "good provider" to afford them for the youngsters. As long as the cost is not too great, he is ready to leave all decisions to his wife. In urging her daughter on with the comment, "If you practice good maybe they'll ask you to play the church organ sometime," the mother reveals the extent of her cultural ambitions.[14]

Still a third corollary insisted that artistic and intellectual activities must conform to local standards of morality. Though not particularly unique in this attitude, country towns succeeded better than cities in enforcing prevailing codes because residents and visitors alike were under constant observation.

Artists and showmen played up to this emphasis on morality. Circuses trumpeted the educational advantages of seeing exotic animals and promised not to offend even the most religious. In deference to moral sensibilities, theatre buildings in country towns were called "opera houses," operas being sufficiently distant and uplifting to escape the damning influence of the word "theatre."

Even then, villagers continued to believe that teaching and preaching were nobler than the arts because they directly promoted religion and morality. Frances E. Willard's career was an excellent example. Daughter of Vermont-born schoolteachers, who held that only religion surpassed education as a "calling," she spent most of her childhood on a Wisconsin homestead where her pious mother taught her the Bible, Shakespeare, and *Pilgrim's Progress*. Although she rashly defied her father by reading novels, a deeply religious experience brought her back to more serious things. Graduating from a small midwestern college in 1859, she taught school until challenged by the work which was to make her famous, the Woman's Christian Temperance Union crusade.[15] As its leader, Miss Willard was idolized by women in small towns everywhere.

In December, 1883, Hillsboro, Ohio, celebrated the tenth anniversary of the founding of the W.C.T.U. locally, an event which aroused much enthusiasm because Miss Willard, the national president, had agreed to be present. Local ministers preached Sunday morning sermons praising her work, and she spoke to citizens at three in the afternoon at City Hall. Miss Willard began her major address with a touching account of the surrender of her cherished pursuits in literature and art to become an evangel to "the great unwashed, untaught, ungospeled multitude." To illustrate her point that the acceptance of Christ's call overshadowed the attractions and importance of following the "vaunted mental culture" of the school of liberal thought, she outlined two widely different scenes. One was the Coliseum in Rome, where the

sweet-spirited Ignatius was thrown into the ensanguined enclosure, the prey of hungry lions, while the typal culture of the day, haughty Roman sire and youthful maiden, looked on with grim and demoniac glee and unfeminine delight. The other a scene in the Moody and Sankey Tabernacle in Chicago, where the renewing power of the gospel was manifest, transforming hearts darkened and debased by sin. . . .[16]

In this measuring of values, the arts took a secondary place; indeed, they were associated with feeding people to the lions, and only by serving the moral values of middle-class villagers could they ever hope to become respectable.

Artists and professional people easily offended local sensibilities. After Theodore Tilton, editor of the New York *Independent*, lectured at Tiffin, Ohio, in 1869, the local paper said that he had thrilled a large audience. Within a few days, however, Tiffin decided to be insulted by Tilton's statement that not enough books could be found locally to make one respectable library. In answering this "very wild" assertion, the local editor named two citizens with libraries of several hundred volumes each and said that others had collections of lesser size. In his estimation, Tilton viewed western people through "eastern and prejudiced eyes," forgetting that the West was old enough in years and had sufficient "vim" to do most things equally as well as Easterners.[17] Even hometown artists had to tread carefully. Though Zona Gale's affection for her own small Wisconsin town led her to produce some of the most saccharine rhapsodizing ever written about the village, her loyalty did not shield her from local criticism in World War I because of her pacifism.[18]

CHOICES OF LOCATION

ARTISTS AND PROFESSIONAL PEOPLE congregated in cities partially according to the degree to which the cult of the immediately useful and the practical made life unbearable for them in country towns. Statistics from the United States census on occupations show that cities attracted more than their proportional share of such people. In 1900, for example, Chicago had some 38 per cent of the gainfully occupied persons in Illinois ten years of age and over. In round figures, however, Chicago had 44 per cent of all people ten years of age and over engaged in "professional service," a term roughly comparable to "artistic and professional employment." [19] Equally significant is the fact that Chicago had 47 per cent of all males and only 38 per cent of all females engaged in such occupations. Men as a rule carried their artistic and professional training to greater lengths than did women, and the concentration of men in Chicago indicates that serious artists found cities especially congenial.

The influence of the cult of the immediately useful and the practical becomes even more evident when census data are examined by individual professions. Although 38 per cent of all gainfully occupied people in Illinois resided in Chicago, that city had only 25 per cent of the preachers and 28 per cent of the teachers. As we have seen, preaching and teaching were considered to possess practical usefulness by people residing in country towns. While Chicago had somewhat more than its share of dentists, journalists, lawyers, and doctors, members of those professions did not congregate in Chicago to the extent that actors, architects, artists, teachers of art, and literary and scientific people did. The percentage difference in residential choice between the two groups arose partially from small-town attitudes in regard to what was immediately useful and practical.

Census figures also reveal some interesting attitudes in regard to participation in artistic and professional life by women. Excluding housekeeping, 16.3 per cent of all women in Illinois ten years of age and over were gainfully employed in 1900. Women made up about 20 per cent of all actors in the state, about 37 per cent of all literary and scientific people, about 40 per cent of all artists and teachers of art, about 55 per cent of all musicians and teachers of music, and about 74 per cent of all teachers. Except for teaching, which fell within the accepted principle of the immediately useful and the practical, women obviously found their greatest occupational opportunities in those arts and professions which were thought to have the least direct material value. Moreover, since women engaged in artistic and professional occupations proportionately more than in other lines of work, the arts and professions were relatively more feminized than other activities. Census figures indicate that female doctors, lawyers, journalists, dentists, and clergymen were inclined to settle in Chicago to a greater extent than were male practitioners of the same calling. These were all eminently utilitarian occupations according to small-town ideas. A greater percentage of female than of male artists, teachers of art, musicians, teachers of music, and literary and scientific people lived in downstate Illinois. These were the less immediately useful and practical occupations according to small-town ideas. While the census figures were offered to the public without interpretation of their meaning, they confirmed the prevailing small-town conviction that women should look after the less immediately useful and practical things. If a citizen in a country town needed a doctor or a lawyer, he selected a man, because men dealt with realities. But if a wife or daughter wanted to play at painting, music or literature, women teachers were adequate, and even appropriate, to provide instruction.

In broad general terms, census figures confirm other data. They show that cities were more attractive to artists and professional people, except for preachers and teachers, who provided the heavy emphasis on education and religion that dominated small-town culture. They indicate that the cult of the immediately useful and the practical exerted a strong influence, perhaps the strongest of all, in determining the distribution of artistic and professional people between cities and the hinterland. And census figures indicate that in general those arts and professions which were considered to be of the least immediate usefulness and practicality were inclined also to be the most feminized of all in smaller places.

VILLAGE BLIGHT?

VILLAGE CONVICTIONS about the nature and value of the arts and professions sustain only in part the implications of Sinclair Lewis' *Main Street*. Carol Kennicott's quest for intellectual companionship in Gopher Prairie met defeat, and the very atmosphere of the place deadened her interest in the finer things of life. Beyond emotional enthusiasm, however, she had little to recommend her for her role of protagonist of culture. Extremely sensitive, over-eager for attention, and virtually devoid of creative ability, Carol Kennicott could easily serve another novelist as a frustrated character—defeated by her own limitations rather than by environment. Any balanced portrayal will show that artists and professional people who were born in midwestern country towns obtained encouragement and even inspiration from the same people who supposedly defeated Carol Kennicott. Moreover, while every country town had citizens who were dissatisfied with local cultural standards, the intellectual and artistic challenges available on Main Street, Mid-America, more than met the wishes of virtually all residents. Those who have asserted otherwise, and who have implied that birth or residence in a country town prevented creative intellects from giving expression to the measure of genius with which they were endowed, must evade or explain away a large amount of evidence to the contrary.

Herbert Quick, Iowa farm boy, taught in rural and village schools, read law, and then gained considerable distinction as a lawyer and novelist. In his autobiography, published in 1925 at the height of the debunking crusade, he commented:

There is a school of writers much in print, and some of them in vogue recently, who have set themselves to the analysis and description of country, village and town communities, with the purpose in mind of displaying to the world their—the localities', not the writers'—sordid drabness, their utter poverty of inspiration, their lack of men and women above the plane of two-legged horses and cattle.

There are too many such in all human societies; but I have spent a good deal of my life in such communities, and I have never failed from time to time and at important crises in my life to make contact with the souls who led me outward and upward. One of our geniuses in gloom, if any such has read this history so far, will be sure that there was no source of light for me in those days. But they are looking for darkness. I, without knowing it, was looking for light. Now the one search is as one-sided as the other; and when it comes to the artist's task, brings forth work just as faulty.[20]

Ed Howe, whose *Story of a Country Town* was one of the earlier realistic pictures of village life, indicated in his autobiography that small-town failings did not include artistic infanticide. Howe's dislike for the phony artist and intellectual, and his respect for small-town intellects is evident in his comment:

It seems to me now that I knew as many smart people in Falls City, an insignificant Nebraska village in 1872, as I have known since anywhere. There was a poet whose verses seemed about as wild, beautiful and worthless as any I have seen in maturer years. This man was a drunkard. . . . A Methodist preacher I knew there was as eloquent a man as I have ever heard. . . .[21]

In recalling his early life, Howe said that he knew outstanding men and profited from the association. He was given access to the best homes in Falls City and was "generally fortunate" in his friendships.[22]

Promising youngsters found books or friends to open new vistas to them regardless of social or economic status. Children of substantial middle-class families like William Allen White and Thomas Hart Benton had access to good literature in their homes or in town libraries sponsored by their parents.[23] An Osage, Iowa, lawyer offered to let Hamlin Garland read law in his office, a common means of entering that profession, and the principal of a little Ohio school gave Sherwood Anderson a key to his own private library when the boy began to show more than passing interest.[24] Even children in country districts of widely scattered homes discovered families with libraries of sufficient size to lead them on if they had an interest in the nature of things.[25]

Incentives did not need to be abundant or profound to awaken those with talent. Though generally disappointed in the intellectual content of the Methodist preaching at Osage, Iowa, Hamlin Garland vividly remembered one sermon on the power of art and its value to man. This, Garland said, awakened his desire to be a scholar. Hard labor and frugal living enabled him to attend several sessions of the Osage academy. It was little above the rank of a modern high school, but Garland entered the door of its one brick building with a feeling of awe. Corinthian columns painted on the chapel walls, a real pipe organ, and a row of bearded instructors seated on the chapel platform during exercises deeply impressed farm and village youngsters. Students dreaded the essays and oratory which challenged their ability to the fullest at the close of the school week.[26] While Garland later recognized the cultural limitations of Osage, it furnished the stimulus and early training behind his literary career.

Benton's challenge came from a less orthodox source. After leaving Neosho for the larger town of Joplin, he became interested in slot machines, saloons, soliciting preachers, and red-light districts, which temporarily delayed his artistic career. While loafing in a Joplin saloon, however, he was driven to announce that he was an artist as a means of silencing others who were tormenting him. To make good his boast, he obtained a job as cartoonist on one of the Joplin papers, for which he drew exaggerated pictures of prominent citizens.[27] Here again the artist found a medium of expression when he had something to say. If he needed training, he moved on to larger cities, but he joined the futile Carol Kennicotts only if he lacked talent.

Edgar Lee Masters convinced himself and many of his readers that Main Street was a barren waste. He had little good to say of anyone associated with his youth, except for his grandparents with whom he lies buried in the cemetery at Petersburg. To him, the Spoon-River country was barren, mean, vicious, and gloomy.

Masters' factual account of his early life does not support his conclusions. Actually, a considerable number of well-educated and sympathetic people encouraged and helped him in spite of his bilious and ungenerous disposition. Mary

Fisher, one of his teachers at Lewiston, Illinois, taught English and American literature, botany, and history. Masters became angry at her because he thought she rated another student above him in ability and also disagreed with his views on literature and the arts. Mary Fisher was not an old-maid pedagogue, addicted to "moral" literature and middle-class standards. Always self-centered, Masters failed to marvel at how a teacher of so many different subjects found time to study French and German on her own. Later on, she wrote novels and literary criticism. After a day in the classroom, Mary Fisher still had sufficient energy night after night to invite four or five of her best students, including Masters, to her hotel room, where they discussed Dickens, Scott, and Emerson, and were introduced to Ingersoll's lectures on the mistakes of Moses.

Well-educated lawyers and doctors also helped Masters. Hostility between his father and a local judge did not stop the latter from encouraging young Masters to associate with his son—a boy who knew three languages and could read Euripides and Sophocles with ease—and to make use of his considerable library of English poetry, prose, and political theory. A country medical practitioner at Bernadotte in Fulton County, Dr. Strode, took Masters with him on visits to country patients and encouraged the boy to join the Fulton County Scientific Association, an organization of teachers and students of literature and science in surrounding towns.

The local Presbyterian preacher, a Princeton man, had a frail, intellectual daughter, Anne, with whom Masters became friendly. This preacher had read widely enough to have favorites. He liked Plato and Berkeley in philosophy, Wordsworth rather than Pope, and the novels of Thackeray and George Eliot over those of Fielding and Sterne. Although Masters' family disliked the preacher and his daughter, they welcomed him to their home. Anne had read more widely than Masters, who grudgingly admired the facility with which she could compose a ballad in imitation of the

Elizabethan dramatists. Eugene Field published one of her ballads in his famous column "Sharps and Flats," although he changed the ending. Instead of having the returning lover rush to kiss a white flag, which he had asked his mistress to display as a token of her fidelity on his return, Field let the hero confuse baby clothing on a line with the flag, and the heroine disillusion him with the remark, "That's not the flag, that's where we dry the baby's things." Another of the girl's poems appeared in a leading anthology published in 1900. When the town began to gossip about the friendship between Masters and Anne, her mother merely suggested that they perhaps should marry at some future time. Even after Masters and the girl quarreled, her father continued to encourage him in his literary ambitions.[28] In contacts such as these Masters found an intellectual challenge, companionship, and tolerance which he rewarded by damning the Spoon River country as barren, mean, and vicious.

Influential as it was, the village cult of immediate usefulness and the practical did not submerge artists and writers in their childhood or cut them off from the stimulus necessary to find themselves. Legal practice and journalism provided incomes for many creative intellects, and made it possible for them to remain directly in touch with their childhood environment or to move on to other places as they chose. Howells, Howe, Eggleston, Bromfield, Twain, Gale, Benton, Quick, White, and Masters are representative of the long list of village youngsters who owed something to one or both of these professions.

Everywhere, at least a few citizens tried to raise prevailing standards of taste. Library associations—either on a subscription or on a free basis—were organized early in the history of many towns. By 1876, a public-library movement had already twice failed in Monroe, Wisconsin, but the local editor and several citizens were willing to try again. Although competition from three local revivals reduced attendance at a lecture by an imported speaker on the value of public libraries, forty citizens signed the call for a meeting to make a third effort. In 1876 the editor of the Chatfield, Minnesota, paper proudly invited young people to visit the new local library and examine the 400 volumes available at a modest rental fee. Supporters hoped that the library would encourage youngsters to abandon dime novels in favor of Scott, Cooper, and Dickens.[29]

In both lyceum work and music every effort was made to improve standards of appreciation by pushing "high-class" programs down the intellectual gullets of protesting local citizens as often as possible, even to the point where audiences reacted with outbursts of boorish rowdiness. In 1865, the Lacon, Illinois, editor complained that while police were available to keep order in cities, he could do nothing more than lecture citizens for having given way to unseemly yelling of "Go it Jase, Go ahead" at nearly every pause in a recent Lacon concert. Three months later he criticized the town for failing to sponsor "brain food" lectures for the young. During the fall one theatrical company and a juggler had appeared in Lacon, and balls regularly educated the "heels" of local residents. At the moment a Mr. and Mrs. Smith were conducting classes in vocal and instrumental music. The editor was distressed over the poor attendance at a concert given by their students, and blamed Lacon roundly when the Smiths left for another town. Conditions seem to have improved little over the years. In 1896 a choral union at Monroe, Wisconsin, attempted to give a series of concerts featuring music by Handel and others, with imported Chicago artists assisting the local performers. In an effort to overcome an apathetic response, the local editor urged citizens to support the singers instead of patronizing "Cheap John" programs to which Monroe was more accustomed.[30]

MINSTRELS, SPIRITUALS, AND MEDICINE SHOWS

MAIN STREET loved simple, non-technical entertainment and responded warmly to its favorites. While Bell Ring-

ers produced music in a sufficiently freakish manner to attract audiences, they did still better if they added comedy
routines and spectacular effects, such as terminating numbers by anvil strokes or pistol shots. Theatrical hits from pre-
Civil War days attracted large audiences. "Ten Nights in a
Bar-Room," featuring angelic little Mary's death at the hands
of her drunken father, was a favorite with both amateur and
professional companies. The popularity of "Uncle Tom's
Cabin" was so great that some troupes specialized in it alone.
While local amateurs often used the play, they were unable
to rival the professional companies in dramatic effects. A
"Tom" company which appeared in Greencastle, Indiana,
in 1894 had bloodhounds, donkeys, jubilee singers, and other
attractions to embellish the performance.[31] Negro minstrel
and jubilee companies were even more popular, but the circus held first place in the hearts of villagers.

Negro minstrels had become established favorites by Civil
War times. Audiences felt superior to the antics of dusky
performers, roared at the simple jokes started by interlocu-
tors, and patted their feet to the tuneful melodies. They
knew the routine and loved it. When the curtain rose on a
line of blackfaced comedians, they were prepared for an
evening of relaxation. The program moved rapidly enough
to dispel boredom and simply enough to prevent mental
fatigue—a pleasant potpourri of jokes, banjo notes, castanets,
the tattoo of jig dancers, and simple lyrics—

> Her lips am sweet as sugah,
> Her eyes am bright as wine,
> Dat yaller little boogah
> Her name am Emiline! [32]

After Arlington's Minstrels performed at the Lacon, Illinois, courthouse in 1865, the local paper called them the
best burnt-cork group in the country, a judgment confirmed
by the turn-away crowd at their performance. Similarly, Al
G. Field's minstrels played before a packed house in Constantine, Michigan, in 1888. Circuses drew larger crowds by

using minstrel troupes as part of the major performance or as an after-show attraction.[33]

Field's minstrels toured small midwestern towns for over a quarter of a century. This "King of Minstrelsy," as the Hillsboro, Ohio, editor called him following a local performance in 1900, prided himself on keeping up-to-date. In the last few years minstrelsy had moved in the direction of high-class vaudeville, with many fine specialties. It still relied on the old songs, jokes, and dances for part of its appeal. When the curtain rose on the Hillsboro performance of Field's group, the crowd saw the usual line of comedians in magnificent costumes. The first part of the program consisted of the standard choruses and solos, with the end man's jokes convulsing the audience. Toward the close, new specialties were introduced—a hoop juggler, the Faust family of acrobats, and dancers.[34] The trend to vaudeville and specialties was associated with a declining interest in minstrelsy, but small-town audiences continued to respond warmly beyond the turn of the century.

In the 1870's student groups from Negro colleges began to sing plantation melodies to enthusiastic audiences all over the Middle West. Troupes from Fisk and Hampton in the South carried on a friendly rivalry with the Wilberforce singers from Ohio, and all found responsive listeners in country towns so long as they limited themselves primarily to the "familiar darky melodies," as the Algona, Iowa, editor put it in complimenting the Nashville group on a local performance in 1886. Earlier appearances of the Hampton and Wilberforce companies at Algona the same year had not lessened local enthusiasm for more of the same kind of entertainment. Performers like Miss Hallie Q. Brown, reader with the Wilberforce group, and "Billy Eldridge," comedian with the Nashville company, were singled out for praise by newspapers from Minnesota to Missouri. Humorous readings, jokes, and "good old plantation melodies" were warmly applauded. Negro jubilee companies could not resist varying their programs with at least some classical music. Invariably, however, newspapers reported that they "lost force" when they did so, or limited comments to a brief statement that "higher grades" of music were also attempted.[35]

Medicine shows toured the Middle West from early spring to fall. The "professor" or "doctor" in charge concocted his own medicines, acted as master of ceremonies and chief spieler for his tonics, and often served as the leading musician of his company as well. He and one or two assistants parked their battered old wagon at some favorite village spot, let down the back end for a platform, lit kerosene-soaked flares, and began to play and sing to draw a crowd. Banjos, blackfaced comedians, and even the line of jokes revealed a kinship to the minstrels on which they were patterned. Retired farmers and their wives were steady customers of such shows. Always complaining of poor health, they spent a dollar for a bottle of tonic and an evening's entertainment rather than pay far more to a real doctor who gave no entertainment at all.

Medicine shows were curbed only by the conscience of their proprietors and the limits of audience gullibility. Neither was a great handicap. Spielers described Indian tonics of secret herbs, barks, and berries, mixed with the purest purling spring water. Professional ethics and a sacred promise to a dying Indian medicine man, however, often prevented proprietors from selling their remedies. In many cases, an old Indian had given the formula for mixing tonics to the spieler's grandfather, with instructions not to let it fall into the hands of evil men and to use it only for the good of humanity. Tonics might be worth thousands of dollars but spielers asked only that listeners contribute a dollar per bottle to enable them to continue their missionary efforts to rid mankind of illness.[36]

THE CIRCUS

OF ALL ATTRACTIONS, the circus held first place, its popularity being so great as to place it in a class by itself. As an old man, Ed Howe listed a performance in 1864 of

Miles Orton's circus at Bethany, Missouri, first among the few wonderful things that had happened to him in his life.[37] Hamlin Garland was equally impressed. To him, and others of his community in Iowa in the 1870's, the circus was India, Arabia, and the jungle:

It was a compendium of biologic research but more important still, it brought to our ears the latest band pieces and taught us the most popular songs. It furnished us with jokes. It relieved our dullness. It gave us something to talk about.[38]

It was no accident that Garland selected the clean-limbed, acrobatic circus performer as the stimulus which led his *Rose of Dutcher's Coolly* to escape the confinements of rural life and to seek perfection and her destiny in cities. As she sat with her lumpy country escort watching a performance, this circus god changed her life: "He wore blue and silver, and on his breast was a gay rosette. He looked a god to her. His naked limbs, his proud neck, the lofty carriage of his head, made her shiver with emotion. They all came to her lit by the white radiance; they were not naked, they were beautiful, but *he* was something more." [39] Nor was it an accident that William Dean Howells, Ed Howe, and Mark Twain all described similar occurrences in recalling the delights of a circus for small boys. Their accounts varied in details, but they all remembered the drunk or country bumpkin who staggered into the ring and announced to the lofty performer that he could ride a horse standing erect. And he did it, even though he swayed perilously as he began! Wonderful though it was, even boys became slightly abashed when the braggart started to remove his clothing in the presence of a large mixed audience. Layer after layer came off—sometimes patriotic costumes of various countries, sometimes a series of long union suits. As he approached the final layer, his audience choked with apprehension, but the last layer was nothing but circus tights, and he was only a circus performer after all![40] When a twentieth-century reader comes across such stories in the works of writers as different as Howells

and Ed Howe, he immediately senses the universal enthusiasm for circuses. The circus was indeed India, Arabia, and
the jungle to Midwesterners, whether they had a literary
destiny ahead or not.

Even the prose of country newspaper editors became
more animated when they described circus day. In 1893 the
proprietor of the Gallatin, Missouri, paper wrote a first-page
article, "Under the Canvas." Opening with the simple statement, "The circus has come and gone," he penned an account which would have done justice to the best reporter in
the country. Five thousand people had crowded Gallatin
streets the preceding Tuesday, many of them arriving early
to watch the rise of the big tents in the west part of town.
Carriages, buggies, and wagons began to appear by seven
in the morning, and by nine the streets were black with people. Long before the parade, the "ossified" man was placed
on display on the southwest corner of the square, and along
with numerous other attractions kept the motley crowd in
confusion. A few minutes before eleven, the sound of a big
bass drum was heard, and someone yelled "parade!" But
alas! It was only the Gallatin drum corps. Within another
few minutes music was heard in the distance and another
stampede for vantage points took place. Shortly thereafter,
the street parade came into view, circled the square, and returned to the show grounds. The big tent was filled long
before two in the afternoon, and ten minutes past the hour
the show opened with a "grand entre march." In the editor's
opinion, there was "something about a circus that makes all
the world akin." [41]

At the height of their popularity, as many as twenty-six
circuses a year were on the road,[42] and they simply overwhelmed the imagination of townsmen with their glitter and
pageantry. Knights rode on Main Streets in a land committed
to the ideal of a classless society. Roman chariots raced within view of Protestant church steeples, and exotic animals,
Tom Thumbs, cannibals, steam pianos, minstrels, plays,
comedies, legerdemain, peanuts, candy, lemonade, and or-

anges tantalized people already drunk with excitement. Only a circus publicist could find the language to describe such entertainment, and only a circus owner could make it come true. Screaming posters and newspaper advertisements preceded the arrival of show day, and by the 1870's were hurling challenges at rival circuses. Cooper, Bailey and Company's circus announced a fifty-thousand-dollar challenge in the Monroe, Wisconsin, paper in 1876 that they alone owned a certain select list of features, and a five-thousand-dollar bet that no other circus in America had five trained elephants representing all species. The description of their street parade indicates the flamboyant nature of their advertising:

A Brilliant, Gorgeous, Imposing and Magnificent Living Panorama, resplendent with glitter and Gold, introducing 60 cages of Wild Animals, Huge Massive Chariots and Golden Tableau Cars, 5 Elephants in harness, 10 Dromedaries, Zebras and Camels in harness; also the Gorgeous Moving Temple of Juno, 30 feet high with the living Elephant Topsy, only 38 inches high, on the top of the same; a Genuine Steam Piano; three separate and distinct bands of music, forming altogether the Most imposing, Brilliant and Grand Street Procession ever witnessed. Excursion rates on railroads.[43]

Menageries and small circuses had been common before the Civil War. The early strolling menageries generally owned a few caged animals, an elephant or pony for youngsters to ride, and pony-riding monkeys. In the same period, circuses had a limited number of performing animals, a clown, and perhaps a bareback rider. Their small size permitted an intimacy which disappeared when they turned to more spectacular entertainment. Spectators and circus employees alike often lounged near the single ring while acts were under way and clowns added to the folksiness of the occasion by inserting the names of prominent local citizens in their jokes. Small boys fed bits of apple and cake to the elephants, and even tobacco, though all knew that elephants had long memories when it came to mistreatment. These early shows moved ten to fifteen miles a night over country roads by horse-drawn transportation and thus included many small towns in their schedules.[44]

A number of factors contributed to the shady reputation of circuses from the very first. Puritanical reservations in regard to theatrical performances handicapped all of them. Moreover, financially embarrassed circus owners occasionally left feed bills unpaid as they moved on to new villages and circus slickers fleeced country boys in the ancient shell game.

To offset village distrust, circuses played up their educational features, a task made easier by the prevailing ignorance of exotic animals. In an 1857 Reader, for instance, William Holmes McGuffey struggled hard to describe elephants, but was reduced to saying that they looked something like hogs, which all youngsters knew.[45] Advertisements like that of Van Amburgh's "Grand Moral Exhibition," which showed at Greencastle, Indiana, in 1867, thus contained a very real educational appeal:

Here people can see that immense and docile animal, Typpo Saib, who moves his great carcass or applies his extraordinary strength at the beck and nod of his master. See the angry lion, the terrible tiger, and the treacherous and cat-like leopard subdue their nature at the bidding of their superior, man. Bring the children and let them see, as God made them, the animals about which they read so much, and know so little.[46]

An "Equescurriculum" circus at Lacon, Illinois, in 1865 invited farmers to examine its 150 fine horses, and manufacturers and artisans to see the new wagons and carriages which the company had purchased from a Concord, New Hampshire firm. In the 1860's some circuses even refused to include women performers in deference to a common prejudice against them.[47]

In spite of their tremendous popularity and their mystic, exalted appeal, circuses ceased to visit many country towns even before the turn of the century. By the 1880's circus advertising boasted of payrolls of several thousand dollars a day, which meant that sizable audiences were needed for both afternoon and evening shows to make such ventures profitable. At smaller towns, farm families attended afternoon performances but night shows often failed to pay out. Circuses began to travel by rail, which enabled them to pitch their tents in only the larger, more profitable towns. Dog and pony shows or smaller circuses continued to visit villages, but one who had seen a really first-rate circus scoffed at such drab organizations.[48]

Since railroad excursions and, later still, automobiles, enabled people to attend circus performances in larger cities, circuses did not lose their unique hold on the village mind simply because they no longer visited smaller places. A steady diet of radio music ultimately dulled the appeal of the circus band, and zoos within driving range of farms and towns taught boys and girls that elephants had little resemblance to hogs.

THE OPERA HOUSE

AMATEUR AND PROFESSIONAL entertainers used courthouses, churches and schools for their performances on the early town frontier. Lodge and municipal halls rapidly expanded the range of accommodations for such activities. Town halls were not simply meeting places for city councils. Many were equipped with stages and platforms for dances, exhibitions, lectures, community-wide celebrations, and amateur and professional theatricals.[49]

"Opera-houses" were being built by the 1860's, and before long all progressive villages wanted one. When first introduced, the term "opera house" was a complete misnomer, for villagers had little knowledge of opera and apparently little inclination to learn. Within a few years, however, companies performing light operas, especially excerpts from the works of Gilbert and Sullivan, began to tour country towns. The Andrews Opera Company, often described as "The Mikado Company," visited Algona, Iowa, in 1886 and again in 1896, and at Monroe, Wisconsin, in the latter year. This company apparently found it profitable to tour relatively small towns and to give summer performances at Lake Tetonka, where it owned a hotel. In the summer of 1896 it presented H. M. S. Pinafore every evening from a barge stationed in the Lake. The Tetonka resort had a track for bicycle and horse racing, a high diver who performed from a fifty-foot platform, yacht racing, and fireworks at night. For evening performances, the bay was illuminated by calcium lights of ten-thousand candle power. Perhaps extravagant showmanship rather than light opera accounted for the popularity of this company, but citizens of smaller towns like Luverne, Iowa, were willing to pay as much as two dollars for a round-trip excursion to the Lake in 1896 to witness the spectacle then being presented.[50]

Without doubt, however, the term "Opera House" was first introduced to midwestern villages because the word "theatre" was in bad repute. An occasional place used the term "Academy of Music," [51] but the word "opera" seems to have been the more satisfactory choice. An incident at Lacon, Illinois, in 1865 illustrates the prejudice against theatrical performances. Several local young men and women staged a series of romantic plays to raise money badly needed for the relief of Union soldiers. Though audiences liked the thrilling love scenes and money poured in, pious local citizens brought pressure against the group. The local editor, who had endorsed the plays at first, now supported the more sanctimonious citizens in suggesting that dialogues addressed to the moral sense, patriotism, and valor of the people would serve just as well in the future.[52]

Prejudice arose in part because professional actors sometimes ignored local standards. The summer stock companies which performed at a casino near Louis Bromfield's boyhood home in Ohio often were embarrassed by drinking bouts or even more sinful displays on the part of resident actors. Though citizens hated to support such wayward people, they nonetheless thrilled to plays like *Camille* and *East Lynne*, thus enabling the companies to continue season after season in spite of local gossip. Perhaps the reaction of Bromfield's aunt to a dance given in a play called "Salome" explains why the theatre survived at all. She and a younger member of the family were present under the impression that they would see a religious mystery—the play having been so advertised. Instead, the whole audience was shocked by a female performance of the "Dance of the Seven Veils." Although the woman still wore a flesh-pink union suit at the close of her act, the local Baptist preacher and others demanded that the dance be omitted from future performances. Many, however, may have been inclined to agree with Bromfield's salty old aunt, who thought the act safe enough because the dancer's advanced age left her little to display.[53] Whatever the process of rationalization, midwestern country towns supported both home-talent and professional companies. Audiences justified themselves on the grounds that plays were similar to church tableaus and cantatas, that part of the proceeds went for good causes, or that actors generally tried to tailor their performances to local standards of morality. And, of course, an opera house was not the same as a theatre.

Opera houses were financed in various ways. Some were erected by wealthy citizens, moved by local pride or desirous of perpetuating family names. Ambrose A. Call, banker and real-estate promoter, built the Call Opera House at Algona, Iowa, in 1892, which operated largely as a family enterprise for many years. Another banker and real-estate dealer, Dr. H. DeGraw, agreed to build a twenty-five-thousand-dollar structure bearing his name at Brookfield, Missouri, in 1905 if local citizens would agree to underwrite a five-thousand-dollar opening night, an offer which was met within forty-eight hours. Some opera houses were financed directly by city governments. Probably the most common procedure of all was for a group of citizens to subscribe shares. In the 1860's, Charles M. Croswell, later governor of Michigan, and another Adrian citizen each subscribed over a thousand dollars toward a local opera house. The remainder of the thirteen thousand dollars needed was pledged by thirty-eight men in subscriptions of as little as fifty dollars each.[54]

In spite of limited financial returns, opera houses existed everywhere. Villages like Jamesport, Missouri, and county-seat towns alike agreed that they were as essential as hotels and stores. In smaller communities, they were often two-story affairs, with ground floors rented out to shops and stores. At Hampton, Iowa, a county-seat town of some 3,000 people, the first floor of the opera house was rented to business firms, and only the words "Opera House" in gilded letters against the cornice of the building indicated its dual purpose.

A stairway carved with initials of patrons and small boys led to the second story of the Hampton Opera House, where kitchen chairs, removable for dances, rose tier by tier on a series of platforms until they reached the rear ceiling. On entering the room, patrons immediately noticed the combined odor of chewing gum, dried tobacco juice, heated foul air, and grease-paint perfume, the seductive opera house smell. A GAR veteran served as janitor, and on show nights bustled about—trimming and lighting the row of kerosene footlights, keeping the two potbellied stoves red hot, and watching for small boys who tried to sneak in to see the play. The small stage was surrounded on three sides by paneled advertisements of local merchants. A front drop curtain, covered with a painting of the Rock of Gibraltar, concealed the stage and the meager equipment with which touring companies had to contend.

At least one Hampton boy found the opera house almost as exciting as the circus. He joined other youngsters around the door in hopes of obtaining a free ticket in return for distributing handbills, generally, of course, in company with some member of the cast who went along to see that he did not stuff the advertisements in the cracks of board sidewalks or throw them away. Professional companies charmed audiences with a combination of easy informality and aloofness. They knew that Hampton loved jokes on neighboring towns, especially when told by outsiders. And when some member of the cast, usually the villain, stepped before the floodlights during intermission, with apologies for appearing "in the costume of the evening," to announce the bill for the following night, they were delighted at such close association with glamorous personalities.[55]

Larger towns had more elaborate buildings and equipment. During the late 1870's and early 1880's many Iowa opera houses contained elevated dress circles, which curved in horseshoe fashion to boxes on both sides of a proscenium arch. Ornate Corinthian iron posts supported enormous balconies. Garishly decorated side walls and ornate gilt scrollwork on boxes, on the railings in balcony and gallery, and sometimes on the proscenium arch itself, impressed audiences with the rich abandon of their surroundings. A dome of gas jets in crystal globes gave off a dazzling display when lighted by ushers with tapers on long poles before audiences assembled and again between acts. Advertisements of local mercantile firms bracketing the sides of the stage were dwarfed to proper size by competition from stage curtains of rich blue or red, caught and draped back in gorgeous folds by painted, gold ropes with enormous tassels. Iowa's elite occupied the better seats in such opera houses—men with sideburns, walrus mustaches, or full beards, only a few smooth shaven. They wore stylish clothes—long-skirted coats, trousers from which the crease had been carefully removed, straight, stiff collars, and wide four-in-hand ties. Their feminine companions were partial to bangs, and dressed in funny little bonnets, tight waists, voluminous skirts, and enormous bustles.[56]

Some opera houses had printed rates and contract forms. At Adrian, Michigan, charges ranged from eight dollars for a half day to thirty for day-and-evening.[57] During the spring and summer of 1869 the Adrian building was used by a great variety of local and travelling organizations—Miller's travelling theatre; Catholic festival; Miltonian tableaux; Hamlet; dancing school; velocipede performance; dance; lecture on the twelve apostles; Episcopal Church fair; Arlington Minstrels; Union School exhibition; Tyrolean Troupe Singers; Catholic lecture; Episcopal strawberry festival; The Continentals; temperance strawberry festival; amateur play; Union School graduation exercises; theatrical company; the Rice acrobatic troupe; Universalist preaching; citizen's meeting; temperance meeting; Othello; Catholic Fair; concert company; peach festival; fireman's dance; Enoch Arden; panorama of Ireland; magic-and-gift show; and the Presbyterian Sunday School being representative. Elizabeth Cady Stanton, Edwin Forest, Anna Dickinson, Susan B. Anthony, and Neal Dow were among the more famous personages who appeared in 1870. Plays, concerts, lectures, freaks, minstrels, dances, local group meetings, and an occasional wrestling or "glove" contest were popular over the years.[58]

Famous players occasionally visited small towns, especially those with good rail connections. The Beckwith Memorial Theater in Dowagiac, Michigan, a town of some 5,000 people, presented May Robson, John Drew, and Ethel Barrymore.[59] Actors from Chicago theatres made summer vacation tours to country towns. Bray Sisters and Company from McVicker's Theatre in Chicago visited Monroe, Wisconsin, in July, 1876. On February 13, 1896, the Algona, Iowa, opera house presented "A Trip to Chinatown," staged by a Chicago company which was making a two weeks' series of one-night stands in Iowa and Illinois to fill in during a break in Chicago engagements. The better seats for this performance at the Call Opera House sold at a dollar each. During the same season the director of the Call Opera House negotiated, with the managers of the famous name player, Keene, for a local appearance in spite of the heavy guarantee required. Enthusiastic crowds during the 1896 winter season had encouraged the manager to seek the best available talent.[60] As a rule, of course, smaller towns had to rely on minstrel shows and the lesser dramatic companies.

Literary and lecture associations were common everywhere. The editor of the Independence, Iowa, paper expressed prevailing sentiment in 1867 when he said, "To be without a lecture course is considered a reproach to any progressive town of the West." [61] Many relied primarily on local talent, but all hoped to obtain at least a few professional speakers. The demand for lecturers led to the formation of the Associated Western Literary Societies in Chicago, with the purpose of providing winter lecture courses for affiliated organizations in villages and towns.[62] Lyceum series were justified on the grounds of instruction, moral uplift, the fostering of libraries, and entertainment, with entertainment becoming progressively more and more dominant. Personalities as different as P. T. Barnum, Mark Twain, Ralph Waldo Emerson, Josh Billings, and Frederick Douglass appeared on western lecture circuits. The Dubuque, Iowa, Young Men's Library Association in the 1860's and 1870's commonly paid as much as one hundred dollars for a lecture and often as much as two.[63] Little towns, on the other hand, had to be content with less expensive performers who discussed the need for prohibition, offered feats of magic with their dialogue, or told of travels in foreign lands.

At the very time when the Opera House seemed most secure as a leading small-town institution new and destructive competitors were being born. On August 20, 1896, the editor of the Chatfield, Minnesota, paper reported that a "fellow" with a phonograph had spent most of the preceding Friday and Saturday at the corner of Main and Third streets constantly surrounded by a group of grinning men and boys who furnished nickels to hear his machine play. Some of the more sedate citizens became suspicious of his great popularity and called the town marshal to investigate. Sure enough, the fellow was playing smutty records for the amusement of his listeners, and he found it advisable to leave town so hurriedly that he forgot his grip.[64] In the same decade the Ediscope appeared among the other curiosities and freaks on midwestern opera-house stages. The Croswell, Michigan, paper on November 5, 1897, announced that Andres and Reithmiller would be at the Gaige Opera House on the twelfth to exhibit "moving scenes" on the Ediscope. As an added feature, they had a phonograph which played between scenes.[65]

When even Edison himself misjudged the real possibilities of his inventions, it is not surprising that Main Streeters also failed to see their great importance for the future. But the movies, of course, explain the decline of the opera house. Second-story opera-house auditoriums in smaller towns were unsuited for movies, which had to conform to state laws requiring the use of ground-floor space because of the danger of fire. Although opera houses held on as centers for civic affairs, occasional plays, and home-talent shows, they became progressively less profitable. Some changed over to roller-skating rinks or dance halls; others became storage centers. The phenomenal growth of excellent high school auditoriums weakened the opera house's position as a community center all the more, and high school athletic contests, the auto and the radio worked toward the same end. Gaunt, weather-beaten walls on some side street may still remind the visitor to midwestern towns that community entertainment once centered there, but citizens now hurry by on their way to the first show at the Main Street movie.

For half a century the opera house symbolized the varied programs, both intellectual and amusing, which pleased Midwesterners. Most of the entertainment by necessity attempted to meet prevailing standards of taste, but always a combination of ambitious professional entertainers and culturally inspired local citizens stood ready to promote "higher" artistic and intellectual standards. The rank-and-file residents of Main Street thus had little reason to consider their environment either barren or sterile.

5 ❖ Arts and Professions

THE LESS REWARDING ARTS

VILLAGERS SAW NO NEED for the services of architects when building new homes or new stores. Carpenters' handbooks or builders' manuals supplied simple designs for the popular one-story, rectangular frame houses, flanked with ample porches. Owners wanting a measure of individuality were advised to add jig-saw railings and gingerbread decorations. These embellishments supposedly made a plain house "tasty" and could be purchased in any quantity and intricacy simply by referring to the published catalogs of planing mills.[1] Their use was determined primarily by the size of the owners' purse, which meant that cheaper homes often had a simplicity and honesty lacking in grander mansions. The banker's home at the edge of town was likely to be a two-story, brick affair, crippled with towers, mansard roof, or some other crossbred mongrel type of architecture. Set well back from the street, it was often enclosed by an iron fence, possessed a few evergreen plantings, and perhaps some statuary in the form of dogs or deer on the front lawn.

Sculptors and painters also obtained little encouragement in midwestern country towns. The G.A.R. succeeded in putting commemorative statues of Civil War generals on most courthouse lawns, and prosperous families erected elaborate gravestones on family lots in village cemeteries. Beyond this, it was hard to conceive of any useful purpose that the sculptor could fill. Very few had family portraits made in oils when a local photographer could provide a satisfactory substitute so much more reasonably. Nudes were suitable for display only in saloons, and the more religious subjects which adorned family homes could be obtained in cheap reproductions that satisfied the critical sense of Main Street. Even culturally ambitious citizens, who shuddered at preferences for dime novels when better writers were available in the local library, voiced no criticism of the pictures in village homes.

Artists reacted to this indifference in various ways. Most of them seem to have remained in the larger cities and to have thought of smaller towns as hopeless prospects. Around 84 per cent of all male artists and teachers of art in Illinois, and over two-thirds of all women so engaged, lived in Chicago at the turn of the century. A few travelling art teachers managed to make a living through superior powers of salesmanship and ingenuity. An eloquent salesman, who happened to visit Ed Howe's boyhood town just after Ed earned five dollars picking blackberries, persuaded him to invest his money in an art course. A woman teacher furnished the instruction and helped him turn out one "flower piece," which local citizens remembered forever after as a prime example of Ed's gullibility in the field of investments. In 1886, "Professor" W. W. Wheelock of Decorah, Iowa, conducted a series of classes in Chatfield, Minnesota. After accepting his advertisement, the Chatfield editor cautiously announced that as far as he could tell from the work shown him, the "professor" was well trained. By teaching an afternoon class in "velvet painting" for ladies and a writing school in the evening hours, Wheelock obtained enough pupils to sustain him for a few weeks. It was far more common, however, for some local woman to teach art classes on a part-time basis. The wife of a successful local doctor at Hampton, Iowa, gave instructions in the copying of reprints of still life, many of which adorned the homes of her pupils, and the principal's wife at Chatfield, Minnesota, conducted classes much along the same lines in the 1870's.[2]

Since the cheapest prints satisfied the universal liking for pictures, creative artists had to do something striking to win attention. Enormous "panoramas," several hundred feet in length, served this purpose even before the Civil War, and men were willing to listen to illustrated lectures based on them. In the fall of 1867, Willard's Panorama, consisting of 6,300 square feet of Grecian oil paintings on ten-by-twelve-foot canvas, was exhibited at Algona, Iowa.[3] But painting had no real place in a man's world insofar as Main Street was concerned.

Music and the closely related declamatory arts were far more popular. Unlike the fields of painting and sculpture, where mechanical contrivances offered substitutes for the artist himself, music and public speaking demanded flesh-and-blood performers. A good reader or musician thus attained social prestige among his neighbors because of his contributions to the success of many public occasions.

Music and oratory thrived on even the newest of town frontiers. Benjamin F. Mackall, of Moorhead, Minnesota, just across the line from Fargo in Dakota Territory, helped organize a singing society in 1873, and seriously considered taking piano lessons during the winter months. He also helped train the local Episcopal choir in preparation for a visit from Bishop Whipple. During the winter Mackall took an active part in the Red-River-Congress debating society, an organization which emphasized public speaking. Local musicians played for dances in Fargo and for those given by the Moorhead Cotillion club. Mackall generally disliked "socials," especially those sponsored by the more evangelistic Protestant church groups, but there were exceptions. On one occasion he accompanied two ladies to a sociable at Fargo, where the group had a most enjoyable evening of tableaux, readings, recitations, and social "confab." Mackall himself read Miss Carleton's "Over the Hill to the Poorhouse," others furnished vocal and instrumental music, and a lady pianist provided the musical accompaniment for a male guest who whistled "The Mocking Bird."[4] In such musical and oratorical activities Moorhead and Fargo simply repeated common patterns from older frontiers. As towns increased in size they provided greater opportunities for expression, but oratory and music arrived with the earliest settlers.

Except for a few men who wandered from town to town teaching singing classes, women or amateurs, who earned their living at more serious activities, dominated musical and declamatory affairs. Small midwestern colleges offered classes in mandolin, guitar, orchestra and band instruments, and in declamatory and oratorical methods.[5] Girls who had received this training and older ladies in reduced circumstances conducted classes for children of the local community. At the turn of the century, three-fourths of all male musicians and male teachers of music in Illinois lived in Chicago, but only about 44 per cent of the women so employed resided in the city. Moreover, music and the teaching of music was the only full-time profession apart from public-school teaching in Illinois in which more women than men engaged. Downstate Illinois obviously had a great many female music teachers.

Sheet music and musical instruments were widely publicized. Piano manufacturers advertised in country newspapers, and music stores provided a constant supply of new tunes. In 1865, a Lacon, Illinois, bookstore advertised several new numbers just received. Some have long since faded away, except for occasional revivals in guessing contests or on give-away radio programs. Such was the fate of "Wake Nicodemus," "Ring the Bell, Watchman," "All Hail to Ulysses," and "Goodby Jeff," but two of the advertised offerings were destined to survive: "Tramp, Tramp, Tramp," and "Tenting on the Old Camp Ground." Over the years other favorites entered the field: "Silver Threads Among the Gold" and "Sweet Genevieve" in the 1870's, and still later: "Oh, Promise Me," "After the Ball," and "In the Shade of the Old Apple Tree."[6]

Local amateur orchestras furnished music for dancing parties just a cut above the country hoedowns for which fiddle and guitar sufficed. In addition to running a store for many years at Algona, Iowa, Theodore Chrischilles gave much time to local musical organizations. In 1877 his orchestra contributed musical preludes to dramas presented by the local dramatic club, played for various club dances, and, at opportune times, such as Washington's Birthday, engaged a hall and charged admission to dinner dances.[7]

The local band outranked all other musical organizations in popularity. Its brilliant uniforms, flashing instruments, and military cadence stimulated town pride and spirit. It was a fixture in Fourth of July and Memorial Day processions, at Old Settlers' Reunions and the County Fair, at Firemen's Tournaments and Lodge picnics. Weekly concerts at the local bandstand were popular by the 1870's.[8] Bands furnished music for holiday excursions and at Masonic funeral services; accompanied baseball teams in those frenzied periods when some local boy was pitching a hot streak of games and the town was bursting with pride in victories over neighboring villages; played for visiting companies of professional actors in need of musical support; and provided the rallying music necessary to summon people for the announcement of important community events. They even participated in the fun of practical jokers. William Allen White's parents were embarrassed on their return to Emporia, Kansas, in 1867 from their honeymoon to find the local band present to serenade them as they descended from the stage coach.[9]

As a rule, bands came into being on a wave of local enthusiasm, functioned well for a time, and then gradually declined, with the process starting over again within a few months. Inadequate financial aid caused much of the trouble. Though city councils occasionally gave some support to bands, citizens disliked being taxed for such a purpose. When the Chatfield, Minnesota, town council in 1886 voted twenty-five dollars to the local band, the Chatfield editor suggested that citizens privately contribute another hundred dollars, in return for which the band was willing to give free concerts the remainder of the summer. Public donations and benefit dances also added to their income. Bands relied almost wholly on what they could earn at paid performances, however, and they were fortunate when they received enough to cover transportation and meals on out-of-town trips and for wages lost when playing locally. Members often had to provide their own instruments and uniforms. In a day when silver instruments were thought to have sweeter tones than brass, and uniforms cost forty dollars, bands were expensive luxuries for their members. In 1902, Rockville, Indiana, determined to provide a new organization with ample income. In the course of the next three years this band received over two thousand dollars from donations and concerts, but new instruments, new uniforms, and the director's salary had reduced the money on hand to $2.23 in 1905. Once again, Rockville had to stage a campaign to prevent the community from losing its major musical organization.[10] Even financial prosperity failed to guarantee success because directors were prone to move to other towns and key personnel joined circus bands at the very season of the year when most needed.

HIGH PRIESTS OF FINANCE

MAIN STREET'S POOR RECORD in the arts contrasted sharply with its encouragement of some professions. Banking was the outstanding example. The banker's withdrawn existence in his own day, and his failure to leave revealing records for future generations, arose from no sense of guilt or feeling of insignificance, but came instead directly from the symbolic functions which he performed. A new and acquisitive society emphasized material things, and money thus symbolized basic aims. It meant so many hogs or cattle or acres of land to the farmer; it measured store goods and business buildings for the merchant. In handling it, the banker manipulated the symbols which identified successful men and eased the way for younger people. He was expected

to be conservative, closemouthed, wise and dignified, as be-
fitted the position of one so powerful, and to honor the con-
fidences which reached his ear.

The external pattern of the banker's life harmonized with
his calling. As a temple of wealth, the bank building often
had classic columns and pediments, though extravagant display was avoided in over-all effects. Figures stating capital
and surplus appeared in gilt on the front of the building,
again with just the proper emphasis and dignity. The business day within proceeded at a leisurely pace, in keeping
with the gravity of the ceremonies taking place. President
and employees alike dressed in serviceable and conservative
garb, and many of the lesser hierarchy donned black, cloth
jackets during working hours to conserve their street coats.
Bearded, conservative farmers sat on the board of directors,
thus emphasizing the source of banking wealth and the stress
placed on age and experience. Unlike twentieth-century
banks, which often belong to a chain and are subject to the
heavy hand of government supervision, nineteenth-century
institutions were relatively sovereign so long as they operated within the limits of their mildly restrictive charters.
Though many towns had more than one bank, rules of competition were sufficiently well understood to enable bankers
to maintain their full dignity in dealing with customers.
Banking cards in newspapers were as sedate and professional
in nature as those of doctors and lawyers. J. C. Easton's announcement in the Chatfield, Minnesota, paper in 1886 read:

> Root River Bank
> Established in 1856
> J. C. Easton   Banker [11]

Bankers generally were prosperous or even wealthy in
their own right. Some gained wealth through successful real-
estate ventures, as did Easton at Chatfield, Minnesota, and
the Calls at Algona, Iowa. Others started out as storekeepers
in frontier towns but turned to banking as the economy became more specialized. All were acquainted with real-estate

loans and investments, the major source of village banking wealth in the nineteenth century. Bankers all had opportunities to purchase town lots, buildings, and farms in the surrounding countryside at bargain rates. Interest charges of 8 to 10 per cent on good security added to their wealth, if they could avoid the optimism which ruined many small banks in periods of national depression.

Though highly respected because of their power, bankers were seldom popular. People knew that they stood at the very center of the small group of local men who manipulated village affairs. At death, they received long-and-laudatory obituary notices,[12] and their families moved in the best social circles. Beyond that, the banker remained an enigmatic character whose ceremonial shell concealed his inner thoughts.

Even novelists have failed to agree on a banker "type," although one can easily point out stock characteristics which writers have assigned to other small-town occupations. Ruth Suckow's novel, *The Folks*, presents Fred Ferguson, the country banker at "Belmond, Iowa," as a pillar in the Presbyterian Church, a stabilizing factor in the bank, and a benevolent guardian of less fortunate members of the Belmond community. He was the fictional counterpart of a real-life banker at Atlantic, Iowa, Franklin H. Whitney, who founded both the town and its first bank. When the bank failed in 1896, his son devoted fifteen years to paying off all obligations and then continued as a local banker for many years. In marked contrast, Allen Seager's novel, *The Inheritance*, gives a most unpleasant picture of the third generation of a banking family in the little town of "Athens, Michigan." Rude, arrogant, high-handed members of this family possessed the necessary toughness to subdue the frontier, but, once it was conquered, they turned to drinking, seducing innocent girls, and flouting other local decencies under the protection of their wealth. When their bank failed, surviving members became aware of the depths of local hatred.[13]

Novelists have agreed only that bankers symbolized the

power of wealth in country towns. Their sons have been pictured as wild and irresponsible because money shielded them from local discipline. Scheming mothers supposedly have rated the scions of banking families as "best catches" for their daughters in spite of any moral taint arising from financial power.[14] As high priests of materialism, bankers have never been allowed to depart from their symbolic roles and to become flesh-and-blood individuals.

LEGAL PERSONALITIES

LAWYERS also played a prominent role in midwestern country towns. At the turn of the century over 50 per cent of the Illinois lawyers lived outside Chicago, mostly in county-seat towns where politics and law thrived. Gallatin, Missouri, a county-seat town with a population of slightly over 1,200 in 1882, had nineteen lawyers living within the city limits.[15] They were also found in lesser numbers in other villages, where they filled more than their proportional share of municipal offices and were directly in touch with local clients. Like the bankers, they advertised their name and office location in chaste business cards, which also listed their auxiliary functions as land agents and legal representatives of distant firms.

The high regard for the profession was based on a number of things. Lawyers were respected in eastern states, and needed only to continue their time-honored functions to retain their prestige. Though many were admitted to the bar after limited reading in some local office, they were still much better educated than the rank-and-file citizen. Lawyers also had opportunities to make profitable investments and to move toward high political office. No wonder then that ambitious young men all over the Middle West taught school and then studied for the bar examination in some older lawyer's office as steppingstones to a legal career.

Though many failed to achieve their high ambitions, legal training still gave them a certain distinction. When Hamlin Garland returned to Osage, Iowa, after a long eastern sojourn he saw one of the local lawyers pass on the street and immediately recalled that individual's six-hour speech in a case involving the stealing of a horse blanket worth $4.50. Garland even remembered the look of stupefaction on the face of the accused when the lawyer compared him to Gurth the swineherd and a peasant of Carcassone. Drinking had reduced this lawyer to a shabby existence, but even in defeat he stood a notch higher in Garland's opinion than did other local failures.[16]

Unlike bankers, lawyers often displayed a flair for individual and peculiar mannerisms. Thomas Hart Benton remembered the full-bodied life surrounding his own father's legal and political career at Neosho, Missouri. Politicians frequently dined at the family dinner table. Young Benton marvelled at the ability of Champ Clark and William Jennings Bryan to consume poached eggs on baked potatoes—half a potato and an egg at a bite. Lawyers needed to be tough to withstand political campaigning. In the 1890's when Benton's father spoke in southwest Missouri for himself or a friend, political meetings were much like carnivals. Campaign orators got no rest as they moved from town to town. They shook hands and visited with local citizens, ate a big dinner, and then yelled for two hours against the competition of shooting stands, merry-go-rounds, gypsy fortunetellers, medicine shows, and other attractions which vied with them for attention. Even though young Benton had no interest in a political or legal career, he was fascinated by his father's stamina, his relish for contacts with constituents, and his ability in some undefined way to maintain a dignified superiority over voters, whose goodwill he courted.[17]

Edgar Lee Masters' father, who served as prosecuting attorney and defense lawyer in several Illinois towns, lived as he pleased. An extrovert who was known to his friends as "Hardy," the senior Masters loved horse racing and sports, and played as hard as he worked. After schooling at Illinois institutions and some study at the University of Michigan, he turned to law as a natural outlet for his talents. He refused to attend church, dared to enter saloons for a drink, and defended a murderer against whom the whole community was aroused. In spite of nonconformity he was elected mayor of Lewiston, Illinois, for four terms and prospered financially. In later life he whipped a detractor on the street, and that in spite of the handicap of a crippled arm.[18] Quiet, learned men who engaged in office practice, shysters who preyed on the public, and scholarly individuals who were best suited for the bench, also were attracted to the legal profession. Such diversity has endeared lawyers to the novelists, who have exploited them for themes from Mark Twain's Judge Driscoll, the freethinker in *Pudd'nhead Wilson*, to the present day.

THE HEALING ARTS

DOCTORS, of course, were indispensable, and, being such, lived everywhere. At the turn of the century only about 40 per cent of the medical practitioners in Illinois resided in Chicago, with the remainder widely scattered over the state. In 1870, Mendon, Michigan, a town of one thousand people, had five doctors; in 1880, Gallatin, Missouri, with 1,200 residents, had eight doctors and a dentist.[19] Doctors were available even in small hamlets of fifty to one hundred people.

The "old-fashioned country doctor" still appeals to many people. Towns which once had five to ten doctors, and now have none at all, look back to the good old days when doctors lived directly in the community or only three or four miles away. People also remember that the old-time family doctor knew his patients, spent long hours at their bedsides, and charged them modestly for his services.

In actuality, the picture was not so idyllic. In the absence of telephones, country people rode to town to summon physicians, and long hours were often lost before they reached the patient. Even within towns, citizens often discovered that their favorite doctor was away on a country call and might not return for several hours. Doctors were more widely dispersed partly because of the difficulties in communication and travel which often prevented them from reaching a patient as rapidly as they can today.

The feverish haste and anxiety involved in "riding for the doctor" was a common experience before the age of telephones. In the dead of night a parent roused a sleep-drugged son to saddle a horse and race to a nearby village for medical aid. As a boy, Hamlin Garland made such a ride through rain and mud to summon the doctor for his father, who was in great pain. Urging his mount to the point of exhaustion, he pushed forward as rapidly as possible until the green and red lamps in the village drug store told him that he was nearing his destination. Fortunately, the doctor was at home and agreed to come at once. Hamlin immediately started for home, but the condition of his horse made it necessary for him to travel slowly. As he rode, he worried whether the doctor would really venture out in such weather:

At last the lights of a carriage, crazily rocking, came into view and pulling Kit to a walk I twisted in my saddle, ready to shout with admiration of the speed of his team. "He's driving the 'Clay-Banks'," I called in great excitement.

They came rushing now with splashing feet and foaming, half-open jaws, the big doctor, calm, iron-handed, masterful, sitting in the swaying top of his light buggy, his feet against the dash board, keeping his furious span in hand as easily as if they were a pair of Shetland ponies. The nigh horse was running, the off horse pacing, and the splatter of their feet, the slash of the wheels and the roaring of their heavy breathing, made my boyish heart leap. I could hardly repress a yell of delight.

As I drew aside to let him pass the doctor called out with mellow cheer, "Take your time, boy, take your time!"

Before I could even think of an answer, he was gone and I was alone with Kit and the night.

My anxiety vanished with him. I had done all that could humanly be done, I had fetched the doctor.[20]

Arthur Hertzler, in his book, *The Horse and Buggy Doctor*, and many other medical practitioners have published accounts of the training, life, and philosophy of the nine-teenth-century doctor. In addition to their limited medical equipment, they carried scoop shovels, axes, wire cutters, and lanterns on country calls in winter in order to push through snow-blocked roads. Though poorly trained in medi-cine, they had to contend with many serious diseases which modern research has brought under control—typhoid fever, dysentery or bloody flux, pneumonia, pulmonary tuberculo-sis, diphtheria, and scarlet fever. Fever thermometers were not commonly used until the 1880's and stethoscopes had little place in general practice. In the absence of nurses, doc-tors remained with patients until a crisis had passed because they knew that their greatest contribution could be made in nursing. After looking at the patient's tongue and taking his pulse, they could perhaps make a general diagnosis but were helpless to do much more. They could administer drugs to deaden pain and their bedside presence strength-ened the courage of family members.[21]

They were priest, confidant, and friend rather than skilled specialist, and the services which they had to sell required long hours at the bedside. Their patients still believed in a personal God and lived close enough to nature to understand the cycle of birth and death in the animal kingdom. In con-trast, modern-day patients rely on skilled nurses for part of what the old-time doctor did for them, but often scoff at the possibility that preachers might complete the services which he rendered. They have also lost contact with nature's les-sons. The medical specialist now sells strictly medical serv-ices and the religiously emancipated patient has lost both his God and his old-time friend. But the fault does not lie wholly with the practice of medicine. The life span has been length-ened and doctors can check the ravages of many killers of the past. Perhaps the patient who yearns for the long visits at the bedside and the personal interest of the old-time doc-tor is really seeking some meaning in the extra years of life which medicine has given him and renewed faith in a personal immortality. And neither of these can modern medicine provide.

Medical costs were cheap before the turn of the century, moreover, because demands were limited. Kitchen surgery rather than hospitals, home nursing instead of professional care, and the use of doctors only in major illness would reduce modern medical costs quite as effectively as they did in the nineteenth century. Early medical associations discussed fees as well as other matters. In 1865, the six doctors at Lacon, Illinois, announced a common schedule of charges: Obstetrics, $10.00; one visit in city, $2.00; two visits in city on same day, $3.00; night visit in city, $3.00; mileage in country—first mile, $2.00, and fifty cents for each additional mile; country visits at night, double the day rate; for prescriptions, $1.00 exclusive of medicine.[22] Such charges were not as reasonable as nostalgic memory would have us believe.

Country practitioners were generally willing to accept payments in kind. Some had farms at the edge of town where they could keep animals and feed taken in payment for accounts. Doctors who lived within city limits still had room to fatten pigs and house chickens, and could store farm produce in the family cellar. Villagers graveled their doctors' driveways, cut their yards, worked their gardens, or performed other services in return for medical care.[23]

Many small-town doctors also operated drugstores. William Allen White's father, who practiced medicine at various times, owned a drugstore in the early 1870's that earned him more than his slender practice. The store had the usual five- or ten-gallon bottles of red, blue, or green water on display in the front window, a trade-mark of the druggist in much the same way that barber poles and wooden Indians symbolized other occupations. On the left as one entered was the soda fountain with its half-dozen flavors—among them, lemon, strawberry, raspberry, and "don't care," which was a mixture of odds and ends from all the others. On top of the screen shielding the prescription case stood a huge mortar and pestle. Gold-labeled bottles of drugs with names on the outside occupied shelves on one side of the store,' and the other was given over to an amazing array of patent medicines. A short stationery counter and a cigar case stood opposite the soda fountain. A barrel of whiskey and several of wine, ranging along the sides of a back room beyond the prescription case, gave White, a mild prohibitionist, the usual trouble that druggists experienced from customers who were convinced that drugstore, prescription whiskey surpassed that obtainable in saloons. In spite of instructions to the contrary, White's clerks were generous with sales. On one occasion, when a drunk was lying in the gutter facing his store, White's cronies poked their heads through the front door to taunt him with ribald remarks. He immediately started to revive the drunk with a bucket of water. As the gathering crowd began to object, he roared, "Is freedom dead in this country, that a man has no right to water his own liquor?"[24]

After a tour of the United States, Lord Bryce observed that doctors took little interest in politics, an observation that would have applied to most other community activities as well. Irregular hours excused them from joining community organizations if they wished, and the number who took advantage of this indicates that perhaps they enjoyed their freedom. Because of their standing, however, their wives often dominated the organized social life of the community.[25]

Professional ethics varied widely when it came to advertising. Resident doctors limited themselves almost wholly to brief cards stating their preparation and office locations. The announcements of two Centreville, Michigan, doctors in 1879 were typical:

M. Sabin, M. D., Physician and Surgeon.
Office at Residence, West end of Burr Oak Street.

J. D. Freed, M. D., Homeopathic Physician and Surgeon.
Office over First National Bank.

On the other hand, patent medicine companies ran huge advertisements in country newspapers, which made fantastic

claims for their products. As soon as people became conscious of scientific developments in electricity, charlatans began to advertise electric belts designed to restore manhood
and to perform other miracles by sending gentle streams of
health-giving electric current through the body. Of this there
could be no doubt, since advertisements of such devices contained pictures of their mysterious rays.[26]

Travelling doctors also trumpeted extravagant claims of
unusual skills and miraculous cures. Some followed the same
circuit of towns for two or three decades, an indication that
exaggerated advertising paid off. As time went on, their
claims became wilder. A long advertisement in the Rockville,
Indiana, paper in 1905, announcing the impending visit of a
doctor, claimed that he had cured 53,000 patients since 1872
on his travels in Indiana, with perfect success in every case.
He had deposited one thousand dollars in a bank as "forfeit"
that he had treated more chronic cases and performed more
remarkable cures than any other three "specialists" in the
state. A short time later, another travelling doctor ran an
even bolder advertisement—he had treated over 70,000 cases
with great success since 1872, and had outdone all other
physicians in a list of specific accomplishments which he
named. Local doctors must have been most irritated by advertisements like that of a Dr. Miner of Chicago in the Chatfield, Minnesota, paper in 1876. According to his pious,
suave claims, he had been a travelling doctor for four years,
during which he had treated primarily only the most helpless
cases. He urged citizens to compare his record with that of
the local doctors. Moreover, since all doctors advertised in
some manner, local practitioners had no right to criticize him
for giving his record. Miner thanked the public for past patronage, and called upon the "Supreme Ruler" to bless his efforts to "do good."[27] Such piety impressed patients in a religious age, but it did not stop advertisements of cancer
cures, and promises to restore without use of the knife manhood lost through youthful indiscretions, or prevent the sale
of opium in general stores.

In spite of the elementary nature of medical knowledge, doctors were plagued by competing systems of medicine— homeopaths, allopaths, and electric doctors all having supporters among practitioners and patients alike.[28] Though such divisions made it difficult to justify any one system of treatment, they seemed not to weaken public faith in the efficacy of medical practice as a whole.

Since the doctor devoted his life to the relief of suffering humanity, a calling which supposedly gave him satisfaction beyond financial gain, some patients were willing to forget financial rewards completely. In 1893 Dr. W. N. Keener of Jamesport, Missouri, presented his long poem, "The Country Doctor's Raven," to the local Shakespearean Reading Circle:

> Once upon a midnight dreary,
> While I slumbered weak and weary
> From a long and tiresome ride through
> Mud and Rain the day before,
> In the midst of soft rain's patter
> Suddenly there came a clatter
> As if someone hard did batter,
> Batter at my bedroom door.
> "'Tis some patient's friend" I muttered,
> Rapping at my bedroom door—
> This I fear means something more.

Twelve more stanzas completed Dr. Keener's story. The rapping was from a "scurvy Poosey granger," who wanted him to come at once to examine a son who had been ill for four days. Although the doctor's bill for treating the granger's wife was long overdue, he expected the doctor to overlook this on the grounds that "We are p'ore." And so the weary doctor travelled eight miles over clay hills and through rain to fulfill his professional oath. As had been expected, the granger never paid for the call, but it was somewhat galling to discover that he had left all his property to his wife to avoid having medical bills collected from his estate.[29]

Although Dr. Keener's poem had a humorous slant, it made its point that medical ethics placed service above financial gain. Since prosperity commonly arrived in due course of time for the successful practitioner, his perhaps was the most satisfying of all professions in small-town Mid-America. Bankers were respected but feared; lawyers were thought to be ambitious and shrewd; but doctors could prosper to a surprising degree without arousing criticism.

Dentistry developed more slowly than medicine and enjoyed little professional distinction before the turn of the century. Up until 1886, for example, not more than 100 dentists were practicing in Wisconsin, an average of less than one to every 8,000 inhabitants. Dentists worked mostly at extracting decayed and aching teeth, at which they had to compete with doctors—who carried turnkeys to gouge out offending molars—and even with blacksmiths, barbers, and drugstore operators. One Indiana pioneer townsman has suggested that many people objected to spending money to improve their appearance as being vain and foolish,[30] but perhaps an almost complete ignorance of preventive dentistry and a relatively low standard of living were more influential in leaving many citizens by middle age devoid of teeth of any sort.

Dentists began to locate in small midwestern towns by the 1860's. In 1865 a resident dentist at Lacon, Illinois, advertised artificial teeth, gold work and fillings, and was prepared to extract teeth under anesthesia. Such men commonly visited smaller towns from central offices in county seats or nearby cities. In 1886, Dr. Ramsey of Winona, Minnesota, advertised a two-day visit to Chatfield to take care of all kinds of dental work and to extract teeth painlessly with "vitilized air." [31] As already indicated, prosperous farm families visited country towns some distance from their rural homes to obtain dental and medical treatment. Bad teeth or none at all among the rank and file, however, were one proof of economic and intellectual gradations in communities committed to the ideal of a classless society.

THE HEIRS OF MILTON AND FRANKLIN

LIKE THE DENTIST, the editor of the weekly newspaper generally ranked below the banker, lawyer, and doctor unless he had an additional claim on community esteem. The Call family ran the first newspaper at Algona, Iowa, only as an adjunct to their real-estate ventures, and a later editor in the same town, A. L. Hudson, was a prominent lawyer. Such individuals conferred distinction on newspaper work because of their other activities. Those who rose through the print shop like Ed Howe, and then used a "shirt-tail full of type" to create still another weekly paper, were honored locally for financial success rather than for their occupation. It is true, as William Allen White suggested, that such men had distinguished antecedents. They were descended from the pamphleteer—John Milton was an ancestor, and Ben Franklin an American progenitor.[32] Such a lineage and the number of distinguished literary people who made their start on country papers have encouraged novelists to picture country editors as individualists, free thinkers, and philosophers. The truth was more prosaic insofar as the Middle West was concerned because the country weekly found its historic position both confirmed and modified as it followed the first settlers into the heart of the American continent.

Idealism and shrewd practicality joined forces to push the rapid establishment of pioneer weeklies on the town frontier. Citizens wanted to extend the blessings of a free press into wilderness areas, and speculators were avid for publicity. Printers themselves knew that contracts with county officials to publish tax lists, land sales, and other legal notices would sustain them while waiting for a town to develop. This led to a phenomenal growth of country weeklies in the post-Civil War era, and continued prosperity for many of them in the twentieth century. In 1927, for instance, Illinois and Iowa, each with more than 500 weeklies, ranked first among the states in number of periodicals of that type, and in 1940 the Midwest had 43 per cent of all the weekly newspapers published in the United States.[33] When Ambrose Call established the Algona, Iowa, *Pioneer Press* in 1861 he was primarily interested in advertising his land holdings. As a secondary objective, he wanted the revenue from printing local tax lists and those of nearby counties which as yet had no paper. Though Call started his paper without subscribers, it more than paid its own way during his short tenure as owner.[34]

Perhaps too much has been made of the old-time editor, with his low financial investment and his freedom to engage in personal journalism without regard to the feelings of advertisers. On the surface, today's masthead, "Largest Circulation in the County," with its appeal to advertisers, seems farther removed from Miltonian pamphleteering than were the mastheads so popular in the years following the Civil War. There was a fine sweeping idealism in mastheads proclaiming "If any man attempts to haul down the American Flag shoot him on the spot"; "Don't Tread on Me"; "With Malice toward none/ With Charity for all"; and even in "A Family Journal, Devoted to Literature, Politics, Agriculture, and News of the day." [35] Though such slogans committed editors to rising above the hucksters of the market place, they were surprisingly subdued in everything but personal editorial feuds and party politics. In an age when men voted as they had shot during the Civil War, country editors naturally supported one of the major political parties, but there was nothing of the heroic in this. Instead, party regularity and hack service assured an editor of the county printing if his side won. As a part of the political game, country editors damned one another, reported political meetings with shameless bias, urged voters to cast straight ballots and to report opposition frauds, bound in long campaign folders from national headquarters with regular issues just before election, and condemned all moves likely to weaken their party.

The venom distilled in efforts to promote party spirit needs illustration lest twentieth-century readers forget its viciousness. Even rural correspondents of the Indiana *Greencastle*

Banner in 1886 belabored the Cleveland administration. In reporting Cleveland's marriage the editor of that paper used language little above that of the barroom: "The President made a remarkable exhibition in marrying a young girl . . . running off to the woods with her, . . . secluding himself, . . . cordon of detectives to keep intruders away . . . able to return to Washington Tuesday." Still another item began "King Cleveland's marriage was conducted with royal exclusiveness." [36] In such "reporting," country newspapers shamed their Miltonian heritage.

Editors endorsed those activities which pleased community sentiment. They favored schools and churches, generally opposed saloons, suggested planting trees and eradicating unsightly spots within city limits, crusaded for railroads and other means of transportation, endorsed local manufactures, reprimanded lower-class drunks and rowdies for disturbing community meetings, warned the younger generation of improprieties, and "boosted" for a bigger and better city. In many of these activities they undoubtedly promoted cleanliness, order, and learning. They generally stood on the side of decency and restraint. But, in doing so, they repeated community sentiments; they were not crusaders battling for unpopular causes.

Novelists may like to depict editors as devotees of Tom Paine and Robert G. Ingersoll, but they wisely concealed any radical leanings which they may have had. The editors at Gallatin and Cameron, Missouri, made short work of the editor of the Princeton, Missouri, paper in 1893 when he dared to defend Ingersoll for "dispelling the dark clouds of religious fanaticism and superstition." Ingersoll's defender was told to move his printing office to some heathen country where people could not even read his remarks, and then see how he liked that! Nothing, said the Cameron editor, was lower in the estimation of thinking people than efforts to tear down the cause of Christ in any way.[37]

As Ed Howe's early career so clearly shows, journalism was neither necessarily profitable nor highly professional-

ized. Howe learned the printing trade in his father's shop at
Bethany, Missouri, and as an employee of publishers at Gallatin and Maysville in the same state. His own father had
been a preacher and a farmer; another employer was a lawyer; and a third was a soldier lately returned from the Civil
War, who bought a paper because he had nothing else to do
and thought perhaps its ownership would aid his campaign
for a county office. At both Gallatin and Maysville the papers
were housed rent free in the courthouse. Editors were looked
upon as mendicants, according to Howe, and people joked
about their living out of paste pots. General stores changed
their advertisements only twice a year in the 1860's to save
money, and even that much advertising was marked off as
charity to the editor.[38] The various Gallatin, Missouri, editors
supplemented their income by job printing, real-estate agencies, magazine agencies, book binderies, and by printing
Christmas cards and marriage announcements.[39] They
"plugged" advertisers shamelessly in the news columns and
did not hesitate to intermingle advertising and news in every
way.

In their struggle to survive, editors quickly learned the
value of indirect attack. Ed Howe's apprenticeship on country papers in Missouri and Nebraska prepared him to deal
with opposition when he bought the Atchison, Kansas,
Globe. A publicity man for a visiting circus gave the major
advertising to Howe's rival, apparently because he thought
that Howe's struggling paper lacked influence. In retaliation, Howe ran a large advertisement of the circus without
cost, so that no one would suspect his purposes, and in the
same issue included items about smallpox in Hiawatha, the
town from which the circus would come. Additional items
stressed the importance of vaccination and the danger of being in crowds, with the result that the offending circus had
a very small attendance in Atchison.[40] Howe ultimately became a distinguished country journalist, and his services to
his adopted town outweighed the shoddy acts which he so
freely admitted. Nonetheless, John Milton and Tom Paine,

if they were privileged to watch Ed Howe's progress from some printers' Valhalla, must have doubted their influence on him at times in his earlier years.

In the 1860's, midwestern country newspapers still followed pre-Civil War definitions of the word "news." As yet, editors generally printed a lady's name only three times in the county paper—at birth, at marriage, and again at death. Readers were expected to know community news. As a result, distant events, especially politics, got major billing.

A major revolution in the concept of news occurred in the 1860's and 1870's, which to a great extent sustained country weeklies after they declined in importance as disseminators of national news and as political party instruments. Editors began to realize as never before that ladies liked to see their names in print, and that men responded to the same appeal. By the 1870's, weekly newspapers were featuring reports from country correspondents. In 1875 the Lacon, Illinois, paper published "Buzzings from Bennington," signed by "Frank," the "Crow Creek Crowings," and items furnished by residents of Washburne, La Rose, Sparland, and other local communities. The practice was now so prevalent that an Indiana country editor contrasted rural and city papers. According to him, city papers published only paid notices of marriages and deaths, obituaries, society notes, Sunday School reports, commencement programs, and political tickets, all of which appeared free in country weeklies. Even then, this particular editor approved the practice, if readers would only cease to expect country editors to wait forever to collect for subscriptions.[41]

As a whole, country editors quickly learned the value of local news. Even though the Lacon, Illinois, paper had at least a dozen correspondents in the 1880's, it ran an article urging people from every township in the county to "Write for the Journal:"

If you haven't but four or five items a week, let your town be represented by all means. Tell us who has died, got married or sold out. Tell us who is building a new house, who is going to

move West, who has bought a farm, begun to plow, or had a run-
away. Tell us when schools begin, about the plays, the parties
and the church and political meetings. Don't forget to tell us who
is engaged to teach your schools, who has an extra large crop,
who can't take a country paper, and give us notes of your literary
societies, balls, institutes and shows. Give us the news. We know
you can do it if you only think you can. It will teach you to write
and do you good. We furnish stationery and stamps free to all
who contribute regularly. Finally give your name (not for publication) that we may know who sent it.[42]

Editors had already learned the dangers in such invitations. A seemingly harmless or humorous item from a country correspondent sometimes contained a cruel jibe. In 1875
the editor of the Lacon paper corrected a recent report of
the marriage of Lyman Andrews and Annie Mitchell which
a correspondent from their community had submitted either
maliciously or through a perverted sense of humor. It was
true, the editor said, that they went to Peoria to get married,
but the ceremony was performed by a Methodist minister
and not by a judge as originally reported. Moreover, when
they returned home they were served a "bounteous supper"
and received a number of presents. The story that the groom
had given the official who performed the marriage a nickel
for his services had hurt the worst, and the editor wanted
all readers to know that it had no foundation in fact.[43] Although Milton and Paine, if they again looked down from
printers' Valhalla, may have thought that the editor had received his just deserts for printing trivial details, weeklies
had found their strongest justification for existence in handling exactly that type of news.

The country newspaper dignified the lives of common people by assuming that their activities were important. The
sorrows of death were eased by kindly words of sympathy:
"Horace was an only son, the darling of the family. The little
hat, the vacant chair, the toys of innocent childhood are
there, but he is gone. Silently they point to the grave—and
then to Heaven." [44] The ill looked forward to having their

condition noted in the weekly paper—"Lafayette Lumpkin has had another spell of heart trouble, and is very poorly." [45] There was even a sense of "belonging" in impersonal items mentioning common activities or common observations. In the spring of 1876 the Chatfield, Minnesota paper reported a change in the color of butter since cows were grazing the new grass, and that farmers had turned from sowing spring wheat to planting corn. In the spring of 1879 the Centreville, Michigan, paper said that housecleaning was now the major occupation, with citizens engaged in pounding carpets, putting away stoves, knocking soot out of stovepipes, and carrying out rotten apples and potatoes from their cellars. [46] By the 1890's country weeklies had developed the art of personalized news to a fine point. In April, 1893, the Gallatin, Missouri, paper mentioned "the girl with the red buttons who will be married shortly." [47] Life was sweet to such a lass when she read the weekly paper. Here was proof that people knew her well enough to need no mention of her name, and yet, the red buttons preserved her personality intact. No city girl could hope for such distinction.

As a matter of fact, readers liked local news so well that editors had trouble keeping reports within manageable limits. Obituaries grew longer and longer in their praise of departed citizens, and marriage notices began to include a multitude of details. To curb this alarming development, some papers began to publish schedules of charges. The Cambridge, Ohio, paper announced in 1876 that it would print notices of deaths and marriages free but would charge for obituaries and society news at half its usual advertising rates. [48] Such threats were never strictly enforced, since country weeklies stood ready to glorify common people to the extent of their abilities.

Ironically, while novelists have fostered the myth of iconoclastic newspaper editors, they have been highly critical of the rural press for bucolic, folksy writing. In his novel, *Sons of the Puritans,* Don Marquis satirized both style and content of the imaginary Hazelton *Weekly Banner:*

Our thriving and progressive little city, which now numbers some eleven hundred and twenty-seven active and enterprising souls, proffers exceptional inducements for all those who would wish to have a look about them before going ahead and buying land in this part of the most up-to-date corn-raising county of the finest state ever settled by our sturdy pioneers. We refer, as is a well-known truism, to the state of Illinois. In the last ten years our little city has greatly increased in population. Westward hoa! the coursers of empire take their sway! . . . A new horse trough at the town pump is sorely needed. City fathers please take N. B.[49]

It is true that the writing in country weeklies was somewhat hackneyed. Citizens attended "social hops" where they "tripped the light fantastic toe;" "death angels" brought sorrow to every home; "bouncing boys" appeared with considerable regularity; and local enterprises had a habit of running "full blast." Booster items were common before the turn of the century. But the country newspaper press was never as bad as Marquis made it out to be. In general, reports were simply written in keeping with the nature of their subject matter. Although country papers abandoned major issues demanding the pen of a Milton or a Tom Paine, and turned instead primarily to the annals of the common man, they were funny only in the sense that the American dream of a classless society was never realized. The aspirations of the common man for recognition, as they are recorded in the rural press, will seem ridiculous only to readers who fail to see in them the hopes and activities of flesh-and-blood individuals.

"FISHERS OF MEN"

COUNTRY TOWNS reserved their highest praise for churches and schools, and downstate communities surpassed cities like Chicago in percentages of population engaged in preaching and teaching. In view of the early appearance of churches and schools on the town frontier, and the number of preachers and teachers in country towns, there can be little doubt as to the honesty of opinions concerning their importance. And yet, preaching and teaching were the poorest paid and generally the least distinguished of all the professions.

James Bryce observed that American preachers were inclined to avoid all controversies except those clearly involving a moral issue.[50] This was particularly true in the small town. The priest of the occasional Catholic church spoke cautiously in part because Protestants were unusually sensitive to rumors of Catholic intentions to dominate the country. Even Protestant clergymen who preached to community leaders soon learned that they must discuss only spiritual-moral issues. A Methodist minister at Chatfield, Minnesota, in 1876 expressed thanks that God reigned in Heaven and that General Grant occupied the White House, sentiments which immediately resulted in a letter of violent protest to the local editor. In the writer's opinion, preachers who were unable to avoid politics in their sermons should change their occupations. The distinction seemed clear enough, but a Methodist minister at Algona, Iowa, in 1876 was severely criticized by the local editor for opposing the election of a judge who had once voted for saloons. Although the minister based his objection on moral grounds, the editor insisted that liquor was no more a moral issue than was the quarantining of an infected ship.[51] Bible-reading members of small-town congregations insisted on individual interpretation of the scriptures, which meant that preachers easily became involved in trouble unless they channeled their efforts narrowly.

This same situation gave point to Bryce's comment that a minister's success depended heavily on his own character and dignity. If individual interpretation of the Bible prevailed, then the preacher had nothing to back him beyond his own intellectual and personal powers of persuasion. An occasional small-town minister impressed people with his leadership and learning. Taylor of Algona, Iowa, was such a man, and even Edgar Lee Masters greatly respected the Presbyterian minister in Lewiston, Illinois. For the most

part, however, village preachers lacked the necessary training and personal strength to dominate their congregations.
The Methodist church filled village pulpits with aspiring
young preachers or old and worn-out men, and those Baptist ministers who had the proper degree of evangelistic fer-
vor often lacked education to go with it.[52] If an individual
felt the "call of God," Protestant churches were inclined to
let him preach. Small towns served as testing grounds from
which promising men rapidly moved to larger places. If they
failed to measure up, they still found part-time preaching
assignments in poverty-stricken churches. One of the ancient
and widely known jokes in midwestern Protestant circles
concerns the farm boy who saw a sign in the sky reading "P.
C." Unfortunately for him and future congregations, he interpreted this as an order from God to "Preach Christ" when
it really meant to "Plow Corn."

Since congregations expected preachers to remain only a
few years, and to accept better-paying jobs whenever offered,[53] stability was as little known in the ministry as elsewhere. American attitudes differed radically from those in
the Swiss colony of New Glarus, Wisconsin, in 1884, where
both minister and schoolteacher had held their positions for
eighteen years.[54] Ironically, by denying teachers and preachers permanent residence, small towns lessened the influence
of the two professions in which they outnumbered cities,
and thus needlessly added to their professional poverty.

Small towns also strained to the limit the Biblical promise
that "where two or three are gathered together in my name,
there am I." In 1870, Mendon, Michigan, had five churches
to care for 1,000 citizens, and in 1884 Gallatin, Missouri,
with 1,250 people had six.[55] Congregations of that size had
to struggle along with inadequate equipment and poorly
paid ministers.

Preachers of an earlier day may seem unduly harsh to a
more worldly twentieth century. Ed Howe's famous novel,
The Story of a Country Town, stressed unforgiving doctrines
and the spirit of melancholy at "Fairview" in the 1880's. Pale,

unhappy women testified at meetings in low and trembling tones of crosses too heavy to bear, and then sat down crying as though their hearts would break, incidents that Howe recalled from his own father's fire-and-brimstone preaching.[56] During a revival at Wixom, Michigan, in the 1870's, the minister plastered the church walls with pictures of sinners burning in Hell. Another Wixom preacher, when asked to conduct the funeral of a drunkard, dwelt on the tortures of the deceased because the Bible had said that no drunkard would go to heaven. During this ordeal the widow sobbed hysterically.[57]

Ministerial diaries reveal the basis for such grimness. As fundamentalists who believed that Adam's sins damned all unrepentant humans, preachers had a compelling sense of urgency to bring sinners to Christ. A Methodist minister at Bluffs and Wyoming, Illinois, in the 1890's worked desperately hard in revivals, holding services for men only, for women only, special prayer meetings, and other group affairs to stir his listeners. Unbelievers might misunderstand this preacher's satisfaction when a saloon keeper in his audience wept, or sympathize with "Brother" Charles Merris, who chided him for criticizing the faithful for not standing up when requested to testify. Nevertheless, deep sincerity and humility characterized this middle-aged minister whose faith alone prevented him from giving up. Brother Merris would have felt more charitable had he seen a diary entry at the close of a revival in which few converts were made: "Again the conviction that I am a failure as a preacher almost crushes me." He was elated when he occasionally "preached with power," fundamentally because it represented a victory for the Lord. In one revival he converted two in one evening, had five more at the altar, and many more obviously were "convicted." "The spirit was upon me in extraordinary power," he wrote, and he was unable to sleep for hours afterwards. When a convert stood up and said "Just as I am" or a young man was won to the ministry, preachers felt rewarded above all other professions.

Their faith sustained them in the face of a great many problems. They took as many as six Sunday services in stride —Sunday school, morning, afternoon and evening preaching, and two Endeavor societies. If a Sunday school teacher or an organist failed to appear, they or their wives took over. A Minnesota preacher struggled against "disintegrating forces" within his church, occasioned by an excitable W.C. T.U. member who balked whenever crossed in any way. Strolling temperance lecturers of doubtful sincerity also irked him by making off with large donations, but he dared not oppose them.

Small-town ministers lived a fairly arduous life. They cultivated their own gardens and repaired their own parsonages. They arranged for W.C.T.U. medal contests, the "arranging" consisting of moving chairs and other equipment needed for the evening. An Illinois preacher exhausted himself in promoting a Harvest Home festival in 1897. He handled all publicity, solicited farmers for ingredients to make ice cream, and helped erect and decorate the stands. On the morning of the festival he arose at 4:30 to make a final check, only to find all decorations ruined and other arrangements sadly disturbed by horses in the surrounding pasture. By working feverishly until nine he restored a semblance of order and then rushed home to make himself presentable. In spite of such intensive work on his part, his church cleared only $32.19. The following Monday at 4:25 in the morning he returned to the Grove to help tear down and return borrowed lumber to its owners. Only a few days later he got a stitch in his back while helping his church prepare a dinner for the local Woodmen's organization.

Scarcely a day passed without some demand being made on the preacher's time. In addition to handling funerals and church calls, they were expected to pray with individuals and to comfort the dying. When old sister Northcut got "very low" at Bluffs, Illinois, in 1879, the local minister was asked to pray and sing hymns with her. Midweek prayer services, meetings of anti-liquor organizations, ice cream sociables, and donation parties automatically required the minister's presence. Fourth of July celebrations demanded a prayer, and even perhaps a short talk, Decoration Day called for a sermon, and one of the local ministers gave the spring commencement address on some theme like "Dream Thou of Higher Things."

Ministers seem to have tried to make amends for their deficiencies in formal education. They ordered field telescopes at "ninety-nine cents" and bought "cyclopedic dictionaries" on the installment plan out of their meager salaries. They clipped stories from religious journals and newspapers to illustrate their sermons. A newspaper account of President Garfield's addiction to work and his devotion to certain goals in life was stored away with pack-rat intensity for future use.

Apart from church activities, a minister's social life was limited. He was expected to oppose "the dancing devil" and to remain away from parties at which people "tripped the light fantastic." Sociables where playing cards appeared were off his list, although he might condone a game of authors. He could enjoy the thrill of horse racing at county fairs in the years immediately after the Civil War, but by the 1880's was beginning to remain away. One minister who attended the horse races at the Griggsville, Illinois, fair in 1897 had his day ruined by the presence of gambling devices and Persian dancing girls for "men only." On the other hand, preachers found unalloyed pleasure in reading, hiking, and swimming. Railroad excursions, lyceums, magazine-sponsored word contests, and even an evening of conversation gave some variety to their lives.

Most of all, perhaps, they found an outlet in lodge activities. They sometimes belonged to as many as three—Odd Fellows, Masons, and Knights of Pythias. The religious slant of lodge ceremonies and their increased effectiveness when conducted by an experienced public speaker enabled ministers to increase their influence and prestige. Lodges presented them with gold-headed canes or five-dollar gold pieces for their loyalty and services, and they in turn responded with an affection that went beyond mere duty.

Only an earnest conviction of their obligations to God and man could have made them patient with their meager salaries and the manner in which they were paid. Congregations often were behind on a preacher's salary, and ministerial diaries record payments of ten- and twenty-dollar sums long after they were due. Ministers commonly received at least one donation party a year to supplement their regular income. The Methodists at Monroe, Wisconsin, gave an oyster supper for the minister's benefit in January, 1869, and a second donation party in the spring at which the local band performed. Occasionally as much as one hundred dollars or more was raised by such means. Instead of being embarrassed by public recognition of their needs, ministers carefully recorded in their diaries the amount of cash contributions and "good" provisions received. The Presbyterian preacher at Chatfield, Minnesota, in 1876 even thanked the community through the local paper for its generous annual donation party, another evidence, he said, of the many attentions to his family which had made his stay so pleasant.[58] Only occasionally was the donation party a surprise. Instead, it was held at the parsonage, in the church, or at some hall, depending on which seemed likely to draw the largest crowd. Christmas baskets, funerals, marriages, gifts from local monument companies in return for names of prospective customers, and substitute teaching in local schools supplemented ministerial incomes. Preachers knew, however, that they were doomed to remain poor men in this world's goods, and, to their credit, their faith seems not to have wavered because of this. They could endure poverty, but indifferent congregations and godless individuals grieved them.[59]

SERVANTS OF THE PEOPLE

TEACHING was the least distinguished of all professions commonly found in small towns. Villagers thought of education primarily in terms of the three "R's" and sound moral beliefs, neither of which demanded highly trained individuals. According to Edward Eggleston's *The Hoosier Schoolmaster*, the "deestrict" teacher needed only to be able to whip the bullies into submission, teach his pupils to read, write, and figure, and hold his own against the district champion in ciphering and spelling matches.[60] His work was honorable and respectable, but, unlike the preacher, he had not been "called" to serve. Ability to pass the annual county examination for teaching certificates admitted a candidate to the teaching profession generally without regard to his previous educational training.

Low prestige and inadequate salaries encouraged teachers to think of their occupation only as a steppingstone to something better. For several years following the Civil War men teachers were preferred, primarily because of disciplinary problems created by great hulking boys who attended for short periods of time when work was slack. Men of ability usually taught just long enough to save money to read law or enter business. Women generally married after a few years of teaching. It was relatively easy to enter the occupation and equally easy to leave it. In 1864, Kossuth County, Iowa, paid male teachers an average of $5.62 a week and females $3.58. As late as 1883 the average age of male teachers in the same county was only twenty-four years and of females twenty.[61]

The occupation had several disagreeable features which contributed to the tremendous turnover in personnel. For one thing, towns preferred to hire teachers from the outside and to change them every few years. Like preaching, teaching was a nomadic occupation, and has remained so largely to the present day. In the spring of 1865 the Lacon, Illinois, editor mentioned the tremendous turnover in prospect for the next term of school. In accounting for this, he said that popular caprice exercised an almost unlimited power, and that teachers in reality competed for public favor. Sword in hand, they were expected to fight for the entertainment of the public.[62] Country towns seem seldom to have felt that permanent preaching and teaching staffs might give better service through a feeling of actually belonging to the community in which they worked.

In spite of the traditional belief that parents preferred teachers who were severe disciplinarians, citizens demanded a combination of order and leniency that was hard to achieve. A disgruntled Chatfield, Minnesota, citizen in 1876 severely criticized the local teaching force. In one room, according to him, the boys showed no respect at all for the teacher and even insulted her by flipping beans at her head. Little girls came home with vulgar language chalked on their coats. The local editor threatened to publish more detailed evidence if such abuses were not corrected at once. On the other hand, the Jamesport correspondent of the Gallatin, Missouri, paper in 1893 labelled one member of the Jamesport board of education a "Judas" for defeating the reappointment of "Professor Jones" to head the local schools for another year. In "quelling insubordination" the "professor" apparently had won the enmity of part of the community.[63]

Petty personal and political exactions added to the discomfort of teachers. They usually were expected to board at the home of one of the directors or with a relative of his. Since county officials who administered examinations for the renewal of teaching certificates also taught the refresher institutes preceding such ordeals, teachers felt that it was wise to pay the annual attendance fee. Lucius B. Swift, superintendent at La Porte, Indiana, in 1875, heartily disliked the pressures and low standards which surrounded the schools. An agent of Harper Brothers offered to influence the board at Evansville to hire Swift as superintendent at $2,500 a year if he would "say a good word" for Harper's books to the local county board. Swift fretted because the local county superintendent, who drew four dollars a day for visiting rural schools, accepted five dollars daily on the side from one particular book company for recommending its maps. After obtaining a better paying job in a state reform school, this same man cleared sixty dollars on his last examination for county teachers by letting them slide through easily. Swift had to fight his own local board of education to prevent it from appointing a politically potent ex-policeman as janitor.

Swift also opposed efforts by local religious groups to invade the public schools. During a union revival in 1877 the minister in charge wanted Swift to use school time to urge students to join the church. When he refused, on the grounds that he had no right to discuss religion in the schoolroom, and also declined to stand up with the saved at one of the evening meetings, the preacher berated him for supporting the devil. Swift was something of a modernist. He believed in separation of church and school, and was also distressed by the preacher's attack on scientific statements concerning the antiquity of man. Unlike the teachers in attendance at the Tiffin, Ohio, Teachers Institute in 1869, who asked that all schools open with devotional exercises and that tobacco-using teachers be dismissed or penalized,[64] Swift wanted to secularize education completely. In favoring this, he ran counter to the wishes of most teachers of the day. Though Swift stood his ground against the local minister, he could not escape bad grades and sleepy classroom performances on the part of several students who nightly served as "workers" in the local revival and then remained at the church to pray with new converts.[65]

Although teachers faced many discouragements, remarkable improvements were made in the forty years following the Civil War. In 1865 most schools still followed an ungraded system of teaching. Two short winter sessions and an abbreviated summer term were common, with women handling the summer teaching when big boys were busy at jobs. Private or church academies gave training beyond the elementary levels. By the 1870's, however, midwestern country towns were boasting of school plants costing several thousands of dollars and were beginning to grade their pupils. In 1872, Gallatin, Missouri, adopted a ten-month school term, although the division of this into a four-three-three month series was based on earlier practice. When some parents objected to having their children assigned to elementary classes, the board mollified them by explaining that brighter students were needed to stimulate the others. Under the new system, students were expected to attend regularly and parents were to receive report cards. Few towns adopted the system tried in Washburn, Illinois, in 1875 of reporting to the newspaper the names of pupils most often absent or tardy,[66] but all began to bring pressure to bear to eliminate infrequent attendance. Gallatin specified the duties of teachers, janitors, parents, and children under the new program, which incorporated many features of the modern-day school. The day opened with a reading of scripture and the Lord's prayer, then moved forward by clock and bell to 4:15 in the afternoon, at which time all pupils were expected to leave the grounds promptly.[67]

High schools began to take over the work formerly given in church-controlled or private academies. Far more girls than boys attended, many of whom taught rural schools for two or three years after graduation and then married. The graduating class of the Tiffin, Ohio, High School in June, 1869, consisted of five girls. Along with the superintendent, several teachers, and the board of education, they occupied the stage of National Hall, which was crammed to capacity with townsmen. Music lightened the serious and philosophical subjects of the five young ladies: salutatory—"My Boat is Launched, Where is the Shore?"; essay—"Clouds will Intervene"; essay—"Times are Changed, and we are Changed with them"; essay—"The Three Charmers—Wealth, Beauty, and Intellect"; valedictory—"What am I? Whence came I? Whither do I go?" As each girl finished, she was showered with bouquets from the audience until the hall was filled with the odor of flowers. The superintendent, Professor Kirkwood, then presented diplomas to the girls, who concluded the program with a class song.[68] For years to come these annual exercises attracted capacity crowds so jammed together that fainting spells were common.

Villages and small towns rapidly forged ahead of the one room, district school system which lasted in rural communities for years to come. Classes might be crowded and the high school course limited to one or two years, but even this was an advance. The superintendent of schools in Green County, Wisconsin, in 1869 reported only eighty-nine of the 120 rural schoolhouses to be in good condition, of which only fifty-four had suitable outhouses, and only seventeen possessed outline maps.[69] The countyseat town of Monroe had already advanced beyond such primitive conditions. The widening gap between rural and village educational systems encouraged the more prosperous rural families to send their children to village schools, at least for high school work. While this tendency reached major proportions only after the turn of the century, its beginning at an earlier date was a forecast of the great part that village educational systems played in winning the allegiance of rural communities.

County teacher institutes were common throughout the Midwest. They most often were held in July and August preceding examinations to renew rural teaching certificates. Running for two weeks, sometimes for a month, they were a relatively cheap and workable substitute for modern-day teachers colleges. Even the small financial outlay necessary to attend an institute often worked a hardship on youngsters preparing for examinations. When Etta May Lacey Crowder and two other little, rural schoolmarms attended an Iowa county institute in the late 1870's, they shared a room with kitchen privileges, for which they paid a dollar a week. Etta May had started teaching in 1877 at the age of fifteen, and the county institute marked her first long stay away from home. She and the other girls brought food from their farm homes to last for the month, and Etta May had a new calico dress and a supply of white aprons.[70]

Institutes were not all hard work. Lighter papers were presented in the evening hours, and musical and declamatory programs occasionally marked their close. William Allen White recalled a teachers' institute in his home town the

summer of his graduation from high school. Ice cream socials given in connection attracted White and other town
boys, all of whom enjoyed sitting on the steps of the local
schoolhouse on clear evenings in company with country
girls who were preparing to teach. During the course of the
evening couples wandered downtown for ice cream and
lemonade. Though some held hands on the way back, schoolmarms did not hesitate to box the ears of village boys who
were too forward.[71] Teaching was only a steppingstone to
marriage, however, and teachers were prized as wives by
farmers and villagers alike.

The cultural and professional life of Main-Street, Mid-
America, ordinarily satisfied such people. If sons or daughters proved queer enough to want professional or artistic
training beyond the dreams of their parents, and even beyond that available in the numerous little colleges which
covered the Middle West, they moved to larger urban centers. Even there, they were refugees from the cult of the immediately useful and the practical which blanketed America. But a normal son or daughter was more than satisfied
with the advantages of the home community. Conviction,
training, and the very inability of local society to support
something different all contributed to the cultural level at
which citizens lived.

6 ❖ Belonging to the Community

"TOGETHERNESS"

SINCE CITIZENS knew the color and shape of every home in town, and could even direct strangers by such means, streets and houses went unmarked until towns grew large enough to obtain house-to-house mail delivery, at which time federal regulations required people to post street names and house numbers. Here was tangible evidence of the closely knit character of village life, of the satisfaction of being so well-known as to need no identifying numbers, of belonging to a neighborhood, of achieving membership in a community simply by living within its boundaries. Early in the twentieth century, and just before the debunking era, Zona Gale published her popular Friendship Village Love Stories, in which she eulogized village life:

In fellowship! I think that in this simple basic emotion lies my joy in living in this, my village. Here, this year long, folk have been adventuring together, knowing the details of one another's lives, striving a little but companioning far more than striving, kindling to one another's interests instead of practicing the faint morality of mere civility; . . . . The ways of these primal tribal bonds are in my blood, for from my heart I felt what my neighbor felt when she told me of the donation party which the whole village has just given to Lyddy Ember:—"I declare," she said, "it wasn't so much the stuff they brought in, though that was all elegant, but it

181

was the Togetherness of it. I couldn't get to sleep that night for thinkin' about God not havin' anybody to neighbour with." [1]

This imaginary village contained characters like "Little Child," a simple, simpering, and angelic being, and her cat, "Bless-Your-Heart." In Gale's words, " 'I'm breathing,' Little Child soberly announced to me that first day of our acquaintance. And I wonder why I smiled." [2] Mark Twain would have guffawed. Miggy and Peter, romantic lovers, extended the gallery of saccharine portraits which Gale created for Friendship Village. In spite of the obvious limitations of her characters, they appealed to a wide reading audience which idealized village life.

Many small-town citizens were less enamored of the "togetherness" of their existence. When a door-to-door salesman in late summer, 1898, sold sixty dollars' worth of house numbers to Gallatin, Missouri, women, the local editor immediately criticized them for being taken in by the "numbers game," which, in his opinion, was "as covered with moss as lightning-rod deals." According to him, women who disliked to live in country towns used house numbers to show that they understood city ways.[3] Although the editor was correct in saying that not one citizen out of ten knew the names of Gallatin streets, and that residents had no need for signs and numbers to direct them, his sharp criticism of dissatisfied women undoubtedly made them no happier over having to live in a community which assumed the prerogative of telling them how to decorate their homes.

Thoughtful writers have noted the influence of "togetherness" on small-town personalities. In his stories of Winesburg, Ohio, Sherwood Anderson included the half-witted town character, Seth Smollett, the wood chopper, who went out of his way to wheel his cart of wood down Main Street for the sheer joy of being shouted at and of returning the hoots and catcalls. They proved that he belonged and had a place in local society. Anderson also described the farm boy who, after moving to town with his father to open a store, learned to dread the attitude of Winesburg people. They called his family queer, or, at least, he thought they did. Under the circumstances, he longed to return to farm life:

When we lived out here it was different. I worked and at night I went to bed and slept. I wasn't always seeing people and thinking as I am now. In the evening, there in town, I go to the post office or to the depot to see the train come in, and no one says anything to me. . . . Then I feel so queer that I can't talk either. I go away. I don't say anything. I can't.[4]

In Anderson's story this boy "escaped" to Cleveland and hid himself in city crowds. Solitude existed on the farm and in cities, but no one could escape the "togetherness" of village life.

Prying eyes, gossip, and pressure toward conformity, which naturally accompanied the "togetherness" of village life, could scarcely have been eliminated in a group which paid that price for membership in a neighborhood—for belonging to a society in its totality. Some loved life in the small town; others found it a severe trial. Hamlin Garland called himself an intellectual aristocrat, incapable of village life, and yet he shared for a time the unalloyed joy of his mother over returning to the village home which he purchased for her:

As I went about the village I came to a partial understanding of her feeling. The small dark shops, the uneven sidewalks, the ricketty wooden awnings were closely in character with the easygoing citizens who moved leisurely and contentedly about their small affairs. It came to me (with a sense of amusement) that these coatless shopkeepers who dealt out sugar and kerosene while wearing their derby hats on the backs of their heads, were not only my neighbors, but members of the Board of Education. Though still primitive to my city eyes, they no longer appeared remote. Something in their names and voices touched me nearly. They were American. Their militant social democracy was at once comical and corrective.

O, the peace, the sweetness of those days! To be awakened by the valiant challenge of early-rising roosters; to hear the chuckle of dawn-light worm-hunting robins brought a return of boy-hood's exultation. Not only did my muscles harden to the spade and the hoe, my soul rejoiced in a new and delightful sense of establishment. I had returned to citizenship. I was a proprietor. The clock of the seasons had resumed its beat.[5]

Village people rose early in the morning and set a pace which saw them through a long working day without ex-hausting their energies. A leisurely tempo with slack periods gave time to enjoy others and to engage in talk, the most pervading of all social activities. Women deserted their can-ning, washing, and housecleaning to gossip over the back fence or to rock in another's home while they discussed de-partures from routine patterns of neighborhood and town life. Marriage, birth, accidents, and death were common topics of conversation. Reports on those ill circulated each morning, and rumors of moral derelictions were passed from home to home. Retired farmers, down town for the morning mail, discussed crops and weather, which had shaped their daily activities for so many years, and then deaths and mar-riages. These were fitted into family and community rela-tionships. Ancestral backgrounds, family connections, prop-erty holdings, and highlights of the career of any recently deceased member of the community were recalled and placed in their proper niche in the oral history of the village, thus giving a sense of continuity.

Town loafers who worked intermittently or not at all gath-ered at another spot to squat against the wall of a business building or to sit hunched over on the ledge extending from the foundation. They alone failed to speak to women pass-ing by on shopping trips to the business section, feigning instead a blindness to matron and girl which was belied by the shifty glance of appraisal and interest in the female body.

At the post office and within the stores conversation was more general and yet more restricted because of the presence of both sexes and of all age groups. Everywhere it concerned people and things. Since art, literature, and abstract ideas were beyond the daily experience of those engaged in making conversation, individuals sought esteem by telling how they had warned another of the proper method of handling some situation which resulted badly through failure to follow seasoned experience. Illness or distress were quickly known and evoked a warmly sympathetic response because people were flesh-and-blood neighbors; wrongdoing or snobbishness aroused an equally quick condemnation for much the same reasons. Gossip served as informal judge and jury, and it sat daily to pass on every individual in the town.

Although this "togetherness" was achieved without numerous, formal social organizations, Europeans have been inclined to call us a nation of joiners and to seek explanations as to why we supposedly dote on organizational activities. In the 1830's Tocqueville suggested that an equalitarian, democratic country required associations to hold society together. In contrast, said Tocqueville, aristocratic societies were somewhat like armies, with relationships clearly defined and recognized by custom or law. In societies committed to equality, in which all were on a common level, men had to band together to accomplish their purposes. In the 1880's James Bryce said that associations were formed, extended, and operated more rapidly in the United States than elsewhere in the world. And this was true in his opinion because Americans were a sympathetic people, capable of such action in spite of nomadic habits which militated against organizational efforts.[6] Still others have traced American interest in joining to the need for associations in which individuals can build their egos by the very act of combining with others and by holding offices of honor. Many observers seem to feel that rank and recognized honors must come either from associations in the American sense or from the clearly defined status of people in aristocratic societies.

The structure and functioning of nineteenth-century midwestern village life confirm European critics in their assumptions that people must have a sense of belonging to the larger society around them and also in their convictions that a mobile, equalitarian age struggles hard to find a sense of permanence and stability. But European critics have misread American history when they assert that we have achieved such ends and must achieve them by being a nation of joiners, for nineteenth-century villagers were satisfied with a limited number of organizations which admitted *all* members of the community. Before automobiles permitted people to seek distant associations, they had to find them locally. "Togetherness" before 1900 came from a few community-wide organizations, from informal community life, and from local association. Americans are not necessarily "joiners"; they do want to "belong."

CHURCH AND LODGE

CHURCHES AND LODGES were the focal points of organized social life before the 1890's, and they were open to all. Many did not belong, it is true, but only because they preferred to find their social outlets through informal, community activities. The few formal organizations had no rules which excluded a portion of the community, and since membership was a matter of choice and not of necessity, little stigma was attached to limiting one's participation to affairs involving the whole community.

On Sunday morning church bells were heard throughout the town, a reminder that religion had passed beyond the usual informality of village social life and functioned throughout the year. Morning and evening preaching services on the Sabbath, Sunday school, and midweek prayer meeting were common among Protestant sects by 1865. Unlike twentieth-century arrangements, however, Sunday school might follow preaching, and varied enough among churches as to meeting time to enable gregarious individuals like William Allen White to display their knowledge of the "Golden Text" in several different places every Sunday. Though parents sometimes left infants at home with older children or the hired girl, the basic church services stressed family worship. All could participate in Sunday school, and babies were put to sleep on back benches during evening services. Young ladies attended Sunday-night preaching and the midweek prayer service as a means of meeting their beaus. When the services ended, boys gathered at the church door or along the walk to escort their favorite girls home.[7]

Sunday school has remained fairly standardized in the smaller churches since 1865. Then, as now, the Sunday-school superintendent called the group together for opening exercises, generally a prayer and a song, and then the classes, sectioned according to age or sex, adjourned to their assigned places in the main auditorium, which in the small churches constituted the one and only meeting place. Though some churches had curtains to separate classes, they did little to deaden the low drone of voices from the various groups. As individual teachers got discussion of the lesson under way, a symphony of sound like that of several hives of bees swarming at one time rose throughout the auditorium. The secretary-treasurer moved from class to class to receive pennies and nickels. Total attendance and total contributions were announced when the superintendent brought the groups together again for a final word pointing up the lesson, another hymn, and a prayer of dismissal. Louis Bromfield remembered the Biblical pictures on the walls, the small chairs, and tiny children marching twice around the room to the tune of "Onward Christian Soldiers," but he obviously belonged to a congregation rich enough to afford separate Sunday School rooms which permitted greater individuality.[8]

Sunday-school teaching left much to be desired. All could memorize the Golden Text, and all could listen to someone comment verse by verse on the scriptural subject matter of the lesson. All were expected to carry away with them a central thought or principle, generally moralistic in nature, but this objective often failed of realization. Teachers of adult classes concentrated on colored maps of the Holy Land and translated shekels and cubits into American money and inches. But if an inquiring youngster asked who made God, he was likely to have a scriptural passage—such as, "In the beginning God created the heavens and the earth. And the earth was waste and void; and darkness was upon the face of the deep. And the Spirit of God moved upon the face of the waters"—read to him in explanation.[9]

Church women maintained a Ladies Aid or a missionary society, and supported temperance groups like the W.C.T.U. While young people's groups like Christian Endeavor and Epworth League became popular around the 1890's, churches did not begin to stress auxiliary organizations of men and boys before the turn of the century.[10]

Various fund-raising and social activities were popular everywhere. One was the donation or pound party, already described, to collect money or foodstuffs for the minister. Socials or sociables also were common. On such occasions, whole families met at some private home, at the parsonage, or in the church for entertainment and fellowship.

Churches used still another type of activity, the festival, to raise money. At Chatfield, Minnesota, in 1876, Presbyterian ladies held a centennial festival in "Ye Whytee's Halle," at which they presented "ye Courteship" of Miles Standish. Also, "Ye Musicke of ye Olden Tyme." Doors opened at "Earlie Candleliting" and admission was fifteen pennies.

The Unitarians, Universalists, Episcopalians, and Catholics often combined dancing with a church dinner as a means of raising money. In February of 1867, some 200 Chatfield people attended a festival of that type. About half of them engaged in dancing but the rest limited themselves to the "delicious refreshments." In reporting the event, the local editor said that all local churches sent delegations and that none seemed unduly shocked at the dancing going on at one end of the hall. Nevertheless, it took a generous and liberal spirit for some to approach so close to wickedness, and the editor was pleased at their courage.

"Festivals and fairs," or, simply, "fairs," as they were sometimes called, were the most ambitious of all church undertakings. On such occasions, the church women sold food, entertainment, and articles donated by members and friends. When the Ladies Sewing Circle of the Algona, Iowa, Baptist

Church in 1867 staged a festival and fair to help complete their church building, they raised almost a hundred dollars on a cold, blustery day by selling tea and coffee, and a choice of oysters or meat at the Harrison hotel, and music, entertainment, and donations of quilts, clothing, books, pictures, nuts, and candies at the town hall.

Catholics and Protestants of less rigorous bent also used lotteries as a part of their fund-raising activities at festivals and fairs. The Catholic young ladies at Lacon, Illinois, in 1884 visited local political meetings to sell chances on articles which they had collected for their fair at Rose's Hall. They had donated a clock for that purpose, the Sisters of Mercy had given a set of silver teaspoons, and Father O'Brien a rug and table.[11] Many local Protestants must have grumbled at such brazen gambling being permitted within the city limits.

Fraternal organizations appeared very early on the town frontier. Masons and Odd Fellows remained most numerous, even after insurance programs of the various orders of Woodmen began to exert a strong appeal around the 1890's. Although a Masonic Eastern Star auxiliary was organized in 1867, it achieved great popularity only after social cliques and clubs began to grow in numbers a generation later. Lodge halls in second-story rooms above business buildings served as regular meeting places for the conduct of routine business and initiation of new members. Lodges were popular in part because they emphasized mutual help and accepted respectable men regardless of wealth or prominence. The religious and moralistic nature of their rituals appealed to churchmen, and even to many who believed in God and morality without being affiliated with churches.

Lodges engaged in a variety of activities. At Monroe, Wisconsin, in 1869 the Masons celebrated St. John's Day with an afternoon and evening program of speeches, toasts, a dinner, and a grand ball. The Odd Fellows of Algona, Iowa, welcomed the New Year in 1877 with a musical and dancing party, an indication of the greater liberality of lodges in regard to dancing. Lodge anniversaries called for something special. The fiftieth anniversary of the founding of Odd Fellows was commemorated at Monroe, Wisconsin, in 1869 by a street parade and banquet, at which toasts, speeches, and tableaus entertained the diners and any citizens who cared to pay twenty-five cents to look on from the gallery. Lodges frequently held public installations of officers, and lodge members occasionally attended church as a group to hear a sermon in their honor. They also made much of funeral ceremonies, one of their strongest appeals. The emphasis on fellowship and informality in modern-day service clubs, like Rotary, contrasts sharply with the dignity and solemnity which dominated nineteenth-century lodge meetings. As one writer has said, the difference is seen in the modern tendency to address a fellow member as "Bill" instead of "Worshipful Grand Master." [12]

RECOGNITION FOR THE COMMON MAN

ALTHOUGH THEY DEFERRED to the "togetherness" of village life by freely admitting applicants to membership, lodges and churches represented a beginning drift toward our highly organized, twentieth-century social life. For the time being, however, most social relations followed a simple, informal pattern. For the individual, this involved birth, marriage and death as assured moments of prominence in the life cycle. For the village, it meant adjustment to seasons of the year and to state and national holidays. For all, it meant activity involving the whole community—celebrations in which individuals participated without waiting for invitations from various inner circles to join in setting social boundaries. And for all it meant that most social life was so informal as to need no organization to make it work.

Rank-and-file citizens were honored at various times. Relatives and neighbors were invited to family birthday dinners, where they joined the honored member in eating and visiting, usually without thought of presents or candles and cakes. Although weddings were scheduled to interfere as little as possible with the groom's job and honeymoon trips were for the few, dinner with the bride's parents, an "infare" visit to the home of the groom's family, and perhaps a charivari by neighbors honored newly married couples. Golden Wedding celebrations had great appeal partly because the death rate prevented so many couples from reaching that goal, but also because people liked to think that Golden Weddings proved the greater stability of marriages in small towns. When relatives and friends of Mr. and Mrs. Peter Berdan of Chatfield, Minnesota, gave a dinner for them in 1876, their son made a trip from Chicago to present his father with a twenty-five dollar gold-headed cane, and the mother received a silver cream pitcher and sugar bowl. Friends contributed a purse of gold coins totalling forty dollars. In reporting the affair, the local editor quoted the Berdans' son to the effect that Golden Weddings were unknown in Chicago; divorces were the order of the day there.[13]

Death touched an entire community because virtually all knew the deceased. Before undertakers built their lavish parlors, a death called for many activities on the part of relatives and friends. The corpse must be washed and laid out, with its hair combed, and in its best suit or dress. A cabinet maker got busy on a casket, unless some furniture dealer carried ready-made stock. Friends began pouring in to the bereaved home as soon as the news reached them, and members of the family seated in the living room received their condolences. Each caller tiptoed into the parlor to see the corpse, as everyone was expected to perform that rite, and all commented on how natural and peaceful it looked. Cakes and pies and meats began to appear in the kitchen in profusion, the gifts of friends and neighbors. A summer death was always easier to honor because home-grown flowers were available, but even in winter one could count on a five-dollar wreath from the lodge. Some member of the family hurriedly arranged for black-edged cards announcing the hour and place of the funeral to be run off at the printing office for display in business houses. A spray of flowers or black ribbon on the front door and small groups of neighbors sitting at night in a dimly lighted room with the corpse signified that death prevailed within.

Since custom favored large funerals, citizens generally turned out in numbers. While the bereaved family would not have had things otherwise, they were in for a rough hour. A long eulogy by the preacher and doleful hymns by a quartette only served to weaken those closest to the deceased and to leave them defenseless for the final ordeal at the grave. White gloves for pallbearers and a plumed hearse gave solemn pageantry, which often was enhanced by uniformed GAR or lodge groups participating in the funeral ceremony. Unseemly haste must be avoided at all costs, and horses in the funeral processions were not permitted to move faster than a walk. When the mourners returned home, they generally found that neighbors had swept and dusted and restored a semblance of order to the house. In return for such neighborly services they inserted a card of thanks in the local newspaper informing all of their appreciation for help in their time of trouble. Widows then donned black mourning garb for a year and widowers moved with circumspection, for the sympathy which had been so evident early in their bereavement could quickly disappear if they departed in the slightest from community customs involving respect for the dead.

FADS, FANCIES, AND NATIONAL HOLIDAYS

CRAZES or temporary fascinations appeared in country towns then as now. Enthusiasm waxed and waned for many things like croquet, hunting clubs, bicycles, roller skating, and even baseball.[14] National influences, individual leadership—a very successful baseball pitcher, for example—and ennui explain much of the variation.

Midwestern enthusiasts joined the rest of the country in pushing membership in the National League of American Wheelmen, originally created in 1880, to an all-time high just before the turn of the century. Iowa had some 1,400 members in the League in 1897, many of them from small towns, and conservative citizens deplored the popularity of divided skirts for female riders just when some had hopes of curbing the growing tendency of mail-order catalogs to include pictures of men and women in underwear.

Other fads seem to have arisen and declined primarily because of local conditions. Croquet, "the courting game," was highly popular in Greencastle, Indiana, in 1867. During the summer a group of men played daily in the courthouse yard, and the local paper mentioned the game's influence on younger people:

> Out on the lawn, in the evening gray,
> Went Willie and Kate. I said, "Which way?"
> And they both replied, "Croquet, croquet."
>
> . . . .
>
> I saw the scamp—it was light as day—
> Put his arm round her waist in a loving way,
> And he squeezed her hand. Was that croquet?
>
> . . . .
>
> Silent they sat 'neath the moon of May;
> But I knew by her blushes that she said not nay,
> And I thought in my heart, "Now *that's* croquet."

In a similar way, moonlight croquet parties became the rage in Coffeysburg, Missouri, in the late summer of 1893. Roller skating rinks had a similar history. During the fall and winter of 1884-85, citizens of Washburn, Illinois, skated in great numbers, the proprietor of the local rink encouraging the fad by giving free lessons one afternoon a week for ladies who wished to engage in the sport. During a similar peak period in Monroe, Wisconsin, the local band furnished music twice a week and masked skating parties were popular.[15]

In spite of ups and downs, a well-recognized annual calendar of events geared to national holidays and weather conditions prevailed in small-town Mid-America. Year after year from January 1 to December 31 this pattern repeated itself with varying intensity but with sufficient emphasis to enable all citizens to know what lay ahead in the way of social life and recreation.

As early as 1862, for instance, Iowa followed the national pattern in making January 1 a legal holiday, along with July 4 and December 25. In 1880 Memorial Day was added to the list, in 1890 Labor Day, and in 1897 Washington's Birthday. Not until 1909, the hundredth anniversary of his birth, was Lincoln's Birthday given the same recognition in Iowa. With the exception of Lincoln's Birthday, Iowa followed the pattern of federal statutes,[16] and other midwestern states did much the same. Of these legal holidays, only July 4, December 25, and Memorial Day were observed with any degree of consistency in small towns, and even then business houses remained open part of the day.

NEW YEAR'S

NEW YEAR'S EVE and Day meant little to the small fry except that they were free from school and could ice skate, go sledding, or hunt rabbits to sell to local produce dealers. For teen-agers and adults it was a different story. Drunkards continued their Christmas spree through the New Year's since winter weather and the holiday season provided only casual labor, if any at all, for the element most heavily addicted to the bottle. Respectable people could choose among a number of well-recognized activities. Retired farmers and their wives generally limited themselves to a dinner with relatives and friends on New Year's Day, although some broke over and attended the New Year's Eve watch party at a local church. Methodists most often observed this practice. Such parties kept respectable people up beyond their usual bedtime hour, however, and differed very little from the regular church services to which they were accustomed. The Monroe, Wisconsin, editor in 1884 reported that sermons, songs and prayers had kept the brethren and sisters awake at a number of watch meetings in the local churches. Though lacking in novelty or excitement, the watch party continued to have a place in village life.

Oyster suppers and dances provided a more lively time for those who had no religious scruples to the contrary. A program at Monroe, Wisconsin, in 1883 started off with musical numbers by the young people and then dancing. The Universalist ladies served supper to the group during the evening. At the hour of midnight all paused to welcome the New Year, and then, it being Leap Year, the season was inaugurated with a grand waltz, the ladies having the choice of partners. All over the Midwest church groups with liberal leanings, lodges, young ladies intent on celebrating Leap Year when they could, and even "club" dances, sponsored by temporary groups formed for that purpose alone, added to the tendency to "trip the light fantastic" on New Year's Eve. Since teen-agers from pious homes could not engage in dancing, most of them ended up at the church watch party in a disgruntled state of mind.

Fortunately, many devout church members permitted their offspring to participate in play parties. Even though group singing eliminated the need for musical instruments in party games, and the tempo of action was somewhat less than in dancing, they came close to being an adequate substitute. "Weevily Wheat," for instance, had many of the elements of the Virginia Reel, and Texans added a stanza recognizing this:

> Take a lady by her hand,
> Lead her like a pigeon,
> Make her dance the weevily wheat,
> She loses her religion.

A whole series of party games were well known everywhere: Skip-to-My-Lou; Pig in the Parlor; Here We Go Round the Mulberry Bush; Oats, Peas, Beans, and Barley Grow; Needle's Eye; London Bridge; Miller Boy; and King William was King James's Son were among the more popular. Some were combined choosing and kissing games and others depended primarily on group rhythm for their appeal.[17] Youngsters could forget the strictures of strait-laced parents when they became immersed in these along with the partner of their choice:

> Oh, Charley, he is a fine young man;
> Charley, he is a dandy.
> Oh, Charley, he's a fine young man,
> For he buys the girls some candy.
> Oh, I won't have none of your weevily wheat,
> I won't have none of your barley,
> But I'll have some flour in half an hour
> To bake a cake for Charley.

Such games seem to have had a rural origin and were popular longest in isolated farming communities, but they also lightened the gloom of village youngsters who could not take part in outright dancing.

From George Washington's administration to January 1, 1934, when Franklin Roosevelt suspended the practice, the President always held a public reception on New Year's Day. Midwestern country towns imitated this custom with varying degrees of intensity, but it was sufficiently common to merit attention in many local papers. Printers encouraged the idea of receptions in order to sell calling cards, and some advertised that they would remain open to print orders until noon on New Year's. Most of the ladies in Lacon, Illinois, kept open house or joined with friends in doing so on New Year's in 1875. In reporting this, the local editor complimented the sobriety of callers, the "toilettes" of the ladies, and the generous refreshments. The custom was observed at least intermittently in Lacon as late as 1894. Generous supplies of eggnog undoubtedly contributed to the rush of callers in Chatfield, Minnesota, in 1867 and to compliments "as thick as blackbirds." There, too, the custom lasted for a considerable period of years.[18]

WINTER AND SPRING

THOUGH JANUARY and February were cold, raw months on the Middle Border, they failed to halt social life. At Coffeysburg and Jamesport, Missouri, in 1893 the temperature dropped to twenty-one below zero, and village boys found the daily chore of filling the wood box after school more time-consuming than usual. Still, the correspondents of those two villages had much to report to the county paper —marriages, deaths, chicken pox among the children, and hog cholera. Harness makers were busy preparing for spring trade, and one of the postmasters received a new stock of notions to occupy his time when not handing out mail. Boys braved the cold to kill rabbits, for which they received ten cents from the local produce dealers. A Christian Endeavor Society was organized at one of the churches. Farm sales were common. Burt Ford moved into Grandma Coffey's place, since she intended to live with her children the rest of her days. The GAR gave a bean supper; young people attended informal parties in private homes; and a citizen captured a bald eagle measuring seven feet from tip to tip. The ground hog failed to see his shadow on the second of February. Preaching services, lodge meetings, and an occasional itinerant lecturer helped to vary life in the dead of winter.[19]

Valentine's Day provided an excuse for a dance and for the sending of sentimental greetings or ugly, joshing caricatures, depending on one's age and inclinations. Volunteer fire companies and other local organizations gave dancing parties on Washington's Birthday, but otherwise it seems not to have been widely observed.[20]

March and April could be bitter cold, but they also were likely to bring sudden shifts to mild, clean-smelling days when all the earth seemed ready to burst with lush, new vegetation. Small towns like Jamesport and Coffeysburg, Missouri, began to turn to outdoor activities. March first was moving day for farm renters who were thinking of sowing spring oats, and townsmen cleared away debris so gardens could be plowed and prepared for early vegetables. Spring thaws meant a battle with mud. People were both amused and sympathetic toward the two sisters who suffered accidents in the spring of 1893—one receiving a mouthful of mud kicked up by the horse which she was driving; the other a scorched back from dropping a curling iron with which she was frizzing her curls. Though revival meetings, oyster suppers, birthday parties, and sociables were common, the approaching termination of school left no doubt that activities were shifting to the outdoors.[21]

Easter Sunday was the only occasion consistently and widely observed in these two spring months. Some women made a practice of growing flowers to decorate their churches at the Easter season. Special music, new dresses and hats for the ladies, and sermons prepared with greater care than usual combined with callas, ferns, gloxinias, and Easter lilies to make Easter Sunday a memorable day. Even before the Civil War children looked forward to dyeing Easter eggs. William Dean Howells remembered the soft, pale green colors obtained by boiling eggs with onions, and most of all the calico eggs which resulted from boiling them wrapped in multi-colored calico cloth.[22]

Youngsters had to have their fun on April Fool's Day. In 1869 the Tiffin, Ohio, editor recommended concealing a stone under an old hat on the sidewalk for passers-by to kick. In his estimation, All Fool's Day gave every sort of license to play tricks on one's friends, and no one had any right to be angry at the custom. Some village schools celebrated Arbor Day, of Nebraska origin, and editors occasionally urged citizens to plant trees in honor of the occasion.[23]

IN THE STEPS OF HUCKLEBERRY FINN AND TOM SAWYER

MOST OF ALL, people looked forward to freedom from hovering within the small areas of heat generated by stoves in homes and public buildings. During the winter it was possible to be warm in front or behind, but uniform temperatures were unknown. Approaching freedom from school and access to woods, caves, and swimming holes within walking distance of town gave the small fry a feverish itch to be about their summer business of foraging, the activity best remembered by writers who spent their childhood in mid-western villages. The antics of Huckleberry Finn and Tom Sawyer, as seen through the eyes of Mark Twain, have immortalized this phase of village life, and here indeed was the glory of small-town existence for youngsters. Farm boys had too many chores, too few companions, and too much nature to enjoy it to the limit; city boys lacked the opportunity. But no one complained of the vistas which lay before village youngsters who could be in open country or the woods in a matter of minutes.

The pattern of childhood activity within the village itself was set before the Civil War. William Dean Howells remembered the sequence of events in Ohio towns—marbles in early spring, followed by foot races, tops, and swimming, and then kites during the sweltering heat of summer. Though Howells became a literary dictator in Brahmin New England with the passage of the years, he never forgot the pets of his youth—coons, dogs, goats, rabbits, and chickens around the yard, and fish and turtles in the hogshead of rain water at the corner of the house. Howells owned a pony for a time, which he stabled in part of the family cow shed. Since guns were scarce, seven or eight boys took turns shooting a muzzle-loader on hunting trips. Howells went to the woods with others to obtain May apples, blackberries, chinquapins, red haws, pignuts, black walnuts, and sugar water from maple trees. As fall approached, boys built a cart and planned to haul in several bushels of nuts, but like all foraging activities the planning of this was more important than the execution.

Thomas Hart Benton revelled in similar pleasures at his home town of Neosho, Missouri, in the 1890's. Neosho had creeks where the gang learned to swim, and on whose banks they practiced chewing and smoking, and added to their linguistic powers. A railroad siding near Neosho enabled youngsters to steal two-mile rides on passing trains. There were caves to explore, horses to ride, cottonmouth moccasins and copperheads to kill. In the autumn, Benton took part in possum hunts west of town, where one ran with a kerosene lantern in hand, trying to beat his companions to the treed possum, with only the bark of the dogs as a guide. A large barn on the Benton lot was a magnificent place for amateur shows and circuses.

Although William Allen White was never a great outdoors man, his small-town boyhood made him fond of nature. Besides his family home, White listed three major influences on his childhood. One was the family barn, with its trapeze, haymows, ancient lores and skills. A second was the river, which provided fishing, swimming, rowing and skating. And the third was "roaming"—roaming in the timber, trapping quail and songbirds, foraging for nuts, and exploiting the changing seasons of the year.

Nostalgia for one's youthful kinship with the spirit of Tom Sawyer never departed from adults who grew up in midwestern country towns. When Herbert Hoover later spoke of the swimming hole under the willows by the railroad bridge near his boyhood home in West Branch, Iowa, of trapping rabbits with box traps, of fishing with willow poles, and of spitting on the bait to assure success, he plumbed the very heart of the Midwest.[24]

Girls were more limited in their play, but they too enjoyed the pets which inhabited outbuildings of the family home, found a ready circle of neighborhood friends, and joined the boys in the nightly game of hide-and-seek. When parents called their children in after dusk of a long summer evening, boys and girls found kinship in a common fatigue and in wondering at the unreasonableness of adults who wanted youngsters to wash their feet after a day of barefooted play.

"TAKE ME OUT TO THE BALL GAME"

MAY AND JUNE quickened the tempo of outdoor life still more for all ages. Men and older boys discussed the prospects for baseball, which had become the great American game by the 1860's. In December of 1865 delegates from Illinois, Indiana, Michigan, and Iowa met in Chicago and adopted the name "Northwestern Baseball Convention," with the intention of obtaining for western clubs some voice in the national movement. State associations were formed in Iowa and Minnesota in 1867, and league play rapidly developed among larger towns all over the Middle West.

Though smaller places were unable to maintain regular schedules, they participated to the extent of their ability. In May of 1867, for example, the Algona, Iowa, paper asked those interested in forming a local team to meet on the public square at three the next Saturday afternoon. Before the end of the month a diamond had been laid out and practice games were under way. Plans for the summer called for games at five on Wednesdays and at two on Saturdays. By the 1870's small towns like Washburn, Illinois, were holding three-day baseball tournaments at the close of the summer season, with cash prizes for the winning team. In general, teams operated on a purely amateur basis and on the smallest possible margin of cost. In 1897 the Croswell, Michigan, Grays beat Center, Michigan, on the latter's diamond fifteen to thirteen, although earned runs stood only five to three. "Jollying, singing, and jostling" helped the Croswell team forget its muddy ride to Center for the contest. After dinner at the Center hotel and a stroll around the village, the team reached the playing grounds at three. As the contest got under way, a drummer drove by and inquired what was going on, a ball game or a yacht race, and was rewarded by a jeer from the small boys hugging the sides of the diamond—"ball, you d—d fool."

Baseball did little to cement good will among competing towns. If one can believe reports in small-town newspapers, umpiring changed little over the years, for the beaten team and its supporters almost invariably agreed that decisions had been intentionally biased. Towns accused one another of playing ringers, of employing crooked umpires, and of unfair noisemaking to rattle opponents at crucial moments. But Babe Ruth never equalled the slugging record of many a midwestern small-town team. Freeport beat Monroe, Wisconsin, on July 5, 1869, by a score of sixty-six to thirty-nine.

In explaining the loss, the Monroe editor pointed out that the score was thirty-all at the end of the fifth, but since Freeport had three pitchers and Monroe only one, the latter naturally dropped behind in the later innings.[25]

MEMORIAL DAY AND FOURTH OF JULY

MAY AND JUNE encouraged villagers to live outdoors. Churches and lodges held so many ice cream and strawberry lawn festivals that papers merely noted the hour and date. Children's-day Sunday-school exercises were occasionally held as early as 1869, and had become fairly common by the 1880's. May-day customs, including baskets for sweethearts and picnics, appealed only to a scattering of towns,[26] but all observed Memorial Day. First proclaimed in 1868 by General John A. Logan, commander-in-chief of the recently formed Grand Army of the Republic, Memorial Day rapidly developed as a major ceremonial occasion.

Two heavy fieldpieces on the river bank fired a sunrise salute at Lacon, Illinois, on Memorial Day in 1884, and shortly thereafter country people began to arrive. At one o'clock the Peru band, a military company, fifty veterans, and citizens on foot and in carriages went in procession to the local cemetery, where eight little girls placed sprigs of evergreen on graves of Union soldiers. Prayers, songs by a quartette, and the firing of a military salute completed the cemetery program, after which the group marched to a grove to hear more band music, more singing, and the orator of the day. Several short talks were also made, one of which stressed the politically useful, time-honored theme of the Republican party—that the Democrats were traitors and that Jeff Davis should have been hanged at the close of the Civil War. Elaborate celebrations of this type were costly, flannel for the powder sacks, and powder and gun primers alone costing fifteen dollars. The program at Minonk, Illinois, the same year showed that Memorial Day celebrations were similar everywhere, and yet the variety of details that could be worked in. The Minonk procession contained a brass band, a drum corps, a wagon holding an organ and a quartette, 200 school children carrying flowers for the graves, the usual assortment of veterans, and forty carriages of civilians. An additional crowd, estimated at one thousand people, straggled along the sidewalks on foot. After visiting the cemetery, the group returned to the local opera house for music and recitations by school children and an oration by a local preacher. The day closed with an "elocutionary entertainment" to raise $150.00 to pay for the celebration.

Memorial Day rapidly surpassed even the Fourth of July as the outstanding ceremonial honoring American national traditions, partly because of the great strength of the Grand Army of the Republic and its auxiliaries like the Women's Relief Corps. Perhaps, too, the "Boys in Blue," and their honored dead, symbolized American conviction that preservation of the Union had ended the last threat to national safety. Since America, and especially the Midwest, was heading toward an era of peace and constantly increasing material growth, one needed only to honor the dead who had made this possible. An occasional citizen like William Allen White's father, irritated by the constantly increasing pension raids and GAR bias toward the Republican party, muttered that Memorial Day parades included "a lot of damn bounty jumpers." But Memorial Day remained supreme until national and world events, starting with the Spanish American War, and the thinning ranks of the GAR, encouraged Americans to divide their attention more evenly among national holidays.[27]

American seaboard villages began to observe the Fourth of July early in the nineteenth century with public prayer, a reading of the Declaration of Independence, and a patriotic speech by an "orator of the day." Many villages also held public dinners at which leading citizens drank patriotic toasts. Although music and entertainment were not wholly eliminated, these early celebrations were basically commemorative in nature. As native-born Americans moved on into the Middle West it was only natural for them to adopt the same kind of program.

Although the effort and cost involved in serving as host on the Fourth of July encouraged towns to pass the honor around, major celebrations were usually held in sufficient numbers to enable farm families everywhere to attend. Special efforts were made to provide an outstanding program on the hundredth anniversary of the signing of the Declaration of Independence, July 4, 1876. The celebration at Algona, Iowa, in that year was typical of the many held. Anvils, cannons, and guns began to fire at sunrise, and by nine o'clock the walks were jammed with people. Township delegations in carriages and on foot milled around, hunting assigned places in the parade line. The Algona silver cornet band headed the morning parade, followed next by two floats of girls arrayed in fitting costumes, one representing the colonies and the other the states. Although muddy roads reduced the number of floats, Algona businessmen and the local newspaper entered enough to make a mile-long parade to Judge Call's grove. Between 450 and 500 vehicles and over 3,000 people were present. Although only half the crowd could be seated at the grove, the rest stood through a long sequence of prayers, band music, glee-club songs, a reading of the Declaration of Independence, an historical sketch of the county, and the oration of the day, all of which preceded the basket dinner. In spite of intermittent rain during the afternoon, the program went on—sack races, tub races, wheelbarrow races, running-and-trotting horse races, drills by a militia company, and a baseball game. Heavy rain ruined the fireworks display at night and reduced attendance at the courthouse ball and festival, sponsored by the local band for the purpose of buying new uniforms and a band wagon.

Many years later, Kin Hubbard wrote a humorous sketch based on the celebrations held in 1876. Hubbard described Alex McGee, the grand marshal of the day, with

a calico Oregon pony an' th' fierce, stern expression o' a fiery rear admiral. "Stand back! Git back! Ever'buddy git back!!" he roared as he galloped around th' public square while th' liberty pole wuz bein' raised. In times o' peace Alex wuz as tame as a kitten, but on a big day he could crush enough women an' children t' keep himself in hidin' th' year around.

Hubbard also mentioned the town drunk who had a reputation to sustain on every public occasion: "Most as many folks used t' come t' town on a big day t' see Buck Taylor taken t' jail as they did t' hear th' music an' see th' sights." In Hubbard's sketch, courtship proceeded apace between bashful country girls and the band boys. A balloon ascension and a hook-and-ladder race, staged by the local volunteer fire company, greatly pleased the crowd. And, sure enough, Buck had to be hauled off to jail with ten or fifteen fellows standing on the dray to hold him down. After this, many went home, but the young blades remained in town to see the "ten thousand dollar" fireworks display.

Elaborate celebrations were held less frequently after 1876. In 1886 Luverne, Iowa, welcomed the Fourth with a sunrise cannon salute which was audible three miles away. An oration, band music, and fireworks featured the day-long celebration. Algona repeated much the same pattern as in 1876, except that the cannon blew up from an overload of gunpowder through failure to discover that someone had choked its mouth with clay, and a "bowery dance," staged in a brush-covered arbor competed with one at the courthouse.

More and more, towns took the day at a less strenuous pace or turned to sheer amusement. At Centreville, Michigan, in 1888 people used the daylight hours for fishing and picnics, and waited until sundown to drift downtown to hear the band and see the fireworks. The Centreville program on July 4, 1897, revealed the changed emphasis when towns celebrated elaborately. The mayor issued a proclamation asking citizens to display large flags and to wear smaller ones or strips of red, white, and blue cloth in their lapels. The program consisted almost wholly of contests—running, jumping, vaulting, catching a greased pig, and egg, sack, and wheelbarrow races, with prizes for winners in each. Because of the current bicycle craze, the largest prizes were given to winners in that division.[28] Within another few years, small-town, Mid-America, responded to the national crusade for a safe-and-sane Fourth in protest against a yearly toll of youngsters maimed by exploding firecrackers and to protect adult nerves. By then, however, the whole pattern of life was shifting.

As torrid heat began to settle over the Middle Border, and more and more farm crops were laid by or harvested, farmers and townsmen alike slowed to a snail's pace in response to a brassy sun by day and humid nights. The Protestant churches of Monroe, Wisconsin, even started union services in the courthouse park for the remainder of the summer in July, 1876, but Baptists at Centreville, Michigan, in August of 1879 still boasted of "Baptists not yet on Vacation" to show that they could endure two regular Sunday preaching services in hot weather. Lawn socials and Sunday-school picnics increased in popularity at this time of year as did railroad and steamboat excursions for those who could afford the expense. Small boys found the scum and stagnant water of their favorite swimming holes less inviting and spent more time resting on the muddy banks, unwittingly storing strength to meet the penalty of illness which many of them would pay. The eastern Chautauqua movement was beginning to invade the Middle West, and citizens of Iowa and Wisconsin towns began to attend the Monona Lake Assembly, while others within easy driving distance went to the Old Salem Chautauqua grounds in Illinois to hear inspirational lectures.[29]

OLD SETTLERS' ASSOCIATIONS

SEPTEMBER AND OCTOBER revived community activities. As graded schools became the rule, more and more youngsters found themselves back in class by early September, and adults looked forward to the three great community efforts of the early fall—the Old Settlers' Celebration, the county fair, and election campaigns.

Old Settlers' Associations appeared quickly on the agricultural frontier and had an enormous popularity with elderly people, who sensed the rapidly changing nature of life around them. The founders of such an association in Van Buren County, Iowa, in 1872, thanked Providence for sending them to Iowa and for lengthening their lives so that they might see the great advances in civilization made by their adopted state. They hoped also to "cultivate a more fraternal feeling" and to pass on to their descendants a history of their own early "trials and tribulations." The founding of numerous county organizations, and even of state federations, should have stimulated a sense of continuity, but most efforts had disappeared or were taken over by 1900 as adjuncts of county fairs or city celebrations.

They had difficulty in surviving because Middle Border ideals of progress held that everything old was inferior. In seeking "advantages" for their children and in emphasizing *growth* in size and numbers, the pioneers themselves had disdained the past. Why, then, should a new generation, swollen with conceit over its advanced civilization, do more than humor the elderly by enabling them to get together to recall the days of their youth? Some local bard wrote a long poem for the souvenir pamphlet published by the *Lacon Home Journal* in 1888 to commemorate the old settlers' meeting held on August 28. Although meant to be complimentary, the poem's jocular, patronizing tone was that of an adult preparing to help somewhat backward children have a good time:

> Nothun like the ole times now—
> Time goes back'ards anyhow!
> Ole folks mostly passed away
> With the good times o' their day,
> When we all wore homespun clothes,
> Jist as happy, I suppose,
> As the young folks air to-day,
> Jist as peart, too, ever' way!

Uncle Johnny took the prize
As the oldest settler heur,
An' he dainced a hornpipe thur,
Right on the platform 'fore our eyes;
Yessir, an' 'at man knows more lies
'N any feller anywhur!
Killed more Injuns, wolves an' bear—
Built fust cabin, raised first corn,
Hilt first meetin, fit first fight,
Got up the first county fair—
Brung first circus'n' side-show there,
His son Ben first sucker born,
Uncle Johnny's jist a *sight!*

. . . .

Then ole Uncle Johnny got
A feller—kindo heavy sot—
Majors was his name—to play
Fiddle-chunes the rest o' the day;
Played ole "Rye Straw" an' "Gray Eagle."
'N'en the geurles commenced to giggle
When they called fur "Leather Britches,"

. . . .

Lord! our feet commenced to go
'Fore he'd hardly drawed his bow!
Cur'us how a feller feels
Daincun them ole ratlun reels!
Wusht ye could'a' seen them folks
Hoppun round an' crackun jokes,
Gray ole Womern an' *ole men*
Jist as young's they'd ever be'n,
Rakun up the old-time fun:

. . . .

Never thinkun of the sun
Till they noticed it wus gone
An' the night wus comun on!
An' ole Johnny says to me,
As we started home, says 'e:
"Now, dog-on, ef't didn't seem
Ole times come back in a dream!"

Uncle Johnnies in their second childhood, incapable any longer of getting the truth straight, ignorant and outdated, apparently were all that the Middle Border saw in the environment from which it sprang.

While the pioneers still lived, the annual reunion attracted large crowds. Although it was occasionally held in other months, late August or September became the favorite time of meeting. People sometimes talked of erecting and equipping pioneer cabins, and old settlers occasionally baked corn pone, displayed old newspapers, and exhibited "relics" of early days, but nothing of a permanent nature resulted. In general, such gatherings took place at a county seat or village, with a morning oration, followed by a basket dinner, and then music, games, reminiscences of the past, and a reading of the names of those who had died during the preceding year. As pioneer ranks thinned, leadership passed to younger people. Algona, Iowa, solved the problem in 1898 in a common way by calling one day of the county fair "Old Settlers' Day." When Algona celebrated its Jubilee in 1904, citizens gathered pioneer relics into a temporary museum and honored the few remaining early settlers,[30] but there as elsewhere concrete remains and traditions had disappeared within half a century almost as completely as the herds of deer that once ranged the county.

THE COUNTY FAIR

COUNTY FAIRS survived because they could be modernized from time to time to meet shifting interests and changed conditions. The period preceding the 1870's has been called the golden age of midwestern fairs because of its heavy emphasis on educational activities, with amusement strictly subordinated to instruction. Midwestern county seat towns awarded generous premiums on farm exhibits,[31] and serious-minded farm folk looked forward to vying with one another for prizes and to visiting with neighbors.

Between 1870 and the turn of the century considerable change occurred. Increasing co-operation with newer educational agencies, like agricultural colleges and farmers' institutes, and more scientific methods of stock judging gained widespread approval. Other changes were more debatable. Horse racing became more prominent and racing circuits were arranged to coincide with a series of county fairs. Opponents of horse racing argued that it had nothing to do with the real business of agriculture; instead, it absorbed an undue proportion of premium funds, distracted attention from farm exhibits, and encouraged gambling. Defenders were not lacking, however, and their arguments impressed a countryside that loved horse racing. They insisted that the development of fine horses of all kinds was a legitimate branch of stock breeding, and that gambling could be controlled, if people really wanted to check it. Moreover, attendance would decline, especially among townsmen, if racing was eliminated.

A rapid growth of shows, carnivals, and other midway features aroused opposition from puritanical citizens. The secretary of the Michigan county fair association in the early 1880's vividly described existing abuses. According to him, "honest grangers" were shocked when they accidentally stumbled into the presence of the "Circassian beauty" while looking for something less exciting. The president of the Wisconsin State Fair Association in 1883 also denounced "the gaudy shows, gambling devices, organ-grinding, conjuring, mountebankism, and every species of graceless vagabondism, which we have admitted to our grounds." [32] Rural newspapers echoed similar sentiments. In spite of a successful fourteenth annual fair at Algona, Iowa, in 1886, the local paper criticized those in charge for admitting travelling shows staffed with "blacklegs and swindlers." The Preston, Minnesota, paper in 1896 even questioned whether fairs were worth while, morally or financially. On Thursday night of fair week Preston streets had been crowded with young men, many of whom were drunk. Some of them had won considerable money betting on the horse races and had drunk too much while treating their friends.

County fairs continued to draw large crowds to the turn of the century in spite of criticism. Some towns held a short, spring racing program, at which grandstand weddings, mule races, and ladies' riding contests vied with the pacers and trotters for attention. The main fair came in the early fall, with a program lasting from two to three days. Directors of the Algona, Iowa, fair in 1877 required all exhibitors to have their entries in place by Wednesday, September 12. Thursday morning was devoted to showing brood mares, jacks, and mules, and to a shooting match with glass balls as targets. The afternoon program opened with an exhibition of horses, which was followed by a pulling contest at two, and then trotting and running races. Awards on farm produce, stock and machinery were announced at ten on Friday, and the rest of the day was given over to horse racing.

Weather-beaten, high board fences enclosed the fair grounds that adjoined the city limits of virtually every county-seat town on the Middle Border. Grandstand, race course, stock pens, and a "floral hall" to shelter the exhibits entered by the ladies were common features, and all towns had hopes of financing enough buildings to shelter crowds and entries alike in bad weather.

The midway asked only for room to pitch its tents and stalls, which moved from fair to fair during the season. As early as 1875 fairs had balloon ascensions, glass works, monkey shows, shooting galleries, and minstrel troupes. In time the midway featured attractions for every age. All bought "candy cream," long strips of a sweet confection which were cut with scissors and wrapped in tissue paper as they emerged from vending machines. Music from a wheezy hand organ—often the same tune over and over—and the thin, shrill whistle of a small steam engine, which emitted puffs of black coal smoke in its efforts to move a heavy load of customers, drew attention to the merry-go-round. Burly countrymen, bashful but proud of their strength, fell easy prey to barkers who challenged them to bet a dime against a good cigar that they could sledge-hammer a lead weight into ringing a gong topping a pole.

Even the most abject gained confidence as they gave way to the frenzied spirit of the midway. Boys twirled canes won at some booth and purchased feather dusters to poke into girls' faces, and were showered with confetti in return. The more daring donned hatbands with snappy slogans and purchased soft rubber balls fastened to India-rubber strings, which enabled them to pop a girl and retrieve the balls virtually in one motion. Small boys exchanged information about sideshow freaks and the strength of the lemonade before investing their nickels and pennies. And all stood in line for access to the one shallow tin cup attached to the fairground pump, even though individuals far back in the milling mob tried to drive other parched throats away by yelling that a dead cat had been found in the well.[33]

Country people brought basket dinners with them and townsmen were sure to arrive in time for the afternoon racing. Herbert Quick has described the excitement of the crowd when horses neared the finish:

The crowd in the grand-stand rose to their feet as the field of trotters came down the homestretch. The marshals yelled at the track-side throng to keep back and give the horses room—and when they came to the wire, with the sorrel still taking the pole, the black leading him by a neck, and roan and bay hurling themselves forward in great surges to close the gap by which they were losing, you should have heard the roar which arose from that Iowa crowd.[34]

VOTING A STRAIGHT TICKET

ALTHOUGH ELECTIONS were important any time, country towns seethed with excitement and debate in presidential-election years. As soon as national conventions announced their tickets, local ratification meetings enthusiastically endorsed the candidates and township political clubs prepared for early fall campaigning. Marching clubs performed at political rallies and in torchlight processions, their members garbed in some distinctive manner such as blue capes and blue helmets topped with white feathers, or white plug hats and canes. Bands, drum corps, blazing torches, flamboyant oratory, and victory barbecues stimulated partisan spirit.

The Monroe, Wisconsin, band played while a crowd gathered at the local Turner's Hall for a Republican rally in 1884. The campaign glee club opened the program by singing "Hold the Fort for Blaine and Logan," after which an abbreviated speech only forty minutes long was given by an embarrassed young man. A seasoned speaker from Janesville held the crowd for two hours, however. He contrasted the American laborer's favorable status under tariff protection with conditions under the caste system and free trade in Europe, compared the records of the presidential candidates, and then finished off with "clever imitations" of "dudes" in the opposing party. The Democrats won that election, and on November 26 staged a local demonstration in honor of their first President in many years. Again the cornet band was called into action to head a parade containing men carrying brooms marked "solid South." Others were dressed as tramps, intended as takeoffs on Blaine and Logan. Mottoes and transparencies, uniformed juvenile marching clubs, fireworks and prismatics on all sides of the public square, shots from improvised cannon, Chinese lanterns everywhere in the courthouse park, speeches, and then a bonfire featured the local celebration.

The Bryan-McKinley campaign aroused even more excitement than usual. An elderly retired farmer of Athens, Illinois, estimated the crowd at a local Republican rally at 5,000 people. Marching clubs from at least ten other towns, some of them as far away as Springfield, were in line. Glee clubs, women's clubs, bands, and all the other paraphernalia of political campaigning were in evidence. Everyone, of course, was excited over Bryan's campaign for free silver and against the "interests." Even youngsters could not ignore the contest when they played their annual Halloween pranks. At Wesley, Iowa, the morning after Halloween the local banker discovered a sign on the front of his bank reading, "I believe in the free and unlimited coinage of silver at the ratio of 16 to 1, G. B. Hall," and an outhouse which had been moved in front of the livery stable bore a placard reading "Free Silver Headquarters."

As soon as the voting ended, citizens began to gather in local opera houses for telegraphic returns. At Athens, Illinois, voters had been excited for months and had talked nothing but politics. By midnight Athens knew pretty well the results and the crowd became wild with excitement. People paraded the streets, shouted, tooted horns, and danced for the rest of the night. While the Republicans were receiving returns at Atlantic, Iowa, a well-known Democrat whose enthusiasm was greater than his information stuck his head in the door, and was informed by some wag that the Argentine Republic had just gone for McKinley, but, being equal to the occasion, he promptly retorted, "It's a d—d lie, for we just got word it went for Bryan." [35]

CHRISTMAS—THE MAJOR FESTIVAL

DURING THE EARLY FALL some churches staged Harvest Home festivals to show their gratitude for bountiful crops, and lyceums and literary societies resumed their winter tempo. Sportsmen who had hunted deer and elk near Algona, Iowa, and other midwestern towns in the 1860's now turned to smaller game or even to trapshooting. Thanksgiving-morning union church services, turkey dinners, and visiting among relatives and friends were common from the 1860's on.[36] But Christmas remained the last and greatest festival of all the year.

William Dean Howells recalled his pleasure in Santa Claus and in hanging up his stockings on Christmas Eve in the small, pre-Civil War Ohio town where he lived as a boy, an indication of the basic continuity of the Christmas pageant. Minor variations existed from place to place, it is true, and church groups occasionally experimented with substitutes for even the Christmas tree. These included paper ships and mills loaded with presents; arches and pyramids; and even illuminated crosses, but invariably congregations used a tree the next year. An editorial in the Lacon, Illinois, paper in 1865, headed "Christmas next Monday," could appear in a country paper today without needing any change to modernize it. Christmas, the editor said, was a day for children, but all had visions of Santa Claus, peanuts, plum puddings, fat turkeys, and genial companions. Children would retire on Christmas Eve with tantalizing visions of Santa Claus in mind and would rise early on Christmas morning to explore the recesses of their stockings suspended from the branches of the family tree. And everyone should spend the day in the real spirit of the occasion, not in "guzzling rot gut."

Local schools dismissed for as much as a week, which alone would have endeared Christmas to children. College boys, schoolteachers, and distant relatives arrived to spend the vacation with their families; dances, marriages, and drinking increased; and youngsters drilled on their songs and recitations for the Christmas program. Already filled with wonder and excitement, children saw fairyland when they entered the church door holding to their parents' hands. There, at the front of the church, stood a magnificent tree, reaching almost to the ceiling, its branches strung with ropes of beauty made from threading pop corn kernels and cranberries alternately on twine. Tin-foil streamers, tapers, and a gold star at the very top added to its splendor. Even the odor of the place seemed changed, a mixture of the smell of wet snow on clothing, of evergreens, of wax and tinsel, of oranges, all nicely mixed and flavored by drafts of hot air from stove or registers and the sharply biting cold which swept inside each time the door was opened.

Children knew that they were sure to receive one of the net stockings crammed with dyed candies, nuts and oranges, and they hopefully eyed the dolls, packages, and curious parcels hanging from branches of the tree or piled at its base. But first the program. Some went through that ordeal with brazen aplomb and loud voice but more hitched at trousers or skirts and twisted handkerchiefs in knots to conceal their agony of embarrassment. The program at the Algona, Iowa, Congregational church in 1886 opened with a song by the entire Sunday school, which meant the whole audience. This was followed by the minister's invocation, and then a song by Mrs. McCoy's class. Georgie Horton gave a recitation, "What Santa Claus Saw," and Howard Robinson followed with another called "The Orphan's Christmas." Master Lee Reed recited "My First Pants," and the program went on through recitations, dialogues and songs until all children had made an appearance. At the Methodist church the program consisted of a cantata, "Catching Kriss-Kringle," but there too the parts were numerous enough to give all fond parents a chance to see their children perform.[37]

In just a few more days the annual cycle of social life would start over again and citizens would have to decide whether to attend the Methodist watch party or a dance on New Year's Eve. By the 1890's small-town social clubs were growing in numbers, state federations of women's clubs were joining the national federation, and the "togetherness" of nineteenth-century country towns was shifting toward a twentieth-century pattern. For the time being, however, citizens automatically belonged to neighborhood and to community, around which social life revolved.

7 ❖ Exit the Horse

CHANGING RELATIONSHIPS

IN 1923 a distinguished American economist, Thorstein Veblen, concluded that country towns had become mere tollgate keepers for vested interests in the background. Manufacturers and jobbers in metropolitan centers now controlled the activities of village retailers through use of national-brand names, package goods, advertising, and agency contracts. According to Veblen, even country bankers had become mere agents of outside financial groups.[1]

Veblen might have pointed out that declining independence had been the lot of country towns since Civil War days. As long as villages grew in numbers and real-estate values, the two accepted measuring sticks of progress, people paid little attention to slowly changing relationships. With the passage of time, however, cumulative change became more evident, and the drift toward national conformity far more evident. Trends of long duration now seemed new only because their effects were so clearly apparent.

PUBLIC UTILITIES COME TO MAIN STREET

PUBLIC UTILITIES were still relatively unimportant in 1865. Town pumps often marked the extent of municipal waterworks; street lighting generally was limited to business districts; and telephones were unknown. Volunteer fire-fight-

217

ing companies exemplified the charm, inefficiency, and local independence which prevailed in the early days. The Iowa state code of 1873 exempted members of volunteer companies from militia duty, jury service, and the poll tax, and ten years of active service excused a man from such obligations forever.[2] While most midwestern states made concessions similar to Iowa's, more appealing considerations accounted for the universal popularity of fire-fighting companies. Members liked the uniforms, the feeling of comradeship, and the social life resulting from sponsorship of parades, picnics, banquets, and the annual fireman's ball, which raised funds for the year ahead. They also competed in regional and state tournaments for awards that added to the richness of their equipment. When fires broke out, members hastily donned their uniforms, dragged their engine by hand from the fire house, and fought the blaze in full view of an admiring crowd. To be elected captain of such a company, and to have the privilege of shouting instructions to its members through the silver trumpet that served as a badge of authority, was one of the great honors of the day. During the course of a fire, some prominent local citizen served refreshments to the volunteers, and still another furnished a team to pull the engine back to the fire house. In view of such rewards, it is understandable that even in New York City members of volunteer companies fought against the establishment of professional departments until 1865. Since smaller towns could not afford such a step, volunteer companies remained the more numerous for years to come. As late as 1944 Iowa's volunteer departments far outnumbered the salaried, professional companies.[3]

Nevertheless, volunteer companies gave way to paid departments wherever towns could afford the cost, and everywhere glamor lost out to efficiency. Skill, training, and permanence were necessary to operate new equipment like the steamers which began to replace hand-operated pumpers from the 1850's on. Citizens learned by bitter experience that volunteers often failed in an emergency, as evidenced

by complaints which developed after the Lacon, Illinois, hotel burned in 1865. The volunteer company had made some
progress in checking the fire by pumping water from the
"pork-house" cistern before their engine choked up with
gravel.[4] Paid companies were expected to avoid such calami-
ties, and lower insurance rates proved that they generally
managed to do so. In return for greater security of property
and cheaper insurance, the midwestern country town sur-
rendered a considerable measure of independence. It celebrated national fire-prevention week, accepted outside advice on methods of fire control, and insisted that its local
firemen model themselves on national patterns of efficiency.

In the years immediately following the Civil War street
lighting differed from town to town. Sauk City, Wisconsin,
depended on kerosene lights, which were serviced nightly
by a one-armed lamplighter equipped with a ladder and a
kerosene can. Atlantic, Iowa, used gas lights. There, too,
a lamplighter, equipped with a small ladder to climb the
corner lamp posts, had to turn on the gas and light each
individual unit. Towns economized by turning off street
lights as soon as people went to bed, and dispensed with
them completely during a full moon. The practice had its
limitations. Local citizens intent on catching early morning
trains stumbled as best they could through dark and dangerous streets, and then wrote letters to the local paper demanding that the city fathers give more attention to actual
needs and less to economy and to calendar predictions of
moonlight nights.[5]

Electric lights began to gain favor before the turn of the
century, even though the early plants were both inefficient
and limited in capacity. Athens, Illinois, celebrated the opening of its first plant in the fall of 1892 with the firing of cannon and a street parade headed by a brass band. The plant
was said to be a fine one. In the winter of 1897, however,
the town was plunged into darkness by a breakdown and
not until the turn of the century did the prospects for lights
seem good again. Cassville, Wisconsin, had an equally bitter

experience. In late summer of 1903 the Cassville plant supplied electricity for twenty-eight lights in the business district. The owner expected to pay thirty dollars a month for an "engineer" to run the plant from dusk to midnight, except on moonlight nights, and to handle all repairing, new installations, and collections of monthly accounts. The engineer was also expected to dismantle all lights during full moons. No skilled engineer could be obtained at the salary offered, and by December the dynamo had ceased to function. This brought a frantic appeal for help to the firm from which it had been purchased, and a leisurely reply. The industry simply had not developed to a point where emergency repairs could be made without serious interruption. Cassville had no lights for several months, and the owner of the plant himself became philosophical about the delay in restoring service.

The growing popularity of electric lights brought greater uniformity to Main Street's appearance. Around 1906 California introduced "white ways," consisting of clusters of globes mounted on ornamental posts, and the idea spread quickly to the Middle West.[6] Unskilled help and frequent breakdowns disappeared as both knowledge and machinery improved. Corporations began to seek franchises to supply electricity to smaller towns, and what had once been a local and rather unimportant activity became big business.

Other public utilities developed in much the same way. In the beginning, telephone service was confined within town limits and was locally financed. As a boy, Edgar Lee Masters spent one summer helping the owner of the Lewiston, Illinois, telephone exchange. Between calls he and the proprietor bottled "Cherry Pectoral," a patent medicine which the latter sold to supplement his income.[7] Subscribers naturally wanted connections throughout the countryside, and within a few years were demanding distant hookups. Local businessmen had to finance the necessary expansion or give way to corporate organizations which could. Many towns preferred municipal ownership. In 1914 the midwestern state of Minnesota led the nation in municipally owned public utilities,[8] and everywhere on the Middle Border towns debated the issue before permitting outside corporations to assume control.

In the end, however, public utility corporations serving many towns within a single system became common. And whether municipal or private ownership prevailed, the trend away from coal-oil lamps, and even away from coal-fired heating systems, made the individual citizen aware that he was becoming part of a larger world. In times of crisis this growing dependence on others was especially evident. In 1935, Hillsboro, Illinois, was affected by a strike of the International Brotherhood of Electrical Workers against the Illinois Power and Light Company which furnished electricity to Hillsboro and other towns in that vicinity. Since another company was willing to service the town during the emergency, Hillsboro was without power for only an hour. It was not so fortunate ten years later when a washout of a natural gas main near Fredericktown, Missouri, interrupted service. Some 900 citizens who depended on the conveniences of Texas natural gas had to turn to other sources for three days. Cold food, cold baths, and cold homes were common complaints during the emergency. Many had to prepare meals in fireplaces and furnaces.[9] After such an experience a resident of a midwestern country town knew for certain that the independence of his father's day had disappeared.

This turning to outside sources became increasingly important in every phase of life. The old family doctor, who had possessed both the knowledge and the equipment necessary to administer the medical lore of 1865, began to take serious cases to larger cities. In 1897 when an Athens, Illinois, doctor could not stop the flow of blood following an operation to remove an abnormal growth from a patient's nose, he rushed the unfortunate man to a sanitarium in Springfield. From the 1880's on, country papers frequently mentioned such trips,[10] evidence that doctors and patients alike were coming to depend on the equipment and skill available in cities.

THE BATTLE OF THE BRANDS

MANY CHANGES occurred without people realizing that they were under way. When brand names began to appear in country newspapers shortly after the Civil War, they aroused little comment and disturbed few, if any, local businessmen. Nonetheless, they revolutionized merchandising procedures. During the first half of the nineteenth century, shoes, clothing, groceries, machinery—all types of goods— were almost always sold without brand names. Merchants shopped where they pleased and bought from the manufacturer or jobber of their choice. Manufacturers gradually learned, however, that newspaper advertising could force storekeepers to carry specific brands of goods. Once Singer Sewing Machines had been widely advertised, for instance, women demanded to see them before making a final choice, and retailers had to carry Singer models or lose trade to stores which did. Any item whose quality and price had been widely praised in advertising literature had to appear in local stores even though merchants felt that a competitive product was better. In this way, manufacturers and wholesalers influenced selection of goods, prices, and even methods of salesmanship in retail stores.

Evidence of the effectiveness of such advertising had been available for many years. Patent medicine companies spent enormous sums on advertising before the Civil War, with testimonials of the wonder-working powers of such remedies appearing as paid advertisements in country newspapers everywhere. As soon as such a campaign opened, customers began to ask their local druggists to supply them with the product. Patent medicine firms thus clearly proved that a market could be created and stores compelled to stock specific items by aggressive advertising in country weeklies. Other manufacturers may have been slow to adopt the same technique because of the chicanery associated with the patent medicine business. An essay on the subject by Josh Billings in 1865 concluded:

P. S. Let me advise you as a friend, if it is indispensably necessary to cheat a little in the manufaktur ov the "Salvashun Bitters" let it bi all means be in the rutes; don't lower the basis. [11]

Such jibes at the heavy alcoholic content of patent medicines did not retard their sale. Another essay in 1890 described the fabulous career of "Drake's Plantation Bitters," which first appeared while the heavy, Civil War excise on whiskey made the price of tax-exempt "bitters" more attractive. Drake's slogan, "S. T. 1860—X," soon appeared in newspapers, and on fences, barns, billboards, and rocks. Pointers suspended over yawning chasms directed the eye to Drake's slogan, painted on beetling precipices and seemingly inaccessible mountain cliffs. One day the sign mysteriously appeared on an exposed rock in Niagara Falls. Along the Pennsylvania railroad a forest of trees on a mountainside was cut down so the letters four hundred feet high could be seen from the car windows. Drake was said to have gotten in trouble over sending men abroad to paint his advertisement on the pyramids and on Mount Ararat, where Noah's Ark had landed. After his retirement, "rich as Croesus," Drake explained the meaning of his slogan—"Started trade in 1860 with $10."

Comparable herculean efforts in many other fields were long delayed but basic skirmishing for what became a twentieth-century "Battle of the Brands" developed in the 1860's and 1870's in durable goods like pianos, farm machinery, and, most of all, sewing machines. Manufacturers of such products went over the heads of retailers by offering to send goods on approval to customers, by seeking local salesmen to represent them, and by offering agencies to any local store willing to carry their merchandise.[12]

The growing volume of brand advertising seems to have pleased country towns. Editors liked the increased revenue, and storekeepers were more than willing for manufacturers to underwrite advertising costs. Additional help with store displays, salesmanship procedures, and accounting methods impressed merchants who often knew little about such things. Customers also reacted favorably. Standardization of quality was essential for brands to mean anything. Once achieved, this made shopping easier for the consumer. If he liked a particular grade of goods, he could purchase it under its brand name where once he had been compelled to rely on the judgment of the storekeeper or his own limited knowledge of merchandise.

Measured in column inches of advertising in country papers, brand goods were not overly important in the 1870's and 1880's, but readers and businessmen alike were adjusting to them. In the spring of 1876, for instance, the Monroe, Wisconsin, paper contained identical advertisements by two local jewelers, both praising the virtues of Elgin watches and both listing exactly the same prices.[13] As yet, such advertising was unusual, though not unique. While local businessmen seldom mentioned brand names in their advertising, manufacturers put more and more money into advertising specific brands of pianos, sewing machines, patent medicines, and other products that did not have local representatives. By the 1890's these campaigns had succeeded in turning local stores toward brand advertising, and each decade of the twentieth century saw it forge rapidly ahead.[14]

Promoters of durable goods invaded new territory by advertising in local papers their desire to establish agencies. An advertisement of the Excelsior Manufacturing Company of St. Louis in the Brookfield, Missouri, paper in 1868 invited dealers and housekeepers to write for catalogs and price lists on its line of Charter Oak stoves. Once some local retailer accepted an agency, the manufacturer was then inclined to deal strictly through his store.

Exclusive agencies on style or durable goods and even on grocery items were quite common at an early period. Hughes Brothers grocery of Greencastle, Indiana, in 1886, for instance, had the only local advertisement of the "celebrated brand" of Diamond Light Oil put out by the Cleveland Refining Company. Its high gravity and high fire test supposedly eliminated all smoke, smell, charring of wicks, and gumming of burners, and thus avoided the major causes of explosions. Edwin Clapp shoes, W. L. Douglas Shoe Company, and even Chase and Sanborn Coffee made exclusive-agency contracts with local stores in the 1890's. Similar arrangements applied to automobiles, electric refrigerators, and other durable items as they came on the market. The Dickinson Motor Company in 1914 proudly announced that no other Brookfield, Missouri, dealer could sell the "Car of Mystery," which Dodge Brothers was bringing out. There had been a scramble to obtain Dodge agencies, and successful applicants obviously expected to profit greatly from their connections with that enormous corporation.

Manufacturers of convenience goods, which were frequently and widely demanded, generally preferred to have their brands available in all retail stores, even if this meant paying all local advertising costs. The manufacturers of Price's Baking Powder spent large sums in the 1870's and later to call attention to its virtues and to announce that it would be available at all grocers.[15] Postum, Grape Nuts, Wrigley's Chewing Gum, Bayer Aspirin, and Yeast Foam followed the same policy in long and costly advertising campaigns in local papers.

Brand advertising prepared the way for startling changes. In the years immediately following the Civil War every country town had its own flour mill, owned and operated locally. Farmers deposited wheat with the miller and drew on him for their yearly supply of flour as needed. Though country editors cited local millers as prime examples of the strength and possibilities in village industry, national brands began to offer serious competition in the 1880's. Advertisements of the consistency and baking qualities of Minneapolis Pillsbury Flour impressed housewives everywhere, and storekeepers began to announce receipt of carload lots for sale locally. An Algona, Iowa, citizen in 1896 claimed to have filled a Pillsbury flour sack with the local mill's "New Daisy" brand and to have taken it home to his wife in place of the Pillsbury flour which she had requested. When she pronounced it the best that she had ever used, her husband had trouble "keeping a straight face at home," but reported the incident to the local paper.

In less than half a century the makers of Pillsbury and other national brands virtually eliminated village flour mills and now competed only with one another. Rockville, Indiana, celebrated "Pillsbury Flour Week" in November, 1937. Eight Rockville stores, including the chains, and a number in smaller towns over the county held special sales, the week ending with a distribution of prizes to housewives who had won baking contests sponsored by the Pillsbury Company. As a climax the weekly national radio program sponsored by the Pillsbury Company saluted Rockville merchants, the president of the local commercial club, and the county as a whole in a short ceremony. In an article headed, "Pillsbury Plugs Rockville and Parke County over WMAQ" the editor of the Rockville paper expressed appreciation for the free advertising.[16] Local mills no longer existed, no local loyalties were involved. The country miller now belonged to history.

Some campaigns centered on poorly prepared foods. Country stores had sold soggy crackers out of cracker barrels long before the National Biscuit Company started an extensive advertising campaign near the turn of the century to popularize soda crackers. Large advertisements informed readers that the story of Uneeda Biscuit came from two ideas: soda crackers could be made better, and they could be conveyed to the home fresh, crisp, and clean. For the first, one needed the best materials, best equipment, and the highest skill; for the second, tradition must be foiled. Older bakers argued that it was impossible to keep a cracker clean, but younger minds invented the "in-er-seal" package. Conservatives claimed that workers wanted solid foods—potatoes, cabbage, and beef—instead of daintily packed crackers, which were as foreign to them as winter strawberries. But facts upset such theories. Conservatives also said that prosperous people would not eat cheaply priced crackers, but they were wrong again. The wealthy began to eat crackers for their delicacy as the workers ate them for their goodness. United States government reports were cited as proof that soda crackers contained all elements necessary to make fat, muscle, and tissue. Crackers should be a part of every meal. And, of course, they should be purchased in clean, sealed packages, free of kerosene smells and other noxious odors which had permeated the old cracker barrel.[17] In words such as these small-town, Mid-America, was coaxed to change its buying habits.

As early as the 1890's advertisements of national brands of clothing began to make men style conscious. By 1896 Hart Schaffner and Marx was furnishing country retailers with advertising material stressing quality, style, and proper buying habits. Such advertising encouraged customers to buy several pairs of trousers on the grounds that frequent changing of clothing made it last longer. From this it was only a step to emphasis on being in style. Readers of country papers were thus thoroughly prepared to appreciate cartoons like that in the Algona, Iowa, paper in 1908 which lampooned styles being worn by the younger set. At the moment, high collars, string ties, balloon trousers, and cigarettes were in fashion.

The appeal to style was not to be denied. Pictures of properly dressed men leaning on golf clubs while being admired by beautiful women and Russian wolfhounds appealed to village boys who wanted the same attention. Older men liked the luxurious fabrics and "executive-type" cut of expensive brands. In 1907 Rummel's store at Brookfield, Missouri, featured Kuppenheimer Clothes, "in a class by themselves," at sixteen to twenty-five dollars, and also sold the Majestic brand at ten to fifteen dollars. A competing store in 1908 warned readers that last year's suits would not do. Within twelve months, 1907 suits had become passé—lines, seams, lapels, pockets, and sleeves were all wrong.[18] The growing volume of such advertising indicated that small-town, Mid-America had begun to respond. Father's black broadcloth and mother's best silk dress no longer marked the boundary between proper dress and merely getting by.

The number of early brand names which have survived to the present are legion. Bissell Sweepers, Pepperell Sheets, Baker's Chocolate, Ivory Soap ("it floats"), and Aunt Jemima's Pancake Flour were winning converts in the 1890's. Quaker Oats, Victor Talking Machines ("His Master's Voice"), Red Cross Shoes, and Stearns and Foster Mattresses were not far behind. Three generations of small-town citizens have succumbed to brand names going back to the 1890's and even earlier.

Many brands won their way against bitter competition, and not all efforts were successful. Some, like Battle Axe Chewing Tobacco, "the largest piece of good tobacco ever sold for 10¢," were widely advertised until consumer habits changed, thus seriously impairing the good-will value of their name. Other brands disappeared from the market as rivalry for the consumer's dollar became more intense. Manufacturers of baking powders spent thousands of dollars in bitter competition for supremacy. A bar graph in an advertisement of Dr. Price's Baking Powder in 1891 showed the comparative worth of various brands as determined by Professor Peter Collier, late chemist-in-chief of the United States Department of Agriculture. Brands named were Royal, Unrivaled, Taylor's, Spoon, Monarch, Snow Ball, Calumet, Hotel, Yarnall's, Milk, Shepard's, Bon Bon, Forest City, Chicago Yeast, Crown, Silver Star, and Dodson and Hils. Professor Collier declared that all but Dr. Price's contained ammonia or alum, and that some contained both. Manufacturers naturally became disturbed when chain stores began to push their own manufactured products, thus endangering brand supremacies which had been won at great financial cost. But the "Battle of the Brands" preceded the arrival of the chain stores. Chase and Sanborn Coffee competed heavily with

Lion Coffee in the late 1890's and early twentieth century. Promoters of Lion Coffee spent thousands of dollars on advertising and on premiums to purchasers while Chase and Sanborn depended solely on heavy advertising. Of the two brands it alone has survived as a household word.[19]

As storekeepers joined with manufacturers in advertising particular brands week after week, consumers began to accept their claims as valid. At least, they wanted to try the products. The manufacturer of Majestic Ranges sent factory representatives to hold a week of demonstrations in local stores and to distribute free cooking utensils to purchasers; free cocoa and servings of new food lines, with an orchestra playing as an additional attraction, became commonplace in village grocery stores on Saturday afternoons.[20] In thus accepting brand goods the local merchant ceased to block the path between manufacturer and consumer. He had let the outside world in. As never before, customers could compare his prices with those of his competitors. When he sold Baker's Chocolate for a penny more than the price being asked in a competing store, he no longer could insist that his product was superior and therefore worth the extra sum. Consumers could compare brands as well as prices, for standardization of products developed quickly. As soon as a means of rapid, short-range transportation appeared, the storekeeper faced competition the like of which he had never seen before.

RAILROADS AND MAIL-ORDER HOUSES

IMMEDIATELY FOLLOWING the Civil War, when railroads were building everywhere to keep pace with an expanding population, every country town exerted itself to become a railroad center. Citizens raised almost unbelievable subsidies to obtain railroad lines, no matter how ridiculous their extent or how little they had advanced beyond the paper stage. Local newspapers campaigned ardently in support of new lines and everywhere the arguments advanced were much the same. The editor of the Tiffin, Ohio, paper in 1868 gave many reasons for supporting the current campaign to raise $80,000 locally to obtain a station on the Columbus, Tiffin and Toledo Railroad. Doubters were assured that every citizen would profit from the venture. Tiffin merchants would be able to obtain cheaper goods and to pass their saving on to customers. Canton, Ohio, which had passed Tiffin in population, was cited as proof of what railroads could do for a town. Factories had moved to Canton. Only recently one valued at two million dollars had located there. In the editor's opinion, if Tiffin obtained the new railroad, she would double in population within ten years and local real estate would boom.[21] Factories, population, and rising real-estate values—here was the constant dream of every midwestern town—and railroads were the Aladdin's Lamp for achieving it.

Since railroads handled primarily long-distance transportation, farmers living along their right-of-way still had to drive to town for goods. Any improvement in transportation lessened isolation, however, and railroads were no exception. Towns with good rail connections began to feel the competition of larger places. In 1894 people could leave Lacon, Illinois, at 8:30 in the morning and arrive at Peoria by 11:00. This enabled them to shop almost four hours and then catch the 2:55 train, which put them home again at 5:30. Since Peoria merchants advertised dry goods, clothing, and jewelry heavily in Lacon papers, they apparently obtained considerable patronage from customers who came by rail. Greencastle, Indiana, in 1886, tried to obtain a special-fare "excursion train" on Saturdays so that villagers and country people in the northern part of the county could spend the whole day shopping in Greencastle. Even small-town merchants gained some trade by rail. An aggressive storekeeper at Gallatin, Missouri, in 1886 offered to refund railroad fares to customers from a distance who bought quantities of goods at his clearance sales.[22]

Railroads also enabled metropolitan centers to invade the retail trade of country towns to a minor extent. In the fall of 1893, Bullene, Moore, Emery and Company of Kansas City advertised the Inter-State Fair and Priests of Pallas entertainment shortly to take place in that city. The store invited residents of Gallatin, Missouri, to come for the entertainment and also to visit the 102 departments in the seven-floor building which it occupied. It also offered to send out samples of dress goods by mail order so that customers could have dresses made while visiting in the city. Another Kansas City firm offered free transportation to every person within one hundred miles who bought five dollars' worth of merchandise.[23]

While hundreds of people took advantage of excursion trips to cities, and many undoubtedly purchased goods, direct competition from city department stores remained only a minor irritant to country storekeepers. Excursion trains were likely to depart at inconvenient hours and to deliver the exhausted traveller back home late at night. Crowded to the point where people had to stand in the aisles, they defied all but the bravest and most resolute shopper to board them for the return trip burdened down with parcels from city stores. Generally he needed all his energy to survive the rigors of the trip, and he travelled light with that in mind.

The great cities needed something more before they could directly tap rural, midwestern retail trade. Montgomery Ward and Company pointed the way as the first of the great mail-order houses. Starting business in the period of Granger discontent, the company developed rapidly to the point where country merchants everywhere feared its influence. Sears, Roebuck and Company entered the field in 1886. These companies selected goods with the rural market in mind, and by purchasing in volume obtained reduced prices from manufacturers. Attractively illustrated catalogs permitted farmers to examine at leisure the bargains offered for sale.

National magazines began openly to discuss the panic generated by mail-order competition. They pictured the country storekeeper as "Standing before the door of his long-established but modest emporium, his ample form flanked by windows displaying hoes and pancake flour, boys' suits and writing-paper, washboards and cigars, while a garish sign, 'General Merchandise' creaked above." [24] He was looking at the heap of freight recently dumped on the depot platform by a passing train. Three sacks of catalogs had arrived at the local post office the preceding week, and now goods were pouring in from mail-order houses. They had been bought for cash, whereas customers demanded credit when buying locally. Moreover, city catalogs displayed goods far more attractively than did local stores. Since farmers living ten miles from town could now buy groceries in Chicago or New York, local retailers were seriously considering closing their stores. They were convinced that if mail-order houses continued to prosper, every country town would be reduced to a post office, blacksmith shop, doctor's office, and a grain elevator. Land values would decline and monopoly would rule the land. Only the railway depot would grow in size under the new regime.

This fear of mail-order houses created much ill will between merchants and farmers. When rural free delivery routes were started at the turn of the century, farmers naturally agitated for their extension, but village storekeepers offered no support for fear that mail-order houses would benefit. Merchants openly opposed the passage of a parcel post law on the grounds that the government would thus be subsidizing mail-order houses in their efforts to deliver large packages directly to the farmer's door for nominal charges. The issue was debated in the pages of the *Outlook* in 1910. Those opposed to parcel post argued that mail-order houses had already ruined "tens of thousands" of local merchants. A parcel post law would reduce transportation rates and provide special, rural-delivery wagons for the benefit of monster corporations. This threatened the very existence of towns. Country merchants supported public improvements, libraries and churches, the professions, and civic progress in general. Destroy them, and the prosperity and individual welfare of the rural population would be endangered.

"A Professor in a State University" outlined the other side of the issue. Local merchants asked twenty to twenty-five dollars for the same suit that mail-order houses sold for $13.75. Groceries and other supplies varied equally as much in price. Why shouldn't people buy from mail-order houses when their profit margins were smaller? Though midwestern farmers were less vocal, they resented seeing delegations of businessmen from their communities attend state conventions called to oppose cheap postal rates.[25] The battle against parcel post stretched out for a ten-year period. Although the final passage of the law helped mail-order houses, country merchants perhaps lost even more in customer good will, for farmers deeply resented any effort to keep them isolated from the outside world. Today, in many midwestern towns mail-order houses operate retail stores or branch offices at which customers may place catalog orders.

STEAM, GAS, ELECTRICITY, SPRINGS, OR COMPRESSED AIR?

AS NEVER BEFORE, small-town merchants needed to foster community solidarity and good will between farm and town for agencies of short-range transportation were rapidly developing. By enabling farmers to shop at greater distances from their homes, they increased the potential market possibilities everywhere, thus encouraging big business to establish chain stores directly on Main Street itself. They even made it convenient for farmers to shop in various county-seat towns and in metropolitan department stores.

Electric interurbans illustrate the rapidity of change in short-range transportation. By the 1890's electrical research had demonstrated their feasibility, and cheaper roadbeds and more economical operation made them superior to railroads for local traffic. They spread rapidly in the early twentieth century, only to be blighted by the automobile and truck. In spite of the great hopes held out for them they were important for no more than two decades. The first Indiana electric road was built in 1898 and by 1911 the state had 2,018 miles of trolley lines. Though expansion continued for a short time beyond that date, motor passenger and bus service had wrecked virtually all lines by the 1930's. Some states, like Nebraska, scarcely got beyond the planning stage before the era of electric railroads had passed. In 1916 a bill was prepared for introduction in the Nebraska legislature permitting stock issues of fifty thousand dollars a mile for interurbans, but cooler minds pointed out that automobiles were rapidly gaining in favor.[26]

This was a far cry from the early twentieth century when interurbans were making history and every town hoped to have one. The Hillsboro, Illinois, editor in 1905 listed numerous advantages of electric lines. Passengers would like them because they were cleaner than trains and could be flagged down anywhere. Towns would benefit. Interurbans would give them all the advantages which cities now had in churches, schools, colleges, lectures, and theatres. By making the countryside easily accessible, interurbans would bring a flock of money-spending city dwellers on Sundays and would boom local real-estate values by enabling city people to purchase country homes. Village storekeepers were told that their advantages in cheaper clerk hire, rent, and taxes would protect them from the competition of city stores. And, of course, people would not go to cities to buy ordinary needs. On the other hand, interurbans would encourage city residents to live in smaller towns, thereby increasing the number of local customers. Storekeepers could replenish their stock quickly, thus needing less money tied up in goods and less insurance. Farmers would benefit because competition between steam and electric roads would lower transportation rates and facilitate marketing of vegetables, poultry, and dairy products. It was only a matter of time until every farm home bordering an interurban line would have electric lights and electric power to grind feed and to pump water. This was not altogether a flight of imagination since interurbans furnished some advantages. In 1905, in order to meet competition from an interurban which paralleled its tracks, the Chicago and Alton Railroad installed a "bob-tail" passenger train which charged the same rates per mile as the interurban cars and stopped at all public road crossings and small stations to take on passengers.[27]

Even towns like Brookfield, Missouri, which relied heavily on trade arising from the presence of railroad machine shops, were anxious to share in this new form of transportation. The town became excited in 1903 over prospects of an interurban running from Brookfield to St. Louis. Communities along the proposed line tried to interest eastern capitalists in the project, the president of the University of Missouri at Columbia being especially desirous to see the line completed so that students could come and go more easily. In 1904 Brookfield pledged money to obtain a station on a proposed route connecting Kansas City and St. Louis. In 1905 the town again raised money for a short line to Marceline, twelve miles away. Light enough to run on curves, and capable of using gas, gasoline, naphtha, or electricity, it was to be a most versatile road, if only it could be financed. When pledges failed to materialize, the local editor threatened to print the names of prosperous businessmen who had not subscribed. In 1907 the local paper supported still another project which proposed to combine electric lines with waterways.

Even slippery promoters failed to dampen the Brookfield editor's enthusiasm. He supported the proposed "Sellers Route," named after the optimistic promoter in Mark Twain's *Gilded Age,* and continued to back still another project after its promoter was exposed as a former convict, who had also frequently been jailed for failure to pay his board and had falsely posed as a member of General Sherman's Civil War staff. Yet, according to the editor, even promoters of that type could be useful in getting sound projects under way!

The agitation continued for another ten years. In 1913 an article headed "Trolley Lines," asked "Why not one to Linneus? to Marceline?" Cars could run every hour, even every half hour. Such lines were inexpensive to build. Some seemed to think that they would not pay. "How do they know? What do they know about such lines anyway?" Later editorials attempted to dispel local ignorance of such matters. In 1916 the editor insisted that the Missouri State Legislature should enact legislation favorable to corporations. If that were done, Missouri would rival Illinois in electric railways. In spite of such agitation and numerous financial campaigns, Brookfield failed to obtain a single electric system. By 1925 the local editor was convinced that the proposed "Pike's Peak Ocean-to-Ocean" highway would mean as much to North Missouri as another railroad.[28]

It is difficult to estimate the influence of the interurbans because of the rapidity with which they lost out to motor transportation. As early as 1909 Cicero, Indiana, was said to be losing trade to Noblesville because of new interurban connections.[29] Similar consequences perhaps were felt elsewhere because any widening of the market increased competition for the country merchant.

As one looks back, the constant change and improvement in transportation takes on a pattern of certainty, and it is easy to say that country towns should have planned accordingly. To those looking forward, the future was far less certain. In 1900 the motor car was starting its bid for supremacy and many saw its future importance. Others were more doubtful. An article in the *Bookman* in 1901 pointed out that bicycles had been very fashionable three years before, and that everyone had talked of new models, century races, and road conditions. Many had expected the bicycle to eliminate the need for horses. The bicycle craze was rapidly passing but cable cars and trolleys had recently supplanted horse-drawn cars, and automobiles now appealed to the wealthy and the fashionable. Nevertheless, automobiles would suffer the same fate as bicycles when they too became cheaper:

The *cachet* of exclusiveness will have been removed and with it half the charm of ownership. . . . The popularity of the horse rests, indeed, upon a sound and lasting basis; for bicycles and automobiles are fads of the moment, while the love of the horse is rooted in something which is immutable.[30]

Even those who saw the possibilities of improved transportation could not be sure of its direction. One commentator predicted that the "horseless age" would be propelled neither by "gasolene, nor gas, nor kerosene, nor steam, nor springs, nor compressed air. There is not the least doubt, in the minds of the progressive, that its energy will be furnished by electricity."[31]

REVOLUTION BY CAR AND TRUCK

CONFLICTING PROPHECIES concerning the horseless age and the rapid development of motor transportation made it impossible for country towns to plan with any certainty. In the twenty-five years ending in 1929, the United States built 506,500 miles of surfaced rural highways, twice the total existing railroad mileage. Registered motor vehicles climbed dizzily from 468,500 in 1910 to 9,232,000 in 1920 and again to 26,718,000 in 1930. Since one-half of the American people lived within fifty miles of cities of 100,000 or more by 1930 and 80 per cent within an hour's motor trip of cities of 25,-000,[32] Main Street had to learn to compete with the outside world.

The automobile solved the problem of short-range transportation. Railroads had connected major cities without seriously affecting local transportation, but highways served another purpose. They bridged the gaps existing in the railroad structure and rounded out the city's hinterland. In spite of the emphasis on major highways traversing the whole of the United States which came with federal aid, American highways still lead *to* cities from all directions instead of serving as single-line connections between metropolitan centers.

Country towns are still adjusting to this tremendous revolution. Trade territory has shifted decade by decade as new highways have altered town and country relationships and as improvements in cars and trucks have extended the range of comfortable travel. In order to share in newly created trade territories, the country town has had to develop greater efficiency. Though national brands of flour eliminated local flour milling in the railroad age, local bakeries still supplied fresh bread. The bread truck was another matter. A bread war in Rockville, Indiana, in 1926 revealed the extent of outside competition with the two local bakeries. The Atlantic and Pacific chain store stood first in weekly bread sales, disposing of 1,900 of the 6,000 loaves consumed in the Rockville community. Since A. & P. had its own purchasing facilities, it did not rely on Rockville bakeries. In addition, bakeries in Indianapolis, sixty miles away, and in Clinton, Terre Haute, Crawfordsville, and Frankfort sent bread trucks to Rockville stores.

Motor trucks reduced the importance of country towns as assembly points for farm crops, since farmers began to haul their own livestock and produce to urban markets. A government survey in 1930 reported that 85.8 per cent of all trucks were owner-operated, while only 5.5 per cent were common carriers like railroads. Stockyards ceased to bustle with activity as they did when railroads alone competed with horse-drawn transportation. By 1930 trucks were coming an average distance of fifty miles to the Chicago livestock market and some travelled as far as 300 to reach the Chicago stockyards. An Irwin, Iowa, farmer pointed out the great changes which had occurred by the early 1940's:

Years ago to haul hogs to market, I had to get the help of five of my neighbors. In 6 wagons we would carry 30 hogs. We went 5½ miles to the railroad stop in Irwin. I had to buy a meal for the men and myself. Generally it cost me about 50 cents apiece. Those men ate a real meal, not a lunch. That's 3$. To put the 6 teams in the livery barn cost $1.20. Because I had the men come and help me, I had to go and help them, which meant 5 days of work off the farm for myself and my team. The cash cost alone was $4.20. Today, I can hire a trucker to take 25 or 30 hogs to Harlan, more than twice as far, for only $2.50. He can get them there and be back in 2 hours. And I don't have to spend any time off the farm.[33]

Community relations, stockyards, bakeries, eating places, livery barns—every aspect of village life felt the impact of truck and automobile. By the early 1940's residents of the Irwin, Iowa, community frequently drove to the county seat at Harlan, a town of some 3,500 people fourteen miles away, and trucked their produce and livestock directly from the farm to metropolitan centers. Omaha and Council Bluffs supplied newspapers and radio broadcasts to the Irwin community, which, in turn, bought clothing, furniture, and other goods and services of a somewhat specialized nature in those cities. Irwin now was closer in time to Omaha, sixty miles away, than it had once been to Harlan. As one farmer said, it had once taken all day with horse and buggy to shop in Harlan, fourteen miles away, but he could now visit Omaha or Council Bluffs in his automobile during the course of an afternoon.[34]

Though competition had existed among towns in the age of horse-drawn transportation, it had been competition among equals. When country merchants everywhere stocked goods with a limited market in mind and knew that customers would come only the distance that a horse and buggy could travel in a day, they had less to fear in the way of ruinous competition.

The influence of the automobile became increasingly evident in the advertising and news columns of country newspapers. In 1916 the Clinton, Wisconsin, editor drove to Chicago, 108 miles away, in six hours. He arrived early in the afternoon and spent the rest of the day window-shopping and attending a Chicago theatre. At the time, and for years to come, Clinton had several prosperous merchants but competition from other and larger places was closing in. Delavan, Janesville, and Beloit stores advertised in the Clinton paper. The Beloit Retail Merchant's Association invited Clinton people to attend Beloit's "Dress-Up Week" in the spring of 1916, which featured live models in the store windows and band music. During the same spring Bostwick's Store in Janesville advertised an extensive stock of clothing, including garments made expressly for large women, who ordinarily were hard to fit. When roads were good, shoppers could visit a half-dozen towns, several of which were much larger and better stocked with merchandise than Clinton. As transportation improved the competition became even more intense. In 1936 Beloit's Majestic Theatre featured Major Bowes' Amateurs for two days and a Beloit store operated a Mickey Mouse Toyland for several months preceding the Christmas season. Santa Claus and Mickey greeted children in person and showed them toys "from every country on the globe." [35] Clinton people who listened to Major Bowes weekly on the radio and whose children loved the movie character, Mickey Mouse, visited Beloit to see the advertised attractions. Smaller towns lacked the resources to meet such competition and could only adjust to the inevitable.

THE CHAIN STORE

BIG BUSINESS itself came directly to Main Street through the chain store movement. Chains began to gather momentum around 1910 and made remarkable gains in the 1920's. For the country as a whole, the Atlantic and Pacific grocery chain grew from 1,726 stores in 1915 to 10,000 in 1923 and increased its volume of business from $44,441,000 to $302,880,000 in the same period. [36] In 1947 national and regional chains were estimated to have some 38 per cent of the country's retail trade, [37] a considerable share of the whole, but far below the doleful estimates by independent retailers in the 1920's. At the end of that decade, W. K. Henderson of Shreveport, Louisiana, was operating his "Hello World" radio station with the intention of destroying the chain store movement and, incidentally, of selling his "Hello World Coffee" at one dollar a pound. Merchants were distributing some twenty-four trade journals with titles like "Chained," "Chain Store Menace," and "The Booster" to customers in hopes of checking the new competition, and close to 300 trade associations were fighting the chains. Many of them were parasitical organizations created to prey on the already highly excited independent retailers, but their very numbers showed the frenzy of despair.[38]

Merchants had many reasons for disliking the chains. As national organizations managed from a distance and selling directly in the local market, they violated a cherished small-town tradition that business by right belonged to locally owned and locally managed stores. For decades, country papers had praised local businessmen because of their public spirit and their gifts to community organizations. Since chains emphasized price competition rather than community service, they necessitated a complete reorientation of thinking. Chains also brought greater efficiency and economy to the retailing field, a threat to those merchants who preferred to continue using the methods that they had learned from still older men. Even those willing to adopt more efficient business methods feared the size and power of the chains.

Whatever their preferences, merchants could not escape the stark reality of weekly, chain-store-price advertisements in country papers everywhere. Both A. & P. and Piggly Wiggly opened stores in Brookfield, Missouri, in 1926, and both stressed low prices. When Piggly Wiggly listed Van Camp's B4 size pork and beans for nine cents, Folger's "Golden Gate" or Hill's Coffee for fifty-nine cents a pound and its own brand for thirty-nine,[39] it laid down a clear-cut challenge to local grocers to meet its prices or give way to chain supremacy.

Even though towns began to realize that each new improvement in transportation intensified competition, they never abandoned hopes of gaining more than they would lose by additional connections with the outside world. Brookfield, Missouri, became excited in 1930 over prospects of being on a new airline running to Kansas City, and its neighbor, Chillicothe, was trying to raise the necessary bonus to acquire an airplane factory and aviation-training school.[40] Both towns still wanted progress in the time-honored sense of more people and higher real-estate prices. As always, those ends stood higher than independence of action or individuality of spirit. No town dreaded to be like another that was booming in population and real-estate prices.

8 ❖ Rootless As Ever

NEW SIDE-PATHS?

By 1925 automobiles had become commonplace. In response to advertisements urging them to leave main-travelled highways and explore "alluring side-paths," people everywhere were investing the necessary $290, "F. O. B. Detroit," to obtain a Ford touring car. On a July Saturday night in 1925 Buster Clements and Corbin Croy went sparking with Fae and Rae Whitehead in the Clements family Ford. While returning home at evening's end, they ran into the back of a wagon which had pulled out to permit an approaching car to pass. Drivers of the two cars were blinded by one another's lights, and the resulting accident severely injured occupants of all three vehicles.[1] Though wagons soon ceased to venture on highways at night because of the frenzied speed of automobiles, other dangers continued to worry parents when their children were out in the family car. As never before, young people were free to imitate what they saw in other places, for automobiles quickly carried them away from the watchful eyes of adults in their home neighborhoods.

There was, of course, the possibility that increased contacts between communities would make them all alike. Perhaps, after all, the opportunity offered to all the Buster Clements' to pilot their dads' Fords to more distant cities

243

than those known by the preceding generation was only a mirage. Once arrived, perhaps they would find themselves in the same old environment with nothing gained beyond greater freedom among strangers to exercise their interests in taboos. At least, country newspapers reported many evidences of growing similarities. In June, 1935, the Gallatin, Missouri, American Legion Post sponsored a baseball game, with players mounted on donkeys. The animals were the famous Bar-X-Ranch veteran troupe of "mountain canaries," and answered to names like Mae West, Moon Mullins, Popeye, Huey Long, Andy Gump, Madam Queen, Wimpy, Pretty Boy, Amos and Andy.[2] These names had become prominent within the past decade and a few of them disappeared from common circulation almost as quickly. For the moment, however, they were well enough known everywhere to require no identification. The movies had made Mae West and her trade mark, "Come Up and See Me Sometime," a part of the national culture. Thousands listened to Amos and Andy on the radio, and Andy's "I'se regusted" had become a household phrase. Metropolitan newspapers had introduced Moon Mullins, Popeye, and Andy Gump to all the Main Streets in Mid-America. Although an efficient FBI would shortly liquidate "Pretty Boy" Floyd, currently "Public Enemy No. 1," newspapers, radio, and the movies were equal to the task of seeing that he became thoroughly known before his brief career ended. Even more convincing evidence came from studies by serious students of American culture who compared country, village, and city in numerous ways and then concluded that Americans everywhere had become more alike in the first three decades of the twentieth century. Even metropolitan centers displayed the same tendencies.[3] Everywhere, everybody knew a host of characters, slogans, and ideas foreign to nineteenth-century America, all of which had been created largely by agencies unknown to nineteenth-century civilization.

Even in the 1930's, however, country towns still differed greatly from cities in basic ways. Already known as the "old people's homes of rural America" because of the presence of so many retired farmers, they generally were strongholds of conservatism. Among employed village men the relative number of proprietors, officials, and managers was at least 70 per cent greater than among city men. Villages also had greater percentages of unskilled labor, of preachers and teachers, of native-born whites of native-born parents, and of home ownership.[4] If McGuffey's old cluster of moralistic ideas exists anywhere in the twentieth century, villages offer the most direct and unbroken connection with them. Although farm, village, and city have experienced much cross-fertilization in the past fifty years, fundamental differences still exist.

Whatever the future may hold, it is thoroughly evident that Main Street has been living in the midst of sharp cultural conflicts between the old and the new. One can find marked survivals of the old in the Chautauqua movement which flourished in country towns until the late 1920's, in high school commencement addresses preceding World War I, in the practices and convictions of small-town preachers and itinerant revivalists, in the still active W.C.T.U. movement, and in the voting and talking record of retired farmers who gather daily to exchange views at some favorite loafing place. One can find marked indications of the new in service clubs, social clubs, metropolitan newspapers which circulate daily in small towns, radio, television and motion-picture programs, and in Boy Scout, Girl Scout and Camp Fire groups.

THE QUEST FOR FELLOWSHIP

COUNTRY TOWNS began to participate in a national trend toward organizational activities in the late nineteenth century. This new spirit was well expressed by the Hastings, Michigan, editor in 1910 when he described current efforts to create a local "Booster's Club." According to him, leaders in the project were thinking along "associational lines:"

Why can't the men folks do something to help boost good things? Here are the women getting better acquainted with each other, doing lots of good, and performing real social services to the people, and helping good causes along through their organizations, and the men folks doing nothing, or at least very little.

In this spirit fifty "delighted" men attended an organizational meeting in the local Methodist church where they got "next" to each other in a social way as they had never done before. They sang "inspired" songs and listened to "soulful" talks on: 1. The need of a larger fraternal spirit in Hastings. 2. Plans to meet that need. 3. "Getting Next." During the meeting it became more and more evident that those present wanted to know more about people living in the local community and to welcome newcomers. They felt an urge to visit the sick and to finish the basement of the new church. Coffee, doughnuts, and sandwiches strengthened them for the task of working out the details of a new organization. On Sunday evening, some three weeks later, over sixty members of the new Booster's Club marched in a group to one of the local churches where the Reverend J. W. Sheehan spoke on man as a social being and Christianity as a social religion. Fourteen men from the club served as a choir during the services and all the "brothers" "joined heartily" in the singing. The preacher concluded the evening by reading a poem written by Sam Walter Foss, "The House by the Side of the Road." [5] Thus spoke the growing spirit of organization.

In McGuffey's age, church, school, and home taught the young and administered the accepted way of doing things for all ages. One Indiana town, for instance, had virtually no clubs before 1879. In that year the number increased from one to three, and was never less than five after 1883. In 1910, the town had a dozen club organizations.[6] Professional organizations of doctors, lawyers, or businessmen usually came first in point of time, then serious study groups, and, finally, restricted social clubs. But organized groups, either for community service or for social entertainment, were few in number before the 1890's.

The twentieth-century cult of joining owes much to man's increasing inability to identify himself with the community at large. Nicknames and first names still come easily to residents of small towns where all are acquainted and speak to one another on the street. Cities have lost this easy familiarity, and even farm and village feel the impact of widening trade and social connections. One or more members of a family may belong to one organization locally, another in a consolidated school district, a third in the county seat, and so on. Fragmentation of social life results. Psychologists and social philosophers now preach the necessity of "joining" for personal fulfillment, but organization is piled on organization in an effort to achieve satisfaction when specialized organizations cannot take the place of the whole community to which man instinctively wishes to belong.

As community boundaries widen or disappear, the urge to join becomes intensified. World citizenship is simply too terrifying to contemplate unless the individual can have something smaller and more personal to sustain him. The cult of joining in America started in our larger towns and cities first of all to meet that need.

Rotary, the first of many current-day service organizations for men, was founded in Chicago in 1905 by Paul H. Harris and four other bachelors, all of whom missed the sense of companionship which they had known in boyhood village communities. In the beginning, the Chicago club fined members for using "Mr." instead of first names and spent much time on group singing. This nostalgia of small-town boys in a large city rapidly won converts to Rotary in other American communities affected by the drift to rootless, impersonal relationships. As smaller places in turn felt the same pressure they, too, turned to Rotary or similar organizations. In 1934, 42 per cent of all Rotary Clubs were located in towns under 5,000 in size,[7] and Kiwanis and Lions were also prominent in the smaller places.

The modern-day woman's club movement also originated in the great cities. In 1889 the Sorosis Club of New York City took the lead in developing a national federation of all existing women's clubs. A speaker at the first biennial meeting in Chicago in 1892 said:

The two great factors of modern civilization are cooperation and centralization. The greatest proof of this truth is the fact of this meeting of the General Federation of Women's Clubs. The value of one person's mind or one person's work is steadily diminishing; it is the associative mind, the many hearts beating as one, that now move the world; and this is so well understood by women that they are rapidly learning what can be accomplished in economic, social and intellectual life by the power of an educated public opinion.[8]

Millions of women and thousands of clubs have testified to the power and attractiveness of organizational life. And again, the movement has spread from larger places to smaller towns. In 1919, for instance, 361 Missouri clubs belonged to the organized federation movement, of which 107 were located in country towns and villages. While St. Louis had forty and Kansas City twenty-two, all levels of population were represented. Moreover, the clubs differed little in purpose according to size of community except that city clubs emphasized civic work somewhat more heavily.[9]

The impulse to join feeds on many stresses in modern culture. Science and its impersonal God have shaken man's confidence in his own importance as the center of the universe and he feels more than ever the need for companionship of fellow mortals. Aggressive business classes on the make find leadership in local civic and social organizations useful instruments in furthering their ambitions. The middle-class group gains prestige by serving actively in American Legion, lodge, and civic organizations, the greater the number of memberships and offices held, the greater one's local standing. And all country towns seem to have developed a breed of "professional joiners." [10]

Statistics alone can properly indicate the tremendous surge of organizational life. Sixty midwestern villages in 1924 averaged 24.8 community organizations and 17.2 church organizations.[11] Though approximately one-third of these disappeared within six years, several hundred new organizations took their place.[12] This instability arises from lack of permanent and professional leadership and from competition created by the very number of cliques and divisions within communities.

Informal recreation and informal social life have continued to appeal to many in spite of organizational trends. As late as 1930 the tone of social life in some midwestern villages was still being set by informal groups. Many villages were said to be turning to a greater interest in the type of recreation common in the nineteenth century. Modern tendencies also helped in various ways. Community houses, playgrounds, swimming pools, and motoring all made possible an increasing measure of recreation without the necessity of joining specialized groups.[13] Here, again, one notes conflicting trends and contradictory ideas as well as a marked increase in the number and types of organizations pretending to speak the mind of the small towns.

The problem of determining major convictions in this era of conflict is further complicated by class lines. After an evangelist at Maysville, Missouri, in 1915 severely condemned illegal sales of liquor locally, he received a letter threatening him with an "egging" if he did not leave town. "All the best people" immediately rallied to his support and offered one hundred dollars to anyone who would identify the letter writer.[14] Here and elsewhere one notes the continuing existence of a moralistic middle class and also a lower group of ne'er-do-wells who flout respectability as they did in McGuffey's day. Any statement of a prevailing small-town code thus needs to recognize that what prevails in one class level does not necessarily carry over to another.

THE "GLAD GAME"

LASTLY, as in McGuffey's day, citizens of small towns seldom analyze and formally state their code of conduct. As late as 1912 a midwestern sociologist argued on the basis of an analysis of the careers of people listed in *Who's Who* that western occupations which won distinction were practical and concrete rather than theoretical—law, the ministry, teaching, and engineering. Similarly, in 1946, an Englishman who had lived in the Middle West for several years spoke of midwestern practicality and distaste for theory. In his estimation, though this anti-rationalism and distrust of the "clever or cultured" was not unique to the Midwest, it was over-developed there.[15] When one turns the pages of country newspapers with the idea of testing such an hypothesis, he realizes how much midwesterners have been addicted to "things" rather than ideas.

The thinness of what passes for ideas often becomes apparent when midwesterners speak philosophically. High school commencement speakers are a case in point. They have felt called upon to grapple with philosophical problems on such occasions but have succeeded mostly in damning the commencement address by vapid generalizations. This perhaps accounted for the mistake made by the Rockville, Indiana, paper in 1926 when it listed the title of the approaching high school commencement address as "The Cloud" when it should have read "The Crowd." Although the editor apologized for the error, either title would have fitted nicely most commencement addresses. Most often, midwesterners take refuge in the inspirational when asked to deal with abstractions. The play "Pollyanna" fits this to perfection. When it was scheduled on the Duvall, Ohio, lyceum series in the winter of 1916, local advertising stressed its "lesson." It was said to be one of the most beautiful stories in modern literature. The main character was supposed to come into a community like Duvall and to show how by playing the "glad game" even the most menial task could become a joy.[16]

The businessman generally heard the same inspirational theme at his meetings. A speaker at the Chatfield, Minnesota, Commercial Club banquet in 1916 discussed the "Spirit of Brotherhood and Service in Business." Though business used to be disreputable, said he, it had changed completely. Banking had become a benevolent institution and loans were made on character. (Here was the theme of the banker as Pollyanna playing the "glad game.") Commercial Clubs had become the "great balance of the brotherhood people" and everywhere they should strive to make their towns one big brotherhood club. After the travelling representative of the Pillsbury Flour Company, C. E. Nelson, addressed the Kiwanis Club at Brookfield, Missouri, in 1926, the local editor described him as a genius who travelled around the country spreading good cheer and happiness—a "double-barrelled gloom chaser." Nelson's philosophical ideas came from Elbert Hubbard, the poetry of Edgar A. Guest, and from his own writings—perhaps from his major work, a book which he had titled "Let's go." When the president of International Rotary in 1935 made the promotion of happiness his special objective during his year in office, the founder of Rotary suggested to the membership, "help our chief to spread good cheer through smiling more frequently, frowning less frequently, through being more neighborly, friendly, and kindly than we have ever been before." [17] This Pollyanna theme has obscured the many community services performed by business and service clubs and has made them peculiarly vulnerable to ridicule. For our purposes, it demonstrates the seeming inability of Midwesterners to think philosophically. They can be consistently inspirational if compelled to turn to ideas but they prefer not to go beyond this. As a result, they carry an astounding amount of contradictory ideas in their intellectual baggage.

POOR BOY, FARM BOY

THIS CONFUSION or indecision comes to light in every aspect of small-town codes when one attempts to compare them with the earlier McGuffey scale of values. Farmers and townsmen continue to affirm the old McGuffey theme that village and farm life surpass that in cities, and country newspapers readily print syndicated material extolling the virtues of the farm boy. As one article in 1915 put it:

When Wall Street wants good business men she usually goes back to the soil to get them. . . . The active officials of most of the large business organizations of America it is said were, with a few exceptions, raised on the farm, and could swim the creek, pitch hay, chop wood, milk the cows, or slop the hogs as easily as they can run world-wide business institutions.[18]

When Edwin T. Chase, editor of the Atlantic, Iowa, paper, recorded his impressions in 1936, he claimed that most of the world's leaders had been farm or village boys who had learned the value of work. Chase even asserted that none of the world's great literary work had been produced in the rush and roar of a metropolis but rather in the more productive environment of smaller places. Even McGuffey had never gone that far in his defense of hamlet and farm.

In many cases, visits to cities convinced small-town citizens that McGuffey had been correct in implying that the village and farm were purer than the metropolis. In 1915, Mrs. A. R. Canfield, the seventy-year-old mayor of Warren, Illinois, visited Chicago to learn something of the world. In cafes and elsewhere she saw men and women drinking and dancing. Two girls bumped into the table where she was sitting in a cafe and giggled as they danced by. Mrs. Canfield asked, "Where are their mothers?" To a reporter she said, "When I go back to Warren, I will do everything in my power to make the town attractive to young girls. If only I can keep Warren girls in Warren, I shall be happy." [19]

McGuffey and Mrs. Canfield would have been horrified by some of the later defenses of the country town on the basis of sex. In 1932 Phil Stong's novel, *State Fair*, presented an Iowa farm family freed of all the provincialism of country hicks and fully able to hold its own with city slickers. Secure in their love of rural life and fully aware of its values, parents and children attended the Iowa State Fair without any feeling of insecurity in the outside world. While the father and mother were winning prizes on stock and canned goods, their son bankrupted the operators of stands who had fleeced him the preceding year. The attractive and uninhibited daughter of a race-track manager chose him for her partner in a sexual bout of pagan intensity, and his sister enjoyed an equally thrilling departure from normal respectability with a reporter for the Des Moines paper. Though both boys proposed marriage to make them respectable women, the girls knew that country and town life differed greatly. They were wiser than the boys in choosing to remain with the environment which they loved. *State Fair* was an answer to all the sniggering stories told by travelling salesmen about the farmer's daughter and the country yokel types. In 1938 Minnie Hite Moody's *Old Home Week* expanded the theme. A successful city woman, whom father had dated as a boy, saved his business for him, and a Hollywood director begged mother—his childhood sweetheart—to elope with him. Mother and dad stopped short of the fire, but daughter thoroughly enjoyed being seduced by the pilot of a barnstorming airplane.[20] Quite obviously, the time had passed when villagers seemed dull and unattractive to people from the outside world. In an allegorical sense, social purity had been bartered for the social sophistication of the city.

Much concrete evidence has been amassed to challenge the long-accepted belief that farm and village are ideal environments. Apparently, children born in the suburbs of large cities are more likely than farm or village youngsters to become prominent enough to be listed in *Who's Who*.[21] Moreover, statistical examination of 190 business leaders of the early twentieth century has refuted the "poor boy, farm boy" explanation of the source of the business elite:

If men with such backgrounds had been in fact representative of the great entrepreneurs of the later nineteenth century, they must have been supplanted with extraordinary rapidity by the

higher status, more highly educated bureaucrats of the following generation. More likely, poor immigrant and poor farm boys
who become business leaders have always been more conspicuous
in American history books than in the American business elite.[22]

While property is safer in village and rural areas, crimes of
violence rival those in great cities. For instance, Minnesota's
rural (including places of less than 2,500 population) -urban
crime rates based on a three-year average rate (1936-1938)
per 100,000 people were:

Type of Crime	Urban Per Cent	Rural Per Cent
Aggravated assault	3.2	5.6
Rape	0.6	2.6
Murder	0.4	1.5
Manslaughter	0.4	1.5 [23]

Even as early as 1912 some observers who had studied
rural-urban migration in older parts of the United States began to note the same phenomenon in the Middle West.
Though one commentator thought that "moral sag" was
deepest in rural New England, which had been most heavily
skimmed of its best people, he also called attention to the
recent disfranchisement of 1,700 residents of Adams County,
Ohio, for selling their votes. To him, this was only another
example of dry rot in lifeless communities which had missed
the electrifying touch of railroads or cities. Knots of gaping
tobacco-chewing loafers could be seen at railway stations in
Indiana, southern Michigan, Illinois, and even on into Missouri, further evidence of communities which reminded the
observer of "fished-out ponds populated chiefly by bull
heads and suckers." Folk depletion was the answer to the
backward status of such communities. Ambitious and able
citizens had moved on to the city or to newer roles.[24]

Villagers may ignore or deny such evidence but even they
are constantly exposed to urban ways and urban ideas. Mc-
Guffey's Readers devoted virtually no space to city life. In
contrast, The Scott, Foresman and Company Readers, which

are currently popular in midwestern schools, draw heavily on city illustrations. The basic primer in this series is city-centered except for one unit in which children visit their grandparents on the farm. Pictures of autos on grease racks, city busses, and the city zoo are in striking contrast to the McGuffey pictures of the village green of less than a hundred years ago.[25]

THE VILLAGE CHURCH STANDS FIRM

NO ONE CAN DENY the power of the village church. Upper-class citizens generally belong, and the great body of respectable, middle-class people are inclined to participate actively in church work. While the lower classes often belong to no religious group, villagers as a whole still believe that churches sustain law and order and property values.[26]

Nonetheless, fundamentalist-moralistic religion has declined since McGuffey's day. When the Reverend Cecil Scott, minister of the Methodist church in Rose City, Michigan, a farming hamlet of 350 people, started a moral crusade, he split the town wide open. Scott accused adults of dancing and going to movies, and youngsters of playing Sunday baseball. In a letter to Governor Kim Sigler he charged that liquor was being sold openly to school children while city officials, "all drinking men," looked the other way. Through the curtains of the local parsonage, Scott claimed to have seen children taking nips from bottles hidden in snow drifts, and boys and girls undressing and committing indecencies in cars. When local city officials and schoolteachers demanded proof, Scott refused to offer any. Local sympathizers shouted "Hallelujah" as he laid into sin harder still, but many citizens only got madder. A Detroit newspaper discovered that Scott had been arrested in 1931 for drunken driving and had only recently been converted after a nondescript career as salesman, industrial worker, and beer-truck driver. In spite of local protests, the Reverend Bishop J. Wade reappointed Scott to the Rose City church, with an exhortation to continue warring against the liquor interests. Even then, local citizens were not helpless. A woman whose well had supplied water to the parsonage for twenty-nine years cut off the supply. The hardware dealer and the druggist refused to sell Scott anything, and signs appeared in local windows reading "We don't want Scott." [27]

Though less spectacular than local church feuds, some of the long-range religious trends have been more effective in reducing the power of the village church. One observer has suggested the following as the most important trends in twentieth-century religion: a growth of Catholicism and the newer Holiness groups; a drift from country to city and hence a rural church problem; the rise of community churches; enlistment of men through brotherhoods and other means for church work; and, most important of all, the growth of a "social gospel" movement.[28] The social gospel has emphasized service to men socially as well as to their souls. It has demanded an institutional church capable of organizing and directing recreational programs, family advice centers, and other activities that are beyond the financial resources of small congregations.

Religious leaders in country towns had ample warning of the changes which were taking place. Books advising village churches began to appear early in the twentieth century, and conferences were held to discuss church problems. A resident of the Ashville, Ohio, community returned home from one of these in 1916 enthusiastically committed to the community-church idea. He urged other local people to consider the possibility of religious leadership in recreation as well as in theology. In the same period, national periodicals like the *Literary Digest* mentioned, and even briefly reviewed, books promoting the community-church idea.[29]

Unless they merged, village churches simply lacked the necessary membership and financial income to support the social gospel movement. At Bellville, Ohio, in 1917, for instance, the five local Protestant churches had enough seats for 1,675 in a town of only 913 people. The five churches combined had 534 members, 357 enrolled in Sunday school, and total annual income of $4,500, an average of less than a thousand dollars a year for each. Total investment in buildings was $28,000.[30] On the surface, at least, Bellville at the moment seemed capable of utilizing and supporting not more than one church.

Nevertheless, rural and village churches were inclined to stand firm. Observers who visited a good many midwestern towns in 1924 reported that schools were changing rapidly and had assumed considerable leadership in tying farms and villages together but that churches seldom concerned themselves with anything beyond a preaching program. Nearly half of them had only one room, less than half had a full-time resident pastor, and almost three-fifths of them had less than one hundred members. Although many observers were inclined to think that one church for every thousand inhabitants was adequate, the actual ratio was one to every 237 people, and national churches seemed determined to help most of all the weakest and least effective local congregations. Six years later, in 1930, little improvement had occurred. If one church ceased to function, another immediately took its place. Less than half of the towns visited had full-time resident pastors and less than a third of those serving village churches had college and seminary training. Ministers kept a pastorate an average of two and two-thirds years. Average number of churches per village remained at 5.6. Church clubs for youngsters were giving way to 4-H farm clubs and others with active and well-directed programs.[31]

It is not easy, of course, to merge denominations which honestly believe in some unique doctrinal position. Moreover, rural and village churches depend most heavily on older people and the more "respectable" classes, those most committed to preserving existing ways and ideas. James Street's novel, *The Gauntlet*, describes the struggle of one young minister to change village attitudes. Though Street's hero wins his battle, his reward, significantly, is a "call" to a larger town. More typical insofar as doctrinal attitudes are concerned is the fundamentalist preacher pictured in Homer

Croy's novel, *West of the Water Tower*.[32] Lacking in educational contact with the newer criticism, hampered by poverty, and moving from town to town in obeisance to custom, the small-town preacher has lacked both the urge and the opportunity to institute long-range plans for community leadership.

The rural and village church has thus tended to stand still. Here, most of all, fundamentalism challenges forces that would change our ways of thinking. This was shown in a report on Oskaloosa, Iowa, in 1923, a town of 10,000 people, made up largely of retired farmers and tradesmen. Oskaloosa had a Quaker College and a Central Holiness University as well as twenty-four churches, most of which upheld the prevailing code in spite of considerable local rebellion. A girl caught walking the street with a married man asked defiantly, "Where will I spend my evenings? I haven't any money to spend. I can't go to the movies. If I was invited to a dance, the law wouldn't let me go. I can't entertain company at home and you can't make me go to prayer meeting—so there! What are you going to do about it?" In open violation of the law, boys under twenty-one bought cigarettes, girls under eighteen attended dances unaccompanied by their mothers, and liquor was being sold. Nonetheless, fundamentalist ministers said, "We are not pessimists. There is, thank the Lord, a renewed determination on the part of Oskaloosa's Christian workers to see that the laws shall be strictly enforced." Though the Knights of Pythias, Elks, and the Episcopal Church sponsored dances, most of the preachers opposed dancing, even at a supervised community center. In retaliation, youngsters were visiting a nearby "Eddyville" in cars and were choosing between toughness and holiness since there was no middle ground. The righteous traced the conflict to war's aftermath, to breakdown of the home, to God's curse for forgetting Him, or to atheism, which was said to have crept into the modern church; but a member of the younger set labelled it a revolt against old "fogyism." [33]

The McGuffey moral tradition also lived on in efforts to

enforce strict Sabbath observance, Sunday baseball being a favorite target for ministerial criticism. In 1915, the directors of the Hillsboro, Illinois, Chautauqua, a movement always closely related to the church, relented enough to permit boats on the Chautauqua lake on Sundays, and even debated letting children swim on Sunday when nothing else was going on. But such innovations required great liberality of spirit. Ministers at Algona, Iowa, in 1928 opposed Sunday movies locally even though citizens drove to nearby towns to attend. Again, in 1939, when an erroneous report circulated that the Algona Ministerial Association had approved opening the annual fair on Sunday, the ministers made it clear that they were still opposed to Sabbath desecration.[34] A few community churches, men's brotherhood classes, children's day activities, and vacation daily bible schools represent some change since McGuffey's day. These, rather than any great break with past tradition and faith, are the fruits of religious adjustment to twentieth-century life.

WHERE THE SOCIAL GOSPEL REIGNS

ON THE OTHER HAND, the social gospel movement has invaded community and service clubs, Boy and Girl Scout and Camp Fire organizations, and YMCA and YWCA chapters in smaller communities. Examples are legion. In 1913, the Paton, Iowa, Community Club staged a "character-building" banquet for men and boys. In 1928, the Algona, Iowa, Community Club paid $100 on the salary of the playground instructor, donated $100 to the public school nurse to purchase clothing for needy children, furnished free coffee for a local Sunday School picnic, helped maintain the local state park, and contributed financially toward a musical program presented by another local service organization. Similarly, in 1926, the Chatfield, Minnesota, Community Club sponsored chest clinics, rest rooms, clothing for the needy, and programs to check juvenile delinquency. In 1936 the same organization furnished milk for needy school children, backed the annual sale of Christmas seals, and stepped in everywhere to further good causes.

Many overlapping organizations help children, the aged, and the underprivileged. The very active Clinton, Wisconsin, YMCA chapter started its winter program early in October of 1916 so that youngsters could make maximum use of the Y gymnasium. Father and son banquets, boy banquets, and other attractions were held throughout the year. When the Algona, Iowa, Kiwanians held their annual banquet for the Kiwanis "Kweens" at the Algona hotel in 1928, they danced and played bridge, but only after the Reverend Mr. Dibble of Mason City had spoken on Kiwanis' aims. These included aid to the underprivileged child, better citizenship, and closer relations between town and country. The women's Tri Kappa Service Club at Rockville, Indiana, spent six hundred dollars on charity, donations, and community youth in 1948. They helped finance the local youth center, the commencement dance, and a children's bus trip to Indianapolis to hear a symphony orchestra. They gave twenty-five dollars each to the tuberculosis association, the local Christmas Cheer Fund, the Cancer Society, and the infantile paralysis campaign. They helped underwrite the local horse show, donated ten dollars to the Indianapolis Symphony Orchestra, and sponsored an exhibit by Hoosier artists. The radio and two wheel chairs which they owned were in constant use by invalids.[35]

Although ministers did not foster the social gospel movement within their own churches, they strongly supported lay movements which were taking over what once had been primarily duties of church or state. In 1915 the Reverend N. M. Tatum, pastor at Grant City, Missouri, proudly explained how he alone obtained 105 new members for the local commercial club, thus enabling his side, the "Reds," to defeat the "Blues" 143 to eighty in a contest for new members. Although ninety days had been allotted to the membership campaign, Tatum made a list of seventy-five names the very night that the contest opened. The next morning at five the local telephone manager helped him surprise prospective members by ringing their homes. Though some refused to have their early morning slumber disturbed, regardless of their "curiosity" at so early a call, Tatum obtained fifteen new members before breakfast, thirty by noon, and enough within the first two weeks to defeat the opposition. Only his team captain knew of his success until five minutes before the contest closed, when Tatum handed his list of new members to the judges and thus "swept victory" for his side. A huge success throughout, the campaign closed with a banquet, a "spicy" program, twenty gallons of ice cream, and "other good things." Tatum said that three kinds of ministers might criticize his efforts: 1. Those who lacked ability to approach men with a "manly business" appeal. 2. Those who considered such activity foreign to a minister's work. 3. Those who lacked vision. To such critics, he replied that in three months of the campaign he had met more men and made more lasting friendships than would have been possible in three years devoted strictly to church work.[36]

As a matter of fact, communities that opposed the social gospel movement within the church itself often expected their ministers to participate actively in lay organizations. A newspaper article in 1919 explained that community clubs no longer relied solely on businessmen. Clergymen now belonged because they had learned that man's material surroundings affected his spiritual outlook. Physicians interested in health, sanitation, and control of epidemics; teachers who loved the youth of the land; and lawyers interested in progressive legislation had all found the community club movement a valuable aid.

Ministers rapidly became a mainstay of service organizations and community clubs. They opened the meeting with prayer, led the singing, gave clever talks in the absence of other speakers, and took time to push club campaigns for local betterment. At the annual community club banquet in Brookfield, Missouri, in 1925, the pastor of the Christian Church spoke on "How I Love Brookfield," and the Baptist minister gave a "clever" talk on "Get your money first." Many devout preachers joined in such activities without loss of stature but some had difficulty in distinguishing between good fellowship and buffoonery. Some of the local ministers led in joviality when the Brookfield Kiwanis club was chartered in 1926:

Regardless of the fact that it was Friday and the thirteenth nothing could stop the dauntless Kiwanians from Macon, Trenton and Chillicothe. There was no room for the gloom dispenser and the twin omens of bad luck received a K. O. blow in the first round. Besides the visiting Kiwanians and their queens there were many invited guests; 205 were served at the banquet tables. This is said to be the largest number ever served at the Country Club. . . . Rev. Pettibon gave the address of welcome. Brother Pettibon is a loyal Brookfielder as well [as] a true Kiwanian, and he never misses an opportunity to boost the metropolis of Linn County. Rev. Ivan Young verified this by telling us how Rev. Pettibon in conducting a funeral in Chillicothe, after asking the friends and relatives if they had anything to say for the departed one. [sic] Nobody seemed to have anything to say, so Rev. Pettibon said: "I'll say a few words about Brookfield." This is what we call boosting.[37]

NEW GODS

PROTESTANT AND CATHOLIC dissension over the teaching of religion in public schools and the growing influence of science and rationalism make it difficult for one even to discuss religious education without accusations of marked bias. Since church and state were separated by the founding fathers, many conclude that the urge to provide religious education in the public schools must be a comparatively recent development stemming either from growing Catholic influence or from a weakening of liberal ideas of an earlier and more democratic tradition. And yet, one needs only to turn the pages of McGuffey's Readers to realize how much education once served as the handmaiden of religion. From pictures and stories in the primer of children kneeling in prayer, on through Washington learning that God made and controls and loves everything, and on to stories of divine intervention in the affairs of man, McGuffey's Readers were literally shot through with fundamentalist-moralistic, God-centered teaching. McGuffey favored no one creed in his school books and he personally disliked the idea of a state church. But he firmly believed that religion was the basis of society and that school children needed to be taught that lesson over and over.

Right or wrong, the modern grade-school reader carefully omits formal religion from its pages. The widely-used Scott, Foresman and Company Readers illustrate the trend that one will find in other and competitive sets as well. In a careful examination of the readers I was unable to find a mention of human death before the fourth level of the basic readers, *Times and Places,* and then only in a one-line reference to the death of Lincoln's mother.[38] Churches are first mentioned in this same reader, but again only in passing and with no approval or disapproval indicated. These readers do not lack ideals. Good citizenship, group co-operation for the welfare of all, honesty, courage, and resourcefulness, themes that McGuffey endorsed over and over, still find a place in the contemporary reader. Home and school and community are emphasized. But the church is not. Though the "lost son" in McGuffey's returns home from the sea to his mother through God's power to control raging storms, in the modern readers the same son is more likely to be saved by an efficient group of Boy Scouts, who, through the wonders of science, broadcast rescue messages and lift victims from wrecks by helicopters.

It is true that *Times and Places* contains a unit on "Famous People of Other Times" in which biblical heroes like Joseph and David are introduced along with Joan of Arc and Saint George who slew the dragon. Pupils learn that such heroes forget themselves in striving to help others and that persons who are well fitted for a task will generally find some useful service to perform. But again, such stories represent the best literature of past ages rather than a revealed account of God's intervention in the affairs of man.

A unit on "Wonders of Today" in *Days and Deeds* presents fascinating accounts of radio, telegraph, telephone, airplane, and outboard motor, and of how intelligent and trained individuals use them to overcome floods, blizzards, and hurricanes. Youngsters broadcast relief signals after hurricanes and when dams are threatened by floods. Boy Scouts on a snowbound bus use their Scout training to send an SOS from the spot on a telegraph wire and then show adults how to clear the road by rolling snowballs through drifts.

In *People and Progress,* the sixth-grade reader, Tad rescues people from a houseboat by skillful use of his father's ferryboat. In this story, one of the victims keeps repeating, "The Lord never does things halfway! It'll come out all right!" And sure enough, it does. A relief boat from the Red Cross unit arrives with food! The relief supervisor congratulates Tad on his good work, and a newspaper reporter talks about a medal. But when Tad is pushed before the microphone of a broadcasting set, he says only, "I really didn't do anything. It just all came about the way it did." [39] McGuffey too would have pictured Tad as modest, but modest because God strengthened his hand and deserved chief credit for the results. Revealed, orthodox religion was the basic foundation of McGuffey's God-centered world; science and man as a social being are stressed in modern readers, with revealed religion omitted rather than condemned.

This marked and rapid shift in viewpoint furnishes opportunities for approval or condemnation, depending on one's point of view. Orthodox religion and education are separated as never before in the history of our American public school system, and formal religion suffers thereby. On the other hand, the gloomy, fearful, morbid teachings of McGuffey are replaced by a philosophy of achievement within a social order stressing social conscience. School children learn that they have a right to be happy. And what a pleasure it is to read from the world's great literature—from the Bible, from

Grimm's fairy tales, from Aesop's fables, from the folk tales of America—Babe, the Blue Ox and Pecos Bill—from Greek mythology, and from Masefield, Twain, and Irving. Moreover, here is laid bare the great challenge of the twentieth century. With science, invention, material riches, and a democratic system stressing freedom for individual achievement, man is asked to face his problems with his own resources and such strength as he can draw from his associates. If man wishes to take God into consideration, the public schools do not forbid him to do so. They merely have ceased to reiterate from the primer on that God is the center and the source of man's strength.

Villages continue to boss and abuse their schoolteachers as in McGuffey's day. Many places forbid them to smoke or drink or marry. It is advisable for them to remain in town on weekends and to teach a Sunday-school class, although they are not permitted to become real members of the community. Each spring they worry over the renewal of their annual contracts, knowing that towns prefer to seek improvement in the happiness, discipline, and education of children by bringing in a new set of teachers instead of increasing taxes to provide more adequate service.[40]

In spite of this, schools have found means of adjusting rapidly to twentieth-century conditions. Teachers themselves have surpassed preachers in sacrificing to obtain better educational preparation and have also learned the value of state-wide organization. In training the young, they have dealt with the most responsive village groups and they have also been blest with little sectarian division. Though villages averaged 5.6 churches in 1930, they had only one school system to support. A Minnesota report in 1916 spoke of new school buildings in towns like Grand Meadow, Proctor, Ortonville, Chatfield, and Two Harbors costing seventy-five to one hundred thousand dollars each and of consolidated school plants in villages like Hitterdal and Clontarf, Adams, Nicollett, Waldorf, Lindstrom, Center City, Nelson, and New Richland valued at thirty to forty thousand dollars. The new

Chatfield school building had a gymnasium equipped with shower rooms and a stage, and space for manual training, domestic science, vocational agriculture, and a commercial department.

Schools also expanded their social activities to meet the desires of the younger generation. On November 20, 1936, the Millington, Michigan, paper announced two events for the coming Friday night. If they wished, young people could attend a potluck supper at the Baptist church being given in honor of those whose birthdays came in October, November, or December. The only charge was a voluntary offering for a new church roof. The first all-school party was held the same evening in the I.O.O.F. Hall, which had been decorated with Thanksgiving themes. Fred Gunnell's orchestra, stunts, square dances to enable the freshmen to "Dosie-Doe," and freedom for both boys and girls to choose partners for round dances promised a maximum of fun. Students were asked to dress informally in keeping with the democratic spirit of the occasion.[41] Here two time-honored village institutions met in conflict on the same evening. No reader needs to be told which "entertainment" was the greater attraction to young people.

Twentieth-century village ideals of home and motherhood have also changed. Women's magazines warn small-town readers against maternal domination, and the ideal mother no longer stays at home. One country editor has described the female leader in his community as tall and well-proportioned, with erect shoulders, white hair, and rimless glasses. Fully informed as to the girlhood name, personality, and ability of every woman in town, she assigns each her proper place in civic campaigns, and if one balks slightly is diplomat enough to add an additional minor honor. Lesser leaders serve as her lieutenants.[42] Women must be active beyond the home if they expect to be chosen "Mother of the Year," even in midwestern rural villages.

Many of the organizations already discussed have assumed duties that once belonged to the family. By the 1920's "Fa-

ther and Son" and "Mother and Daughter" weeks were popular in country towns. Local Rotary clubs observed nation-wide
boy's week with special church programs, free picture shows,
and indoor baseball contests for the youngsters of their own
communities. Far too often a lush comradeship, so typical
of twentieth-century "leaders," marred efforts to strengthen
family ties in an era which valued organizational life beyond
the home still more. In the fall of 1925 the small rural community of Blake, Missouri, staged a father-and-son banquet
in the Blake tabernacle. The Gallatin band and a number of
popular outside speakers assisted. A boy was baptized to
start the evening. This was followed by scripture reading,
the song, "America," prayer, and then "the feed." Enoch Croy
spoke forcefully on "The Dad and his Lad." Carl Shelton
read "The Ten Commandments for Fathers," and Bill Billings "outdid himself" in putting on the "rousements" in song
leading. The evening had not one but two principal speakers. The Reverend Lex Souter of Trenton, "a brilliant young
orator," raised the question "What Makes Success?" "Character building" was his answer. And then came Tom Witten
—"Tom of the tender heart. Tom of the understanding mind;
Tom the eloquent, the inimitable." Lovingly, tenderly, eloquently, from his great heart, he launched on the seas of humanity and hammered home great truths. Organizers honored motherhood as well. Men's service and church clubs
furnished waiters for Mother-Daughter banquets,[43] and
Mother's Day gained rapidly in public favor.

MORAL VALUES—OLD AND NEW

GRADE-SCHOOL READERS have abandoned McGuffey's
open moralizing in favor of an indirect approach to ideals.
They no longer threaten children with death or other severe
penalties for failure to conform nor do they stress a driving,
grim necessity to succeed. Nevertheless, the morals are there,
most often in animal stories which ridicule human foibles or
illustrate desirable traits. Although fantasy lacks direct application of meaning, it gains power through appealing

associations. Moreover, if ideals fail a child in moments of stress, his reaction may be less pronounced. Like his elders, he can console himself with the thought that such ideals represent the world as it should be, not as it is.

Modern-day school readers thus continue to present ideals. The Scott, Foresman series retains many of the old McGuffey values. A greedy billy goat, who demands his share of apples when they are picked and also one of the pies being baked for other animals, discovers that his pie contains only a grass filling. Stories of the golden pears, which symbolize truth, of the North Wind's magic stick that punishes dishonesty, and of discontented rabbits who learn to value their many advantages have a charm and zest for life that McGuffey never expressed. Stories of building birdhouses, putting out feed, sharing dolls with playmates, and taking Christmas trees to sick children teach kindness to all living things.

Even rugged individualism has not disappeared from our public-school books. While the Scott, Foresman Readers recognize society's responsibility to the individual, as did McGuffey, they also emphasize the need to work. "Baby elephant" becomes tired of daily circus parades and runs away to be with other animals who seem freer of irksome tasks. When he finds that mice and bears follow an annual routine of preparing for winter, he is happy to return to his circus duties. Though grandmother mouse warns against dancing both day and night, little mouse refuses to mend her ways until dust threatens her clothing. The "Fairy Shoemaker" teaches that one gets rich quickest of all by useful work, and the old story of the hare and the tortoise reveals the value of steady application. A little engine becomes ashamed of larger and lazier engines who refuse to do their duty in hauling the farmer's wheat and decides to accept the challenge. In his puffing refrain, "I think I can, I think I can, I thought I could, I thought I could," one even senses something of the old McGuffey theme "Try, Try, Again."

Midwesterners continue to believe in work and that adults

should labor as long as health permits. According to one observer in 1912, a leisure class devoted to pleasure or culture had developed in the East, but only the wives of prosperous businessmen followed the same pattern in Mid-America. A successful storekeeper in 1930 said that he considered it unwise for him to retire when he was doing well and liked his work.[44] Like many others, he associated retirement with death.

Before World War I and its aftermath created difficulties for farmers and country towns, high school commencements were fertile ground for rugged individualism. The "Pagan Pastor of the News" in the Hillsboro, Illinois, paper in 1905 could not resist printing his own "Baccalaureate Sermon." Opening on a realistic note, he said that most such talks foolishly encouraged graduates to believe that they could conquer the world. But he too succumbed to the time-honored theme. Men and women were getting more helpless every day. They expected the government, reform societies, and labor organizations to do their work and their thinking for them. In the writer's opinion, government was a pauper and had no right to give away anything but a square deal. Graduates should be self-reliant. In a peroration, they were urged not to emulate the lobster by waiting for the tide to wash them back and forth until they died when a slight effort would save them from that horrible fate. "You with the diploma, don't be a lobster." The Monroe, Wisconsin, graduating class in 1906 took the same firm stand. The class motto was "Rowing not Drifting." Miss Mazie Bowen, class salutatorian, opened her oration on a stirring note: "Hark! the clarion bugle-note is sounding glad reveille to the valiant senior army, whose well accoutered warriors are soon to go forth undaunted to vanquish the mighty hosts of failure and despair. On life's battlefield many a hard-fought contest is awaiting them."

Chautauquas also emphasized rugged individualism. At the Algona, Iowa, Chautauqua in 1908, Dr. James L. Gordon spoke on "The Success of Character or the Character of

Success." In his estimation, the all-around successful man needed moral character, backbone, energy, ability to think quickly and to act promptly, will power, and courage. With these, a man could succeed. The term "red blooded" served as a vague, over-all synonym for anything pleasing to Chautauqua audiences, but found its greatest clarity when linked with rugged individualism. Dr. Benson, platform manager of the Rockville, Indiana, Chautauqua in 1907 gave a Sunday morning "lecture-sermon" on the "Red Blooded Christian." In another talk to the men's Bible class at the Methodist Church he asserted without contradiction that to hold "red-blooded men in the church you must give them red-blooded work to do." [45]

Ralph Parlette, who parlayed rugged individualism into a career for himself, gave his famous talk on "The University of Hard Knocks" at the Rockville Chautauqua in 1926. Originally, this had been a children's talk in which Parlette demonstrated his theme with a jar filled with beans and walnuts. By shaking the jar Parlette would demonstrate that the walnuts would come to the top: "See this poor little bean down there at the bottom? He whines, I ain't never had no chance—you just help me up where them big fellows are and I'll show 'em." Then, with a humorous gesture and grimaces, Parlette would put the bean on top, rattle the jar, and show that it had sunk back to the bottom. In answer to his question on how to get to the top, children would cry in unison, "Change our size and grow bigger." Grownups refused to let him leave out the jar of beans and nuts. Big business hired him at four hundred dollars a night to shake the jar at sales forces. When Parlette died in 1930 he had given the talk over 4,000 times and had sold over 50,000 copies in book form.[46]

Examples drawn from the business world helped preserve rugged individualism in undiluted form. Since the "Local Boy Makes Good" theme was never analyzed statistically by country newspapers, one example became proof of universal application. Under the heading "A Gallatin Boy Promoted," the Gallatin, Missouri, paper in 1909 announced that Alex Irving, who had left Gallatin only three years before, was now general manager for O'Connor and Goldberg, the largest retail shoe store in Chicago. The editor commented, "Who says that the young men of to-day have but few opportunities to rise in the world. It all depends upon the young man as to whether he rises or falls. . . . Alex Irving is of the type that progresses. All honor to such as he." In 1924, the Brookfield, Missouri, paper contained a front-page, column-length article headed "Stories of Success." In this, young men were advised to forget hearsay testimony of "muckrakers" concerning limited opportunities. Examples were given of railroad executives who rose from humble beginnings by hard work, energy, self-denial, and constant preparation. Harding and Coolidge were said to exemplify the same principles in politics. The article closed with the comment, "The future offers ample rewards for builders; it holds only ignominy for destroyers." The self-made men quite obviously constituted the builders.[47]

Henry Ford alone was example enough to sustain a real faith in rugged individualism. Having ridden in his low-priced Fords and joked about them, villagers felt they knew him well. The convenience and appeal of a Ford costing less than three hundred dollars and Ford's five-dollar wage scale also made lasting impressions. Even the 1929 depression could not destroy Ford's appeal. The Hillsboro, Illinois, paper in 1935 told how an interviewer found Ford busy on New Year's Day studying a generator. When asked why he was personally doing this on a holiday, Ford said that looking after details made other things easy. Little matters, said he, are vitally important to success.

The old faith wavered nevertheless during the 1920's, when farmers and country storekeepers began to experience preliminary warnings of the 1929 panic. Chautauquas lost their appeal and were virtually gone before the end of the decade. As depression settled over the land in the 1930's, commencement speakers found it best to emphasize themes other than rugged individualism. Though Hillsboro, Illinois, still admired Ford in 1935, the high school graduating class of that year apparently was in no mood for success stories. The baccalaureate speaker said that production problems had been solved and that young people could best promote "Abundant Life" by working out better methods of distribution. Producers like Ford seemingly were not in demand. The commencement speaker used a strangely new title in that field, "Keeping Adjusted in a Mal-Adjusted World." Even in prosperous 1945 the Hillsboro graduates listened to new themes. A "Global World" of tri-dimensional character was now demanding attention, according to the commencement speaker, and graduates were urged to combine advanced training and faith in the eternal verities in preparation for world citizenship.[48] Ten years of WPA sewing projects and PWA buildings, of local relief, of social security and old-age pensions, and of corn-hog checks to farmers had shaken rugged individualism.

Easy access to many different towns by automobile and surfaced highway perhaps accentuated tendencies already present. Three central Minnesota towns in the midst of good farming land already varied considerably on moral questions in 1940. Dassel was known as a good family town. It had 800 residents but only one poorly-attended movie. Local ministers had prevented public dancing and the sale of beer, and had even succeeded in closing down a skating rink which was heavily patronized by young people for a time in 1939. Social life reached its peak on Saturday nights, when farmers parked their cars in the center of town and listened to a band concert from eight to nine-thirty. Darwin, not far away, had 200 people but almost no business district except for several beer parlors and a dance hall staffed by cowboy bands like Slim Jim and his Rough Riders. Though Darwin too was popular on Saturday nights, mothers tried to keep their daughters away because of its reputation for drunken and rowdy activities. A third town, Litchfield, with some 4,000 people, permitted dancing at its community center on Saturday nights and had two well-attended movies. Even though Litchfield maintained a much higher moral level than Darwin, farmers still liked best of all Dassel's brand of Saturday-night entertainment.[49] Each of these three towns quite obviously catered to a different type of Saturday-night crowd.

Contemporary observers, understandably, could never quite agree on the bootleg-flapper-jazz era's influence on country towns. When in 1923 Bruce Bliven visited "Robertsville," an Iowa prairie town of 2,358 people, to see how much the radio, phonograph, movie, and auto had affected it, he detected little change in moral standards. Although bridge, golf, and motoring had increased, only two or three homes served liquor. A "literary" woman, a preacher, the high school principal, the high school English teacher, and the president of the Tuesday club rigidly censored all books bought for the public library. Any member of the committee could exercise a veto. As a result, Harold Bell Wright's novels had no competition from morally and politically tainted books.[50]

Miss Alice M. Barrows, field representative of a national welfare organization, drew much different conclusions after visiting a number of midwestern country towns in 1922. "Children" were bringing jazz home from college, a form of dancing which an "authority" had condemned for creating physical urges of a most degrading kind. Miss Barrows said this influence was most dangerous in smaller places because country people were less aware of it. Barn-dance places at Marengo and Huntley, Illinois, had indecent trimmings, and fighting and drunkenness were common enough to require constant attention. Miss Barrows urged mothers to remember that supervision was especially necessary after a dance. And again she quoted an "authority": "I wish the mother who trusts her child could realize into what a night she sends that child. We must always expect a few casualties in social intercourse, but the modern dance is producing little short of a holocaust." Miss Barrows roundly condemned Iowa and Illinois river-town dance halls with their modern jazz and bootleg liquor. From such places men took girls to closed, parked cars. River boat excursions with dances held below and on darkened upper decks vied with automobiles as means to an evil end. Girls waited on street corners to be picked up by boys in passing cars and were taken to road-houses. Those who did not "submit" were left stranded on lonely roads. Miss Barrows was morally indignant that people saw anything funny in the vaudeville joke "My wife is a good girl. She went on an automobile ride—and walked back." Miss Barrows mentioned a corn-belt traveller who was looking for evidence of progress like silos, tractors, and hard roads. Puzzled to account for the numerous wooden structures at cross roads and in groves, he asked if they were new agricultural ideas, and was told, "Yes, those are jazz platforms. In some places the saxophones make more noise than the threshing machines. The farmer is getting all the advantages of city life right at home." Nevertheless, the larger the place, the greater the evil. In Kansas City Miss Barrows saw several hundred young people "shimmy and toddle" to "the jazz" in a haze of cigarette smoke.[51]

Other and more moderate criticisms of small-town morals continued to appear throughout the 1920's. One visitor to a midwestern county-seat town of 1,200 people in 1925 noticed the lack of recreational opportunity except for Friday night "jitney dances" and movies of doubtful character. Although the local Lions Club was starting a youth program, loafing groups of boys on street corners smoked cigarettes and criticized those who attended college. Many girls dropped out of school at fourteen and fifteen to parade the streets until they married some transient workman or left for a job in a city factory. Boys of the same type wandered back and forth from city to village and gave exaggerated accounts of their experiences with "swell dames" in the city.[52]

Near the close of the decade Marquis W. Childs presented his version of a "Mid-Western Nights' Entertainment" in the pages of the *American Mercury*. Along concrete highways at intervals one saw signs reading, "Fred Schultz Post of the

American Legion—Dance Saturday Night—The Altoona Opera House." There in crude frame buildings people gathered from distant points to dance the night away. Discontent prevailed everywhere. Cecil B. DeMille's "celluloid fleshpots" had reduced Ringling's yearly show to a mere palliative where once it had satisfied every demand for the bizarre and exotic. Movies flickered in converted opera houses and dingy auditoriums, accompanied by vigorously thumped pianos. At a cost ranging from fifteen to forty cents, Main Street could see Elinor Glyn's "It," which surpassed "Black Beauty" in popularity in midwestern prairie towns. Preachers were trying to explain the period in terms of the Ford car, a crime wave, the movies, and, for a time, as "post-war hysteria." [53]

Country newspaper editors also got excited. In 1928 the Algona, Iowa, paper featured a front-page article headed "College Girls Indorse Free Love." The Women's Forensic Society of the University of Iowa had recently discussed free love and companionate marriage as solutions to the career-versus-children problem. Squalling infants were said to hurt creative art. According to the newspaper report, the group was preparing to discuss birth control as its next topic.[54]

In spite of confusion resulting from lurid charges and counter-charges, certain facts stand out. For one thing, the automobile made violations of accepted standards easier simply by extending the range of travel. Moreover, the movies leaned to risqué themes beginning with the nickelodeon period. In 1907, for instance, Madison Street in Chicago had several all-night nickelodeons, with glaring arc lamps and raucous-ballyhoo phonographs on the outside to attract customers. Typical titles featured by them on April 13, 1907, included "Cupid's Barometer," "Old Man's Darling," "Seaside Flirtation," "Beware, My Husband," "Paris Slums," "The Bigamist," and "College Boy's First Love." [55] Movie titles suggest that Americans seek to remain in a constant state of titillation. In 1916, for example, the Gem theatre in Clinton,

Wisconsin, showed pictures titled "Women and Wine," "A Man and His Mate," and "Gilded Youth." The Gem theatre at Chatfield, Minnesota, the same year advertised Theda Bara in "The Clemenceau Case," the woman "with the most wickedly beautiful face in the world." Three months later Chatfield saw the same actress in "The Devil's Daughter," a picture headlined with the promise, "As this man has done to me, so shall I do to all men. From now on my heart is ice, my passion consuming fire. Let men beware." [56] The current generation giggles at the crudity of these earlier movies but avidly follows the same themes in mechanically improved form. Movie magazines with sultry stories of picture stars vie with "true confessions" for a place on the periodical rack in village drugstores.

Evidences of moral laxity appear in various types of records. Novels of twentieth-century life still retain the town "bad woman," and add the new theme of a "country-club crowd" with its liquor and "wild parties." [57] Residents of country towns can generally identify the country lane or other favored parking spot that serves as a graveyard for chastity. [58] In at least one midwestern county-seat town in the early 1940's youngsters generally knew the "facts of life" by the time they were seven or eight years of age. "Self-abuse" was common among boys from whom information could be obtained, and sexual experience added to one's prestige, at least among lower-class boys. Though lower-class girls were not expected to "sow wild oats," many did have "some fun before settling down." Information concerning ninety lower-class marriages indicated pre-marital sexual relations in 55 per cent of the cases, and at least two-thirds were suspected. Sexual laxity may have been more evident among lower-class people simply because they talked more freely or because upper groups went elsewhere to violate the moral code. [59] Strong taboos surrounding the discussion of sex make any generalizations very doubtful, but "social purity" has trouble withstanding the light of investigation as it did in McGuffey's day.

Smoking and gambling continue to arouse criticism. The youngest member of the Irvington, Iowa, graduating class in 1908 discussed the "Evils of Our Country." These were: trusts, monopolies, and corporations; tobacco; intemperance; and different ways of gambling. Unless all of them were checked, the young man predicted that America would fall as Rome did. Law-and-order leagues in smaller towns have also fought gambling and the selling of cigarettes to minors.

Card playing has gained much wider acceptance. Though good, middle-class, nineteenth-century people refused even to have cards in their homes, the same people today insist on reporting their bridge and other card parties in the weekly society column of the local paper.[60]

Liquor is still roundly condemned in spite of social drinking by the country-club set. Most Protestant churches, especially during revival meetings, favor total prohibition. When a professional evangelist, Dr. Scoville of Chicago, opened a giant union revival at Monroe, Wisconsin, in 1906, the local paper commented that someone needed to dare to be a Joshua in a town with 5,000 people and twenty-six saloons. In spite of Dr. Scoville's converting 425 people in a five-week period, the ticket favoring low taxes on saloons won the fall election. An evangelist preached to 200 men from a box at the end of the bar in a Macon, Missouri, saloon in 1909. The saloonkeeper and his assistants stood with folded arms while he spoke and then joined heartily in the singing when a choir started "Jesus, Lover of My Soul." As the son of Christian parents, the saloonkeeper shook hands with the evangelist at the close of the invasion and assured the church members present that he had a high regard for Christian people.[61]

The W.C.T.U. also continued active in the twentieth century. Spring Valley, Minnesota, held a medal contest for men in 1906, and matrons competed for a gold-medal award at a district convention in Harmony. Orations presented at a silver-medal contest at Hedges Chapel in Ohio in 1926 were as fervent as those given in the 1880's: "Why the Beer Went

Back," "The Convict's Violin," "Why Daddy Signed the Pledge," and "Vote as You Pray, Brother." An affiliated youth organization sold candy and ice cream cones before and after the contest. Most country towns defended national prohibition against all attacks. The Rockville, Indiana, paper in 1926 featured Herbert Hoover's report on six years of national prohibition in which he spoke of declining poverty, greater abstinence, and increased church membership as fruits of the prohibition era.[62]

Dancing has gained ground in spite of opposition from evangelists and fundamentalist preachers. Nineteenth-century public schools dared not sponsor dancing, but many villages and towns now permit school children to hold dances in the school buildings. Occasionally, as in Ashville, Ohio, in 1936, a high school dance will arouse a battle of petitions for and against such activities,[63] and some villages still oppose dancing. Nevertheless, since youngsters can easily go elsewhere to dance, parents are beginning to stress locally supervised dances.

A CLASSLESS SOCIETY

MAIN STREET has continued to assert its faith in a classless society and equality of opportunity. Residents of Irwin, Iowa, and of midwestern "Plainville" in the early 1940's denied the existence of class lines locally.[64] An earlier examination of attitudes in a large number of midwestern villages had revealed the same conviction as well as considerable evidence to sustain it. Though plumbers, garage mechanics, and carpenters seldom mingled with lawyers, doctors, merchants, and bankers in metropolitan centers, villages usually made no such distinctions. There was far greater evidence of class feeling between new residents and old, between denominations, between young and old than between industrial and professional groups,[65] divisions which scarcely fit into the usual concept of class lines. Even in a midwestern town of several thousand population, which contained some

900 factory workers, citizens answered "no" in the 1940's when asked directly if classes existed locally.[66]

Much of this attitude can be traced to American traditions of a classless society and faith in man's ability to improve his status. In commenting on a recent reunion of old citizens, the editor of the Hillsboro, Illinois, paper in 1915 spoke of olden times as being democratic. Old and young, church members and worldlings, saints and sinners, bank presidents and laborers, society belles and kitchen maids supposedly all mingled in old-fashioned quadrilles, waltzes, polkas, schottisches, and two steps which a democratic Hillsboro supposedly danced in the 1890's before the "tango, bunny hug, Boston dip, grizzly bear," and other "modern abominations" took over.[67] By implication, Hillsboro had become less democratic in the interval, although the editor would have denied a class structure.

More than sentiment accounts for the continued emphasis on a classless society, however. Though a study of *Elmtown's Youth* in the 1940's furnished convincing evidence of a local class structure in spite of all denials, almost half of the prosperous families, who ranked close to the wealthy few, had achieved superior positions through their own efforts. The great middle group in "Elmville" believed that a man could rise in the world and that hereditary personal qualities rather than the local social system kept people down.[68] Such evidence must be kept in mind when one evaluates the class structure of midwestern country towns.

Those who have interrogated villagers at length about class lines are inclined to agree that classes exist and also as to the basis for class divisions: Residents of one midwestern town used the following measuring sticks to place citizens in a class hierarchy: 1. The way a family lived—place of residence, type of dwelling, and furnishings; 2. Income and material possessions; 3. Participation in community affairs; 4. Family background—ancestry, kin, and national origin; 5. Reputation or prestige.[69] Citizens in a Nebraska town adopted much the same scale of values in rating their neighbors: wealth and its use; education and its use; community leadership; membership and activity in associations; religious affiliations and activities; occupation; behavior and personal appearance; national origins; kinship affiliations and family reputation; and place of residence.[70]

While newspapers and other community organs continue to pay lip service to a classless society, by silence on the matter if in no other way, detailed questioning proves that citizens of Main Street *do* recognize classes when they think about the matter. Moreover, these classes correlate with patterns of activity. "Elmville's" better residential section and her country club contrast sharply with her poorer homes and taverns. Small villages in strictly rural areas, like Irwin, Iowa, approach much more closely to a truly classless society, or a one-class society, but, again, as in McGuffey's day, the truly "classless society" partakes of myth more than reality.

ONE WORLD

IT WILL BE REMEMBERED that while McGuffey hated war he also glorified leaders who fought for "freedom." He presented Washington and other national heroes as patriots who led America's struggles against old-world tyranny. Moreover, while McGuffey might condemn individual "tyrants," he taught the essential goodness of all peoples. But McGuffey said nothing of power politics, with its great possibilities for both good and evil, and his readers had no inkling that power politics and balance of power maneuvers within this had provided a key to international affairs since the rise of the national state. In McGuffey's opinion, France had come to our aid in the American Revolution because Frenchmen loved liberty, though he did not explain just how a corrupt, absolute, and despotic French monarchy, which still made decisions in French foreign policy, was converted to a love of "liberty." Balance of power maneuvers by France to weaken or even destroy England by aiding her rebellious colonies played no part in McGuffey's explanation of international affairs. As a consequence, his lessons in international diplomacy left much to be desired.

Current school readers have made virtually no change in the McGuffey approach to world affairs. To those who insist that young minds should not be exposed to the "harsh realism" implicit in balance of power politics, one might well ask why the same tender minds are ready for grade-school units on nature study like "The Great Outdoors" and "The World of Nature," which stress the beauty, terror, and grimness of the battle for the survival of the fittest in the animal world. Children learn from these units that animals prey on one another and that every creature must learn to protect itself. A description of a ruthless battle to the death between ants and bees, with the complete destruction of the latter, vividly illustrates the elemental law of survival. Here, too, children are introduced to heroic death in accounts of courageous self-sacrifice by animals in an endeavor to protect their young. In a scientific age we refuse to mislead our children in scientific fields, but truth must not interfere with propaganda in the so-called "social sciences."

In units on "Young Citizens of Other Lands" and on "People and Progress" one widely-used contemporary set of readers stresses the common brotherhood and common worth of children of all lands. American children are led to see that the world is growing smaller and that a new world community demands new sympathies and new understandings.[71] It would be hard to quarrel with the sanity and even the urgency of such a view in a world that has advanced so rapidly in mechanical ways and so slowly in ideas.

Moreover, the modern-day school reader has not omitted consideration of our own national heroes. The Scott, Foresman Readers contain Longfellow's poem on Paul Revere, the exploits of Daniel Boone, and Lincoln's Gettysburg Address. They offer, indeed, a finely balanced presentation of the cultural values of our own national tradition and those of other peoples. But why stop with ideals alone? Why not teach realism in the affairs of men as in the affairs of science or nature? These same readers which do such a fine job on so many aspects of a modern, complex world still present the story of Lafayette coming to the aid of America because he loved liberty and admired Washington. So far, so good. But, when French aid is mentioned in the same story without reference to balance of power principles which motivated the French monarch in that action, the readers fall as short of reality as McGuffey did in his day.

Though Midwesterners displayed a loyal determination to see World War II through to its end, they had little of World War I's enthusiasm and naïve conviction that a new heaven and a new earth would appear with the cessation of hostilities. The second conflict seemed grimmer because people sensed that war itself brought no permanent solutions to problems of international conflict. Unfortunately, such maturity of understanding came from experience alone because our formal agencies of opinion have seldom ventured beyond the realm of make-believe.

A continuation of the old McGuffey pattern of ignorance of the facts of life concerning balance of power politics was fully evident in midwestern life through the 1920's. The Chautauqua movement, which supposedly used well informed speakers, was grievously at fault. Chautauqua orators told their hearers what the latter already believed or what the speakers assumed they wanted to believe. An "authority" told the Hillsboro, Illinois, Chautauqua audience in 1915 that China looked to America for leadership, and wanted most of all American Christian missionaries.

Chautauqua reached a ridiculous peak in explaining world affairs during the actual fighting of World War I. Lieutenant and Mrs. H. R. Peat brought inside information directly to the Rockville, Indiana, Chautauqua in 1917. Lieutenant Peat had risen from private during the course of three years of service in the British army. In a "sunny" talk the Lieutenant admitted that he had never had more fun than he did while serving in the trenches on the western front. Moreover, he "assured" his listeners that German atrocities were 100 per cent worse than pictured. The Germans simply were brutes. Peat was working on a book which he expected to call "The Mad Major," an evidence of the speed with which he was climbing the ladder of army titles. In 1918, "Cyclone" Davis of Texas told the Algona, Iowa, Chautauqua audience how Germany had been plotting to conquer the world for years. The local paper spoke of "Cyclone's" height of six feet four inches, of his whiskers, and of how Washington society closed its doors on him during his service in Congress because he refused to wear a dress suit.[72] All those things of course prepared him to speak authoritatively on foreign affairs.

When the Middle West was being fed on pap by the Davises and the Peats who swarmed across the countryside, little beyond enthusiasm could be expected. And the Middle West measured up. In 1917 a Rockville, Indiana, citizen spoke to his fellow townsmen for a few minutes from the steps of the bandstand during an interlude in the music. He assured his listeners that God would not permit a war to be won by any country which used submarines in an "iniquitous manner." America was fighting the war for idealistic purposes and in the future she would both "propose" and "dispose" in international affairs. Midwestern enthusiasm found outlets in bond-selling campaigns and Red Cross drives. A full-page advertisement in the Algona, Iowa, paper in 1918 urged people to contribute to the Red Cross with exhortations like "You're a regular, red-blooded, true-blue American. You love your country. Your heart thumps hard when the troops tramp by. You're loyal—100 per c.!" In the same year, Oliver Cramer, a Brookfield, Missouri, merchant, supported the current Liberty Bond drive with a full-page advertisement which pictured one of the 32,000 spiked clubs used by German troops to "finish off" wounded enemy soldiers.[73]

Midwestern towns went wild when the holy crusade against the "Beast of Berlin" ended on November 11, 1918. In Algona, Iowa, church bells pealed out word of the surrender and the mayor ordered all business suspended for the day. While an old cannon on the courthouse lawn was being fired, parade after parade of cars with squawking horns passed along Main Street. Many marched on foot behind the Algona band and every type of noise-making device was in demand. A band concert, a short speech by the mayor, and talks by other citizens preceded the final event at the local athletic park where thousands saw an effigy of "Bill Hohenzollern" destroyed in a bonfire.[74] Such was a fitting conclusion to a crusade by a people who believed in the "devil-theory" of history. Burn the devil and the world will have peace!

Failure to appreciate the nature of power politics and the subsequent disillusionment which followed contributed to the rise of the Klan throughout the Midwest. In the middle 1920's, huge advertisements of "Klanklaves" appeared in country newspapers, and junior klansmen and female auxiliaries also flourished. Narrow nationalism and rampant isolationism was in the air. And again, in the absence of attention to basic practices underlying international diplomacy, the Middle West was swept by every passing whim. In 1926 a Rockville, Indiana, clubwoman wrote a paper on Benito Mussolini, large parts of which the local editor reproduced. Since Mussolini, a former blacksmith boy, had lifted Italy out of selfishness, laziness, and indifference to the welfare of her neighbors, Rockville people were urged to join the Italians in saying "Long live Mussolini!"[75]

Main Street is learning from such errors of judgment to temper enthusiasm with a measure of realism. Some day, perhaps, textbook writers and "leaders" may even get around to reconciling "America's mission" in foreign affairs and power politics. When they do, midwestern idealism may flourish once again but in a saner perspective on world affairs.

The City Comes to Main Street

9 *

LOSS OF "TOGETHERNESS"

I N MATERIAL WAYS, midwestern country towns have become more and more like cities, and have departed radically from former patterns of living. Rockville, Indiana, advertised a surprisingly large number of modern services in 1948, including a "mortuary" prepared to handle every detail of funerals, and appliance stores selling various national brands of electric refrigerators and home freezers. Hatcheries, garages, filling stations, home-and-auto radio repair shops, dry cleaners and pressers, a battery shop, a "Beauty Shoppe," and moving-picture houses contrasted sharply with nineteenth-century services. Advertisements mentioned electric sweepers, floor polishing machines, electric wiring and maintenance, ambulance service, and nationally publicized brands of insulating materials.[1] For the term "country town" to continue to have real meaning under such circumstances, Rockville and other claimants to that title need more than a small population in a rural setting, and that need has been expressed in the word "togetherness."

A real country town continues to be a community in which people speak to one another as they pass along the street and a stranger is recognized as such the minute he arrives. In such places people feel that all "belong" and all should be acquainted. When Mrs. Maggie Fugate asked the Gallatin,

Missouri, editor to continue to send the paper to Viola, Illinois, where she then lived, she explained that her husband had recently died from a stroke and that she needed something to remind her of other days, and, as Mrs. Fugate said, there were people around Gallatin whom she once knew. Mrs. Fred Snyder of Altamont felt much the same way. On a Tuesday shopping trip to Gallatin she took time out to renew her subscription because her husband, "the late Fred Snyder," had been a life-long reader of that paper, and she expected to continue the custom as long as she lived.[2]

In real country towns people know one another well enough to recognize the unique in every personality, town "characters" being common for that reason. "Uncle Pat" Snider of Altamont, Missouri, had all kinds of trouble in 1909. Boys first stole his knife and tobacco while he was "taking in the sights" at the local depot; then, while "up town" one evening, he received a handful of "cow itch" down his neck. Although Uncle Pat could not identify the culprit, he swore vengeance on his tormentor. For the moment, however, he could only itch.[3] August Derleth speaks of the "Town Characters Club" which he and another citizen of Sauk City, Wisconsin, have mentally called into being. It includes such likable characters as Mr. Elby, the bibulous pants-presser, Mr. Syllaber, the salesman, Mr. Elgy, the incomparable justice of the peace, Mr. Elky, the kindly religious fanatic, and even Derleth himself. Out of such familiarity with one's neighbors comes the small-town urge to employ nicknames. In Sauk City they generally emphasize physical traits or personal mannerisms. "Butch" is a tough guy, ready to fight; "Dutchy" has a German accent; "Stub" and "Shorty" are simply short; "Pipe" once became ill from smoking; and "Duke" puts on airs.[4]

In a real country town citizens identify themselves with the place through participation in informal social activities which are open to all. When the Clinton, Wisconsin, editor wanted to recall his own days of fun in the local community he remembered the strawberry patch on "Quality Hill," the melon patch near the Northwestern railroad tracks which the boys raided until Old Doc Calvert "doctored" the watermelons, and the swimming hole at the Wyman farm. He recalled the local fires which he had attended as a breathless youngster, the local home-run hitter in baseball, Ed Klenigbeil, the raft on Case's pond, hunting, annual school picnics in Wyman's Woods, and the place in town where one could put on skates and slide all the way to the marsh.[5]

In spite of the tremendous upsurge of organized life and the organizational spirit, informal life still remains important in country towns. Residents have their memories made warm and vibrant by what they see. In Derleth's words,

Coming home this evening, I heard and saw children playing hide and seek in the park, and others playing about a bonfire in the street not far away; and at once I was struck with a pleasant nostalgic memory of how at one time I too played blindman's buff, statue, run-sheep-run, and hide-and-go-seek, always waiting apprehensively for the streetlights to come on, knowing soon we would be called to bed.[6]

Though one cannot determine the relative amounts of formal and informal social life in cities as contrasted with country towns, available figures and estimates indicate that informality exists most of all in small communities. Grownups belong to casual congeniality groups and youngsters make eating a hot dog or a noonday lunch at a local restaurant, or having a coke at the local drug store a major part of their commercial recreation.[7]

Several factors help explain why smaller places emphasize informal social life. For one thing, community-wide participation without extensive planning is much easier to achieve in villages. Moreover, rural towns have been slow to extend organizational activities to children. In the 1920's, 19 per cent of the population in a considerable number of midwestern towns, selected as average for their section, consisted of boys and girls aged ten to twenty, but only 2 per cent of all people enrolled in organizations in these same villages were members of girls' and boys' groups.[8] Lastly, as the home of old people, country towns have been slow to abandon the more informal life of earlier days.

No historian can surpass Ruth Suckow's book, *Iowa Interiors,* in portraying the social life of elderly village people. In spite of airing and cleanliness, their homes are likely to retain an air of mouldiness, of autumn shade, emphasized still more by the old-fashioned look of brown-painted woodwork. Suckow's photographic mind evokes pictures of ancient organs, ingrain carpets, geraniums in tin cans and jars, faded religious mottoes on the walls; of blue, plush-covered albums with steel clasps on center tables, pink shells near the door, and black walnut bedroom furniture; of "shut-off" chilly rooms and front-door screens covered with black oilcloth in the winter season to reduce heating costs.

Suckow sees the tragedy in the lives of these elderly people. Instead of stressing the usual theme of peace, security, and contentment in the little town, she points out that many homes are haunted with fear of poverty and that all face the grim reality of declining independence in old age. Since even the "well-fixed" have worked hard in early life in order to be able to "sit" in later years, they lack the necessary interests to enjoy their new-found leisure. Women fare better with their sewing, cooking, canning, and housecleaning. But husband and wife rise early as they did on the farm, and "she" waits on him at the table as she did in more hurried days until "he" has finished his meal. Beyond attending church functions he and she depend on informal activities for their social life. She may attend a birthday club of elderly women even before she becomes a widow, but does not turn to clubs otherwise. He goes to town for the mail and a package of yeast. Going and coming he stops at the poultry house to chat with his cronies. In a big dingy room littered with slatted poultry crates, a wooden settee and some battered chairs around a pot-bellied stove compete with similar accommodations for retired farmers in stores all over town. Most of the loafers wear woolen caps, old coats, and sweaters which seem to go with their white hair and rough, weather-stained complexions.[9] These people live in the past, and thereby help dilute the heavy emphasis on organizational life.

A real country town also continues to demand obedience to local customs and beliefs from those who expect to share in its spirit of "togetherness." In 1905 a Rockville, Indiana, couple became incensed when their wedding plans were marred by local "hoodlumism." In an effort to stage a fashionably correct ceremony, male members of the wedding party had worn dress suits and a satisfactory number of out-of-town guests had been present. Unfortunately for the peace of mind of those participating, a crowd gathered outside the gates of the home, and, worse still, some of the bolder spirits insisted on using that "relic of barbarism," the charivari, to serenade the bride and groom with raucous noise and village joviality.[10]

Even nostalgic articles recognize that knowing and being known exact the penalty of conformity to local custom. A Mount Pleasant, Iowa, family received gifts of chocolate cake, apple pie, a jar of home-made strawberry preserves, and half of a fried chicken from immediate neighbors their first day in town, an introduction to many happy, satisfying years which lay ahead. Nonetheless, they knew that friendship extended to them on arrival in a new community could rapidly vanish unless they kept "clean," went to church most of the time, and spoke to everybody. Another defender of the small town has recorded examples of disciplinary force in action. When "Judith" in a moment of sentimental forgetfulness said to her friends "Tom and I have such a wonderful love," she was not allowed to forget the comment for a whole year. As the writer remarked, Judith would be an old lady with snow-white hair before she allowed herself to become audibly sentimental again:

After a few years of this, one is trained for the diplomatic service, for court intrigue, for a master's degree in tact, self-control, and valiance. For you have to take it. You have to profit by it. And, at times, you must hand it out. So, only, can the local social group survive without being bored, and so is the whole state enriched by discipline.[11]

Many factors have combined to weaken small-town "togetherness." Rural and village youngsters know and participate in a larger world which no longer thinks of them in unkind moments as rubes, hicks, or hayseeds. In describing the Iowa State Fair of recent years, Phil Stong has stressed the poise and polish of 4-H club boys and girls. Though busy showing livestock and household products during the day, these farm youngsters leave their dormitories on the fair grounds each evening on pleasure bent, the girls garbed in stylish pink and yellow dresses and the boys in clean white flannels—marked contrasts to the daytime blue jeans of both sexes. As Stong says, they look like city folks, and an English photographer, covering the fair for a New York magazine, keeps asking why only city people are present and no farmers in sight.

An expanded curriculum in consolidated rural and village high schools and easy access to cities by automobile put youngsters in immediate contact with urban life as early as the 1920's. Within another decade visits to cities even in the dead of winter became routine. One Monday night in January, 1935, Bernays Seymour and James Cooper of Hillsboro, Illinois, drove to St. Louis, fifty miles away, to attend a performance of "Roberta," and Mrs. H. H. McHugh took her daughters and their chums to the city to spend the night and see the Russian ballet.[12] Unfortunately, the true cosmopolitan has difficulty in developing any feeling for small-town "togetherness." As small towns have become more cosmopolitan, they have lessened their bonds of local unity.

CLUBS AND MORE CLUBS

MOST DEVASTATING of all to small-town "togetherness" has been the advent of organizational life, especially the club movement. Clubs thrive on a sense of exclusiveness or of superiority, which injures community-wide unity. Lions and Kiwanis, Camp Fire Girls and Girl Scouts, Laff-a-Lot bridge club and Twentieth Century bridge club, Professional Women's club and Mothers' club—belonging even to one or more such clubs as these can help to create divisive activities in any town still small enough for people to be generally acquainted. In larger places, where a sense of unity is no longer possible, organizations may unite the individual with a larger whole but they encourage fragmentation and competition elsewhere.

Organized women's clubs, which began to report their activities in country newspapers in the 1880's and 1890's, were formidable organizations from the first, as Dr. Black of Gallatin, Missouri, learned in 1899 after attending the first anniversary celebration of the exclusive Hawthorne Reading Circle. The lady members entertained their husbands by giving excerpts from noted authors by memory and then turned to the "social feature" of the evening, which consisted of looking at pictures of celebrities in recent magazines and naming them. The winner of the contest received a copy of Longfellow's *Evangeline,* but poor Dr. Black, who won the booby prize, received a cabbage head.[13]

Early culture clubs apparently were determined to demonstrate their own superiority and to destroy the tendency of small-town inhabitants to discuss the same humdrum topics over and over. As a result, they favored active programs in which participants rushed hurriedly from one stunt or one number to another, and reported their meetings at length in local newspapers. Although activities varied from party to party, a first-page report in the Croswell, Michigan, paper in 1898 pictures fairly accurately the ancestral background of modern organizations. The account was headed, "Social Event of the Season," and contained a picture of Mrs. J. M. Gaige, president of the local Bay View Reading Circle. On this occasion, lady members entertained their husbands with a program and dinner, forty couples being present. After a reception at the "elegant" home of Mrs. Gaige, the group adjourned to the banquet room of the "finest" hotel in the state, the local Croswell, where the ladies first read papers on Frederick the Great, notable German educators, and Maria Theresa, and then presented musical numbers, and a charade, in which the word "illiterate" was acted out. The banquet itself, starting with oysters, did not get under way until 10:20 and lasted until one in the morning, with an orchestra playing throughout. When the last course had been served and the last conundrum solved, the ladies stood behind their chairs and treated their guests to the following "yell,"

> What's the matter with the gentlemen?
> They're all right!
> Are they all right?
> Well, we should evoke a facial ripple.
> H. A., H. A., Ha!
> Hurrah, hurrah, huree,
> Croswell, Croswell, B. V. C.[14]

As early as 1915 a University of Minnesota report on Ada, Minnesota, and the surrounding farm population, concluded:

There have been two noticeable changes in the development of social life in the village since the early days. These are, first, whereas formerly the village people and the farming population mixed freely in the social activities of the village, to-day there is very little social intercourse between the village and the country; and, second, while the people of the village formerly got together for general good times, to-day they are split up into groups or cliques, each group having its own social activities. . . . The splitting-up into groups within the village has been developed to such an extent as to be unfortunate.[15]

Perhaps this accounts for the wealth of criticism of the club movement, especially of the social club which makes no pretense of social uplift or service. A recent novelist has described the "Friendship Club" which meets in rotation at the homes of eight members. The food served is not only competitive but unwise, since all members are striving to preserve their figures. After a luncheon of canned lobster or crab meat, tuna fish, baked in shells, or chicken patties, lavish salads and New York ice cream, they settle down to bridge with their hats on and their shoes pushed off under the card table. Their voices rise higher and higher, their short-range view of human events becomes crueler and crueler as they double and redouble one another's bids, make grand slams and quarrel over the scoring. No reputation is safe with them, and every member must be present to preserve her own. The innocent are thrown to the wolves, the kind made fun of, and the old stripped of the dignity which belongs to their years. "They say" is the usual phrase when a good name is auctioned off the block. "They say" that she has cancer; "they say" that he was running around; "they say." [16]

Since organizational pressure keeps the small-town social pot boiling the year round, with only a mild decline apparent in the summer months, any attempt to describe twentieth-century social life must stress organizations and still more organizations. Churches and lodges provide their quota: men's Bible classes; Willing Workers among the women; Epworth League, Christian Endeavor, and Baptist Young People's Union; I.O.O.F., Modern Woodmen, Elks, Masons, Order of Eastern Star, Rainbow, and DeMolay. A hasty perusal of any country newspaper will provide long lists of organizations—American Legion and its auxiliaries, Daughters of the American Revolution, SOS bridge clubs and Les LMVL bridge clubs, Rotary, PTA, Self-Culture Club, Book Club, Mothers' Club, Young Mothers' Club, Birthday Club, Boy and Girl Scouts, Camp Fire Girls, YMCA, YWCA, Hi-Y and Tri-Hi-Y, Great Books Seminar, Coon Hunter's Club, Ladies of the Cemetery Association, Home Economics Club, Tri Kappa, Priscilla Needle Club. No one can name them all.

COUNTRY CLUB AND "BIG JACK'S PLACE"

AS COMMUNITY SOLIDARITY weakens under an avalanche of organizations, community pillars join a service club to satisfy their sense of obligation to humanity at large, and then feel free to build their own social life around the country club and other restrictive organizations. The elite dined with the elite in the nineteenth century, it is true, but their class activities scarcely extended beyond the home. Today, they lay out their own country-club golf courses, build their own lakes for fishing and swimming, and their own club-houses for luncheons, dinners, and parties. When the Maddox property at Hillsboro, Illinois, was offered for sale in 1915, some wanted to buy it for a city park and playground but others were more interested in making it into a country club. By 1935, the Hillsboro country-club group was staging its own New Year's Eve turkey dinner and dance, and if an orchestra failed to arrive on time it was easy enough to drive to neighboring Litchfield and dance with the better people there.[17]

The limited financial resources of smaller communities have curbed tendencies toward exclusiveness in such undertakings. The Rockville, Indiana, golf club had to rent grazing rights and operate a skating rink on the golf course in the interest of solvency in 1917, and Gallatin, Missouri, and neighboring towns in 1935 actively campaigned for new members to sustain the "Sho'Me Club," just east of Gallatin, which was said to have a nine-hole golf course, a big lake, and spacious picnic grounds.[18] Though smaller places open membership to all who can pay the annual dues, the country-club movement everywhere stands as a monument to twentieth-century social fragmentation.

Roadhouses of course are open to all. Along midwestern highways one will notice "Big Jack's Place," which offers curb service, and the "Canton Inn," serving beer, ice cream, chili, soft drinks, spaghetti, chicken, and potato salad. Both operated on Highway 16 outside Hillsboro, Illinois, in 1935. "Big Jack's" featured "dining and dancing," with chicken and a fish fry as special features on occasion.[19] Some have only a jukebox for music, enough floor space for a few couples, and a lunch bar serving beer and short orders; others feature huge parking lots, hillbilly bands, colored lights, streamers hanging from the ceilings, and impersonal crowds gathered from little towns in all directions. Everywhere, young men who have money to feed the jukebox, a clean shirt, and a date find evening after evening of entertainment safely removed from the critical stares of elders in their own immediate neighborhoods. Such recreation owes nothing to the twentieth-century cult of joining or to feelings of community solidarity.

PHONOGRAPH, RADIO, AND HILLBILLY MUSIC

ALTHOUGH TRAVELLING SHOWMEN were still charging admission to phonograph concerts at the turn of the century, furniture and music stores began to advertise them for home use within a few years. Pettijohn Brothers held an "Edison picnic" on Saturday evening December 19, 1908, at their Gallatin, Missouri, store to let the public hear the latest records. Advertisements picturing elegantly groomed men and women in dress clothes, standing at the side of Edison disk machines—equipped with horns for amplification—foreshadowed the development of expensive cabinet models supposedly capable of reproducing the human voice to perfection. Proud owners furnished music at school entertainments and elsewhere, a stage which rapidly gave way to one of widespread ownership and nationally known recording artists. One of them, Cal Stewart, became a special favorite of small-town audiences by 1916 with his "Uncle Josh" series —"Uncle Josh at Pun'kin Center," "Uncle Josh and Moving Pictures at Pun'kin Center," "Uncle Josh Playing Golf," "Uncle Josh at the Opera," and Uncle Josh in innumerable other highly diverting situations. Stewart toured small midwestern towns and gave personal performances to boom the sale of his records. By 1925, parents were being urged to make down payments on phonographs early in the fall to give their children every educational advantage in the long winter months ahead, evidence that the phonograph had achieved a secure position in midwestern life. Radios won equally rapid acceptance. As early as 1925 almost 20 per cent of all families in one Ohio county had radios, and cost alone kept the percentage from being very much higher.[20]

The growing popularity of barn-dance "radio stars" with small-town audiences indicates that hillbilly music has become the favorite of Main Street. Lulu Belle of the famous Chicago Saturday night barn-dance program has become the prima donna of small-town musical circles, surpassing even the minstrel show in popularity. Barn-dance "radio stars" from WLS in Chicago performed at the Tuscola County Fair in Michigan in 1936, and Joe Kelly headed a group from the same station in a performance sponsored by the Pythian Sisters in Rockville, Indiana, in 1937. In 1946, the Chatfield, Minnesota, municipal band engaged a barn-dance cast from radio station KSTP to assist in a local benefit performance. The American Legion of Gallatin, Missouri, in 1935 brought in Miss Louise McKay of the Des Moines, Iowa, station, WHO, Barn Dance Frolic cast to work with a local group. Headed by the Gallatin superintendent of schools as master of ceremonies, it gave performances locally and in neighboring towns. Similarly, the Women's Department Club of Rockville, Indiana, sponsored a home-talent WLS barn-dance show in 1936. Success in this venture encouraged them to repeat the idea in 1937 and to hire Miss Betty Anderson of WLS to direct the group. In order to give variety, Miss Anderson proposed to use a Mardi Gras or Mexican Fiesta setting for the hillbilly program, but it followed the same old barn-dance theme—imitators of Lulu Belle and Uncle Ezra, Virginia reels, square dances, and the Ridge Ramblers.[21]

FROM PEEP SHOW TO MOVIE

IN 1887 Edison began work on the kinetograph, the first motion-picture camera capable of photographing a few seconds of continuous action, and the kinetoscope, the popular peep-show device which brought magic-shadow art to the public. Edison concentrated on the kinetoscope, which retailed to showmen at three hundred to three hundred and fifty dollars each, because he feared that screen projections, enabling many people to see pictures from one machine, would quickly destroy the novelty of his inventions. Nevertheless, the motion picture soon invaded vaudeville programs, where it replaced one of the ordinary acts because of its lower price or served as a "chaser" to clear the house when the show ended. In the absence of titles or explanatory phrases, an announcer, garbed in a frock coat, stood at the side of the screen to make appropriate remarks and to identify objects as they flickered into view. As films lengthened, this functionary evolved into a "lecturer," whose services were necessary until producers began to substitute titles to explain the film.

Western audiences, including church societies and Chautauquas, showed an avid curiosity in moving pictures; an interest which travelling showmen from the older carnival, patent medicine, and phonograph fields began to meet with machines, lectures, and films purchased from the Michigan Electric Company of Detroit or Montgomery Ward. They were tall, gaunt personages, addicted to Prince Alberts— often turned slightly green at the back and shoulders by age. Although dependent on novelty and change for audience appeal, such exhibitors must have been astounded at the rapid growth of movies. By 1915 Louella O. Parsons and others were established film critics, stars were becoming nationally known, and movies were rapidly destroying the old operahouse regime.[22]

Old country newspapers—yellow and fragile with age— reveal the ease with which moving pictures invaded older or better established mediums of entertainment. In 1905 the Terre Haute, Indiana, Chautauqua featured a vitascope production of the Russo-Japanese war in appealing to small neighboring towns for patronage. The following year, during a week's stay at Monroe, Wisconsin, the Mardi Gras Carnival Company introduced an "electric theatre" as one of its

midway attractions. This showed pictures of the San Fran-
cisco fire, of Buster Brown and his dog "Tige" in comical
feats, of the Old Maid's mad chase for a husband, of a bank
robbery, a train robbery, a holdup of the Denver stage, and
the capture of the fugitives who committed the crimes. A
company of professional actors who presented a week of old-
style plays to a Gallatin, Missouri, audience in January, 1909,
gave a Saturday afternoon ten-cent matinee for children
which featured moving pictures and illustrated songs.

The mixture of the old and the new was much in evidence
at Algona, Iowa, in 1908. Jubilee singers performed at the
Algona Chautauqua; Ringling Brothers circus came to town;
and the local opera house featured old favorites like "Uncle
Tom's Cabin" and "The Count of Monte Cristo." A brash,
new "Broadway Electric Theatre" offered a program opening with a city "fire run" by a dozen or more fire engines,
and involving scenes of daring rescues and hazardous positions taken by firemen. This was labelled "pathetic and sensational." In addition, patrons could see "The Talisman,"
called "mystic," "The Orphan," described as "pathetic," and
a "Quiet Hotel," said to be "very comic." The program closed
with an illustrated song, "Just Because I Loved You So," by
Mr. Arthur Smith. Admission was ten cents—half-price for
children under twelve—with shows starting at 7:30, 8:30,
and 9:30. Shortly afterwards, the Broadway Electric Theatre
responded to complaints against noisy children in the audience by charging them adult prices, except on Saturday
nights, unless they were accompanied by their parents. All
were urged not to miss the pictures "Are you an Elk?" and
"The Masher." Algonans were debating whether movies
were just a fad of which the public would rapidly tire, but
the local editor insisted that people would always be interested in unusual sights and would look at copies when orig-
inals were unavailable.

Even by 1916 touring play-companies and Chautauqua
programs were beginning to seem dated in comparison with
movie offerings. The Chatfield, Minnesota, Chautauqua in

1916 featured a lecture on "Unseen Forces" by Judge Man-
ford Schoonover, "a rugged, manly man with a virile message." By then, the local Gem Theatre was advertising Vita-
graph's "great five reel masterpiece, the Colossus of Modern
Railway Drama—The Juggernaut," containing a train wreck,
actually staged at a cost of $25,000. Though Chautauquas
seemed solidly entrenched in public favor, within another
ten years they were virtually gone because audiences preferred colossal train wrecks to virile messages.

Those were the days when serials were popular. Pearl
White appeared in "The Perils of Pauline" in 1914, and the
rage was on. In 1915 youngsters at Gallatin, Missouri, could
see the first two reels of "The Master Key" simply by present-
ing a picture of a key, cut from the local advertisement, at
the ticket window of the "Duchess Photoplay House." The
remaining twenty-eight reels were strung out over the course
of the next fourteen weeks. On Saturday nights Gallatin
youngsters gathered on the front rows to chew popcorn,
scream at chilling dramatic moments, and cheer when the
hero overcame seemingly insuperable difficulties with nothing more than the pulsating music of the piano player at
the front of the show house as an aid. In the end, movies
completely eliminated some of the old rivals and surpassed
all others in popularity. When Walworth County, Wisconsin, high school students were asked in 1950 to list their favorite pastimes, movies were an easy first choice, with 93
per cent naming picture shows as their favorite form of
recreation.[23]

CHURCH AND LODGE

AUTOMOBILES, movies, radio, television, and other
mechanically reproduced mediums of entertainment now
operate throughout the calendar year with no interruption
from the marked midwestern variation in seasons. In doing
so, they compete with churches and lodges which almost
alone among nineteenth-century, small-town organizations
maintained their major activities every month in the year.

Basic church activities of a continuous nature have expanded very little over the years. The calendar for the Gallatin, Missouri, Christian Church in March, 1915, announced Bible School at 9:45, morning worship at 11:00, Junior Christian Endeavor at 3:00, Senior Christian Endeavor at 6:30, and an evening sermon at 7:30 on Sundays, with Ladies' Aid on Tuesday afternoons and prayer meetings on Wednesday evenings at 7:30. The United Brethren, the most active church in Ashville, Ohio, in July, 1926, had Bible School, morning preaching and afternoon Christian Endeavor on Sundays, orchestra and choir practice on Tuesday evenings, prayer meeting on Wednesday evenings, and meetings of the "Sisterhood" each Friday evening.[24] Even in the smallest places, Sunday school, a Sunday morning preaching service, and midweek prayer meetings are maintained around the calendar, if at all possible.

Although lodges have suffered from new and competing forms of recreation, they have held on exceedingly well in the Middle West. In 1925, midwestern towns averaged over eight lodges each, considerably higher than the rate in comparable communities elsewhere. At the time, Masons, Eastern Stars, Odd Fellows, and Rebeccas were the most numerous. Lodges continue to appeal to middle-class groups and have emphasized social activities more with the passing of the years. Eastern Star receptions, installations, initiations, and entertainments are leading social events of the season,[25] at which women often appear in evening clothes and the men in business suits.

PROGRESSIVE EDUCATION

ALTHOUGH MECHANICAL INVENTION and organizational life are increasingly important, climatic influences still create seasonal patterns in midwestern social activities. As summer heat gives way to fall McGuffey's schoolboy still turns from summer leisure to more formal education, the transition being all the sharper for him because of the increased importance of schools, especially in the high school field. In contrast to nineteenth-century high schools, where girls greatly outnumbered boys because they planned to teach, and boys saw little reason to continue beyond the grades unless they were preparing for a professional career, the twentieth-century high school has greatly expanded its curriculum to meet "practical" needs of those who intend to remain on the farm or in the small town. Vocational agriculture, domestic science, music, and commercial subjects are now quite common. The Millington, Michigan, high school girls in 1936 received a twelve weeks' course in child care under the direction of a registered state nurse, and boys enrolled in vocational agriculture in the same school carried on supervised and practical farm projects throughout the year. High schools have also expanded their social activities. In 1936 the Millington high school student council planned and supervised a St. Patrick's party devoted to dancing and individual skits imitating established performers in the entertainment world like Phil Baker, Fred Astaire, and Kate Smith.

Progressive townsmen recognize the value of expanded educational programs in maintaining farm loyalty. Some, like Chatfield, Minnesota, have actively sought rural students in order to obtain additional state aid and to build better farm-town relations. The Chatfield paper in 1946 contained a large advertisement featuring state awards won by Chatfield the preceding year in vocal and instrumental music, dramatics and declamation, and most of all, Chatfield's sweep of conference titles in track, basketball, and football. Local graduates were said to have made outstanding records on state board examinations.

Alumni associations have also contributed to the growing popularity of local high schools. The Jamesport, Missouri, High School Alumni Association, which was organized in 1896, had ninety-six people in attendance at a banquet in May of 1909 at the local Odd Fellows Hall, an indication of the interest commonly aroused every spring by the addition of still another graduating class to membership. The Ashville, Ohio, alumni group even held a "lawn fete" in the summer of 1916 to help finance annual publication of a yearbook advertising the local high school. After many smalltown youngsters began to attend college, the glamor of high school declined somewhat, but alumni association spring banquets are still well attended.[26]

Organized athletics have made a phenomenal growth in the twentieth century in every way except perhaps in partisanship, which ran to extremes from the very first. Small colleges in rural towns throughout the Midwest provided immediate and perhaps unfortunate examples for high school athletes. In 1898 a football game between colleges located at Kidder and Gallatin, Missouri, was terminated by the Kidder team walking off the field. The contest was marred by a full quota of imported players, cursing on the field, dirty play, and fist fights, at least one of which started when a professor on the Gallatin team struck an opponent, evidence that the common practice of including able-bodied faculty members and coaches on a team most often simply added to the intensity of play. Moreover, local papers were extremely partisan. Rockville, Indiana, lost to Waveland High 12 to 0 on a Saturday afternoon in October, 1905. About seventy rooters accompanied the Rockville team to Waveland, and about 300 people saw the game, gate receipts totalling almost forty-five dollars. According to the hometown paper, Rockville's more scientific game was of no avail against heavier opponents and unfortunate fumbles. Nonetheless, Rockville got better as the game went along and would have scored if time had not "run out." A Thanksgiving Day game with Kingman later in the season ended in disagreement and a forfeit, possibly because both coaches had been allowed to play by special agreement.

Publication of the local college "yell" in the Gallatin, Missouri, paper in 1898 set· an example for high schools in that locality:

Rah, Rah, Rah, Re
Who are we?
Grand River College
Don't you see?

During the Christmas season of 1905 a Chatfield, Minnesota, high school girl entertained some of the high school alumni, including a number of young people home from college for the holidays. Part of the evening was spent in giving alumni, college, and high school yells, and the group obviously exchanged information on college and high school athletic practices.

An all-victorious season naturally heightened local interest. In the fall of 1936, 140 students registered in the Millington, Michigan, high school, of whom twenty-two reported out for football. Although the high school section of the local town paper urged school authorities to purchase a microphone for use in the fall contests, and forty-five students started practicing for the band, Millington had a new football coach and no one seemed to suspect that a victorious season was in the making. Headlines in the student section of the paper just before the first game in September proclaimed "Millington Lads Play Standish," "Alumni Field Big Spectacle This Friday," "Band Parades," "Amplifying System Used for First Time," "Coach Glaza Worried." The first game ended in a tie, better than expected, and Millington went on to win all of its remaining contests. Excitement mounted game by game. Millington's first football team, the 1914 squad, planned a reunion at Homecoming, and other special features were added. Millington gloried in Coach Glaza's feat and within a few years rewarded him with the greatest honor possible, the superintendency of the local school system.

The Algona, Iowa, and Rockville, Indiana, football homecomings in 1948 were modelled closely on college and university practices. Algona had a homecoming queen, a marching band, and an address of welcome by the president of the student council. Rockville staged a bonfire and a snake dance on Thursday night preceding the big event. On Friday night the school band headed a parade around the public square, through the park and on to the playing field, where the home team lost under the lights to Cayuga, 31 to 6. Even defeat did not destroy interest in the crowning of the queen and her attendants at half-time, or in the homecoming dance that followed the game. School classes, Rotary, Hi-Y, and Y-teens entered floats in the parade preceding the game, an indication of the extent of local interest even in a mediocre season. The following March, the Algona Junior Chamber of Commerce gave a dinner for all high school lettermen, at which official awards in both basketball and football were made. The sports editor of the Davenport *Democrat* spoke to the group about his experiences during twenty years of sports' writing and officiating in the Big Nine Conference. Everywhere university coaches on the prowl for talent are glad to address high school lettermen's banquets, which are now a part of the annual school routine. Track and baseball provide spring competition, thus keeping the athletic program going throughout the year.[27]

Girls shared with the boys in the thrills and rewards of the expanding athletic program. They were ambitious to be homecoming queen, a princess, or an attendant, and vied with the boys for basketball honors everywhere until some states ended girls' inter-school competition for reasons of health. In the fall-winter season of 1905-1906, Chatfield, Minnesota, had an outstanding team of girls. Although the boys lost to Wykoff, the girls won 26 to 1, and kept the Chatfield high school "banner at the very top of the mast." In a later contest, Preston led the Chatfield girls at the half, overconfidence having reared its ugly head, but the rooters challenged impending disaster by opening the second half with a yell,

> Pike's Peak or bust!
> Pike's Peak or bust!
> Chatfield High School
> Win—you—must!

Captain Underleak led her teammates back on the court in the midst of this thundering ovation and demonstrated once again that Chatfield had "the best girls' team in southeastern Minnesota."

Archery was introduced in the Millington, Michigan, high school in 1936. Six fleecy white jackets bearing the red letters CARDINALS were purchased to be worn by girls who succeeded in making the team. The remainder of the uniform consisted of cardinal tams and socks, and skirts of a common color. Archery contests were scheduled with neighboring schools. Intra-mural sports and programs leading to physical fitness awards have become common for all girls enrolled in high school regardless of their ability to play on conference teams.[28]

Other high school activities are legion. Class rings and pins were being ordered as early as 1916. Glee clubs, bands, and high school operettas provide an outlet for those musically inclined, and give training necessary for competition in state-conducted musical contests and in national music week. Literary societies, state debate leagues, and clubs are common.[29]

Graduating classes now often run to a hundred or more, in sharp contrast with the half-dozen of an earlier day, and senior plays and senior pictures come early in the year in order to give time to work in all the ceremonial features which commemorate high school graduation. Valedictorians and salutatorians are being replaced in some schools with awards to the "best all-around" boy and girl. Since the very size of graduating classes makes it impossible to follow the old custom of having every graduate give an essay or oration, most of the class has to be slighted in this respect. Perhaps Ashville, Ohio, was trying to ease any unhappiness occasioned by this situation when her graduating class of twenty-three members in 1916 were seated in comfortable rockers on the platform even though only four performed. Parents still recognize the potted ferns, the class colors in royal purple and gold crepe paper, the class motto "Excelsior," the class flower, the class prophecy, and the class history. While the class play, baccalaureate sermon, commencement exercises, and the junior banquet are all in keeping with traditional practices, senior trips and "Junior Proms" are of more recent date.[30]

"Senior sketches," a feature of the Millington, Michigan, high school section of the town paper for many years, illustrates the very active program of virtually all high school students. Kenneth L. "Mirg" Monroe, who graduated in 1936, played a trombone in the band, belonged to the Future Farmers of America and the student council, took part in dramatics, co-captained the football team, and served as feature editor of the high school annual during his four years in school. Dorothy Bishop, who graduated in the same class, belonged to the Girls' Club and the Glee Club, was pianist of the Glee Club and typist of the "Cardinal Call," the high school paper, was editor-in-chief of the school annual, and chairmaned the junior-senior prom in her junior year.[31] In providing imposing lists of "activities" and an expanded academic program the public school system has tried harder and profited more than most other small-town institutions which have been buffeted by the rapidity of twentieth-century change.

THE DECLINE OF POLITICAL PARTISANSHIP

TWENTIETH-CENTURY VOTERS lack the partisan political interest which characterized their fathers, and have also ceased to devote enormous amounts of time to narrow partisan activities. As the "Boys in Blue" died off, independents began to replace those who voted as "they had shot," and the GAR spirit no longer ruled the land. Newspapers likewise became more moderate politically as advertising by local businessmen and national corporations began to surpass the legal and political advertising on which they once had depended. Radios enabled citizens to hear campaign talks and receive election returns in home comfort whereas once they had been forced to brave mobs of yelling zealots in local opera houses.

The change in tone was quite pronounced. In 1937, when the Rockville *Republican* announced that it had purchased the Democratic newspaper at nearby Montezuma, Indiana, it claimed that it was joining a quite common movement among Indiana editors in publishing both Democratic and Republican newspapers under one ownership, and that it would guarantee to keep the Montezuma paper "militantly democratic." How an old-time editor would have guffawed or stormed at the idea of papers of one political party giving militant leadership to those of an opposing belief! The same hollow ring marked the advertisement of a "big extra special frolic" at the Algona, Iowa, opera house on election night in 1928. A moving picture entertained the audience during the evening and the management furnished confetti, balloons, and noisemakers to be used when election returns by wire were announced at intervals after midnight.[32] In reality, the election was an excuse for people of both parties to attend a midnight show together, not the culmination of weeks of marching, arguing, and even fighting by those who would be present.

COUNTY FAIRS AND TOWN DAYS

COUNTY FAIRS underwent the same mockery of their original purpose during the early twentieth century. As yet, agricultural colleges and other farm agencies had made only minor efforts to invigorate the farm movement whereas urbanism had destroyed much of the old-time appeal of livestock shows. Even farm youngsters, many of whom expected to seek city employment, saw little reason to waste time on the old-type county fair. Subscribers to country newspapers read advertisements of the annual state fair, whose resources enabled it to surpass county efforts along the same lines, and whose entertainment yearly became more accessible to those owning automobiles. Iowa's state fair in August 1908, featured racing, twenty thousand dollars' worth of vaudeville entertainment, nightly pavilion shows, bands, orchestras, free camp grounds, and twenty-five thousand dollars' worth of premiums. In 1910, advertisements of Michigan's state fair promised four flights daily of the Wright Brothers' airplane; harness races worth forty-five thousand dollars in prize money; bands; big, free outdoor acts costing thousands of dollars; nightly fireworks; Barney Oldfield and Ralph De-Palma in a matched automobile race; four additional hours of motor-car racing; the biggest auto show ever, and "Oh, that Midway." [33]

County fairs tried to match this increasing emphasis on entertainment. Green County's fifty-third annual fair at Monroe, Wisconsin, in 1906 had a greatly expanded midway containing two electric theatres; a "lady vaudeville theatre" featuring dancing, singing, and posing; a kicking mule; a snake tent; cane and Kewpie-doll racks; and lunch stands. Daily throughout the fair a man and woman waltzed, imitated drunken squabbles, and performed other feats on stilts fourteen feet high. In spite of such attractions, the fair was only moderately successful. Though the ladies' vaudeville show proved highly popular, it had to be closed down, the ladies having come in "under false pretenses," and two gambling wheels suffered the same fate.

The rage for entertainment gave point to a *Collier's* article in 1913 describing midwestern country fairs in which "barkers" along the midway surpassed the livestock exhibits in drawing power. Spectators watched Congo's keeper punch him with a heavy, iron trident as he lay concealed in a canvas pen, and listened to his occasional roars. "There he is," cried the barker, "a-roarin' an' cryin' for meat! It's all the poor creature knows—to roar an' cry for meat!" Mention of a recent order from the army for his return, with the intention of dissecting him to see if he was man or gorilla, stimulated people to want to see such an unusual phenomenon before it was too late. For the small admission price the audience could also see the seventeen deadly "cober" snakes "a-bitin'" at him. As a final clincher, the barker rushed in to feed the creature ten pounds of raw meat, which averaged something over half a ton a day if he consumed the entire amount at each feeding. Though people knew that they would see nothing more than a boy in a wig and a few blacksnakes, they enjoyed being fooled before passing on to La Belle Fatima, Algeria, and Oskalina in "Paris by Night."

In some places the county fair disappeared completely in favor of town "days" of various kinds, and everywhere it was sadly declining before new forces began to revive its original purposes in the 1920's and 1930's. Businessmen learned that county fairs which honored and promoted farming were excellent means of improving town-farm relations. Most of all, farm youngsters in 4-H and other agricultural clubs began to take a part. In many places they helped with the planning, and everywhere competition among the girls for prizes on canned goods, sewing, and homework, and among the boys for livestock and carpentry awards, gave young people a greater interest than ever before. The midway remains, but exhibits are returning to their former prominence. Horse shows, often staffed with local mounts and riders, provide a pleasant interlude, and displays of new farm machinery and household equipment appeal to many.[34]

While fairs were in the doldrums, a new competitor developed in the form of town "days" which continue to be popular everywhere. By 1925 villages were staging celebrations under a variety of titles—implement day, community day, farmers' spree, poultry show, community mix, ox roast, harvest home, May festival, fiddlers' convention, and so on. Some towns even used national holidays like the Fourth of July and Labor Day for their annual celebration, thus gaining some advantage by exploiting a time-honored but otherwise declining holiday. In most places, they combine exhibits of farm products on a limited scale with the more modern carnival midway.

Several factors account for the continued popularity of town "days." Since county fairs are almost invariably held at the county seat, smaller towns try to offer comparable entertainment to farmers in their own immediate vicinity in order to retain a share in rural trade. In August of 1927, the Algona, Iowa, paper mentioned nearby celebrations of Sauerkraut Day at Lakota, Indian Day at Titonka, and Dairy Day at Ledyard. Such celebrations surpass fairs as trade promotion devices in that midway, stands, and exhibits often are located directly on Main Street or around the square while fair grounds are much farther removed from the heart of business districts. Efforts to make town "days" original or different from all others indicate that they also satisfy an urge along those lines among small-town residents. By 1926, the Circleville, Ohio, annual Pumpkin Show was already in its twenty-third year and had become widely known. Some 60,000 were said to have attended that year. The one distinctive feature of this celebration, the pumpkin contest, had 1,021 entries, with the largest pumpkin weighing seventy-five pounds. Cedar Springs, Michigan, a town of some 1,200 people, had five thousand visitors to its annual "homespun fiesta," "Red Flannel Day," in 1940. Contestants competed in wood splitting, sawing, telling tall tales, and eating blueberry pie. Here again, however, one item set Cedar Springs apart from other towns, this time red-flannel underwear rather than pumpkins. Five years earlier the two "lady bachelor" editors of the local paper had replied to a New York columnist's complaint that red flannel underwear had disappeared by pointing out that a Cedar Springs store still sold it to local "red-flanneled he-men." Local stores suddenly found themselves swamped with orders from all over the United States, and thus Cedar Springs became famous as the home of red-flannel underwear.[35]

When such trivia were becoming the trade-mark of so many country towns, it is not surprising that some places saw nothing incongruous in exploiting the old-settler theme. Since progress was identified with change, old landmarks had been ruthlessly eliminated, but sentimental attachment to one's immediate ancestors offered a good excuse for a town "day," providing, of course, that the past did not intrude too much on the progressive present.

Hillsboro, Illinois, which had taken the old settler to heart as its "day," demonstrated how effectively the old could be submerged in the new when it planned its 1935 celebration. Early in August a committee adopted "Radio Programs" as the old-settlers'-day parade theme. The local paper praised this choice because it provided so many ideas— Amos and Andy, Sisters of the Skillet, Gardens of Tomorrow, WLS Barn Dance, Joe Penner, Eddie Cantor, and other themes peculiarly fitting to the spirit of the day. Though funds were short because of contributions to so many other "good causes," Hillsboro was determined to have a "day," just like the other towns in the county that were known for such activities—Farmersville for Irish Day, Litchfield for the Fourth of July, Witt for Labor Day, Harvel for German Day, and Nokomis for a Farmers-Merchants picnic. Citizens rallied to the cause, and by late August the program was set. Miss Mae Butts, singing hostess of Priddy's Inn in Springfield, was engaged to serve as "hostess" and to present several songs. Bands, vaudeville acts from St. Louis, the "Sunbonnet Girls" from "WDQ" broadcasting station, amateur tap dancing, softball, and speaking were among the many activities. Local picture shows, which planned to run continuously from three to eleven at night, reminded people that they would be a good place to rest. Only the scheduling of a tennis tournament in connection with Old Settlers' Day seems to have impressed the planning committee as being so incongruous as to need justification. Connections with the past were to be recognized only by asking people over sixty-five to ride in cars at the head of the parade and by gifts of one dollar each to the oldest man and oldest woman present and of two dollars to the oldest couple. Rootless as ever, the Midwest saw no incongruity in observing sauerkraut day, red flannel day, and old settlers' day in the same manner.

It would, of course, have been difficult to do otherwise when towns no more than seventy-five years old had obliterated all vestiges of "early days" except perhaps for a few relics, scattered letters, and documents. A crowd estimated at 40,000 people saw the parade of 116 floats depicting the founding of Algona, Iowa, when the town celebrated its seventy-fifth birthday in 1928. A marker was placed on the homesite of Asa C. Call's residence, the first house built in Algona, but early homes and early churches had all disappeared. "Rusty Hinge" quartets and clown bands [36] entertained citizens who had only a passing curiosity about the ancient history of white men who had started the town so long ago, seventy-five years in the past.

FROM HALLOWEEN TO CHRISTMAS

THE SPIRITS of the Calls and the Taylors and the other families who established all the Main Streets in the Middle West find expression in many of the less formal activities, which have changed very little. Though small boys are learning to curb their wilder impulses through pageants and awards sponsored by service clubs and other agencies as a means of lessening age-old vandalism, on All Hallow's Eve, Hillsboro youngsters upset privies and ran rampant on Halloween as late as 1945. On Thanksgiving Day union church services continue much as in the past, small boys still go rabbit hunting, and families and neighbors dine together. Lyceum series sponsored by schools, community clubs, and other local agencies still provide several evenings' entertainment during the fall and winter months. In 1926, the Clinton, Wisconsin, lyceum consisted of five numbers—a three-act comedy drama; the Neapolitan Serenaders; the Pantheon Players; E. J. Powell, orator and wit; and the Gerhardt Duo, entertainers. Although lyceums fell on evil times as the century moved on, they have held on longer in country towns than did Chautauqua. The Clinton, Wisconsin, high school sponsored a lyceum in 1936 consisting of three numbers—Al Priddy of Ringling Brothers circus on "Can Animals Think?"; a naturalist on "Your Friends the Snakes"; and the Dixie Melody Masters—four Negroes who sang spirituals and "plantation" songs. Season tickets ranged from thirty cents for grade-school youngsters to seventy-five for adults.[37]

Always, however, the spirit of organization and change has been evident in twentieth-century life. November poppy sales for disabled veterans, banquets, box suppers and dances mark American Legion ascendancy over the GAR's declining ranks. Armistice Day early in November now seriously challenges GAR Decoration Day, and VE Day of World War II still has to find its proper niche. The Rockville High School band headed a Legion parade on Armistice Day in 1948 to place wreaths on the soldier's statue at the west side of the courthouse lawn and on the World War II memorial at the northeast corner. Then came a silent prayer, taps, a speech, introduction of the commanders of the American Legion and of the Veterans of Foreign Wars, and the benediction. Early in the fall the Twentieth Century Club, Pythian Sisters, Order of the Eastern Star, and the League of Women Voters step up their meetings. While Fire Prevention Week, Employ the Handicapped Week, American Education Week, and all the other nationally observed "weeks" receive passing attention, real effort is devoted to Red Cross drives, Community Chest drives,[38] and other "drives" throughout the year.

As in the nineteenth century, the mystery of the Christmas season still breaks the frenzied pace of modern life for harried club woman and rushing businessman alike, if they can only manage to survive the days immediately preceding. Midwesterners have enriched Christmas pageantry with a sureness of touch almost totally unique to the Christmas season alone. While they can be sold change for change's sake on almost any other phase of life, they choose between phony elves and traditional Santas, evergreens and brassy substitutes with an understanding that maintains unbroken connections with the past. Christmas programs, Christmas trees, and Christmas visiting are the heart of Christmas today as they were in 1865. Even the army turns its fighting men loose by the thousands at the Christmas season in obeisance to the homeward urge.

Those who fear that commercialization will destroy the Christmas spirit perhaps fail to realize how long it has withstood that danger. One Illinois paper in 1905 printed a parody on "The Night Before Christmas":

THE DAY AFTER CHRISTMAS

The day after Christmas the old man was broke,
  And he sat by the fire and attempted to smoke.
His wife was quite happy, though all tired out,
  And Lord! how the kids did frolic and shout.

. . . .

And all were remembered, kids, cousins and wife,
  But did Dad get a thing? No, not on your life.

Letters to Santa in 1905 were concerned primarily with gifts, Master Clement Spinner's note being a model of brevity and directness: "Dear Old Santa: Bring me some candy, nuts, oranges, a gun and a knife for Christmas." As early as 1906 the Monroe, Wisconsin, paper printed a communication recently received from "a weekly journal of philanthropy," published by a New York charitable society:

To Christmas Shoppers: Please buy your presents early; early in the day and early in December. That will be your biggest gift to the holidays—to the workers behind the counters and on the delivery wagon.

Merchants were asked to insert the message in all their advertising. As early as 1911, Brookfield, Missouri, stores were being decorated at the Christmas season with red streamers, holly wreaths, and rosebud lighted globes. And by 1916 banks were operating Christmas Savings Clubs.[39]

Professional Santa Claus troupes were visiting country towns by the 1920's. Ashville, Ohio, invited the school band and all school children to greet Santa at nine A.M. on December 24, 1926, when he arrived with his six reindeer, a fawn, two Eskimos, and a gift for every child. A crowd estimated at 2,500 to 3,000 people crowded the streets that day and watched Santa pass out 1,500 gifts. The Algona, Iowa, Chamber of Commerce sponsored Santa Claus and his circus on December 11, 1939. Fifty-eight hundred candy bars were distributed during the course of the day. This Santa troupe had live deer; Shetland ponies; a trumpeter on a white horse; comical clowns representing toys; and Fairyland Floats— Cinderella, Mother Goose, the Cat and the Fiddle, the Cow Who Jumped Over the Moon, Wynken, Blynken, and Nod, Three Little Pigs, Mutt and Jeff, Ferdinand the Bull, and Humpty Dumpty. Children took free rides on the Shetland ponies, and Santa held open house in his own special log cabin. Despite their popularity with children and merchants alike, such companies failed to make innovations like Mutt and Jeff last. Only Rudolph, the Red-Nosed Reindeer, seems to have much chance of becoming a fixture in the annual Christmas program.

By the 1930's firemen were repairing broken toys for distribution to the poor. Another form of charity was for Boy Scout and other youth organizations to contribute canned goods as admission to picture shows and other entertainments. Christmas caroling and German bands grew in favor. Most of all, business streets were hung with evergreens and strings of colored lights; brilliantly decorated Christmas trees sparkled in public places, and permanent evergreens on front lawns of private homes were dressed in Christmas splendor. Annual sales of Christmas seals had become routine.[40] Nonetheless, all the pageantry and all the lights served only to reinforce the inner core of momentary peace and sense of timelessness which has descended on an otherwise turbulent Midwest at the Christmas season seemingly for years beyond recall.

FROM NEW YEAR'S TO MEMORIAL DAY

WATCH PARTIES at the Methodist Church and dances now have to compete with a country club dance, card parties, and the midnight picture show on New Year's Eve. Although the Binney theatre at Pattonsburg, Missouri, started its "owl show" at 10:30 P.M. in 1935 to give patrons ample opportunity to see "Miss Mercedes" perform the same fan and hula dances which were being featured in Kansas City's gayest night club,[41] the New Year's Eve owl show performance is usually more sedate, and even youngsters from very strict homes are permitted to attend. New Year's Day still goes in heavily for visiting, dinners, and hunting.

Revivals are common throughout the year as they were in the nineteenth century. Fundamentalist preachers stress the old-time religion in union meetings but pay obeisance to the spirit of progress by using hymnals with snappy, syncopated tunes, and by playing guitars, vibraharps or trumpets to accompany the singing. Bake sales are relatively modern innovations, while the older forms of church fairs and festivals have declined in favor. Men's classes hold fellowship dinners and listen to "two-fisted" speakers. And everywhere village churches join the national observance of a week of prayer early in the new year.[42]

Organized winter sports have grown in popularity. Boys join the town team after completing their high school basketball career, while men and women alike enjoy bowling in towns capable of supporting alleys for public use.[43]

National and traditional winter-and-spring holidays provide excuses for social events instead of being observed with commemorative ceremonies. Though the "President's Ball" to raise money for fighting polio was common on Franklin D. Roosevelt's birthday during his administrations,[44] former presidents, like Washington, Jefferson, and Lincoln, seldom received more than passing attention on their natal days. Valentine Day and St. Patrick's Day serve as themes for parties and dances.

Easter alone continues to have widespread ceremonial observance tailored to the spirit of the occasion. Protestant churches with full-time ministers have become more inclined to observe Holy Week preceding Easter Sunday and special Easter music has grown in favor. Some small towns hold sunrise services on Easter morning, and egg hunts for children are more common than in earlier days.[45] Easter rivals Christmas in the extent to which more elaborate pageantry has been fitted to traditional concepts.

America now has fought too many major wars for Memorial Day to retain the unique position which it enjoyed in GAR times. By the 1920's leadership in veterans' affairs had passed from the GAR to the American Legion, a shift which was openly recognized during Memorial Day services at Rockville, Indiana, in 1926. Eleven GAR and two "Johnny Reb" Civil War veterans occupied the platform at the Ritz theatre. Although the older veterans had planned to "charge" the American Legion with responsibility for continuing Memorial Day observances, only a few legionnaires in uniform and a small crowd witnessed the historic ceremony. No longer able to march with ease, the old soldiers rode in cars to the local cemetery for the traditional ceremony of decorating graves of former comrades. By request, the commander of the local GAR gave an abbreviated form of the order's service, after which a squad of American Legionnaires fired a salute and sounded taps. Few, perhaps, realized how thoroughly the haunting sound of the closing trumpet notes marked the end of a colorful phase of American life.

The American Legion and other new veterans' groups have added many new features to the traditional method of honoring America's soldier dead. In May of 1925 groups of young girls at Gallatin, Missouri, sold poppies made of crepe paper to raise money to decorate graves of World War I soldiers buried in France, while the American Legion Auxiliary at Rockville, Indiana, on May 29, 1937, turned over the proceeds of its Poppy Day sales to the relief of disabled veterans who had made the flowers. The poem "Flanders Fields" now rivals Lincoln's Gettysburg Address in popularity on Memorial Day programs, and the number of organizations participating in parades has increased greatly in keeping with the spirit of an organizational age—American Legion, American Legion Auxiliary, Veterans of Foreign Wars, Veterans of Foreign Wars Auxiliary, Women's Relief Corps of the GAR, Spanish-American War Veterans, Gold Star Mothers, Blue Star Mothers, National Guard, Daughters of the American Revolution, Boy Scouts, Girl Scouts, and Camp Fire Girls, to mention only a partial list of those named in newspaper reports. At Winston, Missouri, in 1935 a cold, wet spring held back the peonies, the traditional midwestern flower for Decoration Day, but the American Legion went through with its ceremony nonetheless. A verse from the old hymn "When the Roll is Called Up Yonder" and a basket dinner represented tradition, while "Flanders Fields" typified the new.[46]

SUMMER ENTERTAINMENT

MEN STILL GATHER every spring in barber shops to lay plans for the baseball season just ahead and local merchants decide how much they can afford to give toward supporting the town team. Big league baseball salaries have glamorized the game even more for small-town youngsters who can think of no kinder fate than getting rich playing baseball. As early as 1909, the Gallatin, Missouri, editor, a baseball fan in his own right, called attention to salaries of as much as five thousand dollars for the 154-game season and mentioned particularly Cy Young's fabulous income of $7,800 per year.

Other very modern features had appeared even before the turn of the century. A team of "Bloomer Girls" played the Gallatin nine in 1898, though progress has improved on such stunts as on all other aspects of midwestern life. When the Clinton, Wisconsin, town team faced the "Western Bloomer Girls" in 1916, Princess Hiawatha, billed as "the only lady Indian pitcher in the world," was the opposing hurler. Towns now seem to prefer to form leagues of a half-dozen to eight teams in order to have regularly scheduled opponents, and American Legion sponsorship of teen-age boys has added additional interest to the game.

By the 1920's, "kitten ball" or "soft ball," which had been

played as indoor winter baseball in northern states like Minnesota early in the twentieth century, was becoming something of a rage. When Gallatin, Missouri, installed lights for night games in 1925, the local editor said that softball had been sweeping the country and that several nearby towns had teams. Although Gallatin currently was supporting a junior American Legion hard-ball team, and an adult hard-ball team—for which a local pitcher was having a hot streak of luck—softball was being played several nights a week and was more than holding its own. An admission charge of five cents covered all expenses, and women and men alike could play without having to maintain themselves in top physical condition. Apart from satisfaction arising from town pride, Rockville, Indiana, merchants perhaps gained little by purchasing uniforms for the local hard-ball team in 1937 even though names of donors were stencilled on the backs of sweat shirts worn by the players. On the other hand, softball teams during the same season were garbed in colorful and inexpensive attire, the Lincco Oilers wearing yellow shirts and red caps while the Avalon Veterans were known by their blue and white striped shirts.[47] Softball's universal popularity reflects the Midwest's widespread and growing interest in organized physical activity.

Outdoor picnics have retained their popularity with numerous types of organizations. Churches like to give lawn parties and lawn socials in the summer season and also occasionally join together in one big union picnic featuring contests for all age groups. Modern Woodmen of America, one of the newer fraternal lodges emphasizing insurance benefits, staged elaborate picnics during the first two decades of the twentieth century. The Algona, Iowa, lodge in April, 1908, expected to spend seven to eight hundred dollars in expenses and prize money for its local picnic. Prizes were to be given for the best Woodman drill team, the largest delegation from any "camp," the best Woodman band, and the best-drilled Royal Neighbor team. In 1916 some 3,000 people attended a combined fish fry and picnic staged by the Woodman lodge at Ashville, Ohio.[48] Family and neighborhood picnic groups have also retained their popularity throughout the twentieth century.

Summer concerts have suffered little from new and rival attractions. As early as 1916 an Ohio paper commented that automobiles now made it much easier for farmers to attend weekly concerts. Informally dressed adults sitting at ease in cars around the band stand or courthouse square, milling youngsters with candy and popcorn, and a rather sedate program of music lasting something over an hour characterize the band concert. While listeners express approval of popular numbers by sounding their horns, they seem to like most of all the easy informality of the occasion and the excuse which it provides for a pleasant evening drive.[49]

The modern Fourth of July retains little semblance of its former glory. After national journals carried through an active campaign condemning the noise and bodily injuries resulting from "the old-time Fourth," country towns turned to a "safe and sane Fourth," or none at all, except where fair associations burdened with expensive buildings and grounds or communities desirous of making the Fourth their own special town "day" have gone over to a highly commercialized program involving maximum amusement and a minimum of patriotic observance. In the 1920's Chatfield, Minnesota, boasted of its "enviable reputation" for Fourth of July celebrations. The Chatfield editor claimed that nine thousand people were present on July 4, 1926, to hear the reading of the Declaration of Independence and other brief commemorative ceremonies and to enjoy the day-long bowery dances, parades, vaudeville shows, and band music. The Monroe, Wisconsin, Chamber of Commerce in 1948 sponsored a four-day program including "Crash" Thompson and his "thrill show," a music festival, a "Funzapoppin" revue, and two hours of fireworks. But towns that have selected other "days" to emphasize have come to prefer informal activities on the Fourth of July. The editor of the Hillsboro, Illinois, paper described a more common situation when he said in 1945 that years had passed since the Fourth had been celebrated locally in the "old-fashioned" way. While he understood that cannons, bands, parades and crowds were still popular in some parts of the country, and local citizens had heard plenty of radio oratory during the recent Fourth, Illinois seemed to prefer family reunions, picnics, fishing, boating, swimming, trips to nearby places, victory gardening to help win the war, or just loafing in the shade with a good book. A state anti-fireworks law had helped establish the "safe and sane" Fourth in Illinois.[50]

Travelling tent shows offering a week of dramatic productions, with a new play each night, continue to invade country towns during the summer season. They have changed little from the plan followed by the "Glen L. Beveridge and Associate Players" who visited Hillsboro, Illinois, in May, 1915. An advertisement credited this company with thirty people, including a band and orchestra, and a carload of scenery and electrical effects. A thousand seats at ten cents and a more expensive reserved section were available for the opening play, "The Smuggled Necklace." [51]

Carnival companies tour the Midwest from early spring until late fall, where they surpass second-rate circuses in popular favor and provide businessmen with commercial entertainment to accompany trade-promotion activities. The Mardi Gras Carnival Company, which spent a week at Monroe, Wisconsin, in July, 1906, pitched its tents on the four sides of the town square. Its Amaza Show, featuring the flying lady and sleight-of-hand performances, was located on the northeast corner; on the west was the Electric Theatre, previously described; and on the south the "Old Plantation" tent, devoted to songs, dancing, and acting reminiscent of the older minstrel shows. A ferris wheel was located on the southwest corner, a penny arcade, English gondolas, and a merry-go-round on the southeast, with the snake pit and a show picturing the bombardment and surrender of Port Arthur stationed on the north. Numerous other concessions were sandwiched in around the square. A free, open-air, revolving ladder act was open to all, and the management was trying desperately to obtain a band to replace one recently fired. Admission to Amaza and Port Arthur was fifteen cents, to the merry-go-round five, and for all other attractions ten.

Although it had been sponsored by the Monroe Business Men's Association, and had paid the city $120 for the privilege of coming, this carnival caused considerable local discussion as to the wisdom of promoting such ventures. Earlier in the summer efforts had been made to obtain some other company but the city fathers discovered that a few carnival organizations demanded guarantees instead of paying for the privilege of showing regardless of money taken in. Businessmen themselves were divided. A few thought only in terms of trade promotion, one suggested that people should occasionally be entertained without thought of profits, and others feared that money would be taken out of local circulation.

In spite of their popularity, carnivals have always had trouble over gambling devices and "dancing" acts which run counter to local sentiments. The S. W. Brundage Carnival Company, which had been in existence since 1899, was held up temporarily by an injunction granted to "several hundred" Algona, Iowa, citizens in 1918. After a court hearing, the show was allowed to open, but with restrictions on "gambling, liquor, and lewdness." [52]

CHAUTAUQUA WEEK

FROM THE TURN of the century to 1930 the "better people" could ignore carnivals in favor of annual Chautauquas which lasted for a week or more during the summer season. The name itself was derived from Lake Chautauqua in the state of New York, a popular spot for nineteenth-century camp meetings. Over the years, a Sunday School Teachers' Assembly, lectures, music, and readings became a popular part of the annual Chautauqua Lake Assembly. Any idea with a lineage based on a combination of the old, religious camp meeting, the Sunday school, and the idea of cultural progress [53] was bound to appeal to a generation of Midwesterners nurtured on McGuffey's Readers and "social purity" ideals of the W.C.T.U. Although cities showed little interest in the movement, Chautauqua became very popular in country towns, and even more so with farmers, for whose convenience the annual meeting date usually was set.[54]

Chautauqua emphasized wholesome cleanliness during its period of greatest popularity. When a musical comedy company presented scenes from the opera, "Carmen," on a Kansas Chautauqua circuit, it had the girls working in a dairy instead of a cigarette factory, and Carmen made her entrance carrying a milk pail. Chautauqua also had a "message." Orators demonstrated the eternal verities in speeches labelled "Community Deadheads," "The Tragedy of the Unprepared," "The Man Who Can," and "The High Cost of Low Living." Moreover, Chautauqua was sound psychologically in giving toil-worn and dedicated parents a feeling of happiness and of their own worth as they struggled to lift their children one step farther up the ladder toward achieving the American dream of opportunity. "Sunshine" Bates may have seemed ridiculous to some people but he expressed the fierce urge in many seemingly phlegmatic listeners when he said,

Happiness is the joy of overcoming. It is the delight of expanding consciousness. It is the cry of the eagle mounting upward. It is the proof that we are progressing. . . . Don't stay down in the valley of material things. Go on up to the mountain top where you can look down into the clouds and see their silver lining. Some day my night will come. It will spread over all this valley of material things where the storms have raged. But I shall be on the mountain top.[55]

Thomas W. Duncan's highly critical novel, *O, Chautauqua,* has failed to note that some of the supposedly shoddy tricks of platform managers succeeded only because they met unexpressed audience needs. Managers had a practice of walking on the stage and saying "Hello!" If this elicited a feeble response, they left the platform and then returned to repeat the same greeting until enthusiasm had been stirred.[56] People wanted and needed to be brought together and to have their inhibitions temporarily laid aside.

Instead of being victims of unscrupulous showmen, midwestern audiences knew exactly what they wanted—to feel superior and cultured without being bored in the process. While a speaker at the "Recognition Day Exercises" of the Hillsboro, Illinois, Chautauqua in 1915 impressed listeners as "witty," good-natured, and "brainy" when he complimented them for preferring Chautauqua over moving-picture shows, culture was never allowed to interfere with entertainment for long, even among Chautauqua audiences. To their credit, they did not suffer in silence when programs were over their heads. The Ashville, Ohio, paper summarized the local 1916 Chautauqua by saying that while talent had been of the highest type, customers were displeased with so much solo work. As a result, no effort was being made to engage the same company for another season. Performers at the Ashville Chautauqua in 1926 had learned to reinforce technical competence with showmanship which, though undoubtedly irksome to serious artists, also helped to reconcile culture and pleasure. The Parkinson Ensemble, consisting of two cellists and a pianist, presented one group of numbers while attired in Dutch costumes and wooden shoes. The Harmony Maids, a soprano, a contralto, and a pianist, stressed "character and action" songs, "beautifully costumed novelty numbers," "piano accordion solos," and "effective lighting." The Clinton, Wisconsin, editor in 1916 frankly said that Chautauquas should not try to accomplish a great deal in a week's time. Nonetheless, through a sane combination of instruction and entertainment they could break the monotony of rural life, create interest, stimulate inquiry, promote sociability, and increase knowledge—accomplishments which more than justified their policy of asking local citizens to guarantee them against loss on the week's entertainment.[57]

In the beginning each Chautauqua operated as an independent agency and obtained its summer talent by direct negotiation with individuals and lyceum bureaus. Some places with permanent grounds or strong Chautauqua traditions operated for several weeks during the summer season, with home-talent days supplementing professional performers.[58] In 1904 circuit or tent Chautauquas appeared,[59] which made it possible to employ talent steadily throughout a whole summer by sending tents and performers on a previously arranged circuit. Although this compelled all towns on a circuit to accept a common program, it did enable many small towns to schedule Chautauquas.

The Redpath-Vawter Circuit presented a fairly typical program at Algona, Iowa, from July 6 to 12, 1918. Sergeant Flahiff, an American survivor of the Princess Pat Regiment, and "Cyclone" Davis briefed Algonans on both the diplomatic and human-interest aspects of the current war. Oyapeh (Singing Water) talked on Indian folklore; the Mikado Company sang light opera; professional actors gave the popular play "It Pays to Advertise"; and the Williams Jubilee Singers provided an ever-popular program of Negro spirituals. "Kiddies" of the Junior Chautauqua put on a "circus." Very early, professional Chautauqua companies sensed the advantage in providing a week of supervised play for children, and this became one of their strongest appeals.

Chautauqua probably reached its height in the decade from 1910 to 1920. By then it had become a widespread summer institution, and at many places families camped on local Chautauqua grounds for the duration of the program. Camp facilities at Gallatin, Missouri, in August, 1915, included segregated sanitary toilets, a large dining hall which served reasonably priced meals, electrically lighted grounds and tents, free ice water, an information bureau, a check room for parcels, a telephone to order groceries for direct delivery to the grounds, hitching privileges, and plenty of water for horses. At Rockville, Indiana, in 1916 merchants even furnished "rest" tents for the Chautauqua grounds. Over one hundred families camped at Gallatin in 1916 and fifty at Rockville in 1917. The famous Jeffries band, which had been engaged for the whole week by the Gallatin Chautauqua organization in 1916, agreed with the campers to retire by eleven each night, at which time one of the musicians sounded taps. Fine weather and a complete absence of mosquitoes made the season perfect, so much so that one camper who had rented a two-room tent for the current session applied immediately for five rooms for 1917. People entertained nightly at their tents after the evening program. Twenty-two ladies served a dinner at one tent party, and forty couples enjoyed a chili supper at another tent before playing outdoor games like drop-the-handkerchief. The R. L. Etters erected a tent on their front lawn during Chautauqua week to accommodate fraternity guests of Etter's son, while his daughter entertained sorority sisters in the house. Mrs. Etter kept the young people occupied with parties, luncheons, dinners, and dances. When Champ Clark came to deliver his Chautauqua address, his son, Bennett, later to be a United States Senator, joined the Etter tent party.

Astute advertising agents made advance visits to prepare the way for ticket sales. Although the 1916 Ashville, Ohio, Chautauqua did not open until August, Miss Virginia Titus, a college graduate and the supervisor of Junior Chautauqua on the Ashville circuit, came in June to publicize the children's program. During her stay she engaged three local teachers to help with games, entertainment and preparation of the play which the youngsters were to present on the last day. Miss Titus announced that she wanted seventy-five to one hundred children aged six to fourteen for the program, and also outlined ways in which boys and girls could earn a dollar for their ticket. Since local papers gave generous publicity during the summer and sponsors staged civic campaigns to dispose of tickets, Chautauqua was well publicized. Long before Chautauqua week arrived large advertisements made of bunting swayed back and forth above Main Street, and handbills proclaimed the coming event from store windows and front lawns of homes. Pressure really mounted as opening day approached. An advertisement of the Junior

Chautauqua at Ashville, Ohio, in 1926 opened with the official yell,

> Chautauqua enthusiasm, Rah
> Rah, Rah!
> Johnny has it. Susie has it
> So has Pa.
> Junior Chautauqua, Rah, Rah,
> Rah!

In order to make "Pa" show the proper response, the play director planned to start her part of the program four days ahead of Senior Chautauqua and to admit all children free for that period. At the end, of course, Pa paid for a ticket or visibly declined in his children's estimation.

Chautauqua week itself saw an outpouring of culture, entertainment, and community good will. Although Rockville, Indiana, liked a "scientist's" lecture on chemistry and physics in 1917, he touched his audience most of all by gracefully acknowledging how much a local high school student who had come to the platform to help had added to the program by his marked familiarity with science. People still drove with their automobile tops down much of the time, a practice which enabled Boy Scouts to demonstrate their own worth at this same Chautauqua. When the audience came out on Sunday night after a rain which had fallen during the program, it found that efficient scouts had turned up all car seats before the shower, thus enabling people to ride home on dry cushions.[60] On hot midsummer afternoons as heat waves danced on canvas tents, headliners, like William Jennings Bryan, who had learned how to cope with the weather, moistened their hands on a cake of ice held for them by a boy and then mopped their brows.[61] The famous handkerchief salute, which consisted simply of waving handkerchiefs in the air to indicate approval, became a trademark of Chautauqua audiences.[62] Chautauqua even had its own distinctive odors of sunny canvas, crushed grass, rope, warm humanity, pine lumber, and starched clothing.[63] It was gay and folksy and uplifting and cultured.

Chautauqua declined and then disappeared with a suddenness that was astounding even in the Middle West, where institutions have no guarantee of longevity. Rapid as the decline was, it appeared more so because community leaders refused to recognize loss of interest until such embarrassing evidence could no longer be ignored. By the middle 1920's Chautauqua was in distress; by 1930, for all practical purposes it was gone. The Rockville, Indiana, Chautauqua of 1926 had a "fair" attendance and was probably "our best," according to the local paper, but businessmen who had guaranteed the circuit against financial loss were saddled with an operating deficit. The editor of the local paper bravely remarked that if Chautauqua had "run its day" people should act accordingly, but he would not admit that Parke County lacked progressive folks in sufficient numbers to keep so fine an institution alive. Clinton, Wisconsin, faced the same problem the very same year. Before the local Chautauqua opened the Clinton editor printed an article on "Chautauqua and the Community," in which he mentioned the prevalent opinion that Chautauqua was declining. People supposedly were more interested in player pianos, victrolas, radios, movies, and automobiles. Nevertheless, ran the editorial, the movies had no voice, and other competitors had no sight. Chautauqua provided both sight and hearing and was now on a higher plane than ever. When Chautauqua week closed, the editor said that it had been a big success, with standing room only available on two nights, but then admitted that local sponsors went behind $255 because paid admission fell short of the required guarantee.[64]

Gay MacLaren, historian of Chautauqua, cites the answer which publisher John Temple Graves made to the question "Why does the metropolitan press continually ridicule Chautauqua?" as one explanation for its decline everywhere—"Because Chautauqua is ridiculous." [65] Chautauqua stressed too much its mission of culture and uplift. A provincial society liked Chautauqua, but as Midwesterners became more cosmopolitan they began to smile at red-blooded men and pure

women, so red-blooded and so pure that they were only caricatures of reality.

Sunshine Bates would have raged had he lived to see the
extent to which Chautauqua descended from the "mountain
top" in its death struggles. He might have condoned the increasing emphasis on plays, light music, and straight entertainment, but he probably would have shuddered at the
compromises made in order to operate at Algona, Iowa, in
the summer of 1928, when a Chautauqua circuit accepted
sponsorship from the local American Legion post and tried
to offer a "clean snappy show." In spite of reducing lectures
to a minimum and the joint legion-circuit sponsorship, attendance was disappointing. On the last day, Harry Hibsch-
man of New York City and Sam Grathwell of Portland, Oregon, debated the subject of companionate marriage.[66] What
a way for Chautauqua to bow out in a town where it had
scored some of its greatest triumphs!

The spirit of Chautauqua is not wholly dead. In 1945, a
Boy Scout organization bought the old Litchfield-Hillsboro,
Illinois, Chautauqua grounds as a summer camping site and
for annual meetings. The spirit of organization and uplift has
at last extended rapidly among midwestern youngsters, and
Main Street boys now spend a week at Camp Ro and take
long YMCA hiking and camping trips. Boys and girls learn
to swim in Red Cross classes.[67] Modern Huckleberry Finns
have far less chance than in Mark Twain's day to escape society's ministering hands, and they will have to accept the
undoubted good that comes to them from organizational
sponsorship unless organizations make Chautauqua's mistake. Joining and uplift can become ridiculous if carried to
the extreme. Once that occurs, Huckleberry Finn may return
in part to his foraging; but, for the moment, he is a captive
of the organizations.

10 ❖ Progress—Hopes and Realities

VILLAGE DREAMS

E VERYWHERE ON THE MIDDLE BORDER men enamored with the idea of progress established country towns in order to share in the blessings which lay ahead. To them, the present was superior to the past, and the future held even greater promise. For the town itself, progress meant growth, growth in population and real-estate values. Everywhere, associations of businessmen crusaded in behalf of local progress with arguments paralleling those on the letterhead of an Oakland City, Indiana, business group in 1891 —crusades that gave meaning to Booth Tarkington's novel describing the growth of "Midland City" from a hamlet to a large industrial center at the turn of the century:

They were optimists—optimists to the point of belligerence—their motto being "Boost! Don't knock!" And they were hustlers, believing in hustling and in honesty because both paid. . . . They were viciously governed, but they sometimes went so far as to struggle for better government on account of the helpful effect of good government on the price of real estate and "Betterment" generally; the politicians could not go too far with them, and knew it. The idealists planned and strove and shouted that their city should become a better, better, and better city—and what they meant, when they used the word "better," was "more prosperous," and the core of their idealism was this: "The more prosperous my beloved city, the more prosperous Beloved I!" [1]

Citizens honestly believed that as soon as their town had grown to some unspecified but enormous size it would foster arts, literature, happiness, and leisure, and that future "betterment" justified an emphasis on the immediately useful and the practical until their own community had surpassed all others in population and real-estate values. Even colleges were sought because they added to local payrolls. Growth in population and real-estate values in some college towns encouraged Brookfield, Missouri, in the 1880's to try to expand its own local academy to college level. One interested citizen pointed out that Springfield, Missouri, grew from five to twenty thousand people within eleven years after Drury College opened its doors and that Oberlin, Ohio, was transformed from "bare, open country" to a town of almost eight thousand people within a short time after Oberlin College located there.[2]

Many factors have contributed to this heavy and continuing emphasis on material progress. While America as a whole held similar views, the Middle Border reinforced its faith from the abundant resources and optimism of pioneer days. Men knew that material progress was possible because they saw within a single generation towns grow from one log cabin to sizable communities. Moreover, Main-Street merchants have been reluctant to surrender their booster spirit and their hopes for material growth when metropolitan centers with fabulous records of increase in wealth and population explain their own success in terms of such a philosophy.

A Commercial Club was organized in Kansas City, Missouri, in 1887, for instance, and three years later started a series of annual trade visits to smaller towns. One spring afternoon in 1909 a special train carrying a hundred members of the Commercial Club and fifty other representative businessmen of Kansas City stopped for thirty minutes in Gallatin, Missouri. The visitors wore white hats to identify themselves and all presented individual souvenirs to the large delegation from the Gallatin Commercial Club which met the train. According to the Gallatin editor, the Kansas City

Club had 1,250 members, whose capital investments exceeded ninety million dollars. They expected to travel 1,400 miles during the current week and to visit eighty-three towns in Missouri, Kansas, and Nebraska. They hoped to meet 170,-000 people and to make them aware of the progressive spirit of Kansas City, with its slogans "Make Kansas City a good place to live in" and "Keep something going on." [3]

Towns, which failed to achieve their hopes of greatness through the settling of rich and virgin lands, retain their hopes of "progress," because many places have grown tremendously through more recent revolutions in management, technology, and transportation. In recent years, such varied factors as movie drive-in theaters, television, plans to consolidate high school districts into no more than three or four per county, and the harnessing of atomic energy have all given promise of still another turn of the wheel of fate and the possibility of radically juggling population once again. In a revolutionary age anything can happen.

MEANS OF PROGRESS IN PIONEER DAYS

ALTHOUGH SETTLEMENT of the Middle Border offered abundant reason for establishing towns, promoters stretched such opportunities to the limit. Created in greater numbers than needed, and committed to a philosophy of superlatives that demanded first rank in population and wealth, country towns naturally turned to organization, advertising, and the underwriting of new enterprise to achieve their ends. Organized groups calling themselves Business Men's Associations, Improvement Associations, Retail Merchants' Associations, and other more or less descriptive names fostered such programs. By the 1890's "Board of Trade" had become a popular title for such groups, and the term "Commercial Club" grew in favor around the turn of the century. Later still, such groups became known as Chambers of Commerce, and from the 1920's on they competed with service clubs like Rotary, Lions, and Kiwanis.[4] Most promotional efforts emphasized industrialization, improved transportation, exploitation of mineral resources, and trade-at-home, home-town loyalty.

In 1871, while Brookfield, Missouri, was still an infant, the local editor published "Some Plain Talk about Brookfield." He told citizens that rapid local development depended on manufacturing, which meant giving up the idea of exchanging livestock and grain for manufactured goods. The gristmill, blacksmith, and shoe shop benefited hamlets in the same way that towns and cities profited from planing mill, carriage factory, rolling mill, and foundry. Already, associations in Chillicothe, Macon, St. Joseph, and other Missouri towns were seeking new industry, and some places had voted subsidy bonds. Lagrange, Missouri, had obtained a "$200,000 rolling mill" simply by making a generous donation to promoters. Five thousand dollars, according to the Brookfield editor, would bring the best pottery in North Missouri; three thousand would attract a chair factory; ten thousand a flour mill and carding machine factory; five thousand a tannery or soap factory.

There were some results in the 1870's. According to the Brookfield paper, at least six Missouri towns, including Brookfield, obtained factories by means of subsidies. Still other towns were seeking new industry, and at least one Brookfield firm was encouraged to move elsewhere at the height of the competitive craze. Brookfield's new "factory" was established by William Fay of Grand Rapids, Michigan, in 1873, perhaps because relatives in Brookfield called the town to his attention. In return for a bonus of two business lots and a residential lot, Fay erected a shoe plant which employed as many as fifteen to twenty hands for a time. It ran only spasmodically, however, and had disappeared by the end of the decade, a record which characterized all other subsidized industries in the Brookfield area.

Brookfield modestly considered a new axe-handle factory in 1888, and cheered in 1892 when the Davis Manufacturing Company agreed to transfer from Carrollton, Missouri. The Carrollton paper openly admitted that the loss would have been severe if local citizens had not immediately raised money to open another planing mill. Small towns were happiest of all when they gained something desirable at the expense of a rival community. Brookfield boasted that the Davis Company's payroll of fifty to sixty people would be a permanent asset, but the national panic of 1893 caused the first of several suspensions of activity in which that factory was involved before disappearing from the local scene. In the interval, the Brookfield editor looked around for other enterprises to join the Davis Company in bringing prosperity to the local community. He was enthusiastic about a canning factory at Chillicothe, Missouri, in 1893, which was said to be running day and night, and in which children earned $1.25 a day for a ten-hour shift during the rush season. In his estimation, factories of that type should be encouraged because they would stop the flow of money east for manufactured goods.[5]

Towns became interested in coal veins, fire clay, and other possible mineral assets in their immediate vicinity. In the 1870's and early 1880's petroleum fields in western Pennsylvania began to attract national attention. Natural gas, formerly regarded as a waste by-product of oil, was being extensively used in Pittsburgh by 1880. In the spring of 1884 promoters at Bucyrus, Ohio, became interested in drilling for natural gas, which, in turn, stimulated the rival town of Findlay, Ohio, to do the same. By 1885, Findlay had twelve wells. When the famous "Karg" well was brought in on January 20, 1886, its leaping flames could be seen forty miles away through the clouds. Findlay now staged a strenuous advertising campaign to attract manufacturing and population. Sightseers came on special trains to marvel at green grass growing within a hundred yard radius of the burning well during the winter months. Torches burned day and night along the streets of Findlay and rival towns, which took that means to demonstrate their marvelous and inexhaustible resources to prospective homeseekers. One Findlay citizen boasted in 1888:

Its [Findlay's] people have caught the divine afflatus which came with the discovery of natural gas. . . . that she will continue to progress is as certain as the stars which hold their midnight revel around the throne of Omnipotence.[6]

Although northwestern Ohio's gas supply became seriously depleted within a few years, her success encouraged other places to explore their own local resources more thoroughly. During the summer of 1887, Brookfield, Missouri, leaders tried to raise funds through a joint-stock enterprise to prospect for natural gas, coal, and other possibilities. Macon, Moberly, Mercer, Palmyra, and other neighboring towns were sinking shafts at the same time. As the Brookfield editor suggested, no one knew what underlay the surface of Brookfield, and great profits might be amassed.[7]

Trade-at-home, home-town loyalty was a popular theme from the very first. An article in the Centreville, Michigan, paper in 1869, headed "Buy at Home," repeated arguments heard long before the Civil War. Inhabitants of the Centreville community were told that no town or village could prosper unless purchases were confined to the local market. Money spent with local merchants, mechanics, and manufacturers remained at home and thus found its way back to the pockets of those who spent it in the first place. If spent in distant places, money was gone for good. Country newspapers stressed mercantile donations to churches, schools, and local charities. Storekeepers were praised for exchanging merchandise for farm crops, for granting credit in hard times, and for contributing food to the needy.[8]

FALTERING HOPES

A CONCEPT OF PROGRESS based on constantly and rapidly increasing population and rising real-estate prices would sooner or later reveal its weaknesses. Only a very few cities could find satisfaction in a philosophy of superlatives in which each community had to surpass all others in rates of growth if it expected to achieve maximum possible "progress." By the 1890's, the agrarian age was rapidly giving way to an urban-industrial supremacy in which a country town could no longer hope to surpass all other places in rates of growth. Older sections of the country naturally faced the problem ahead of the Middle Border. New England felt the population drain to cities and to new western areas while the Middle West was still growing rapidly. In 1889 the Reverend Julius H. Ward discussed the plight of rural New England in one of its regional journals. According to him, the problem went back twenty-five years. Rural New England had lost its best blood to the cities, and leadership was sorely needed to revive the countryside.[9]

As population growth in the Middle West slackened in the 1890's, prophecies of despair began to appear. An article in the *Forum* in 1895, "The Doom of the Small Town," pointed out that 3,144 townships out of 6,291 in Ohio, Indiana, Michigan, Illinois, and Iowa had lost population in the decade of the 1880's. Railroad rate discrimination, decline of small-town handicrafts, and rise of city factories were blamed for the decline. This and other early articles set a pattern for an increasing flood of literature describing the "decline" of midwestern country towns.[10]

Because Midwesterners, and Americans as a whole for that matter, believe that progress demands phenomenal material growth, they have concluded that country towns are disappearing from the American scene. Midwestern country towns of less than five thousand population have declined from 18 per cent of the total midwestern population in 1903 to 16 per cent in 1932 and to 10 per cent in 1952.[11] Such figures carry conviction to anyone who believes that progressive communities permit no place to surpass them in rate of population growth.

Even the casual visitor to the Middle West is impressed by empty store buildings and an evident spirit of decay in many villages bordering major highways. What he sees, however, is a process as old as the town frontier itself. As previously indicated, Iowa, which achieved statehood in 1846, had 2,205 completely abandoned towns, villages, hamlets, and country post offices by 1930. Reasons for such a high mortality in less than one hundred years are legion. Loss of the county seat to a larger or more aggressive town, abandonment of military roads, exhaustion of coal veins, declining importance of grist- and sawmills, decline in river traffic, and shifting trade advantages with the coming of the railroad—all these accounted for numerous ghost towns in the very period when midwestern population as a whole and the total population living in country towns were increasing rapidly decade by decade. Town building on the Middle Border has always been a hazardous occupation, with some towns growing, some declining, and some stationary in population, no matter what the movement of population as a whole has been. In such circumstances, it is dangerous to generalize from individual cases.

For the Middle West as a whole, country towns above 100 in population have *grown* in total population during the first half of the twentieth century. Nevertheless, since their own rates of increase have declined below those of previous decades, and many cities continue to have phenomenal rates of growth—and hence of progress—country towns consider their own situation as little short of catastrophic. Every decade they watch the taking of the local census with anxiety. When the figures are announced, they rejoice if the town shows an increase, and they mourn if the town does not. In the 1930 census, Brookfield, Missouri, showed a gain of eighty-five people in the preceding ten years. With a population of 6,389, Brookfield was a fairly stable community, but the Chamber of Commerce "got busy and scared up" 150 more names. In 1940, the town census showed a loss of 287 people over the past ten years. Brookfield was obviously reaching a plateau of stability out of which it might plan for community welfare with greater certainty. But the town leaders were unhappy. Although they could not repeat their earlier feat of finding additional names, they did point out that the 1930 figures were wrong after all. In 1930 the Chamber of Commerce had counted the employees of the Atkinson

Paving Company who were in town temporarily on a construction job! [12] Unwillingness to recognize that they are maturing and that growth in numbers cannot go on forever has reduced country towns to such measures in order to prove that they have not ceased to "progress."

MEANS OF PROGRESS IN AN URBAN, INDUSTRIAL AGE

EXCEPT FOR THOSE TOWNS that have grown spectacularly because of twentieth-century revolutions in transportation, management, and technology, the modern age has been unkind to country towns, unkind, that is, because they have refused in most cases to change their basic philosophies and their basic ways of achieving their desires. As in an earlier day, they still look to industrialization, improved transportation, exploitation of local mineral resources, and trade-at-home, home-town loyalty to bring them happiness. They still believe that the immediately useful and the practical must come first and that they must surpass all others in real-estate prices and population.

Early in the twentieth century, for example, the Brookfield, Missouri, editor published an article headed "Stand Up For Brookfield," in which he urged citizens to establish an "Improvement Association" to foster industry. In his opinion, Brookfield needed to start a pump or gasoline engine factory or to encourage the Burlington railroad to open a car manufactory locally. The local newspaper and the Brookfield Commercial Club were more than ready to act in 1907 when the industrial commissioner of the C. B. and Q. Railroad, which ran through Brookfield, announced that the Brown Shoe Company of St. Louis, Missouri, might consider establishing a branch plant locally capable of employing five hundred workers. The local editor demanded immediate action to raise whatever subsidies might be necessary to bring the plant to Brookfield. Only a few months earlier he had printed a plea from the Mexico, Missouri, newspaper asking towns not to bid against one another for factories. Apparently, Moberly, Missouri, had found out how much Mexico had raised to obtain a branch of the Brown Shoe Company, and had then won the prize by offering ten thousand dollars more. The Brookfield editor demanded an all-out effort to avoid a similar calamity.

The crusade opened in high gear. No one knew how large a bonus would be necessary but the local editor felt that future returns would justify any current sacrifice. Such a plant would boom the price of property; vacant houses would be filled; all would find employment at good wages. The Commercial Club met daily to plan ways to raise the necessary subsidy. They bought land and divided it into lots for sale at $200 each. Buyers thus added to the bonus fund and provided themselves with real estate that was sure to boom in value when the new plant opened. Within two or three days after the campaign started, the Commercial Club sent a delegation to St. Louis to notify the shoe company that Brookfield was offering a free factory site and $40,000 in cash. Within a week, the local paper carried headlines, "Necessary Money Raised."

The shoe company prolonged local tension by examining competing sites. Chillicothe and Macon, Missouri, decided not to compete with Brookfield, a gesture which brought a "Thank you, Sisters" from the Brookfield editor and a promise to return the favor when they wanted something in the future. But Taylorville, Illinois, was still in the running.

Brookfield was not to be denied. She solicited congressmen and county officials for donations. When the venerable Dr. H. DeGraw, a local leader for many years, walked through the rain to address one of the mass meetings at Elks Hall, and then made a liberal contribution, others in the packed building doubled their pledges. Prospects of a factory employing five hundred people to make "fine ladies' shoes" aroused home-town loyalty to feverish pitch. Week by week the cash bonus and other gifts increased in size. When the contract was signed in June of 1907, the bonus had reached $60,000, and the city also agreed to furnish free a factory site, water, and sewage disposal. In return, the shoe company promised to erect a three-story brick building 45 by 250 feet and to start making shoes as soon as labor could be obtained.

A few days after the successful campaign ended the local paper mentioned the suicide of H. B. Clarkson, an eighty-year-old resident. As a younger man, Clarkson had been a butcher, grocer, and livestock dealer, and at one time had been financially independent. Age and financial difficulties had reduced him to the extremity of paying out his last money for board and then to weighting his pockets with stones and drowning himself in Yellow Creek. In that age of rugged individualism, many people were embarrassed if offered public assistance but bonuses to industry were another matter.

The Brookfield branch of the Brown Shoe Company failed to reach the heights predicted for it by zealots during the bonus-raising period. It has produced medium-priced and work shoes rather than fine quality products, mostly perhaps because unskilled labor in the Brookfield area could not handle quality production in the earlier years. In an early defense of the plant against its critics, the local editor granted that many employees received only a small weekly wage but pointed out that they were paid regularly. Without the factory, they would have had only intermittent work or none at all. In reality, many of them had come to Brookfield to work in the factory, and they probably cost the town more than they contributed in taxes from their meager incomes. In 1911, trouble of some sort developed between local workers and "foreigners" imported from St. Louis. During World War I the plant was so embarrassed with unfilled orders that Brookfield's city fathers staged a campaign to recruit workers. When the plant reduced production in the hard times following the War and again in the early 1930's, Brookfield had a surplus of poorly trained workers to add to her problems. Machine shops erected by the C. B. and Q. Railroad helped Brookfield far more over the years, and they had cost the city nothing in the way of a bonus.

Nonetheless, Brookfield has been inclined to defend its investment in the shoe plant. In 1926, the city entertained officers from the mother company in St. Louis and local employees in honor of the plant's nineteenth anniversary. The occasion was marked by goodwill on all sides. When the president of the organization finished his address to plant workers assembled at one of the local theatres, a girl employed by the Brookfield factory proudly remarked to her boy friend, "He ain't a bit stuck up, is he?" Moreover, Brookfield continued to offer subsidies to prospective factories, although none comparable to the shoe plant in size was obtained.[13]

Experience of town after town in the Middle West shows the danger of subsidizing industry indiscriminately. Many promoters prey on small-town enthusiasm, with cash bonuses the real object in mind. As early as 1898, when Gower, Missouri, was said to be seeking a flour mill and a canning factory, the Brookfield editor sourly remarked that Gower might have trouble finding a flour mill, but that promoters kept canning factories and creameries in stock to unload on gullible communities.[14]

Enthusiasm would remain within bounds if city fathers would only remember that subsidized industries as a whole have low capital investments and depend on unskilled, low-paid labor. Towns made up of such workers lack the necessary tax structure to maintain adequate services for their citizens. While untrained workers may gain in skill, industries employing the unskilled will want to move on when that occurs. After towns have subsidized an industry, and have thus become emotionally involved, they often oppose efforts of their own unskilled workers to raise wages by unionization. When danger of unionization threatened a subsidized industry in Warsaw, Illinois, the following announcement appeared in the local paper:

To Warsaw Citizens

For several years citizens have put forth much effort and considerable expense in their endeavor to bring an industry to Warsaw. After several months of negotiation and investigation, the Mirro Leather Goods Company of Chicago has been induced to move its plant to our community. . . .

Unfortunately agitation and intimidation is being attempted by paid organizers who care nothing for our community and who are schooled and trained in the art of creating unrest.

The citizens of Warsaw are capable of handling any situation that may arise without the aid of outside paid agitators, who do not have the best interests of Warsaw and its people at heart. The local Factory Committee will be in constant contact with the situation for the mutual benefit of the Mirro Leather Goods Company and its employees.

Let us stand behind the Mirro Leather Goods Company and give them a chance for our mutual success.

Warsaw Factory Committee.[15]

Such touching loyalty appeals to industries anxious to escape the higher wages demanded by unionized groups in cities.

Professional and literary people who grew up in small towns have recognized the folly of trying to buy industrialization. Ed Howe's famous *Story of a Country Town,* which appeared in 1882, suggested that factories would seek out those towns suited to industrialization. Howe also spoke of the disillusionment and frustration associated with poorly conceived efforts to attract factories:

There was a very general impression that manufactories were needed, and this was talked about so much, and so many inducements were offered, that the people became discouraged, believing that the average manufacturer had a wicked heart and a hollow head to thus wrong Twin Mounds . . . .

The people were always miserable by reason of predictions that, unless impossible amounts of money were given to certain enterprises, the town would be ruined, and although they always gave, no sooner was one fund exhausted than it became necessary to raise another. . . . I have thought that Twin Mounds would have been a much better town but for the fact that it was always expecting improbable disaster, but which never came, for the people were thus prevented from exercising their energy, if they had any.[16]

Other perhaps less realistic critics have emphasized the destruction of creative talent among small-town artisans when factories have taken over. In his *Memoirs* Sherwood Anderson spoke of the "Boss" in an Ohio bicycle factory who was reduced to routine activity when once he had been free to exercise some ingenuity in building carriages one by one:

"Here we paint these bicycles," he said. "Well, you see, we do not paint them. We dip them in these goddamn tanks filled with this stinking stuff. It is true that I do not myself dip them into the tanks. I stripe the damn things. You see how it is, there are thousands and thousands and thousands of them, all striped just alike.

. . . . . .

I tell you, boy, you get out of here as soon as you can. I am getting old and I have to do what I can." [17]

Believing as they did in the immediately useful and the practical, townsmen, of course, paid no attention to people foolish enough to write novels.

Country towns have found industrial opportunities in processing farm crops, and some have profited from diversified industries. Forty Wisconsin towns subsidized a total of 130 industrial plants between 1930 and 1945. An investigation of these subsidized industries in 1947 indicated that they had created a relatively satisfactory amount of new industrial employment and an increase in industrial payrolls. Nevertheless, subsidies were very large in comparison to results obtained in a number of towns, and perhaps improving economic conditions contributed to the favorable overall record. In Wisconsin, as elsewhere, success in subsidizing new industries has depended on the selection of stable firms suited economically to the local community, with financial aid limited to the amount necessary to overcome "economic immobilities and frictions which prevent the operation of basic economic forces." [18] When country towns depart from such principles they generally become involved in expensive and unprofitable undertakings.

Trade-at-home, home-town loyalty campaigns have grown in favor because of increased competition from mail-order houses and chain stores. Syndicates have thus found a market among country newspapers for long series of articles on the virtues of home-town loyalty. In the fall of 1935 the Clinton, Wisconsin, paper ran a series of twelve "editorials" on the virtues of "keeping money at home." These pictured Clinton merchants as the nucleus of a local network of community activities. Once the merchants disappeared, the cement binding the local community together would be gone. Many arguments were advanced to prove that it was cheaper to buy in Clinton stores. Rents and wages were said to be cheaper in smaller towns. Moreover, customers had to pay for the many services offered by city stores. In the end, they paid the salary of

the resplendent man with the brass buttons; of the fashionable information woman; of the floor walker with the wavy, blond pompadour; of the elevator starter with the natty uniform; of the demonstrator of the latest beauty preparations; of the attendant in nurse's uniform in the rest room; of the cash girls; of the force of plain clothes store detectives; of the credit department members with their extensive records that help them decide who shall not be permitted to run a bill and when they err to help them make good the loss.[19]

Such campaigns were never very effective. A comparison of prices and qualities of goods available locally and of those sold in cities and by mail-order houses convinced most customers that they suffered by slavish devotion to one town. When farmers of the Braham, Minnesota, community were asked about home-town loyalty in 1915, they answered: "Business is business; let the local storekeeper handle only those things that he can handle more cheaply than the mail order houses." Likewise, in Pickaway County, Ohio, in 1927: "Farmers bought their supplies wherever they could get them most conveniently or most cheaply. They did not hesitate in going to distant towns or sending to mail-order houses if they thought that it would pay them to do so. When they traded near home they did so because it did not pay financially to go elsewhere, and not because of any recognition of mutual interest with the local dealer." [20]

NEW MEANS OF PROGRESS

MANY OUTSIDE ORGANIZATIONS have been interested in helping country towns. National commissions, universities, and national foundations have all contributed ideas.[21] Since so many different groups have been involved, and the movement has been in existence for so many years, no one agency can be credited with having developed a program strictly on its own. Suggestions have overlapped throughout the whole movement and have waxed and waned in no strict chronological order.

One of the earliest organized movements was devoted to beautifying country towns. Long before Hamlin Garland spoke of "barbed-wire" villages, Susan Fenimore Cooper urged citizens to form village improvement societies and to foster picturesque architecture, vine-covered stone bridges, brick and flagstone sidewalks, "overhanging trees," and street names with some originality.

At times, suggestions have bordered on the ridiculous. Mrs. Cooper thought that the name "Main Street" was fitting and proper, but that "Broadway" was an affectation. Perhaps, however, it served better than some of the names which she proposed to substitute. She preferred names of birds, trees, and animals, such as pewee, woodpecker, sparrow, chickadee, moose, bear, and stag. Midwesterners quite properly have balked at the idea of meeting friends on the corner of Chickadee and Moose or Pewee and Bear streets.

Similarly, so far as the writer knows, no one has ever complimented the architecture of the midwestern Main Street. Highly utilitarian and nondescript, it has been both grim and drab. Nonetheless, it is better than the suggestion offered in *House Beautiful* for the improvement of Main

Street, Wheaton, Illinois. An architect, Jarvis Hunt, was stranded in the local railroad station for a few minutes in 1909, long enough for him to observe the graceless and unimaginative store buildings along the main business street. Hunt submitted plans for altering this to the magazine. He proposed to use brick, cement plaster and wooden cross beams to change the appearance of all store fronts to a new type of architecture which he described as "A little English, a touch of German, all planned by a Yankee—perhaps just 'Wheatonesque.'" Whatever called, the form failed to touch a single indigenous strand in midwestern history, as a glance at the before-and-after pictures will show, and thus failed to improve on the admittedly poor form which it was intended to replace.

Nevertheless, the Middle West had much to learn from eastern sources about village beautification. Local improvement associations, starting with one in Stockbridge, Massachusetts, well before the Civil War, made their own communities beauty conscious. By the 1880's and 1890's periodicals like the *Chautauquan* were offering sensible and inexpensive suggestions for village improvement.[22] And, of course, the charm of old New England villages challenged "barbed-wire" midwestern towns to seek a sense of beauty of their own.

The most popular and most effective programs depend on detailed surveys and detailed planning for more effective use of community resources. In 1917, for example, Bellville, Ohio, claimed credit for having made the first complete community survey, although other towns may have preceded it by as much as two or three years. Bellville felt sure that its revitalized church, school, and community program would make it a model American village.[23] In 1949, five small towns in central Illinois made a similar report on their joint activities during the preceding three years. In co-operation with newspaper editors and the University of Illinois they made detailed surveys of their needs and resources. Mass meetings gave citizens an opportunity to contribute toward the shaping of new programs. At such a meeting in Lexington, Illinois, a teen-ager impressed the group with her comment, "Speaking of *our children,* all you older people think it's wrong of us young ones to go off to Bloomington and Peoria to shows, dances and stuff. Well, what else are we supposed to do? What have *you* got to offer?" [24] Such challenges and much hard thought have stimulated the building of community houses, better farm-town relationships, and an educational curriculum adjusted to the needs of those intending to remain in the local community. Appreciation of relationships with the larger outside world, renewed hope, and energy have also resulted from the community survey movement.

Survey-planning programs have been particularly effective in making towns more conscious of the surrounding farm population on which their prosperity depends. After a survey and planning session in 1915 at Sauk City, Wisconsin, under the auspices of the state university, farmers and townsmen alike recognized the need for greater solidarity. Towns are learning that free picture shows, free band concerts, and give-away contests and drawings will not win farm loyalty. Trite as it seems, the secret of improved relations lies in doing things *with* farmers rather than *for* farmers.

For sixty-nine years, St. Johns, Michigan, wanted to become an industrial city. Large sums of money were raised to subsidize industry but the results were disappointing. Local businessmen gave $150,000 toward the building of a local truck plant in the booming times just preceding the end of World War I, only to see this industry move to Detroit as soon as hostilities ended. Young people left St. Johns; population dipped below 4,000; and two new highways threatened to draw off much of the remaining trade to other towns. At the height of the emergency, in 1924, the town turned to the staff of the state agricultural college for advice. They told St. Johns that its location in the heart of rich agricultural land would guarantee its survival, and that it might grow if it would build first-class schools, up-to-date churches, a modern hospital, efficient wholesale and retail stores, sympathetic banking institutions, and ample recreational facilities.

The city fathers worked out a long-range program to achieve those ends. They built a new community hospital. They constructed a new and modern high school with gymnasium and auditorium to serve a student body of which more than half lived on surrounding farms. They turned sixty acres of land, originally bought by the town for factory sites, into a park. They used brick from abandoned factory buildings to build pavilions, rest stations, and band shells. They dedicated the largest pavilion of all to the use of local 4-H clubs and encouraged country people to feel that the park belonged to them and to use its tennis courts and playing fields. In the eighteen years following inauguration of its new program, St. Johns achieved a new plateau of prosperity.[25] Though many country towns lack the necessary resources to provide all the services available in centers as large as St. Johns, numerous smaller places by conscious planning have increased their attractiveness markedly for the surrounding farm population.[26]

REALITIES

NO PROGRAM has been able to defeat basic forces which are shaping American life anew.[27] Farmers and townsmen alike now patronize a greater number and greater variety of trade centers than ever before. In spite of all the pleas for home-town loyalty and all the claims of economic solidarity within local communities, purchasing habits reveal a different story. Farmers always shopped in as many trade centers as possible, but improved transportation and good roads have given them still greater freedom of choice. Assuming that prices are identical in all trade centers within driving range of a farm home, the *type* of merchandise or service wanted at one particular time will determine the farmer's choice of town to visit.

Marketing specialists have long been accustomed to dividing merchandise into convenience goods and shopping goods. Groceries and work clothing are examples of convenience goods because they are frequently in demand, have little style appeal, and people take little time to compare grades and brands before purchasing. Customers like to buy such goods at convenient points in their own vicinity. On the other hand, shopping goods consist of more expensive items like women's fashionable attire, men's dress suits, and household furniture. Their cost encourages the purchaser to want to shop in various stores and even in various towns before making a selection. Moreover, since shopping goods are subject to the whims of fashion, buyers want them to be strictly in style at the moment, either through pride or a desire to extend their use by buying the newest and therefore the style least likely to be outmoded in the immediate future. From the merchant's point of view, this involves problems not connected with the sale of convenience goods. Since shopping goods come in a greater range of grades and styles than do convenience goods, stores have to carry a considerable stock if they expect to satisfy a customer's desire to compare grades and prices without visiting other shops or other towns.

Farmers now spend a greater portion of their income on shopping goods. Increasing rural standards of living have meant that money left over after buying food, work clothing, and shelter can go for durable goods for the home, such as refrigerators, washing machines, and television sets—which are also shopping goods—and for dress clothing. Farmers no longer shop as a family, with the father carrying the purse and making final decisions on what to buy. Farm women now purchase most of the family clothing and household furnishings, and farmers defer to their wives in matters of quality and style. Though farm families generally select the less expensive grades and the less radical styles of shopping goods, they are unable to escape the common problem posed for all consumers by the rapidly changing styles involved in twentieth-century merchandising. To the extent that they wish to keep abreast of styles, they must increase their purchases of shopping goods.

Differences in the nature of shopping and convenience goods, of consumer buying habits in regard to them, and of mercantile problems involved in selling the two account for much of what has happened to rural trade centers. Larger towns have considerable retail trade with their own inhabitants. When farm demand is added to this, such places find it profitable to offer shopping goods and professional services as well as convenience goods. Smaller towns have been driven more and more to concentrate on convenience goods. Obviously, then, size of town is important in modern-day trade competition, and the country hamlet finds itself at a disadvantage in many ways.[28]

Everywhere on the Middle Border shopping goods and professional services have tended to concentrate in larger towns. In 1927, Circleville, county seat of Pickaway County, Ohio, provided shopping goods and professional services to many people who formerly had patronized surrounding villages. Circleville, in turn, suffered growing competition from still larger and more distant places like Columbus, Ohio. In Iowa, between 1939 and 1948, village business establishments declined in numbers. In the very same period, the number of firms in Iowa county-seat towns tended to increase. Webster City, county seat of Hamilton County, Iowa, for instance, contained 42 per cent of all trade establishments within the county in 1900, 46 per cent in 1920, and 52 per cent in 1945.

Webster City furnishes convenience goods, shopping goods, and professional services to its own immediate trade area. In addition, it draws customers away from the smaller county villages because of its supply of shopping goods and professional services. In 1945, the 187 trade establishments in Webster City could furnish eighty-two different kinds of service. Clothing and dry good stores, specialty shops, printing and publishing plants, jewelry stores, photographers, hotels, restaurants, hospitals, and other agencies which never existed in smaller towns or which have withered there because of insufficient patronage operate quite successfully in Webster City. And again, Webster City shares the trade in shopping goods and professional services with still larger places like Des Moines and Waterloo, and even with neighboring county-seat towns.

Webster City and other county-seat towns have also profited from the growing centralization of governmental functions. Township government has virtually passed away. Federal agencies often use the county as a basic administrative unit and thus increase the frequency with which people visit county seats to transact legal and governmental business.[29]

Towns of less than 1,000 population have been more and more limited to the sale of convenience goods. Grocery stores and general stores in such places handle primarily groceries and work clothes. Although super-markets and chain grocery stores emphasize price appeal and variety of goods, groceries continue to be a major and sustaining item of merchandise in those villages whose businessmen have adopted improved methods. Other convenience goods like hardware, drugs, lumber, cement, feeds, and tractor-and-motorcar fuel often sell well in smaller places. Durable goods of various kinds, like farm implements and farm machinery, also do well in villages when they meet specifications approaching the nature of convenience goods. Retail dealers in farm machinery, for instance, generally act as sales agencies for manufacturers, and sale prices do not vary greatly from store to store. Moreover, farm machinery varies less than furniture and dress goods in styles, sizes and grades, and therefore requires a smaller stock of merchandise on the floor.

The impact of basic forces is most startlingly revealed in the history of individual villages. Irwin, Iowa, had 295 people in 1900. In terms of the standard of living at the time, Irwin came very close to being what sociologists call "a complete service center," because its 295 people could meet most farm demands. The village contained general mercantile stores, a millinery shop, hardware and implement dealers, drugstores, post office, furniture and undertaking shops, banks, grain and coal dealers, lumberyards, blacksmiths, barber shops, hotel, confectionaries, real-estate agencies, livery stable, cream station, a contractor and builder, physicians, veterinarians, attorneys, saloons, a newspaper, and a depot agent.

In 1940, Irwin had grown to 345 people. By then, however, the millinery shop, attorneys, livery stable, furniture store, and hotel had disappeared, and the number of doctors, grain dealers, blacksmiths, and general mercantile stores had declined. Only one bank remained. Goods and services available in Irwin were unspecialized, generally of low cost, and frequently in demand. Though people still bought groceries, overalls, and house dresses at the local general store, they went to the county seat, to Omaha, or to Council Bluffs for shopping goods. Irwin was more fortunate than many small towns. As the center of a rich farming area, it supported a bank and a picture show. A garage and five filling stations had taken over the functions formerly represented by the livery stable and hotel. Pool hall, beer joints, and hamburger stands were also relatively new. By 1940 many farmers drove to Irwin daily, and the majority came at least twice a week—in winter in the afternoon and in summer at night—where once they had made a single weekly shopping trip. Wednesday evening picture shows, Saturday night dances, and school functions drew people to the village. In this, Irwin typified the growing tendency for farm-village social relations to improve at the very time when economic relations were growing more tenuous. At the end of the forty years, Irwin remained a healthy community in spite of competition from larger places.[30]

Many small places have been harder hit. In some of them, a spirit of decay is evident to the visitor the moment he arrives. Empty store buildings—some with broken windows—vacant lots on Main Street, unpainted, warped and dying lumber in sagging business houses—such obvious signs of death can be found everywhere in the Middle West. In such places one or two grocery stores and a filling station still operate. Dad's soda grill offers greasy, quick orders of hamburger and beer. Matt and Marie's place across the street has pool, beer, cigarettes and candy. Elderly inhabitants live by rigid, moralistic creeds while others lounge in and out of the beer joints and make life miserable for themselves and others by deviltry growing out of sheer boredom and despair. In a few, a new note is appearing in gospel missions staffed by newer evangelistic groups which hold forth nightly in some abandoned store building while beer drinkers loaf across the way. Except for the quickness with which one can move from the limited circles of flickering light into complete darkness less than a block from Main Street, Skid Row indeed would seem to have come to many hamlets on the Middle Border.

WHAT LIES AHEAD?

THE TWENTIETH CENTURY continues to be a revolutionary age. Americans now living have seen two world wars, revolutions in technology, management, and transportation, and tremendous upheaval everywhere. In such times, one normally can expect nothing but change. No one knows what atomic energy will mean to American civilization, and even minor influences like the proposed consolidation of high school districts may seriously affect numerous midwestern towns. The road ahead keeps its own secrets.

As yet, most country towns retain their traditional philosophies of "progress." Town fathers continue to think in terms of population growth and rising real-estate prices. They stress the virtues of industrialization, of exploitation of local mineral resources, of improved transportation, and of trade-at-home, home-town loyalty as keys to "progress." In doing so, they are captives of their own past.

Cities, too, have worshipped material growth. By maintaining their phenomenal rates of increase beyond the golden age for village communities, they have bolstered hopes for similar "progress" elsewhere in America. As an integral part of American civilization, country towns, retaining these hopes, find it doubly difficult to change their patterns of thought. American civilization—urban and rural alike—dreads maturity.

Waves of national prosperity and of international calm strengthen America's urge for efficiency, for bigness, and for growth. In the 1920's, for instance, Thomas A. Edison, high priest among American prophets, stressed the values of social engineering. In his opinion, the future lay with the city because people naturally would prefer the greater efficiency of urban ways. Edison suggested that benevolent nature would adjust mankind to city inconveniences, even to blessing them with deafness to shield their nervous systems from the noise of urban traffic.[31] Such ideas appealed in the roaring twenties.

Nevertheless, our national point of view has shifted. Much of our modern economic thinking rests on the premise that human material wants are limited. The great depression undermined convictions that full employment and an ever-expanding economy were our normal and inevitable destiny. Perhaps we have reached the stage where we must invest in non-material things to achieve full use of our resources. Perhaps necessity will compel us to concentrate on those spiritual ends toward which American effort supposedly has been striving all along. Public works in time of economic stress may set an example.

Necessity may compel midwestern country towns to lead the way. Like the New England village of an earlier period, they seem to be passing from the growing pains of expansion to an ultimate stability. Farms and food and service centers for farmers must be maintained. Although additional declines may occur in farm population and in some rural towns, substantial losses seem unlikely. So, too, does growth. Mechanization and scientific methods now enable one farmer to feed several city people. Moreover, as national standards of living rise, relatively less of national income goes for food. Population growth itself perhaps will remain below the phenomenal increases recorded in earlier decades of American history, thus lessening the number of mouths to be fed. Since country towns have always depended on agriculture, they will probably share the farmer's declining but important part in American life.

In reshaping their thinking, small towns have much to learn from their past. Contrary to nostalgic memory they have lacked the stability, the changelessness, and the sense of continuity which people ascribe to them. They too have been buffeted by a revolutionary age. And yet, nostalgic memory is not wholly in error. Small-town residents have achieved a sense of stability through "belonging" to a community in its entirety. In the nineteenth century especially, people were born into the small town as they once were born into the church. They "belonged" by their very presence, and they had something larger than themselves to which to cling.

After declining temporarily in the early twentieth century, this urge to belong reasserted its appeal. As America's relations with the rest of the world expanded rapidly in World Wars I and II; as depression weakened the cult of self-reliance in the 1930's; and, most of all, as Americans became convinced that they really were a part of a world social order, the urge to belong to something a little less imposing and a little less impersonal was intensified. More and more, appreciation has arisen for primary groups, to which the individual can really belong, in which he can feel a sense of security, and in which he is not overwhelmed by the magnitude and the coldness of world citizenship. One writer in 1941 argued that Americans were more lonely and more unhappy than ever before. Radios, movies, and automobiles had not brought happiness. People found no real satisfaction in driving ten miles to sit among strangers in a movie audience. As a solution, the writer suggested neighborhood groups similar to those recently revived by the Ohio Farm Bureau. As one farmer participant said: "Our getting together and working together has made all of us realize that we have the best neighborhood in the country. I guess I'm kind of proud to belong." [32]

People cry out against over-centralization, even when it is in the interest of efficiency. Medical care is a case in point. Article after article in national periodicals stresses the decline in the number of doctors living and practicing directly in rural areas. Specialists thought for a time that hospitals were unnecessary within a fifty-mile radius of a large urban medical center, particularly if good roads and ambulance service were available. They thought of hospitals as workshops for doctors and as hotels for sick people needing bed service. In that opinion they ignored a wealth of evidence that many individuals refuse to patronize distant hospitals because in illness their need for families and friends becomes intensified. Community medical and health centers recognize that need. [33]

Bigness has many limitations. While county seats, like Webster City, have what sociologists call a "high service rating"—which enables them to gain trade at the expense of smaller towns—they almost invariably have a "low group identification." [34] Growing social unity between farm and village has served partially to check trade encroachments from larger places. In this social identification of town and country lies much of the strength of small-town Mid-America. Trade areas have become more stable in recent years, an indication that the automobile may have largely completed its work of reshaping trade and recreational patterns. Factual surveys also prove that individual initiative means much to town prosperity. One town may be in trouble while another of comparable size is fairly prosperous because its businessmen have adjusted to changing conditions. When country towns have held their own so well in a rapidly changing world, and have so many advantages in their favor, why should they distrust the future?

They need only to recognize that the time has come to stress ends rather than means. Like all Americans, villagers became accustomed to living in a feverish state of expansion, in which population, real-estate prices, and prosperity grew at fabulous rates. In the Middle West, as elsewhere, the first settlers stressed the immediately useful and the practical as necessary forerunners of arts, advanced learning, the humanities, literature, and "betterment." Some day, they said, their descendants could afford the better things. The Middle West has prospered greatly and its towns are approaching maturity. Unfortunately, they still spend relatively little of their time and their accumulated wealth on anything beyond the practical, which threatens to become an end in itself instead of a means to an end. The real problem of the country town thus demands only an honest answer to the Biblical question, "For what is a man profited, if he shall gain the whole world, and lose his own soul?"

APPENDIX I

DISTRIBUTION OF WOMEN IN PROFESSIONAL OCCUPATIONS IN ILLINOIS IN 1900

OCCUPATION	PER CENT OF TOTAL IN OCCUPATION	PER CENT LIVING IN CHICAGO	NUMBER OF WOMEN OUT OF TOTAL IN OCCUPATION IN STATE
Actors, etc.	20	over 80	737 out of 3,678
Architects, etc.	less than 3	over 80	70 out of 2,508
Artists and teachers of art	about 40	about 69	1,055 out of 2,713
Clergymen	about 4	about 56	292 out of 6,836
Dentists	about 4	about 60	117 out of 2,605
Journalists	about 9	about 60	240 out of 2,690
Lawyers	about 1	about 58	113 out of 9,030
Literary and scientific people	about 37	about 52	536 out of 1,437
Musicians and teachers of music	about 55	about 44	4,560 out of 8,199
Physicians and surgeons	about 9	about 65	820 out of 9,055
Teachers	about 74	about 30	23,100 out of 31,234

NOTE: Since small towns and villages are not reported separately in this distribution of occupations, it must be remembered that comparisons here and elsewhere given from census figures use only the very rough distribution as between Chicago and the rest of the state.

Table compiled from the 1900 census.

POPULATION GROWTH OF MIDWESTERN COUNTRY TOWNS

FOR EIGHT midwestern states as a whole between 1903 and 1952, the number of people living in towns of

99 or less	declined	from	345,376	to	254,067
100–499	increased	from	1,053,979	to	1,210,118
500–599	increased	from	728,921	to	857,357
1,000–1,999	increased	from	819,626	to	1,012,882
2,000–2,999	increased	from	486,665	to	648,302
3,000–3,999	increased	from	326,715	to	406,183
4,000–4,999	increased	from	280,411	to	366,558
5,000–9,999	increased	from	875,627	to	1,404,772
Over 10,000	increased	from	1,112,855	to	3,584,768

The figures on midwestern country town population were collected by Joseph LaPage under my supervision. The eight states were Michigan, Minnesota, Wisconsin, Ohio, Indiana, Illinois, Iowa, and Missouri. Since small towns within metropolitan areas have been shown to change in population at a different rate than those in non-metropolitan areas, we made a list of all counties included in "standard metropolitan districts" as defined by the 1950 census. These were eliminated from all consideration for the whole period examined. Then, we totalled the population for each of the size ranges as indicated in the table for the years 1903, 1932, and 1952 on the basis of the estimated or census-provided figures appearing in the Rand McNally Commercial Atlases for the three years specified. All towns were thus included. Our thanks are due to the Rand McNally Company for the loan of atlases for the earlier periods. Percentages of decline on the basis of total population came from dividing our totals for all towns below 5,000 by the total population of the eight states, obtained from the official census figures. The "over 10,000" category in the table involves cities of over 10,000 but below the 1950 census requirement to be included in a "standard metropolitan district." Population in towns below 3,000 has tended to decline between 1932 and 1952 but all except those below 100 in population are above the 1903 figure.

Variations within each size group among the eight states and effects of depressed economic conditions after 1929, all emphasize the point of *change* in the population history of country towns.

Confusion resulting from contradictory reports on the health of country towns led the Institute of Social and Religious Research to carry on an intensive investigation in the 1920's. Field workers collected data on 140 villages of between 250 and 2,500 population, sixty of which were in the Middle West. On the basis of these data, and supplementary estimates from the Rand McNally Atlases where census data were incomplete, the Institute pointed out that country towns generally were maintaining their population.[1] The Institute found that census data were inadequate to measure population trends in rural towns. The figure used to divide rural and urban population has been shifted virtually every census. Unincorporated communities are ignored by the census. Hence, the Institute used estimates from the Rand McNally Atlases as a basis for data apart from that for villages where field workers made actual counts of population. The Institute found that the Rand McNally Atlases were fairly close to the figures which the Institute collected directly in the field, and therefore was inclined to feel that population estimates in the Atlases were reasonably correct.

Edmund Brunner, who played a prominent part in the investigations carried on by the Institute, joined with J. H. Kolb in writing *Rural Social Trends*, which appeared in 1933 as a part of the famous Hoover series, "Recent Social Trends." In this book the authors confirmed the earlier conclusions of the Institute after examining all available data: "An examination of the evidence for the 8,900 villages of all types and also for the sample of agricultural villages, therefore gives no support to the theory that the American villages as a class are a disappearing or a declining population type. That is not to say that some villages with their communities do not decline or even disappear. But the evidence indicates that hundreds of villages grow and that thousands hold their own in the general growth of the total population."[2]

A statistical study by S. C. and Agnes Ratcliffe, "Village Population Changes," in *The American Journal of Sociology*, XXXVII (March, 1932), 760-767, reached much the same conclusion. While recognizing that the smaller towns were most subject to population losses, the article pointed out that incorporated places of less than 2,500 people had more than doubled in population since 1890. The following table summarizes the findings:

YEAR	NUMBER OF VILLAGES	POPULATION	PER CENT OF TOTAL POPULATION	AVERAGE SIZE
1930	13,443	9,183,453	7.5	683
1920	12,857	8,969,241	8.5	697
1910	11,832	8,169,149	8.9	690
1900	8,930	6,301,533	8.3	716
1890	6,490	4,757,974	7.6	733

See also the excellent article by Sidney Glazer, "The Rural Community in the Urban Age: The Changes in Michigan since 1900," *Agricultural History*, XXIII (April, 1949), 130-134. Among other things, Glazer shows that a population of at least 300 people seemingly guarantees the continuous identity of a village. Those larger have had a tendency to grow.

APPENDIX III

MOVEMENTS TO AID COUNTRY TOWNS

ORGANIZED movements to aid the small town owe much to President Theodore Roosevelt's appointment of a "Commission on Rural Life" in 1908 to consider means of improving rural living. Though Congress refused to publish its findings, they were made available to later groups interested in the same problem. However, Roosevelt dramatized and stimulated a going movement instead of pioneering new fields. By 1913, literature on the country life movement consisted of more than one hundred books, some two or three hundred pamphlets and reports, and many hundreds of significant magazine articles. Six writers were preparing books on the subject at the time. Some of the "old-timers" present at Baltimore in 1919, when the National Country Life Association was formed, concluded that the flood of advice presented in papers at that meeting differed little from suggestions made at conferences years before. They were sensitive to the need for greater emphasis on leadership and organization, the chief development after the 1920's.[3]

Already, state universities were moving in that direction. University extension divisions started local community institutes throughout the Middle West early in the twentieth century. The University of Wisconsin held two in 1912, seven the next year, and nine in 1914. Iowa held similar meetings in 1913, Indiana University Extension Division conducted nine institutes in 1915, and Minnesota and other states experimented with programs on a more limited scale. The early Wisconsin Institutes lasted for three days, with morning, afternoon and evening sessions. Subjects for discussion came from community leaders and from direct local surveys by members of the university extension division staff. The survey served four purposes. It determined conditions needing immediate attention and the relative importance of each. It discovered local groups and agencies willing to co-operate in the work. It provided information for the use of speakers on the institute program. And, most important, it was a basis for further community study. Community institutes were popular from the beginning, with attendance sometimes reaching several thousand.[4]

Colleges of Business Administration in midwestern universities also rapidly joined the movement to aid country towns. In the 1920's, for example, a Committee on Business Research of the College of Business Administration of the University of Nebraska published a series of business surveys which were distributed through the extension division. These ranged from detailed studies of operating expenses of retail stores in Nebraska for a single year to analyses of the influences of automobiles and good roads on retail trade centers. Bibliographies were made available at a nominal sum to those who wished to obtain further information on banking, insurance, and retailing. The Bureau of Business and Economic Research of the State University of Iowa is currently pursuing retail trade analyses for Iowa towns interested in improving their economy, an indication of the long continuing pattern of specific advice to local communities.[5]

University conferences which bring together specialists from various fields of leadership have also offered help. The University of Minnesota School of Business Administration held a conference on the problems of small cities and towns during the 1929 summer session. Speakers were drawn from the fields of marketing, journalism, agriculture, and forestry of the University of Minnesota and other midwestern campuses, from the business world, and from local, state, and national agencies of government. At the close of the meeting, a final report of the essential material from the various speeches was published for distribution to interested parties.[6]

The United States Department of Agriculture has contributed to the movement through various of its sub-agencies. At the moment, one of the most important programs involves studies of rural organization in representative counties all over the United States, a joint project of the Division of Farm Population and Rural Life, Bureau of Agricultural Economics, Department of Agriculture, and state agricultural college experiment stations. Reports growing out of these surveys reveal changing social, economic and cultural relationships between rural towns and the surrounding farm population.[7]

National Foundations have also contributed to the study and improvement of rural towns. The Humanities Division of the Rockefeller Foundation underwrote a three-year effort in Montana, directed by Baker Brownell, to help communities through self-study and planning. Richard W. Poston in turn was aided in his efforts to report the results of this program by a grant from the Newberry Library in Chicago.[8]

APPENDIX IV

SURVEYS OF MIDWESTERN
COUNTRY TOWNS

THE FOLLOWING are detailed surveys of midwestern communities, counties, or areas: J. H. Kolb, *Service Relations of Town and Country* (Dane County, Wisconsin), Research Bulletin No. 58, Agricultural Experiment Station, University of Wisconsin, Madison, 1923; Committee on Business Research of the College of

Business Administration, University of Nebraska, *The Influence of Automobiles and Good Roads on Retail Trade Centers,* Nebraska Studies in Business, No. 18, published by the Extension Division, Lincoln, 1926; H. Bruce Price and C. R. Hoffer, *Services of Rural Trade Centers in Distribution of Farm Supplies,* University of Minnesota Agricultural Experiment Station Bulletin No. 249, University Farm, St. Paul, 1928; Perry P. Denune, *The Social and Economic Relations of the Farmers with the Towns in Pickaway County, Ohio,* Ohio State University Bureau of Business Research cooperating with the United States Department of Agriculture, Columbus, 1927; John H. Kolb and Douglas G. Marshall, *Neighborhood-Community Relationships in Rural Society* (Dane County, Wisconsin), Agricultural Experiment Station of the University of Wisconsin, Research Bulletin No. 154, Madison, November, 1944; John H. Kolb and LeRoy J. Day, *Interdependence in Town and Country Relations* (Walworth County, Wisconsin, 1911-1913 to 1947-1948), University of Wisconsin Research Bulletin No. 172, Madison, December, 1950; Paul J. Jehlik and Ray E. Wakeley, *Rural Organization in Process. A Case Study of Hamilton County, Iowa,* Agricultural Experiment Station, Ames, Iowa, and Sociology Subsection, Economics and Sociology Section, Division of Farm Population and Rural Life, Bureau of Agricultural Economics, United States Department of Agriculture Cooperating, Research Bulletin No. 365, Ames, Iowa, September, 1949; *Retail Trade Area Analysis: 11 Southwest Iowa Towns,* prepared by Bureau of Business and Economic Research, State University of Iowa, July, 1950; and *Retail Trading Area Analysis: Osage,* prepared by Bureau of Business and Economic Research, State University of Iowa, for Osage Chamber of Commerce, Osage, Iowa, January, 1951.

APPENDIX V

SURVEYS OF RURAL SHOPPING HABITS

QUESTIONNAIRES circulated in Nebraska in the late 1920's showed that small stocks and limited varieties of goods were more important than price in encouraging people to trade outside their home town. The figures are indicated in the following table:

Why people shop out of town:

PEOPLE LIVING IN TOWNS OF	NUMBER OF ANSWERS	BETTER PRICES	GREATER VARIETY	GOODS NOT HANDLED AT HOME	MISCEL-LANEOUS
Under 500	72	25	61	49	4
500–1,000	31	8	26	21	1
1,000–5,000	27	8	23	9	3

The extent to which Nebraskans shopped at home for various items in 1925 is revealed in the following table in which items above the line constitute in order of frequency those goods which were still purchased locally by 60 per cent or more of the people who formerly had done so:

TOWNS OF 500 AND UNDER

1. Groceries
2. Meats
3. Drugs and medicines
4. Men's work clothes
5. Work shoes
6. Kitchen and small hardware
7. Bulky hardware
8. Fresh fruits

---

9. Furniture
10. Tires and auto accessories
11. Rugs and carpets
12. Dry goods
13. Jewelry and silverware
14. Pictures, novelties
15. Dress shoes
16. Sporting goods
17. Millinery
18. Women's ready-to-wear
19. Musical merchandise
20. Men's dress clothes

TOWNS OF 500 TO 1,000

1. Meats
2. Groceries
3. Drugs and medicines
4. Bulky hardware
5. Work shoes
6. Men's work clothes
7. Kitchen and small hardware
8. Fresh fruits
9. Tires and auto accessories

---

10. Furniture
11. Jewelry and silverware
12. Sporting goods
13. Dry goods
14. Rugs and carpets
15. Pictures, novelties
16. Dress shoes
17. Musical merchandise
18. Men's dress clothes
19. Millinery
20. Women's ready-to-wear

TOWNS OF 1,000 TO 5,000

1. Men's work clothes
2. Drugs and medicines
3. Groceries
4. Meats
5. Work shoes
6. Kitchen and small hardware
7. Bulky hardware
8. Fresh fruits
9. Tires and auto accessories
10. Rugs and carpets

11. Musical merchandise
12. Dress shoes
13. Sporting goods
14. Jewelry and silverware
15. Furniture
16. Pictures, novelties

17. Men's dress clothes
18. Dry goods
19. Millinery
20. Women's ready-to-wear [9]

Some surveys arrived at this same conclusion by studying the average size of town necessary to support a particular type of store. A Minnesota report in 1928, based on a study of the types and numbers of stores in 603 towns below 11,500 in population, resulted in the following table:

Minimum size of town in Minnesota for various types of stores:

TYPE	POPULATION OF TOWNS
Drugstores	500
Furniture stores	1,000
General stores	No lower limit
Grocery stores	1,000
Hardware stores	No lower limit
Jewelry stores	1,000
Ladies' ready-to-wear and dry goods stores	3,000
Men's clothing stores	1,000
Shoe stores	2,500
Variety stores	3,000 [10]

One needs to keep in mind that the surveys agree on trends rather than on percentages. In the preceding table, for instance, it would seem that Minnesota towns of 1,000 population in the 1920's were capable of supporting men's clothing stores. Such a finding is contrary to the generalization that shopping goods tend to concentrate in larger towns and also contrary to the findings of other surveys as to size of population necessary for men's clothing stores. Nevertheless, the Minnesota survey agrees with the conclusions of all other surveys that shopping goods have an affinity for larger towns.

Other illustrations of seeming contradictions are resolved when one reduces the findings to the status of trends. The volume in the Hoover series on "Recent Social Trends," which surveyed *Rural Social Trends* during the first three decades of the twentieth century, reported on the basis of detailed surveys of 140 villages that the average number of stores in each *increased* from 44.9 in 1910 to 49.3 in 1920 and to 56.2 in 1930. Midwestern villages listed in the survey made the smallest gain, the figures for that section being 31.6 in 1910, 32.9 in 1920 and 33 in 1930.[11] These figures do not contradict the conclusions of Brunner and Kolb and of all other studies that increased size of town was conducive to growth of function during the twentieth century. They do seem to indicate a different situation from that after 1930, in which the number of stores in smaller places declined. I seriously doubt, however, if the Brunner and Kolb figures show anything more for the earlier period than that the number of automobile accessory and eating places increased enough in smaller places to offset the loss of more basic businesses. Eating places were probably what have been called "hamburger joints," and the automobile accessory places probably had a very small capitalization.

NOTES

CHAPTER I.   EARLY DAYS ON THE MIDDLE BORDER

1. Theodore C. Blegen, "The Competition of the Northwestern States for Immigrants," *Wisconsin Magazine of History*, III (September, 1919), 3–29.

2. *Ibid.*

3. Paul W. Gates, *The Illinois Central Railroad and Its Colonization Work* (Cambridge, Massachusetts, 1934), 148. The preceding material relating to the Illinois Central Railroad is based on chapter 7 of this book.

4. James B. Hedges, "The Colonization Work of the Northern Pacific Railroad," *Mississippi Valley Historical Review*, XIII (December, 1926), 311–342.

5. Letter October 27, 1871, Edwin Clark Papers 1857–1904, Minnesota Historical Society, St. Paul.

6. Letters August 31 and September 5, 1883, Letter Book of Comstock and White beginning May 2, 1883; letter January 5, 1885, Letter Book of Northwest Land Company beginning October 1, 1884, Solomon G. Comstock Papers 1872–1932, Minnesota Historical Society, St. Paul.

7. Harold E. Briggs, "The Great Dakota Boom, 1879 to 1886," *North Dakota Historical Quarterly*, IV (January, 1930), 78–108.

8. *History of Kossuth and Humboldt Counties, Iowa* (Springfield, Illinois, 1884), 237–238; Benjamin F. Reed, *History of Kossuth County, Iowa* (Chicago, 1913), III, 95–96.

9. Algona, Iowa, *The Upper Des Moines*, June 6 and 13, and July 11, 1867. When a Midwesterner had "seen the elephant," he had been everywhere and seen everything.

10. *Ibid.*, December 28, 1876 and February 22, 1877.

11. See, for example, advertisement of southern Minnesota land in Chatfield, Minnesota, *Chatfield Democrat*, May 13, 1876; Canadian and Dakota lands in *Chatfield News-Democrat*, January 4 and 11, 1906; Wisconsin, Arkansas, and Texas lands in Hillsboro, Ohio, *The Hillsborough Gazette*, November 6, 1883 and January 3, 1884; Nebraska, Iowa, Dakota, and Kansas lands in Monroe, Wisconsin, *The Monroe Sentinel*, April 5 and May 3, 1876; southern Minnesota and Dakota lands in *ibid.*, March 5, 1884; Alabama and Wisconsin lands in *ibid.*, November 11 and 18, 1896; Iowa and Nebraska lands in Lacon, Illinois, *The Lacon Home Journal*, January 6, 1875; and Mis-

souri and Nebraska lands in Greencastle, Indiana, *Greencastle Banner,* various issues for 1874.

12. Algona, Iowa, *The Upper Des Moines,* May 27, 1896.

13. *Ibid.,* April 15, 1908.

14. Gallatin, Missouri, *North Missourian,* November 6, 1908 and January 15, 1909.

15. Hastings, Michigan, *The Hastings Banner,* January 12, 1910.

16. Mark Twain and Charles Dudley Warner, *The Gilded Age* (New York, 1915), 13.

17. *Ibid.,* 170 ff.

18. Letters cited in Paul H. Giddens, "Eastern Kansas in 1869–1870," *Kansas Historical Quarterly,* IX (November, 1940), 371–383.

19. Harold E. Briggs, "The Great Dakota Boom, 1879 to 1886," *North Dakota Historical Quarterly,* IV (January, 1930), 78–108.

20. James Bryce, *The American Commonwealth* (New York, 1891), II, 703.

21. *Ibid.,* II, 641.

22. Hamlin Garland, *A Son of the Middle Border* (New York, 1920), 44–45. My factual account of the Garland family is drawn from this and the following additional volumes in the Garland family autobiography: *A Daughter of the Middle Border* (New York, 1921); *Back-Trailers from the Middle Border* (New York, 1928); and *Afternoon Neighbors* (New York, 1934).

23. Garland, *A Son of the Middle Border,* 461.

24. Garland, *Back-Trailers from the Middle Border,* 300.

25. *Ibid.,* 304.

26. *Ibid.,* 368.

27. *Ibid.,* 375.

28. Garland, *Afternoon Neighbors,* 505.

29. *History of Kossuth and Humboldt Counties, Iowa,* 241. Unless otherwise indicated, the account of the early history of Algona and vicinity is based on this history and Reed's *History of Kossuth County, Iowa.*

30. Reed, *History of Kossuth County, Iowa,* 541.

31. Algona, Iowa, *The Upper Des Moines,* advertisements of Asa C. Call, August 8 and 15, 1867.

32. "A Review of Business Done During the Past Year," *ibid.,* January 4, 1877. See also Arthur Weimer, "Outline of the Economic History of Alma, Michigan Prior to 1900," *Michigan History Magazine,* XIX (Winter Number, 1935), 129–138, and "Economic History of Alma Since 1900" (Spring-Summer Number, 1935), 287–295, for a comparable example of aid to Alma by A. W. Wright.

33. C. Taylor, "Schools in Kossuth County," *The Upper Des Moines,* July 18, 1867.

34. Edward Eggleston, *The Circuit Rider: A Tale of the Heroic Age* (New York, 1897), 159.

35. Algona, Iowa, *The Upper Des Moines,* January 3, 10 and 31, 1867.

36. Reed, *History of Kossuth County, Iowa,* 487.

37. Algona, Iowa, *The Upper Des Moines,* August 22, 1886.

38. Franklin Curtiss-Wedge and others, *History of Fillmore County, Minnesota* (Chicago, 1912), I, 66–68.

39. Margaret Snyder, *The Chosen Valley: The Story of a Pioneer Town* (New York, 1948), 183. Unless otherwise indicated, I have followed Miss Snyder's book for facts and judgments concerning the career of Jason Easton. While her book treats the history of Chatfield as a whole, I have gone directly to the sources for my material wherever possible except in the case of Easton's general career.

40. Algona, Iowa, *The Upper Des Moines,* September 26, 1867.

41. Chatfield, Minnesota, *The Chatfield Democrat,* October 30, 1886.

42. Jacob Van Der Zee (translator), "An Eminent Foreigner's Visit to the Dutch Colonies of Iowa in 1873," *Iowa Journal of History and Politics,* XI (April, 1913), 221–247. The visitor was the Reverend Doctor M. Cohen Stuart.

43. Roy W. Swanson (translator and editor), "A Swedish Visitor of the Early 70's," *Minnesota History,* VIII (December, 1927), 386–421. The visitor was Hugo Nisbeth.

44. "Simeon Harding Diary 1863–72," Minnesota Historical Society, St. Paul.

45. Garland, *A Son of the Middle Border,* 99 and 204–205.

46. Herbert Quick, *One Man's Life* (Indianapolis, 1925), 72, 75.

47. Alexis de Tocqueville, *Democracy in America,* edited by Henry Steele Commager (New York, 1947), 292.

48. David C. Mott, "Abandoned Towns, Villages and Post Offices of Iowa," *Annals of Iowa,* XVII (October, 1930), 434–465; (January, 1931), 513–543; (April, 1931), 578–599; XVIII (July, 1931), 42–69; (January, 1932), 189–220.

CHAPTER II. THE HORSE IS KING

1. Item in Gallatin, Missouri, *North Missourian,* August 21, 1873.

2. Lacon, Illinois, *Illinois Gazette,* August 9, 1865.

3. *Ibid.,* June 14 and August 2, 1865; Chatfield, Minnesota, *Chatfield Democrat,* May 8, 1886; Lacon, Illinois, *Lacon Home Journal,* June 5, 1884.

4. Phil Stong, *Horses and Americans* (New York, 1939), 237–238.

5. M. B. Stratton, "The Old Home Town in the Late 70's," fourteen typed pages of reminiscences, Indiana State Library, Indianapolis. His town was Ridgeville, Indiana.

6. *The History of Daviess County Missouri* (Kansas City, 1882), 459–463.

7. Reported by Colon correspondent in Centreville, Michigan, *St. Joseph County Republican*, January 4, 1879.

8. Croswell, Michigan, *Sanilac Jeffersonian*, May 28, 1897.

9. Monroe, Wisconsin, *Monroe Sentinel*, March 15, 1876.

10. Reported by Chillicothe correspondent in Lacon, Illinois, *Home Journal*, December 22, 1875.

11. Algona, Iowa, *The Upper Des Moines*, January 25, 1877.

12. Statistics and description in *ibid.*, January 4, 1877. See also Gallatin, Missouri, *North Missourian*, June 26 and September 25, 1873.

13. See description of livery stable at Mason City, Iowa, in Algona, Iowa, *The Upper Des Moines*, August 2, 1877. Also, Chet Shafer, "The Old Livery Stable," *Saturday Evening Post*, CXCIX (February 5, 1927), 20–21, 158.

14. Louis Bromfield, *The Farm* (New York, 1933), 219–221.

15. In the issue of August 24, 1867, the editor of the Chatfield, Minnesota, *Chatfield Democrat* called attention to a "gentleman cow," as certain refined local citizens called it, running at large within the city limits and suggested that the animal should be confined.

16. Bromfield, *The Farm*, 219–221; William Allen White, *Autobiography* (New York, 1946), 40, 123–124; *Sherwood Anderson's Memoirs* (New York, 1942), 77–78.

17. Stratton, "The Old Home Town."

18. Cited in Gallatin, Missouri, *North Missourian*, June 19, 1873.

19. Day Book of Meek and Brothers 1873–1874, entries Saturday, September 20, 1873. Indiana State Library, Indianapolis.

20. *Illinois Gazette*, September 11 and October 11, 1865. See announcement of sale of business by J. L. Mohler and Company in *Lacon Home Journal*, June 5, 1884.

21. This description of the general store is based on newspaper accounts. Also, Will Rose, "The Passing of the Country Store," *Scribner's Magazine*, LXXX (October, 1926), 362–367; Phyllis Fenner, "Grandfather's Country Store," *American Mercury*, LXI (December, 1945), 672–677; Thomas H. Pederson's Reminiscences, Minnesota Historical Society, St. Paul.

22. Pederson's Reminiscences. Similarly, Peter Schuster's family, German immigrants of the 1840's, husbanded its resources to develop the family farm in Dane County, Wisconsin. In the early 1870's they disposed of eggs at from five to ten cents a dozen in trade. In turn, they took small amounts of coffee, unbleached muslin, a few hanks of thread, and yards of calico for dresses and aprons. In the late sixties they were able to replace their oxen with horses, and the mother acquired a sewing machine in 1871. Now she could buy unbleached

muslin by the bolt for sheets. Rose Schuster Taylor, "Peter Schuster, Dane County Farmer," *Wisconsin Magazine of History*, XXVIII (June, 1945), 277–289; (September, 1945), 431–454.

23. Thorstein Veblen, "The Country Town," *Freeman*, VII (July 11, 18, 1923), 417–420, 440–443.

24. Bryce, *American Commonwealth*, II (New York, 1891), 301.

25. *Tiffin Tribune*, June 19, 1869.

26. *Monroe Sentinel*, November 17, 1869.

27. Lacon, Illinois, *Illinois Gazette*, January 4, 1865.

28. Lacon, Illinois, thus faced retail competition from Peoria and Chicago; Monroe, Wisconsin, from Janesville, Milwaukee and Chicago; Greencastle, Indiana, from Terre Haute and Indianapolis; Algona, Iowa, from Cedar Falls and Chicago; Chatfield, Minnesota, from Winona and La Crosse; Centreville, Michigan, from Three Rivers and Kalamazoo; Tiffin, Ohio, from Toledc and Zanesville; and Gallatin, Missouri, from St. Joseph. See issues of Lacon, Illinois, *Illinois Gazette* for 1865 and of *Lacon Home Journal* for 1875; of Monroe, Wisconsin, *Monroe Sentinel* for 1869 and 1876; of Greencastle, Indiana, *Putnam Republican Banner* for 1867 and *Greencastle Banner* for 1874; of Algona, Iowa, *The Upper Des Moines* for 1867 and 1877; of Chatfield, Minnesota, *Chatfield Democrat* for 1867 and 1876; of Centreville, Michigan, *St. Joseph County Republican* for 1869 and 1879; of Tiffin, Ohio, *Tiffin Tribune* for 1868; and of Gallatin, Missouri, *North Missourian* for 1865 and 1873. Almost any issue for the years indicated will reveal advertising of the type specified.

29. *North Missourian*, September 7, 1865.

30. *Lacon Home Journal*, January 6, 1875. See issues of papers for years cited in footnote 28 for examples of advertising by competing small towns. Gallatin thus competed with Pattonsburg and Hamilton; Tiffin, Ohio, with Fostoria; Centreville, Michigan, with Burr Oak, Colon and Mendon; Chatfield, Minnesota, with Fillmore, Hamilton and Preston; and Lacon, Illinois, with Washburn, Chillicothe, Lawn Ridge and La Rose.

31. Garland, *A Son of the Middle Border* (New York, 1920), 91–93.

32. Fred Downer Diaries 1873–1891, Illinois Historical Society Library, Springfield. The same pattern of trading is revealed in the John E. Young Diaries 1843–1904, Illinois Historical Society Library. See also for the same pattern farther west, Powell Moore (editor), "A Hoosier in Kansas: The Diary of Hiram H. Young, 1886–1895," *Kansas Historical Quarterly*, XIV (May, 1946), 166–212; (August, 1946), 297–352; (November, 1946), 414–446; XV (February, 1947), 42–80; (May, 1947), 151–185.

33. Thomas S. Berry, *Western Prices Before 1861: A Study of the Cincinnati Market* (Cambridge, Massachusetts, 1943), 128–129.

34. See, for example, Wallace and Fenn advertisement in Lacon, Illinois, *Lacon Home Journal,* March 17, 1875; account of trip to eastern markets by J. B. Treat in Monroe, Wisconsin, *Monroe Sentinel,* August 23, 1876; and advertisement of Johnson's dry-goods wholesale house of Quincy, Illinois, in Brookfield, Missouri, *Brookfield Gazette,* with editorial comment to the effect that it offers advantages equal to those in Chicago and eastern wholesale centers, March 18, 1868. Also, Isaac F. Marcosson, "The Country Merchant Comes to Town," *World's Work,* VII (November, 1903), 4141–4144.

35. See, for example, complimentary book for written orders issued by Joseph A. Brigel and Company of Cincinnati, labelled "Account Book 1888–1889," in Account Books of William Schneider and George Naas of Saint Wendells, Posey County, Indiana, 1854–1892, Indiana State Library, Indianapolis.

36. Day Book 1873–1882, Wisconsin Historical Society, Madison.

37. Forrest Crissey, "The Modern Commercial Drummer," *Everybody's Magazine,* XXI (July, 1909), 22–31.

38. Numerous examples are available in newspapers cited in note 28.

39. See January-February and July-August issues of newspapers cited in note 28 for numerous examples.

40. *Monroe Sentinel,* January 6, 27, 1869.

41. Will Rose, "The Passing of the Country Store," *Scribner's Magazine,* LXXX (October, 1926), 362–367.

42. Daniel M. Storer Diary 1849–1905, Minnesota Historical Society, St. Paul. Thomas H. Pederson's Reminiscences reveal much the same picture of his life as storekeeper and clerk at Hendrum, Minnesota, and other villages.

43. Fred L. Holmes, *Side Roads Excursions into Wisconsin's Past* (Madison, 1949), describes an old-fashioned barbershop at Hustisford, Wisconsin. See also Ferdinand Reyher, *I Heard Them Sing* (Boston, 1946), a novel of small-town life with a barber as the central character. Also, notice in Chatfield, Minnesota, *Chatfield Democrat* on January 30, 1886, that barbershops would be closed on Sundays in the future; announcement of opening of combination billiard hall and barbershop in a basement in Washburn, Illinois, in Lacon, Illinois, *Illinois Gazette,* December 22, 1875.

44. *North Missourian,* June 14 and 22, and August 31, 1865.

45. Clyde Brion Davis, *Jeremy Bell* (New York, 1947), 43. See also account of old-time saloon in Holmes, *Side Roads Excursions.*

46. Holmes, *Side Roads Excursions.*

47. *Monroe Sentinel,* May 19, 1869.

48. See reference to Charley Peterson's establishment in Algona, Iowa, *The Upper Des Moines,* January 11, 1877.

49. *St. Joseph County Republican,* June 30, 1888.

50. Edgar Watson Howe, *Plain People* (New York, 1929), 73.

51. See descriptions of hotels in Mary H. Catherwood, *The Spirit of an Illinois Town* (Boston, 1897), 63; in Sherwood Anderson, *Winesburg, Ohio. A Group of Tales of Ohio Small-Town Life* (New York, 1919); and in Fred Oney Sweet, "An Iowa County Seat," *Iowa Journal of History and Politics,* XXXVIII (October, 1940), 339–408. Also, advertisement of Clinger House in Gallatin, Missouri, *North Missourian,* January 6, 1865, and references to the Mendon, Michigan, hotel by the correspondent from that town in the Centreville, Michigan, *St. Joseph County Republican,* February 12, 1870, and April 19, 1879.

52. Advertisements of J. H. Roberts and of Thomas Freeman in Chatfield, Minnesota, *Chatfield Democrat,* January 5, 1867.

53. Advertisement in *Illinois Gazette,* June 21, 1865.

54. *North Missourian,* February 13, 1873.

55. Advertisement of D. A. Shepherd in Brookfield, Missouri, *Brookfield Gazette,* March 5, 1885.

56. *Putnam Republican Banner,* January 10, 1867.

57. *St. Joseph County Republican,* April 10, 1869.

58. See advertisement of house painting, papering, and graining in Lacon, Illinois, *Illinois Gazette,* January 4, 1865.

59. Sherwood Anderson's father turned to such work in his later and less prosperous years. *Sherwood Anderson's Memoirs,* 26. One of Zona Gale's most effective novels, *Birth* (New York, 1924), centers on the life of a village paper hanger and laborer.

60. See advertisement of G. F. Dockstader in Centreville, Michigan, *St. Joseph County Republican,* April 10, 1869.

61. "Memoirs of William George Bruce," *Wisconsin Magazine of History,* XVII (September, 1933), 3–71. See especially pages 25–26.

62. Ruth Suckow, *The Bonney Family* (New York, 1933), 157.

63. See, for example, contracts awarded by the town council of Tiffin, Ohio, for repair of the local market house, *Tiffin Tribune,* June 10, 1869.

64. *North Missourian,* June 12, 1873. See also discussion of the Chatfield Woolen Mill in Chatfield, Minnesota, *Chatfield Democrat,* May 13, 1876.

65. *Putnam Republican Banner,* April 2, 1874.

66. Garland, *A Son of the Middle Border,* 191.

67. Purchase Book, March-June, 1888, in Joseph H. Osborn Papers 1855–1890, Wisconsin Historical Society, Madison.

68. "Was She a Boy?" story in Maurice Thompson, *Hoosier Mosaics* (New York, 1875).

69. Edward O. Moe and Carl C. Taylor, *Culture of a Contemporary*

Rural Community: Irwin, Iowa, U. S. Department of Agriculture, Bureau of Agricultural Economics, *Rural Life Studies* No. 5, December, 1942, p. 61.

CHAPTER III. ETHICS, FOLKLORE, AND MORALITY

1. Richard D. Mosier, *Making the American Mind: Social and Moral Ideas in the McGuffey Readers* (New York, 1947), 168. I am indebted to this study and to Harvey C. Minnich, *William Holmes McGuffey and His Readers* (New York, 1936) for biographical detail concerning McGuffey and for suggestive leads. The material cited in this study comes from the 1857 edition of McGuffey Readers, the titles of which follow: *McGuffey's New First Eclectic Reader: For Young Learners* (Cincinnati, 1857); *McGuffey's New Second Eclectic Reader: for Young Learners* (Cincinnati, 1857); *McGuffey's New Third Eclectic Reader: For Young Learners* (Cincinnati, 1857); *McGuffey's New Fourth Eclectic Reader: Instructive Lessons for the Young* (Cincinnati, 1857); *McGuffey's New Fifth Eclectic Reader: Selected and Original Exercises for Schools* (Cincinnati, 1857); and *McGuffey's New Sixth Eclectic Reader: Exercises in Rhetorical Reading, with Introductory Rules and Examples* (Cincinnati, 1857). In the absence of graded schools the titles lacked the same significance that they would bear today. For instance, many pupils got no further than the third reader. Material in the sixth reader was very advanced in nature and would be read today not earlier than junior high school.

2. *Third Reader,* 201–202.

3. See *Sixth Reader,* 206–211, 398–400, and *Third Reader,* 118–120.

4. Edgar W. Howe, *Plain People* (New York, 1929), 305.

5. Roger S. Galer, "Recollections of Busy Years," *Iowa Journal of History and Politics,* XLII (January, 1944), 3–72.

6. *Fifth Reader,* 280–282.

7. *Fourth Reader,* 82–83.

8. *Ibid.,* 180–183.

9. *Third Reader,* 139–142.

10. Galer, "Recollections of Busy Years."

11. *Fifth Reader,* 306–307.

12. *Sixth Reader,* 421–423.

13. *First Reader,* 26.

14. *Second Reader,* 81.

15. *Fifth Reader,* 150–153.

16. *Third Reader,* 21–22.

17. See, for example, article on value of schools in Algona, Iowa, *The Upper Des Moines,* March 7, 1867, and a similar article in Gallatin, Missouri, *North Missourian,* March 10, 1893.

18. Comment on removal of H. C. Callison from Jamesport to Gallatin, in Gallatin, Missouri, *North Missourian,* September 1, 1893.

19. For the state of Illinois as a whole in 1900, for instance, only 46.6 per cent of adults were church members. United States Bureau of the Census, *Religious Bodies, 1906* (Washington, 1910), I, 305–308.

20. Edward O. Moe and Carl C. Taylor, *Culture of a Contemporary Rural Community: Irwin, Iowa, Rural Life Studies* No. 5 (Washington, 1942), 61.

21. *Sixth Reader,* 167–168.

22. *Second Reader,* 151–152.

23. *Ibid.,* 101–103.

24. *Fifth Reader,* 51–52.

25. *Fourth Reader,* 172–174, 239–241.

26. *Fifth Reader,* 65–69.

27. *Second Reader,* 84–85.

28. See Chapter II and Chapter V.

29. Kate Milner Rabb, "A Hoosier Listening Post," feature section of Indianapolis *Star,* March 14 to May 24, 1935. During this period the column carried the Shroyer diary which may also be found in a folder of clippings from the column, Indiana State Library, Indianapolis.

30. August Derleth, *Still Small Voice: The Biography of Zona Gale* (New York, 1940), 27–28.

31. Don Marquis, *Sons of the Puritans* (New York, 1939), 30–33.

32. Louis Bromfield, *The Farm* (New York, 1935), 157–162.

33. Centreville, Michigan, *St. Joseph County Republican,* November 27, 1869.

34. Gallatin, Missouri, *North Missourian,* April 14, 1893.

35. See accounts in Monroe, Wisconsin, *Monroe Sentinel,* January 13, 27, February 3, March 3, April 7, May 5, and December 8, 29, 1869, for activities of the group and comments by the editor of the local paper.

36. Van Wyck Brooks, *The Ordeal of Mark Twain* (New York, 1920).

37. Bernard De Voto, *Mark Twain's America* (Boston, 1932).

38. *Sixth Reader,* 212.

39. *Ibid.,* 215–217.

40. *Fourth Reader,* 231–236.

41. *Ibid.,* 95–96.

42. See *Third Reader,* 233–236, 110–113, 144–148.

43. *Ibid.,* 215–217.

44. *Ibid.,* 335–336.

45. *Second Reader,* 99–101.

46. *Third Reader,* 80–81.

47. *Sixth Reader,* 217–218.

48. Centreville, Michigan, *St. Joseph County Republican*, January 15 and 22, 1870.

49. Chatfield, Minnesota, *Chatfield Democrat*, September 17, 1896.

50. Monroe, Wisconsin, *Monroe Sentinel*, June 3, 1896.

51. *Sixth Reader*, 246–250; *Second Reader*, 115–118.

52. *Third Reader*, 203–206.

53. *Sixth Reader*, 205–206.

54. See *Fourth Reader*, 111–112, 63–65; *First Reader*, 51.

55. *Fourth Reader*, 31–32.

56. Algona, Iowa, *The Upper Des Moines*, January 10 and February 28, 1867.

57. Centreville, Michigan, *St. Joseph County Republican*, November 27, 1869.

58. Gallatin, Missouri, *North Missourian*, May 26, 1893.

59. Brookfield, Missouri, *Brookfield Gazette*, September 2, 1899.

60. *Fifth Reader*, 88–90.

61. Entry, December 31, 1868, John E. Young Diaries, 1843–1904, Illinois Historical Society Library, Springfield.

62. Benjamin F. Reed, *History of Kossuth County, Iowa* (Chicago, 1913), II, Chapter 27, "Some Evidences of Progress."

63. Algona, Iowa, *The Upper Des Moines*, January 1, 1896.

64. *Fifth Reader*, 83–85, 155–160, 192–193.

65. *Ibid.*, 204–208.

66. Don Marquis, *Sons of the Puritans*.

67. Logan Esarey, *A History of Indiana from 1850 to 1920* (Bloomington, 1935), 589.

68. John E. Young Diaries 1843–1904, Illinois Historical Society Library.

69. William Allen White, *Autobiography* (New York, 1946), 52.

70. Centreville, Michigan, *St. Joseph County Republican*, April 10, 1869.

71. Fred L. Holmes, *Side Roads Excursions into Wisconsin's Past* (Madison, 1949), 59.

72. Greencastle, Indiana, *Star-Press*, March 3 and July 28, 1894.

73. Gallatin, Missouri, *North Missourian*, November 3, 1893.

74. See, for example, *Fifth Reader*, 169–170, and *Sixth Reader*, 76.

75. See Zona Gale, *Miss Lulu Bett* (New York, 1920) for an excellent treatment of the plight of the unmarried female, and Rose Wilder Lane, *Old Home Town* (New York, 1935), for a shrewd but sympathetic account of the life of the small-town woman.

76. Gallatin, Missouri, *North Missourian*, February 23, 1865.

77. Alexis de Tocqueville, *Democracy in America*, edited by Henry Steele Commager (New York, 1947), 393.

78. Gallatin, Missouri, *North Missourian*, August 26, 1898.

79. Ledger of the Attica (Indiana) Baptist Church 1870–1901, Indiana State Library, Indianapolis.

80. David Leigh Colvin, *Prohibition in the United States. A History of the Prohibition Party and of the Prohibition Movement* (New York, 1926), 116–119.

81. See, for example, such advertisements in Tiffin, Ohio, *Tiffin Tribune*, November 5, 1868; Cambridge, Ohio, *Cambridge Jeffersonian*, May 18, 1876; Centreville, Michigan, *St. Joseph County Republican*, April 10, 1869, January 4, 1879, and September 1, 1888; Croswell, Michigan, *Sanilac Jeffersonian*, May 28, 1897; Algona, Iowa, *The Upper Des Moines*, April 7, 1886; Chatfield, Minnesota, *Chatfield Democrat*, January 5, 1867, May 20, 1876; Monroe, Wisconsin, *Monroe Sentinel*, August 5, 1896, January 5, 1906; Greencastle, Indiana, *Putnam Republican Banner*, January 10, 1867; Greencastle, Indiana, *Greencastle Banner*, January 8, 1874; Lacon, Illinois, *Illinois Gazette*, January 4, 1865; Gallatin, Missouri, *North Missourian*, January 2, 1873, March 11, 1898.

82. Card contained in Fred Downer Diaries, 1873–1891, Illinois Historical Society Library, Springfield.

83. Herbert Quick, *One Man's Life* (Indianapolis, 1925), 150–151.

84. Reminiscences of Mrs. C. A. Davis of Carrollton, Missouri, who participated in medal contests, in personal possession of the author.

85. Minutes of Woman's Christian Temperance Union of Thorntown, Indiana 1885–1892, Indiana State Library, Indianapolis.

86. In 1900 the figures were: Michigan, 40.5%; Ohio, 42%; Iowa, 35.2%; Indiana, 37.4%; Wisconsin, 48.35%; and Missouri, 38.5%, for example. Figures compiled from U. S. Bureau of the Census, *Religious Bodies, 1906*, Part I (Washington, 1910), 308–372.

87. *Sherwood Anderson's Memoirs* (New York, 1942), 63–64.

88. William Allen White, *Autobiography*, 40, 46, 67. Quotations on pages 40 and 67.

89. Herbert Quick, *One Man's Life*, 147–150.

90. Monroe, Wisconsin, *Monroe Sentinel*, January 6, 1869. See also advertisement of "pessaric remedies" in Chatfield, Minnesota, *Chatfield Democrat*, January 5, 1867.

91. Hamlin Garland, *A Son of the Middle Border* (New York, 1920), 175–176.

92. Chatfield, Minnesota, *Chatfield Democrat*, August 19, 1876.

93. Report of Mendon correspondent in Centreville, Michigan, *St. Joseph County Republican*, December 13, 1879.

94. Centreville, Michigan, *St. Joseph County Republican*, September 10, 1897.

95. John E. Young Diaries, 1843–1904, entries October 24, 1894, March 27, 1896, March 2, 1898, and March 18, 1900.

96. Gallatin, Missouri, *North Missourian,* June 2, August 4, and December 29, 1893; March 11, 18, and July 29, 1898.

97. George B. Vold, "Crime in City and Country Areas," *The Annals of the American Academy of Political and Social Science,* CCXVII (September, 1941), 38–45.

98. As early as 1900 F. W. Blackmar of the University of Kansas published an article questioning the purity of the village green. Blackmar emphasized the weaknesses leading to "social degeneration" in smaller communities. Village police forces were inadequate to cope with local problems. Gangs of idle village boys loafed on street corners, shot craps and played cards, were guilty of profane language and indecent remarks on Main Street, and engaged in long, leisurely conversations on smutty subjects. Blackmar's article pioneered a sociological trend toward a more realistic appraisal of village morals. F. W. Blackmar, "Social Degeneration in Towns and Rural Districts," *Proceedings of the National Conference of Charities and Correction,* XXVII (1900), 115–124.

99. *Fifth Reader,* 271–274.

100. *Ibid.,* 182–184.

101. Minnich, *William Holmes McGuffey,* 179.

102. Dorothy Canfield Fisher, *The Squirrel-Cage* (New York, 1915).

103. Alexis de Tocqueville, *Democracy in America,* edited by Henry Steele Commager, 146, 316–317.

104. James Bryce, *The American Commonwealth* (New York, 1891), II, 618.

105. William Dean Howells, *A Boy's Town* (New York, 1890), 116.

106. *Mark Twain's Autobiography* (New York, 1924), I, 120.

107. Thomas Hart Benton, *An Artist in America* (New York, 1937), 10.

108. Edgar Lee Masters, *Across Spoon River: An Autobiography* (New York, 1936), 74–75.

109. See, for example, references to "Slab Town" in Chatfield, Minnesota, *Chatfield Democrat,* April 29 and May 6, 1876, and reports of invitation dance at Court House and of "Ole's" ticket dance in Algona, Iowa, *The Upper Des Moines,* January 1, 1896.

110. William Allen White, *Autobiography,* 64, 75. Quotation on page 75.

111. Edgar Watson Howe, *Plain People,* 76.

112. William Dean Howells, *A Boy's Town,* 197–204.

113. *Sixth Reader,* 444–447, 319–322, 401–403.

114. *Fifth Reader,* 275–277.

115. *Fourth Reader,* 113–114, 228–230, 241–242.

116. *Third Reader* (1853 edition), 69–70.

117. Ralph H. Gabriel, *The Course of American Democratic Thought: An Intellectual History Since 1815* (New York, 1940), 365.

CHAPTER IV. ". . . WHERE YOUR TREASURE IS . . ."

1. *Democracy in America*, Chapter 22.

2. *Fourth Reader*, 86–91.

3. *Culture of a Contemporary Rural Community: Irwin, Iowa*, 16.

4. Algona, Iowa, *The Upper Des Moines*, October 20 and November 3, 1886.

5. "House-Building in America," *Putnam's Monthly*, X (July, 1857), 107–111. See also article by John W. Root, "The City House in the West," *Scribner's Magazine*, VIII (October, 1890), 416–435, for comments on newness of the country as a factor in delaying architectural development.

6. Thomas Hart Benton, *An Artist in America* (New York, 1937), 12, 23–28.

7. Edgar Lee Masters, *Across Spoon River: An Autobiography* (New York, 1936), 99.

8. William Allen White, *Autobiography* (New York, 1946), 58–59.

9. See comments on intellectual companionship in cities in Hamlin Garland, *Back-Trailers from the Middle Border* (New York, 1928), 299–300; also comment on golden fraternity of intellectuals in Chicago, in Floyd Dell's autobiographical novel, *Moon-Calf* (New York, 1920), 362. Garland spoke repeatedly in his autobiographical volumes of the value of living in New York City in proximity to his publishers. Benton attended art school for a time in Chicago before moving on to Paris.

10. Benton, *An Artist in America*, 31–41.

11. This short story is contained in a collection by Willa Cather, *Youth and the Bright Medusa* (Boston, 1937). Quotation on p. 271.

12. James Bryce, *The American Commonwealth* (New York, 1891), II, 612.

13. Laurence E. Schmeckebier, *Art in Red Wing* (Minneapolis, 1946), 1.

14. Dora Aydelotte, *Full Harvest* (New York, 1939), 23–24, 200–201.

15. Katharine Anthony, "Frances Elizabeth Willard," *Dictionary of American Biography*, XX, 233–234.

16. Hillsboro, Ohio, *The Hillsborough Gazette*, January 3, 1884.

17. Tiffin, Ohio, *The Tiffin Tribune*, March 18 and 25, 1869.

18. August Derleth, *Still Small Voice: The Biography of Zona Gale* (New York, 1940), 118–120.

19. The term "professional service" was broken down in occupational terms but in many cases failed to provide satisfactory classifica-

tions. Thus, "literary and scientific" statistics of occupations often failed to distinguish between those in certain scientific lines and those engaged in creative writing. The figures given here are all from Department of Commerce and Labor, Bureau of the Census. Special Reports. *Occupations at the Twelfth Census* (Washington, 1904). For a table showing distribution of women in professional occupations in Illinois in 1900 see Appendix I.

20. Herbert Quick, *One Man's Life* (Indianapolis, 1925), 164.

21. Edgar Watson Howe, *Plain People* (New York, 1929), 106.

22. *Ibid.*, 106–107.

23. White, *Autobiography*, 44, 60; Benton, *Artist in America*, 10–11.

24. Garland, *A Son of the Middle Border* (New York, 1920), 213; *Sherwood Anderson's Memoirs* (New York, 1942), 58–59.

25. Vernon J. Brown, "Country Life in the Eighties," *Michigan History Magazine*, XVII (Spring Number, 1933), 175–191.

26. Garland, *A Son of the Middle Border*, Chapter 17.

27. Benton, *Artist in America*, 18–21.

28. Edgar Lee Masters, *Across Spoon River: An Autobiography.* Masters read a paper on Whitman at a meeting of the Fulton County Scientific Association and found an outlet for his verse in Quincy, Bushnell, and Chicago papers.

29. See, for example, account of exhibition at courthouse in Lacon, Illinois, in 1865 to raise money to improve the local school library, *Illinois Gazette*, December 13, 1865; of library association in Algona, Iowa, in *The Upper Des Moines*, January 4, 1877; of Centreville, Michigan subscription-library movement in *St. Joseph County Republican*, June 21, 1879. Also, Monroe, Wisconsin, *The Monroe Sentinel*, January 26 and March 8, 1876, and Chatfield, Minnesota, *Chatfield Democrat*, April 1, 1876.

30. Lacon, Illinois, *Illinois Gazette*, August 9, November 8, 15 and 29, 1865; Monroe, Wisconsin, *The Monroe Sentinel*, April 29, 1896. The phrase "Cheap John" was descriptive of anything lacking in quality.

31. Chatfield, Minnesota, *Chatfield Democrat*, December 25, 1886; "Fairview Items" in Cambridge, Ohio, *Cambridge Jeffersonian*, May 18, 1876; Monroe, Wisconsin, *Monroe Sentinel*, January 6, 1869; Algona, Iowa, *The Upper Des Moines*, January 18, 1877; Centreville, Michigan, *St. Joseph County Republican*, March 8, 1879; Greencastle, Indiana, *Star-Press*, advertisement, February 3, 1894.

32. Quotation in story "Trout's Luck," in Maurice Thompson, *Hoosier Mosaics* (New York, 1875).

33. Lacon, Illinois, *Illinois Gazette*, August 2, 1865; Centreville, Michigan, *St. Joseph County Republican*, March 10, 1888; Chatfield, Minnesota, *Chatfield Democrat*, July 6 and September 7, 1867.

34. Hillsboro, Ohio, *Hillsboro Gazette*, May 11, 1900.

35. Algona, Iowa, *The Upper Des Moines*, October 20 and December 22, 1886; Chatfield, Minnesota, *Chatfield Democrat*, June 12 and 26, and October 23, 1886; Gallatin, Missouri, *North Missourian*, September 8, 1893. See also announcement of Nashville singers as part of college lecture course, Greencastle, Indiana, *Greencastle Banner*, March 4, 1886, and entries January 16, 1878, concerning Louisiana jubilee singers at Rochelle, Illinois, and December 23, 1882, at Shabbona, Illinois, Fred Downer Diaries 1873–1891, Illinois Historical Society Library, Springfield.

36. Victor Holmes, *Salt of the Earth* (New York, 1941), Chapter 12, describes medicine shows.

37. Edgar Watson Howe, *Plain People*, 44–45.

38. Hamlin Garland, *A Son of the Middle Border*, 137.

39. Hamlin Garland, *The Rose of Dutcher's Coolly* (New York, 1895), 46.

40. Howe, *Plain People*, 44–48; William Dean Howells, *A Boy's Town* (New York, 1890), 100–101; Mark Twain, *The Adventures of Huckleberry Finn* (New York, 1931), 204–207. Twain and Howells were writing of the ante-bellum period and Howe of the 1860's, but all were recalling incidents of their own past.

41. Gallatin, Missouri, *North Missourian*, June 2, 1893.

42. Gil Robinson, *Old Wagon Show Days* (Cincinnati, 1925), 195–211.

43. Advertisement, Monroe, Wisconsin, *Monroe Sentinel*, July 12, 1876.

44. Howells, *A Boy's Town*, 93–109.

45. *Fourth Reader*, 192–195, 201–203.

46. Greencastle, Indiana, *Putnam Republican Banner*, May 30, 1867. I have changed the original quotation here slightly in the interest of clarity.

47. Lacon, Illinois, *Lacon Gazette*, August 2, 1865; comment of editor on "Occidental Circus," Chatfield, Minnesota, *Chatfield Democrat*, July 6, 1867.

48. See advertisement of Barnum's circus in Greencastle, Indiana, *Greencastle Banner*, March 4, 1886, boasting of a four million dollar capitalization and a payroll of seven thousand dollars a day. See discussion in Monroe, Wisconsin, *Journal-Gazette*, July 20, 1906, concerning why large circuses no longer wanted to appear in small towns. Also comment on dislike for having to rely on small circuses in Oney Fred Sweet, "An Iowa County Seat," *Iowa Journal of History and Politics*, XXXVIII (October, 1940), 339–408.

49. See description of local town hall in Tiffin, Ohio, *The Tiffin Tribune*, December 17, 1868.

50. Algona, Iowa, *The Upper Des Moines*, April 1, 1886, July 29 and November 4, 1896; Monroe, Wisconsin, *Monroe Sentinel*, May 6, 1896.

51. Willis F. Dunbar, "The Opera House as a Social Institution in Michigan," *Michigan History Magazine*, XXVII (October-December, 1943), 661–672. Dunbar speaks of an opera troupe which gave H. M. S. Pinafore, Mikado, Bohemian Girl, and Rigoletto on a circuit of opera houses including the towns of St. Johns, Ithaca, St. Louis, Alma, and Mt. Pleasant.

52. Lacon, Illinois, *Illinois Gazette*, March 8, 15, 29, 1865.

53. Louis Bromfield, *The Farm* (New York, 1935), 130–132.

54. Benjamin F. Reed, *History of Kossuth County Iowa* (Chicago, 1913), I, Chapter 26; Brookfield, Missouri, *Brookfield Gazette*, December 2, 1905; Calumet, Michigan, built its Opera House as a civic project, Dunbar, "The Opera House as a Social Institution"; Box of Papers relating to Adrian Union Hall Company, Governor Charles M. Croswell Papers 1825–1886, Burton Historical Collection, Detroit, papers dated November 25, 1863, January 28, 1866, and September 30, 1867. A financial report in 1869 to the stockholders of the Adrian, Michigan, opera house showed that it had grossed over $2,500 a year for the past three seasons but still had been unable to pay interest on indebtedness, and, of course, no dividends to contributors. The building was in use as much as a third of the time in some years but it apparently never yielded satisfactory net returns because of the heavy costs for upkeep, janitor service, heat, and the manager's salary. Papers dated January 25, 1869, report for year beginning October 1, 1870, and "Theatrical Date Book for the Year 1884–85."

55. Oney Fred Sweet, "An Iowa County Seat," *Iowa Journal of History and Politics*, XXXVIII (October, 1940), 339–408.

56. Bruce E. Mahan, "At the Opera House," *Palimpsest*, V (November, 1924), 408–423.

57. Box of Papers relating to Adrian Union Hall Company, contract dated April 3, 1883, and card of local rates in back of "Theatrical Date Book 1885–86."

58. *Ibid.*, Annual Report March 9 to October 2, 1869; Report for year beginning October 1, 1870; Theatrical Date Books, 1884–85 and 1885–86.

59. Dunbar, "The Opera House as a Social Institution."

60. Monroe, Wisconsin, *Monroe Sentinel*, July 12, 1876; Algona, Iowa, *The Upper Des Moines*, January 1, February 12, and March 11, 1896.

61. Independence, Iowa, *Cannon County Bulletin and Garden*, May 17, 1867, cited in Hubert H. Hoeltje, "Notes on the History of Lectur-

ing in Iowa, 1855–1885," *Iowa Journal of History and Politics,* XXV (January, 1927), 62–132.

62. Loula M. Wright, "Culture Through Lectures," *Iowa Journal of History and Politics,* XXXVIII (April, 1940), 115–163.

63. Hoeltje, "Notes on the History of Lecturing in Iowa, 1855–1885."

64. Chatfield, Minnesota, *Chatfield Democrat,* August 20, 1896.

65. Croswell, Michigan, *Sanilac Jeffersonian,* November 5, 1897. These dates do not represent the earliest appearance of movies and phonographs in small midwestern towns, although both appeared first in the decade of the 1890's.

CHAPTER V. ARTS AND PROFESSIONS

1. See, for example, discussion in Laurence Schmeckebier, *Art in Red Wing* (Minneapolis, 1946), and John W. Root, "The City House in the West," *Scribner's Magazine,* VIII (October, 1890), 416–435. This latter article was properly critical of current practices but its suggestions for improvement indicated the continued poverty of architectural ideas.

2. Edgar Watson Howe, *Plain People* (New York, 1929), 52; Chatfield, Minnesota, *Chatfield Democrat,* March 18, 1876 and January 2, 1886; Oney Fred Sweet, "An Iowa County Seat," *Iowa Journal of History and Politics,* XXXVIII (October, 1940), 339–408.

3. Algona, Iowa, *The Upper Des Moines,* September 10, 1867.

4. Benjamin F. Mackall Diary 1873–1874, Minnesota Historical Society, St. Paul.

5. See, for example, notice of Professor Nourse's singing school at Janesville in Monroe, Wisconsin, *Monroe Sentinel,* January 6, 1869; notice of organization of singing school at Chillicothe, Illinois, in Lacon, Illinois, *Lacon Home Journal,* October 27, 1875; and notice of Professor Thompson's vocal classes at Algona, Iowa, in Algona, Iowa, *The Upper Des Moines,* October 13, 1886. Grand River College which operated at Gallatin, Missouri, for a few years had orchestra, brass band, and mandolin and guitar clubs in 1898. Gallatin, Missouri, *North Missourian,* November 25, 1898.

6. Advertisement, April 19, 1865, in Lacon, Illinois, *Illinois Gazette;* Philip D. Jordan, *Ohio Comes of Age 1873–1900* (Columbus, Ohio, 1943), Chapter 11.

7. See, for example, Algona, Iowa, *The Upper Des Moines,* January 11, 18 and February 8, 1877, and October 13, 1886.

8. See announcement of Centreville people attending Friday night concert by Constantine band in Centreville, Michigan, *St. Joseph County Republican,* May 17, 1879; request of Tiffin, Ohio, editor for weekly concerts, *Tiffin Tribune,* July 30, 1869; similar request by

Chatfield, Minnesota, editor in *Chatfield Democrat*, April 15, 1876; announcement of completion of bandstand at Algona, Iowa, in *The Upper Des Moines*, June 28, 1877, and comment on Saturday night band concert in *ibid.*, October 13, 1886. Weekly concerts seem to have been given most often on Saturday nights before the turn of the century, after which a midweek evening became more popular.

9. William Allen White, *Autobiography* (New York, 1946), 19.

10. Chatfield, Minnesota, *Chatfield Democrat*, July 10, 1886. A benefit dance for the local German band was given at Monroe, Wisconsin, in 1869, *Monroe Sentinel*, December 8, 1869; the Young America Hose Company at Tiffin, Ohio, in 1869 gave a benefit dance for the local band, *Tiffin Tribune*, August 6, 1869; Washburn, Illinois, citizens pledged eighty dollars toward band instruments in 1875, Lacon, Illinois, *Lacon Home Journal*, January 6, 1875. The Tiffin, Ohio, band was paid eighty dollars for several performances at the fair given by the local fire company in 1869, *Tiffin Tribune*, January 21, 1869; the Peru, Illinois, band was paid $66.80, and nine dollars for dinner, for playing in the Memorial Day parade at Lacon, Illinois, in 1884, *Lacon Home Journal*, June 5, 1884; Rockville, Indiana, *Rockville Tribune*, November 15, 1905.

11. Chatfield, Minnesota, *Chatfield Democrat*, January 2, 1886.

12. See long obituary of Mrs. Emma J. Thompson, wife of a local banker, in Lacon, Illinois, *Lacon Home Journal*, August 7, 1884; obituary of R. J. Wheeler in Brookfield, Missouri, *Brookfield Gazette*, March 18, 1905.

13. Ruth Suckow, *The Folks* (Garden City, New York, 1934); Edwin T. Chase, "Forty Years of Main Street," *Iowa Journal of History and Politics*, XXXIV (July, 1936), 227–261; Allen Seager, *The Inheritance* (New York, 1948).

14. See comment on banker's son as good catch in Rose Wilder Lane, *Old Home Town* (New York, 1935), in Virginia Dale, *Honeyfogling Time* (New York, 1945), and in Dora Aydelotte, *Full Harvest* (New York, 1939). Also, account of banker's sins in Sterling North, *Night Outlasts the Whippoorwill* (New York, 1936), in Virginia Dale's novel, and in Seager's novel.

15. *The History of Daviess County Missouri* (Kansas City, 1882), 480–481.

16. Hamlin Garland, *A Son of the Middle Border* (New York, 1920), 359–360.

17. Thomas Hart Benton, *An Artist in America* (New York, 1937), 6–8.

18. Edgar Lee Masters, *Across Spoon River: An Autobiography* (New York, 1936), passim.

19. *The History of Daviess County Missouri*, 480–481; report by

Mendon correspondent in Centreville, Michigan, *St. Joseph County Republican*, February 12, 1870.

20. Hamlin Garland, *A Son of the Middle Border*, 143.

21. Arthur E. Hertzler, *The Horse and Buggy Doctor* (New York, 1938); J. B. Stevens, M.D., "The Pioneer Wisconsin Family Physician," *Wisconsin Magazine of History*, XVII (June, 1934), 377–392.

22. Daviess County, Missouri, formed a county medical society in 1877, for instance, and this soon expanded to include five counties, *The History of Daviess County Missouri*, 422–423; Lacon, Illinois, *Illinois Gazette*, January 4, 1865. Doctors at Algona, Iowa, in 1877 published a notice in the local paper that they would not treat delinquent patients who were able to pay their bills, *The Upper Des Moines*, January 25, 1877.

23. See a description of an old-time doctor in Victor Holmes, *Salt of the Earth* (New York, 1941), Chapter 14.

24. William Allen White, *Autobiography*, 32–33.

25. James Bryce, *The American Commonwealth* (New York, 1891), II, 293; Mrs. Dr. Boal, for instance, was credited with instituting the custom of New Year's calls in Lacon, Illinois, *Lacon Home Journal*, December 29, 1875; Dr. and Mrs. G. C. Smythe gave a reception at their residence to celebrate an anniversary of a local literary club in Greencastle, Indiana, *Greencastle Star-Press*, February 17, 1894. Doctors' wives seem to have taken a lead in creating social organizations which did not include the whole community within their membership.

26. Centreville, Michigan, *St. Joseph County Republican*, January 4, 1879. See advertisement of Dr. Owen's Electric Belt in Gallatin, Missouri, *North Missourian*, January 6 and April 7, 1893.

27. Advertisement of Dr. Gillespie, September 13, 1905, and of Dr. Younge, November 15, 1905, Rockville, Indiana, *Rockville Tribune*. Advertisement of Dr. Miner in Chatfield, Minnesota, *Chatfield Democrat*, May 20, 1876.

28. Of the five Mendon, Michigan, doctors in 1870, for example, one was a homeopath, three were allopaths, and one was an electric doctor. See Mendon correspondence in Centreville, Michigan, *St. Joseph County Republican*, February 12, 1870. See also letter by a reader on the superiority of homeopathic over allopathic treatment in Lacon, Illinois, *Illinois Gazette*, January 25, 1865.

29. Gallatin, Missouri, *North Missourian*, June 2, 1893.

30. Herbert W. Kuhm, "Pioneer Dentistry in Wisconsin," *Wisconsin Magazine of History*, XXVIII (December, 1944), 154–168; M. B. Stratton, "The Old Home Town in the Late 70's," Indiana State Library, Indianapolis.

31. Lacon, Illinois, *Illinois Gazette*, January 4, 1865; Chatfield, Minnesota, *Chatfield Democrat*, January 9, 1886.

32. *History of Kossuth and Humboldt Counties, Iowa* (Springfield, Illinois, 1884), 295; William Allen White, "The Passing of the Free Editor," *American Mercury*, VIII (May, 1926), 110–112.

33. Jesse F. Steiner, "The Rural Press," *American Journal of Sociology*, XXXIII (November, 1927), 412–423; Charles E. Rogers, "The Role of the Weekly Newspaper," *Annals of the American Academy of Political and Social Science*, CCXIX (January, 1942), 151–157.

34. *History of Kossuth and Humboldt Counties, Iowa* (Springfield, Illinois, 1884), 290–291.

35. See, respectively, Gallatin, Missouri, *North Missourian*, September 15, 1864; account of Algona paper in 1879 in *History of Kossuth and Humboldt Counties, Iowa*, 295; Lacon, Illinois, *Lacon Home Journal*, January 6, 1875; and Centreville, Michigan, *St. Joseph County Republican*, February 1, 1879.

36. Greencastle, Indiana, *Greencastle Banner*, February 11, April 8, May 6, and June 10, 1886.

37. Exchange item from Cameron, Missouri, *Observer* in Gallatin, Missouri, *North Missourian*, November 17, 1893.

38. Edgar Watson Howe, *Plain People*, 66–67.

39. For advertisements of these services see Gallatin, Missouri, *North Missourian*, January 6 and February 2, 1865, and January 6, 1893.

40. Edgar Watson Howe, *Plain People*, 267.

41. Lacon, Illinois, *Lacon Home Journal*, January 6, 1875; "What Country Papers Do," an item from the Marion *Chronicle* in Greencastle, Indiana, *Greencastle Banner*, February 5, 1874.

42. Lacon, Illinois, *Lacon Home Journal*, June 5, 1884.

43. *Ibid.*, January 6, 1875.

44. Gallatin, Missouri, *North Missourian*, November 24, 1864.

45. *Ibid.*, January 6, 1893.

46. Chatfield, Minnesota, *Chatfield Democrat*, May 6, 1876; Centreville, Michigan, *St. Joseph County Republican*, May 3, 1879.

47. Gallatin, Missouri, *North Missourian*, April 7, 1893.

48. Cambridge, Ohio, *The Cambridge Jeffersonian*, May 18, 1876.

49. Don Marquis, *Sons of the Puritans* (New York, 1939), 10–11.

50. James Bryce, *The American Commonwealth*, II, 293, 581–582.

51. Letter signed "Civis," Chatfield, Minnesota, *Chatfield Democrat*, December 9, 1876; Algona, Iowa, *The Upper Des Moines*, December 28, 1876.

52. Roger S. Galer, "Recollections of Busy Years," *Iowa Journal of History and Politics*, XLII (January, 1944), 3–72.

53. Ruth Suckow, daughter of a preacher, speaks of this in her novels. See *The Bonney Family* (New York, 1933); *New Hope* (New York, 1942).

54. *History of Green County, Wisconsin* (Springfield, Illinois, 1884), Chapter 26.

55. Report of Mendon correspondent in Centreville, Michigan, *St. Joseph County Republican*, February 12, 1870; *History of Daviess County Missouri*, 455.

56. Edgar W. Howe, *The Story of a Country Town* (New York, 1917), 37.

57. Henry O. Severance, "The Folk of Our Town," *Michigan History Magazine*, XII (January, 1928), 50–55.

58. Monroe, Wisconsin, *Monroe Sentinel*, January 27, 1869; Chatfield, Minnesota, *Chatfield Democrat*, March 18, 1876.

59. Unless otherwise indicated my account of ministers is based on the 59-volume diary of Charles E. Thayer, Presbyterian minister, in Charles E. Thayer Papers, Minnesota Historical Society; also, Charles A. Reichard Diary for 1897, Methodist minister, Burton Historical Collection, Detroit Public Library.

60. Edward Eggleston, *The Hoosier Schoolmaster: A Story of Backwoods Life in Indiana* (New York, 1892). This story first appeared in 1871.

61. *History of Kossuth and Humboldt Counties, Iowa,* Chapter 10.

62. Lacon, Illinois, *Illinois Gazette*, June 28, 1865.

63. Chatfield, Minnesota, *Chatfield Democrat*, January 29, 1876; Gallatin, Missouri, *North Missourian*, May 12, 1893.

64. Tiffin, Ohio, *The Tiffin Tribune*, April 8, 1869.

65. Lucius B. Swift Diary 1875–1888, Indiana State Library, Indianapolis.

66. Report of Washburn correspondent in Lacon, Illinois, *Lacon Home Journal*, April 21, 1875.

67. Gallatin, Missouri, *North Missourian*, August 21 and September 4, 1873.

68. Tiffin, Ohio, *The Tiffin Tribune*, June 10, 1869.

69. Monroe, Wisconsin, *The Monroe Sentinel*, January 6, 1869.

70. Etta May Lacey Crowder, "Pioneer Life in Palo Alto County," *Iowa Journal of History and Politics*, XLVI (April, 1948), 156–198.

71. William Allen White, *Autobiography*, 97.

CHAPTER VI.   BELONGING TO THE COMMUNITY

1. Zona Gale, *Friendship Village Love Stories* (New York, 1909), 6.

2. *Ibid.*, 24.

3. Gallatin, Missouri, *North Missourian*, August 5, 1898.

4. Sherwood Anderson, *Winesburg, Ohio. A Group of Tales of Ohio Small-Town Life* (New York, 1919), 237–238.

5. Hamlin Garland, *A Daughter of the Middle Border* (New York, 1921), 14–15.

6. Alexis de Tocqueville, *Democracy in America*, edited by Henry Steele Commager (New York, 1947), 323; James Bryce, *The American Commonwealth* (New York, 1891), II, 269, 281–282.

7. William Allen White, *Autobiography* (New York, 1946), 44; Rose Wilder Lane, *Old Home Town* (New York, 1935). The "Golden Text" consisted of a short scriptural passage pointing up the central idea of the lesson. All were supposed to memorize it.

8. Henry O. Severance, "The Folk of Our Town," *Michigan History Magazine*, XII (January, 1928), 51–65; Louis Bromfield, *The Farm* (New York, 1935), 145.

9. Don Marquis, *Sons of the Puritans* (New York, 1939), 41–42.

10. See, for example, a detailed analysis of the origins of such organizations in Newell L. Sims, *A Hoosier Village: A Sociological Study with Special Reference to Social Causation* (New York, 1912), 68.

11. Chatfield, Minnesota, *Chatfield Democrat*, February 26, 1876, April 1, 1876; Algona, Iowa, *The Upper Des Moines*, March 7 and 21, 1867; Lacon, Illinois, *Lacon Home Journal*, October 30, 1884.

12. Monroe, Wisconsin, *Monroe Sentinel*, April 21, 1869, June 30, 1869; Algona, Iowa, *The Upper Des Moines*, December 21, 1876, announcement of plans for New Year's; Earnest Elmo Calkins, *They Broke the Prairie: Being Some Account of the settlement of the Upper Mississippi Valley by religious and educational pioneers, told in terms of one city, Galesburg, and of one college, Knox* (New York, 1937), 25.

13. Chatfield, Minnesota, *Chatfield Democrat*, February 19, 1876.

14. A detailed study of an Indiana town has shown the extent of this pattern over a long period of years. For instance, the town had a baseball team in the years 1869–70, 1883–84, 1888–90, 1893, 1895, 1897–99, 1902–5 and 1910; a shooting club 1872–78, 1884, 1898–1902 and 1909–10; a roller skating rink 1883–85 and 1905–6; and a bicycle club 1883–85, 1888 and 1890–92. Newell L. Sims, *A Hoosier Village*, 114.

15. Dorothy W. Regur, "In the Bicycle Era," *Palimpsest*, XIV (October, 1933), 349–362; Greencastle, Indiana, *Putnam Republican Banner*, July 4 and August 7, 1867; Report of Coffeysburg correspondent in Gallatin, Missouri, *North Missourian*, September 1, 1893; Lacon, Illinois, *Lacon Home Journal*, January 1, 1885 and October 9, 1884; Monroe, Wisconsin, *Monroe Sentinel*, January 2, 9, 30, 1884.

16. William J. Peterson, "Legal Holidays in Iowa," *Iowa Journal of History and Politics*, XLIII (January, 1945), 3–68 and (April, 1945), 113–191.

17. Monroe, Wisconsin, *Monroe Sentinel*, January 2, 1884; Henry

O. Severance, "The Folk of Our Town," *Michigan History Magazine,* XII (January, 1928), 51–65; Leah Jackson Wolford, *The Play Party in Indiana* (Indianapolis, 1916), 105. See also article and bibliography by Bruce E. Mahan and Pauline Grahame, "Play-Party Games," *Palimpsest,* X (February, 1929), 33–90.

18. Advertisement, Monroe, Wisconsin, *Monroe Sentinel,* December 31, 1884; Lacon, Illinois, *Illinois Gazette,* January 6, 1875; *Lacon Home Journal,* December 27, 1894; Chatfield, Minnesota, *Chatfield Democrat,* January 5, 1867 and January 2, 1886.

19. See reports of correspondents from Coffeysburg and Jamesport in Gallatin, Missouri, *North Missourian,* January-February, 1893.

20. See discussion and advertisements of ugly Valentines, Algona, Iowa, *The Upper Des Moines,* February 17, 1886, and February 12, 1896, and Croswell, Michigan, *Sanilac Jeffersonian,* January 28, 1898. Also, balls and dinners, *ibid.,* February 11, 1898, and Lacon, Illinois, *Lacon Home Journal,* February 10, 1875. See also balls and dinners, Tiffin, Ohio, *Tiffin Tribune,* February 4, 1869; Chatfield, Minnesota, *Chatfield Democrat,* February 16, 1867, and Monroe, Wisconsin, *Monroe Sentinel,* February 27, 1884.

21. See reports of correspondents from Coffeysburg and Jamesport in Gallatin, Missouri, *North Missourian,* March-April, 1893.

22. Gallatin, Missouri, *North Missourian,* April 7, 1893. See also William Dean Howells, *A Boy's Town* (New York, 1890), 113, for a description of Easter eggs before the Civil War. Also, Ruth Suckow's novel *New Hope* (New York, 1942), for an excellent description of Easter services.

23. Tiffin, Ohio, *Tiffin Tribune,* April 1, 1869; Chatfield, Minnesota, *Chatfield Democrat,* April 24, 1886; Gallatin, Missouri, *North Missourian,* April 7, 1893.

24. William Dean Howells, *A Boy's Town,* 80–92, 133–147, 152, 161–170; Thomas Hart Benton, *An Artist in America* (New York, 1937), 9–10; William Allen White, *Autobiography,* 44; Herbert Hoover, "Boyhood in Iowa," *Palimpsest,* IX (July, 1928), 269–276.

25. Writers Program of the Iowa W. P. A., "Baseball! The Story of Iowa's Early Innings," *Annals of Iowa,* XXII (January, 1941), 625–654; Cecil O. Monroe, "The Rise of Baseball in Minnesota," *Minnesota History,* XIX (June, 1938), 162–181; Harold C. Evans, "Baseball in Kansas, 1867–1940," *Kansas Historical Quarterly,* IX (May, 1940), 175–192; baseball reports in Algona, Iowa, *The Upper Des Moines,* May 16 and 23, 1867, August 11 and 25, 1886; Report of Washburn correspondent in Lacon, Illinois, *Lacon Home Journal,* August 25, 1875; Croswell, Michigan, *Sanilac Jeffersonian,* June 11, 1897; Monroe, Wisconsin, *Monroe Sentinel,* July 7, 1869.

26. Monroe, Wisconsin, *Monroe Sentinel,* June 30, 1869; Chatfield,

Minnesota, *Chatfield Democrat,* June 16, 1886. See, for example, reports of the custom of holding a May-day picnic at Jamesport, Missouri, in Gallatin, Missouri, *North Missourian,* May 19, 1893.

27. Lacon, Illinois, *Lacon Home Journal,* June 5, 1884; William Allen White, *Autobiography,* 73.

28. Algona, Iowa, *The Upper Des Moines,* July 6, 1876 and July 7, 1886; for the Kin Hubbard quotation, see "Abe Martin on an Ole-Fashioned Fourth O' July," *American Magazine,* LXXIV (July, 1912), 356–358; Centreville, Michigan, *St. Joseph County Republican,* July 7, 1888 and June 11, 1897.

29. Monroe, Wisconsin, *Monroe Sentinel,* July 19, 1876 and August 5, 1896; Centreville, Michigan, *St. Joseph County Republican,* August 9, 1879; Algona, Iowa, *The Upper Des Moines,* August 18, 1886; John E. Young Diaries 1843–1904, entry August 11, 1899, Illinois Historical Society Library, Springfield.

30. "Pioneer Association of Van Buren County," *Annals of Iowa,* XI (January, 1873), 375–399; early volumes of the *Annals of Iowa* are full of material relating to Old Settlers' Associations. See also "The Michigan Pioneer and Historical Society," *Bulletin* Number 3, Michigan Historical Commission (Lansing, 1914), 12–62; "Proceedings of Old Settlers of Cass County, Indiana 1870–1888," scrapbook in Indiana State Library, Indianapolis; and *Proceedings of the Old Settlers' Meeting held at Catlin, Illinois, Saturday September Twenty-Sixth, 1885* (Danville, Illinois, 1886). See also account of founding of county society at Monroe, Wisconsin, *Monroe Sentinel,* January 13, 27 and February 3, 1869; and founding of county society at Tiffin, Ohio, *Tiffin Tribune,* February 4, 1869. See *Souvenir of the Old Settlers' Association of Marshall County,* published by the *Lacon Home Journal* (Illinois), 1888, Illinois Historical Society Library, Springfield; Benjamin F. Reed, *History of Kossuth County Iowa* (Chicago, 1913), I, Chapter 22 and pp. 470–471.

31. See lists in Algona, Iowa, *The Upper Des Moines,* July 4, 1867 and in Monroe, Wisconsin, *Monroe Sentinel,* July 21, 1869.

32. Quoted in Earle D. Ross, "The Evolution of the Agricultural Fair in the Northwest," *Iowa Journal of History and Politics,* XXIV (July, 1926), 445–481. Quotation on p. 473. Unless otherwise indicated, material relating to fairs has been taken from this study.

33. Algona, Iowa, *The Upper Des Moines,* August 9, 1877 and September 29, 1886; item from Preston paper in Chatfield, Minnesota, *Chatfield Democrat,* October 1, 1896; Maurice Thompson, *Hoosier Mosaics* (New York, 1875), story titled "Trout's Luck"; Oney Fred Sweet, "An Iowa County Seat," *Iowa Journal of History and Politics,* XXXVIII (October, 1940), 339–408.

34. Herbert Quick, *The Invisible Woman* (Indianapolis, 1924), 294.

35. See, for example, Monroe, Wisconsin, *Monroe Sentinel,* September 22, 1876, September 24 and November 26, 1884; Lacon, Illinois, *Lacon Home Journal,* September 11, October 9, 23, and November 27, 1884; Hillsboro, Ohio, *Hillsborough Gazette,* October 9, 1884; Chatfield, Minnesota, *Chatfield Gazette,* November 25, 1876; Centreville, Michigan, *St. Joseph County Republican,* June 30 and October 20, 1888; Algona, Iowa, *The Upper Des Moines,* November 4, 1896; John E. Young Diaries 1843–1904, entries October 13, 23, 30, November 3, 4, 1896. Illinois Historical Society Library, Springfield; Edwin T. Chase, "Forty Years on Main Street," *Iowa Journal of History and Politics,* XXXIV (July, 1936), 227–261.

36. Centreville, Michigan, *St. Joseph County Republican,* November 27, 1869, November 29, 1879 and September 24, 1897. See also the description of the Harvest Home festival by Ruth Suckow, *New Hope.* See also Algona, Iowa, *The Upper Des Moines,* April 18, 1867, November 21, 1867, January 9, 1868, August 2, 1877, June 23, 1886, and November 24, 1886; Monroe, Wisconsin, *Monroe Sentinel,* November 17, 1869 and August 2, 1876; Hillsboro, Ohio, *Hillsborough Gazette,* January 3 and December 4, 1884; Lacon, Illinois, *Illinois Gazette,* November 29, 1865 and *Lacon Home Journal,* November 24, 1875; Greencastle, Indiana, *Greencastle Banner,* November 25, 1886; and Tiffin, Ohio, *Tiffin Tribune,* November 19, 1868.

37. Centreville, Michigan, *St. Joseph County Republican,* January 4, 1879; report from Bainbridge in Greencastle, Indiana, *Greencastle Banner,* December 30, 1886; Chatfield, Minnesota, *Chatfield Democrat,* December 25, 1886; Lacon, Illinois, *Illinois Gazette,* December 20, 1865; and Algona, Iowa, *The Upper Des Moines,* December 29, 1886.

CHAPTER VII. EXIT THE HORSE

1. Thorstein Veblen, "The Country Town," *Freeman,* VII (July 11, 1923), 417–420; (July 18, 1923), 440–443.

2. Carl B. Cone, "The Iowa Firemen's Association," *The Iowa Journal of History and Politics,* XLII (January, 1944), 227–265.

3. See "Minutes of Meetings 1863–1879" of Lawrence Fire Engine Company No. 1 of Appleton, Wisconsin, for an account of social and other activities of a volunteer department, Wisconsin Historical Society, Madison. Also, Cone article in footnote 2.

4. Lacon, Illinois, *Illinois Gazette,* August 30, 1865.

5. August Derleth, *Village Year: A Sac Prairie Journal* (Sauk City, Wisconsin, 1948), 90–91; Edwin T. Chase, "Forty Years on Main Street," *The Iowa Journal of History and Politics,* XXXIV (July, 1936), 227–261. See editorial in Hillsboro, Ohio, *Hillsborough Gazette,* January 3, 1884.

6. John E. Young Diaries 1843–1904, Illinois Historical Society Library, entries November 3, 1892, August 25, 1896, December 7, 1897, and October 1, 1900; "Letter Book of Klindt, Geiger and Company 1903–1907 and of John A. Klindt 1907–8," Otto F. Geiger Papers 1854–1908, Wisconsin Historical Society, letters dated August 25 and December 23, 28, 1903, and January 12, 1904; J. R. Cravath, "The Replacement of Old Style Street Lamps and Lighting Fixtures," *The American City* (town and country edition), XIV (January, 1916), 58–63.

7. Edgar Lee Masters, *Across Spoon River: An Autobiography* (New York, 1936), 70.

8. Gerhard A. Gesell, *Minnesota Public Utility Rates. Gas-Electric-Water.* Bulletin No. 3, Current Problems, University of Minnesota (Minneapolis, 1914), 1.

9. Hillsboro, Illinois, *Montgomery News*, April 11, 1935 and April 19, 1945.

10. John E. Young Diaries 1843–1904, Illinois Historical Society, entry June 7, 1897. By 1915 such reports were everyday occurrences. See report of Dr. Foster's trip to Kansas City, Missouri, with a female patient in 1915, in Gallatin, Missouri, *North Missourian,* January 14, 1915.

11. Gallatin, Missouri, *North Missourian,* May 25, 1865.

12. Brookfield, Missouri, *Brookfield Gazette,* April 16, 1890. See also issue for May 6, 1871. This issue contained an advertisement of some twenty different brands of sewing machines in price ranges of twelve, thirty-eight and fifty dollars.

13. Monroe, Wisconsin, *The Monroe Sentinel,* May 31, 1876.

14. A fairly representative issue of the Algona, Iowa, paper in 1896 contained approximately 125 column inches of advertisements by local merchants in which brand names were mentioned and 150 column inches of local advertisements without mention of brands. By 1908 brand advertising by local merchants was in the lead, 170 column inches to 150. In 1918, the ratio was 650 to 465; in 1928, 640 to 380; and in 1948, 1,100 to 600. See Algona, Iowa, *The Upper Des Moines,* December 27, 1866, December 28, 1876, April 7, 1886, April 15, 1896, April 15, 1908, August 28, 1918, August 29, 1928, and April 20, 1948. Exact measurement of the extent of brand advertising is virtually impossible. Many stores which carried brands did not mention them in all advertisements, notably in clearance sales, for instance. The figures given are only rough approximations. Other country papers, however, present much the same pattern.

15. Brookfield, Missouri, *Brookfield Gazette,* April 1, 1868, January 6, 1893, October 28, 1914, February 6, and April 14, 1879; Greencastle, Indiana, *Greencastle Banner,* January 7, 1886; advertisement

of Palace Shoe Store, Gallatin, Missouri, *North Missourian,* October 20, 1893.

16. Brookfield, Missouri, *Brookfield Gazette,* September 8, 1887, advertisement of Dean and Chapman; Algona, Iowa, *The Upper Des Moines,* January 1, 1896; Rockville, Indiana, *Rockville Republican,* November 4, 11, 1937.

17. For examples of advertising see Hillsboro, Illinois, *Montgomery News,* February 10 and March 17, 1905; and Brookfield, Missouri, *Brookfield Gazette,* April 11, May 9, and June 20, 1903, and September 16, 1905.

18. See series of advertisements by W. E. Cross and Company of Chatfield in Chatfield, Minnesota, *Chatfield Democrat,* January 3, 10, 16, 23, 30, February 6, May 21, 29, June 4, 18, 1896; Algona, Iowa, *Upper Des Moines-Republican,* August 19, 1908; Brookfield, Missouri, *Brookfield Gazette,* April 27, 1907; advertisement of H. Tooey Mercantile Company, Brookfield, Missouri, *Brookfield Gazette,* May 2, 1908.

19. Algona, Iowa, *The Upper Des Moines,* January 1, 1896; Brookfield, Missouri, *Brookfield Gazette,* October 2, 1891. For a series of Chase and Sanborn advertisements see announcements of the Chapman grocery store in Brookfield, Missouri, *Brookfield Gazette,* September 7, 14, 1895, May 2, 1904, and April 25, 1908. For Lion coffee advertisements see the same paper for October 7, 1899, January 27, February 10, 24, March 10, 24, 1900, and August 12, 1905.

20. For examples see Brookfield, Missouri, *Brookfield Gazette,* February 1, 1896; Hastings, Michigan, *The Hastings Banner,* September 14, 1910; Ashville, Ohio, *The Pickaway County News,* February 4, 1916 and September 30, 1926.

21. "The New Railroad—Shall We Have It?" Tiffin, Ohio, *The Tiffin Tribune,* December 3, 1868. In subsequent issues the editor maintained a question and answer column in which he explained the virtues of the proposed line to doubtful citizens.

22. Train schedule and Peoria advertisements in Lacon, Illinois, *Lacon Home Journal,* May 10, 1894; Greencastle, Indiana, *Greencastle Banner,* May 20, 1886; advertisement of Etter's O. P. C. H. Store, Gallatin, Missouri, *North Missourian,* January 7, 1886.

23. Advertisements in Gallatin, Missouri, *North Missourian,* September 15 and 22, 1893.

24. Charles M. Harger, "The Country Store," *The Atlantic Monthly,* LXXXXV (January, 1905), 91–98.

25. J. H. Brown, "How We Got the R. F. D.," *Michigan History Magazine,* VI (1922), 442–459, discusses the forces behind establishment of rural free delivery; letter of George P. Engelhard, "The Parcels Post," *The Outlook,* LXXXXVI (December, 3, 1910), 794; "A

Professor in a State University," "The Parcels Post and Mail Order Business," *The Outlook*, LXXXXVI (December 31, 1910), 1033. In 1900 forty Brookfield, Missouri, retailers attended a state convention called to oppose parcel post, Brookfield, Missouri, *Brookfield Gazette*, July 21, 1900.

26. Fred B. Hiatt, "Development of Interurbans in Indiana," *The Indiana Magazine of History*, V (September, 1909), 122–130; Harry Osborne, "History of the Electric Railroads in Indiana—Brief History of Transportation in Marion County, Indiana," Federal Writers Project, 1940, Typed Copy, Indiana State Library, Indianapolis; E. Bryant Phillips, "Interurban Projects in Nebraska," *Nebraska History*, XXX (June, 1949), 163–182 and "Interurban Projects in and Around Omaha," *Nebraska History*, XXX (September, 1949), 257–285.

27. Hillsboro, Illinois, *Montgomery News*, January 27 and April 14, 1905.

28. Brookfield, Missouri, *Brookfield Gazette*, February 14, 1903, September 24, 1904, July 1, 1905, June 2, 1906, July 6, 1907, July 3, 1909, August 28, 1909, February 18, 1911, July 26, 1913, November 25, 1916, and December 4, 1925.

29. Hiatt article cited in footnote 26.

30. H. T. P., "The Return of the Horse," *The Bookman*, XIII (July, 1901), 425–427.

31. Henry W. Fischer, "The Horseless Age," *Munsey's Magazine*, XIII (May, 1895), 143–146.

32. R. D. McKenzie, *The Metropolitan Community* (New York, 1933), 140–141; 311.

33. Edward O. Moe and Carl C. Taylor, *Culture of a Contemporary Rural Community: Irwin, Iowa*, United States Department of Agriculture, Bureau of Agricultural Economics, *Rural Life Studies* No. 5, December, 1942, pp. 78, 86.

34. Rockville, Indiana, *The Rockville Republican*, March 18, 1926; McKenzie, *The Metropolitan Community*, 90, 92–93.

35. Clinton, Wisconsin, *Rock County News*, May 25, September 14 and October 12, 1916; Clinton, Wisconsin, *Times Observer*, February 20 and November 10, 1936.

36. By a Member of the Staff, "Do You Buy From a 'Chain'?" *World's Work*, XLIX (December, 1924), 212–218.

37. "Two New Chains," *Business Week*, October 2, 1948, 50–51.

38. John T. Flynn, "Chain Stores! Menace or Promise?" *The New Republic*, LXVI (April 22, 1931), 270–273.

39. Brookfield, Missouri, *Brookfield Gazette*, January 7 and August 2, 1926.

40. *Ibid.*, January 2, 1930.

CHAPTER VIII.   ROOTLESS AS EVER

1. Gallatin, Missouri, *North Missourian*, July 23, 1925.
2. *Ibid.*, June 6, 1935.
3. Edmund Brunner and J. H. Kolb, *Rural Social Trends* (New York, 1933), Chapter 5; R. D. McKenzie, *The Metropolitan Community* (New York, 1933), 120.
4. Brunner and Kolb, 23–24; C. Luther Fry, *American Villagers* (New York, 1926), 66–67, 94–95, 97–100, 113, 115, 118; William F. Ogburn, *Social Characteristics of Cities: A Basis for New Interpretation of the Role of the City in American Life* (Chicago, 1937), 1–4, 16. As a matter of fact, insofar as all treat the same topics, Brunner and Kolb, McKenzie, Fry, and Ogburn all agree fundamentally on differences between village and city and also on a tendency for the two to become more alike.
5. Hastings, Michigan, *The Hastings Banner*, November 2 and 24, 1910.
6. Newell L. Sims, *A Hoosier Village. A Sociological Study with Special Reference to Social Causation* (New York, 1912), 126–127.
7. Silvester Schiele (first president of the Chicago Rotary Club), "When Rotary Was a Stripling,"—as told to Karl K. Krueger, *Rotarian*, LII (May, 1938), 40–43; Fred H. Clausen, "Small Towns Need Rotary," *Rotarian*, XLV (November, 1934), 28–29.
8. Mary I. Wood, *The History of the General Federation of Women's Clubs for the First Twenty-One Years of Its Organization* (New York, 1912), 48. State federations of women's clubs appeared in Iowa in 1893, in Illinois, Ohio, and Nebraska in 1894, in Minnesota, Michigan, Kansas and Missouri in 1895, and in Wisconsin in 1896. Only Indiana of the Midwest group of states was fairly late in forming a state federation by waiting until 1906, but this did not materially affect the increase in Indiana clubs.
9. *Year Book 1919–1920* of Missouri Federation of Women's Clubs, published by the Federation, 1920. The figures cited are based on my analysis of club listings by towns and on the brief statements of purpose submitted by each club reporting.
10. August B. Hollingshead, *Elmtown's Youth: The Impact of Social Classes on Adolescents* (New York, 1949), 90–91, 100; E. Brunner, G. S. Hughes, and M. Patten, *American Agricultural Villages* (New York, 1927), Chapter 7.
11. Brunner, Hughes and Patten, *American Agricultural Villages*, Chapter 7.
12. Brunner and Kolb, *Rural Social Trends*, Chapter 9.
13. *Ibid.*

14. Undated item from Maysville, Missouri, *Pilot* in Gallatin, Missouri, *North Missourian*, August 12, 1915.

15. Edward A. Ross, "The Middle West—Being Studies of Its People in Comparison with Those of the East," *Century Magazine*, LXXXIII (February, 1912), 609–615; (March, 1912), 686–692; (April, 1912), 874–880; (May, 1912), 142–148; David Graham Hutton, *Midwest at Noon* (Chicago, 1946), 195.

16. Rockville, Indiana, *The Rockville Republican*, June 3, 1926; Ashville, Ohio, *The Pickaway County News*, November 17, 1916.

17. Chatfield, Minnesota, *Chatfield News-Democrat*, March 30, 1916; Brookfield, Missouri, *Brookfield Gazette*, August 5, 1926; Paul H. Harris, "Rotary is Thirty Years Old," *Rotarian*, XLVI (February, 1935), 5.

18. Gallatin, Missouri, *North Missourian*, July 22, 1915.

19. Edwin T. Chase, "Forty Years on Main Street," *Iowa Journal of History and Politics*, XXXIV (July, 1936), 227–261; Gallatin, Missouri, *North Missourian*, July 1, 1915.

20. Phil Stong, *State Fair* (New York, 1932); Minnie Hite Moody, *Old Home Week* (New York, 1938).

21. Roland S. Vaile, ed., *The Small City and Town: A Conference on Community Relations* (Minneapolis, 1930), 19, relying apparently on the studies conducted by Albert S. Visher of Indiana University.

22. William Miller, "American Historians and the Business Elite," *Journal of Economic History*, IX (November, 1949), 184–208.

23. George B. Vold, "Crime in City and Country Areas," *Annals of the American Academy of Political and Social Science*, CCXVII (September, 1941), 38–45.

24. Edward A. Ross article cited in footnote 15.

25. William S. and Lillian Gray, *Fun With Dick and Jane* (Chicago, 1946–47).

26. Hollingshead, *Elmtown's Youth*, 88, 94, 98; Edward A. Moe and Carl C. Taylor, *Culture of a Contemporary Rural Community: Irwin, Iowa, Rural Life Studies* No. 5 (Washington, December, 1942), 61; James West (Carol Withers), *Plainville, U. S. A.* (New York, 1945), 142.

27. "The Preacher and Rose City," *Time*, XLIX (June 30, 1947), 17.

28. Benjamin H. Pershing, "Religion in the Twentieth Century," Chapter 14, in Harlow Lindley, compiler, *Ohio in the Twentieth Century 1900–1938* (Columbus, 1942).

29. Wilbert L. Anderson, *The Country Town* (New York, 1914), Chapters 16 and 17. The book was first copyrighted in 1906. See speech, reported in full, in Ashville, Ohio, *The Pickaway County News*, May 19, 1916. In 1917, Miss Jenness Wiat read a paper on commu-

nity churches to the men's Bible class of the Rockville, Indiana, Methodist church. In reporting her paper, the local editor suggested that she must have gone to considerable work as she presented figures to show the duplication and financial waste resulting from the currently large number of churches. Rockville, Indiana, *Rockville Tribune*, March 6, 1917. "To Merge Denominations in a Community Church," *The Literary Digest*, LXIV (February 21, 1920), 37. This was a brief review of a new book by Henry Jackson, *The Community Church*.

30. "An Old Village on a New Model," *Survey*, XXXVII (March 24, 1917), 726.

31. Brunner, Hughes, and Patten, *American Agricultural Villages*, Chapters 2, 3, and, especially, 6; Brunner and Kolb, *Rural Social Trends*, Chapter 8.

32. James Street, *The Gauntlet* (New York, 1945); Homer Croy, *West of the Water Tower* (New York, 1923).

33. "The Caller from *Collier's*," "What the Folks Are Thinking About in Oskaloosa, Iowa," *Collier's*, LXXI (June 2, 1923), 26.

34. See petition against Sunday baseball in Monroe, Wisconsin, *The Journal-Gazette*, May 18, 1906; Hillsboro, Illinois, *Montgomery News*, August 17, 1915; Algona, Iowa, *The Upper Des Moines-Republican*, April 11, 1928; *Algona Upper Des Moines*, March 9, 1939.

35. Fred M. Hansen, "The Practical Program of a Village Commercial Club," *The American City*, VIII (April, 1913), 397–398; Algona, Iowa, *The Upper Des Moines-Republican*, March 7 and April 11, 1928; Chatfield, Minnesota, *Chatfield News-Democrat*, April 1, 1926; *Chatfield News*, January 30, May 7, December 10, 1936; Clinton, Wisconsin, *Rock County Banner*, April 20, October 12, 1916; Rockville, Indiana, *Rockville Tribune*, September 20, 1948.

36. The Reverend N. M. Tatum, "How a Minister Added One Hundred Members to a Village Commercial Club," *American City* (Town and Country edition), XIII (September, 1915), 193–196.

37. Brookfield, Missouri, *Brookfield Gazette*, December 13, 1919; January 30, 1925; August 16, 1926.

38. All references are to the 1946–1947 edition of this series unless otherwise indicated. The volumes are published by Scott, Foresman and Company, Chicago, Atlanta, Dallas, and New York. The title are as follows: By William S. and Lillian Gray, *Fun With Dick and Jane; Our New Friends; Friends and Neighbors; More Friends and Neighbors; Streets and Roads; More Streets and Roads;* William S. Gray, Marion Monroe, and May Hill Arbuthnot, *Times and Places; Days and Deeds* (1947–1948 edition); *People and Progress* (1947–1948 edition); *Paths and Pathfinders* (1946 edition); *Wonders and Workers* (1947 edition).

39. Gray, Monroe, and Arbuthnot, *People and Progress*, 39–40.

40. A novel by Sophia Belzer Engstrand, *Miss Munday* (New York, 1940) gives a good picture of the schoolteacher's life in small towns. See also Hollingshead, *Elmtown's Youth*, 142–147.

41. Chatfield, Minnesota, *Chatfield News-Democrat*, July 27, January 27, 1916. Gymnasiums also were used as community centers in some towns. See, "A Community Center is the Hub of Town Progress," *The American City* (Town and Country edition), XIV (January, 1916), 10–11. Also, Millington, Michigan, *The Millington Herald*, November 20, 1936.

42. Victor Holmes, *Salt of the Earth* (New York, 1941), Chapter 11,

43. Gallatin, Missouri, *North Missourian*, April 30, November 15, 1925; Chatfield, Minnesota, *Chatfield News*, May 7, 1936.

44. Edward A. Ross article cited in footnote 15; "The Corner Grocer talks about chain-store Competition to Freeman Tilden," *World's Work*, LIX (April, 1930), 61–62.

45. Hillsboro, Illinois, *Montgomery News*, May 26, 1905; Monroe, Wisconsin, *The Journal-Gazette*, June 12, 15, 1906; Algona, Iowa, *Upper Des Moines-Republican*, July 8, 1908; Rockville, Indiana, *Rockville Tribune*, August 7, 1917.

46. Rockville, Indiana, *Rockville Republican*, August 12, 1926; Gay MacLaren, *Morally We Roll Along* (Boston, 1938), 176–177.

47. Gallatin, Missouri, *North Missourian*, July 30, 1909; Brookfield, Missouri, *Brookfield Gazette*, April 25, 1924.

48. Hillsboro, Illinois, *Montgomery News*, January 3, 1935; May 27, June 3, 1935; May 28, 1945.

49. Doris A. Pearson, "Dassel: Past and Present. A survey of Recent Changes in an Agricultural Community," typewritten manuscript, 1940, Minnesota Historical Society, St. Paul.

50. Bruce Bliven, "A Stroll on Main Street," *The New Republic*, XXXVII (December 12, 1923), 63–66.

51. John R. McMahon, "Our Jazz-Spotted Middle West. Small Towns and Rural Districts Need Clean-Up as Well as Chicago and Kansas City," *The Ladies' Home Journal*, XXXIX (February, 1922), 38, 181.

52. Elsie Baier, "How a Small Town Educates Its Youth," *Survey*, LIV (April 15, 1925), 90–92.

53. Marquis W. Childs, "Mid-Western Nights' Entertainment," *The American Mercury*, XV (October, 1928), 169–174.

54. Algona, Iowa, *Upper Des Moines-Republican*, March 14, 1928.

55. Terry Ramsaye, *A Million and One Nights: A History of the Motion Picture* (New York, 1926), I, 391–392, 473–474.

56. Clinton, Wisconsin, *Rock County Banner*, March 9, April 20, 1916; Chatfield, Minnesota, *Chatfield News-Democrat*, September 14, November 2, 1916.

57. See, for example, Emerson Price, *Inn of that Journey* (Caldwell, Idaho, 1939); Paul Corey, *County Seat* (Indianapolis, 1941).

58. August Derleth, *Village Year: A Sac Prairie Journal* (Sauk City, Wisconsin, 1948), 149.

59. Hollingshead, *Elmtown's Youth*, 414–436.

60. Algona, Iowa, *Upper Des Moines-Republican*, June 24, 1908; Hansen article cited in footnote 35.

61. Monroe, Wisconsin, *The Journal-Gazette*, August 14, September 11, 21, 1906; Macon, Missouri, report cited in Gallatin, Missouri, *North Missourian*, February 12, 1909.

62. Chatfield, Minnesota, *Chatfield News-Democrat* (supplement to *News*), May 24, 1906; Ashville, Ohio, *The Pickaway County News*, August 19, 1926; Rockville, Indiana, *Rockville Republican*, February 4, 1926.

63. George M. Elwell, "How One Small Town Has Acquired a Community House," *The American City*, XXV (November, 1921), 392–393; Moe and Taylor study cited in footnote 26; Ashville, Ohio, *The Pickaway County News*, January 16, 1936.

64. Moe and Taylor study and West book cited in footnote 26.

65. Brunner, Hughes, and Patten, *American Agricultural Villages*, Chapter 7.

66. Hollingshead, *Elmtown's Youth*, 83.

67. Hillsboro, Illinois, *Montgomery News*, February 9, 1915.

68. Hollingshead, *Elmtown's Youth*, 90, 95.

69. *Ibid.*, 29.

70. Wayne Wheeler, *Social Stratification in a Plains Community* (Minneapolis, 1949), 38–54.

71. See unit five in Gray, Monroe and Arbuthnot, *Times and Places* and unit five in Gray, Monroe and Arbuthnot, *Days and Deeds* and unit five in Gray, Monroe and Arbuthnot, *People and Progress*. Unit six in *Times and Places* and unit six in *Days and Deeds* present a realistic treatment of the animal world.

72. Hillsboro, Illinois, *Montgomery News*, August 6, 1915; Rockville, Indiana, *Rockville Tribune*, August 7, 1917; Algona, Iowa, *Upper Des Moines-Republican*, July 17, 1918.

73. Rockville, Indiana, *Rockville Tribune*, August 7, 1917; Algona, Iowa, *Upper Des Moines-Republican*, May 15, 1918; Brookfield, Missouri, *Brookfield Gazette*, April 6, 1918.

74. Algona, Iowa, *Upper Des Moines-Republican*, November 13, 1918.

75. See, for example, Klan advertisement in Sandusky, Michigan, *Sandusky Tribune*, May 29, 1925; Rockville, Indiana, *Rockville Republican*, November 25, 1926.

CHAPTER IX.   THE CITY COMES TO MAIN STREET

1. Rockville, Indiana, *Rockville Tribune*, March 4, 1948.
2. Gallatin, Missouri, *North Missourian*, October 22, 1925.
3. Altamont news in *ibid.*, February 5, 1909.
4. August Derleth, *Village Year: A Sac Prairie Journal* (Sauk City, Wisconsin, 1948), 13, 161.
5. Clinton, Wisconsin, *Clinton Times Observer*, December 10, 1926.
6. Derleth, *Village Year*, 114.
7. Paul J. Jehlik and Ray E. Wakeley, *Rural Organization in Process. A Case Study of Hamilton County, Iowa*, Agricultural Experiment Station Bulletin, Iowa State College Research Bulletin No. 365, Ames, Iowa, September, 1949. These researches found that during 1948 farm families exchanged 53 visits, village families 37, and county-seat families only 33 visits.
8. E. Brunner, G. S. Hughes, and M. Patten, *American Agricultural Villages* (New York, 1927), Chapter 7.
9. Ruth Suckow, *Iowa Interiors* (New York, 1926).
10. Rockville, Indiana, *Rockville Tribune*, September 20, 1905.
11. Mary Jean Nesbitt, "Small-Town Girl," *Ladies' Home Journal*, LXIII (July, 1946), 136, 157. See also Margaret Weymouth Jackson, "This is My America—A State that is one proud family of Home-Town Folks," *American Magazine*, CXV (February, 1933), 38–39, 138–142. The state is Indiana, and the author draws her illustrations of town discipline from Spencer, Indiana.
12. Phil Stong, "State Fair," condensed from *Holiday* in *Reader's Digest*, LIII (October, 1948), 33–37; Hillsboro, Illinois, *Montgomery News*, January 3, 1935.
13. Gallatin, Missouri, *North Missourian*, February 3, 1899.
14. Croswell, Michigan, *Sanilac Jeffersonian*, January 14, 1898.
15. Louis Dwight Harvell Weld, *Social and Economic Survey of a Community in the Red River Valley*, University of Minnesota, Current Problems No. 4, Minneapolis, January, 1915, 74–75.
16. William Maxwell, *Time Will Darken It* (New York, 1948), 199–201.
17. Hillsboro, Illinois, *Montgomery News*, April 27, 1915, January 3, 1935.
18. Rockville, Indiana, *Rockville Tribune*, July 3, 1917; Gallatin, Missouri, *North Missourian*, February 21, 1935.
19. Hillsboro, Illinois, *Montgomery News*, January 3, February 7, 1935.
20. Gallatin, Missouri, *North Missourian*, December 11, 1908, and

October 1, 1925; Clinton, Wisconsin, *Rock County Banner*, September 7, 1916; see also Allen D. Albert, "Where the Prairie Money Goes," *Scribner's Magazine*, LXXXII (October, 1927), 476–480. This is a report on a survey of Edgar County, Illinois, in the middle twenties for manufacturing plants interested in the midwestern market. At the time, two-thirds of the citizens of the county were said to have phonographs, and half owned radios. See also for a 1925 survey Perry P. Denune, *The Social and Economic Relations of the Farmers with the Towns in Pickaway County, Ohio*, Ohio State University Bureau of Business Research, Columbus, 1927, table on page 30.

21. Millington, Michigan, *Millington Herald*, August 21, 1936; Rockville, Indiana, *Rockville Republican*, March 18, June 10, and July 15, 1937; Chatfield, Minnesota, Chatfield News, October 10, 1946; Gallatin, Missouri, *North Missourian*, April 4, 1935.

22. Martin Quigley, Jr., *Magic Shadows: The Story of the Origin of Motion Pictures* (Washington, D. C., 1948), 133–134, 137; Terry Ramsaye, *A Million and One Nights: A History of the Motion Picture* (New York, 1926), I, 260–267, 301, 313–314, 362, 391–392, 603–606, 681.

23. The preceding account is based on Rockville Indiana, *Rockville Tribune*, June 28, 1905; Monroe, Wisconsin, *Journal-Gazette*, July 24, 1906; Gallatin, Missouri, *North Missourian*, January 29, 1909 and February 11, 1915; Algona, Iowa, *Upper Des Moines-Republican*, March 11, April 22, July 15, and September 2, 16, 23, 1908; Chatfield, Minnesota, *Chatfield News-Democrat*, May 25 and June 15, 1916; John H. Kolb and LeRoy J. Day, *Interdependence in Town & Country Relations in Rural Society*, University of Wisconsin Research Bulletin No. 172, Madison, December, 1950, 46.

24. Gallatin, Missouri, *North Missourian*, March 11, 1915; Ashville, Ohio, *Pickaway County News*, July 22, 1926.

25. Brunner, Hughes, and Patten, *American Agricultural Villages*, Chapter 7; see also Gallatin, Missouri, *North Missourian*, March 5, 1925, for Eastern Star activities.

26. The preceding pages relating to high schools are based on Millington, Michigan, *Millington Herald*, February 21, 28, March 13, June 19 and 26, 1936; Chatfield, Minnesota, *Chatfield News*, September 12, 1946; Gallatin, Missouri, *North Missourian*, May 7, 1909; Hillsboro, Illinois, *Montgomery News*, May 12, 1905; Ashville, Ohio, *Pickaway County News*, July 14, 1916.

27. Gallatin, Missouri, *North Missourian*, November 4, 11, 18, 1898; Rockville, Indiana, *Rockville Tribune*, October 11 and December 6, 1905, and October 7, 1948; Chatfield, Minnesota, *Chatfield News-Democrat*, January 4 and April 26, 1906; Millington, Michigan, *Millington Herald*, September, October, November issues, 1936 and

January 11, 1946; Algona, Iowa, *Algona Upper Des Moines*, March 23, April 13, and November 9, 1948; Hillsboro, Illinois, *Montgomery News*, May 12, 1905; Monroe, Wisconsin, *Journal-Gazette*, June 15, 1906; Algona, Iowa, *Upper Des Moines-Republican*, April 10, 1918.

28. Chatfield, Minnesota, *Chatfield News-Democrat*, January 18, February 22, 1906; Millington, Michigan, *Millington Herald*, March 27, April 3, October 2, 1936, and January 25, 1946.

29. Chatfield, Minnesota, *Chatfield News-Democrat*, January 27, 1916 and January 21, 1936; Ashville, Ohio, *Pickaway County News*, February 25 and October 7, 1926; Millington, Michigan, *Millington Herald*, January 25, 1946, February 21, 28, and September 18, 1936.

30. Millington, Michigan, *Millington Herald*, June 5, 1936, January 25, February 22, and October 11, 1946; Algona, Iowa, *Upper Des Moines-Republican*, May 2, 1928; Ashville, Ohio, *Pickaway County News*, June 2, 1916; Clinton, Wisconsin, *Clinton Times Observer*, May 28, 1936.

31. Millington, Michigan, *Millington Herald*, January 31 and February 7, 1936.

32. Rockville, Indiana, *Rockville Republican*, September 30, 1937; Algona, Iowa, *Upper Des Moines-Republican*, October 17, 1928.

33. Algona, Iowa, *Upper Des Moines-Republican*, July 29, 1908; Hastings, Michigan, *Hastings Banner*, September 7, 1910.

34. Monroe, Wisconsin, *Journal-Gazette*, September 11 and 18, 1906; Arthur Ruhl, "At the County Fair," *Collier's*, LI (August 16, 1913), 20–21; Chatfield, Minnesota, *Chatfield News-Democrat*, August 19, 1926; Rockville, Indiana, *Rockville Republican*, January 28 and September 2, 1937; *Rockville Tribune*, September 27, 1948.

35. Brunner, Hughes, and Patten, *American Agricultural Villages*, Chapter 7; Algona, Iowa, *Upper Des Moines-Republican*, January 4, 1928, reporting summaries of news from preceding year; Ashville, Ohio, *Pickaway County News*, October 28, 1926. For a good description of the daily program of one of the Pumpkin Shows see the same paper for October 6, 1916. See also novel by Minnie Hite Moody, *Old Home Week* (New York, 1938) for a picture of town "days." See also Michael Costello, "The Clipper Girls," condensed from *Independent Woman* in *Reader's Digest*, XXXVIII (March, 1941), 64–66.

36. Hillsboro, Illinois, *Montgomery News*, August 1, 5, 8, 22, 26, 1935; Algona, Iowa, *Upper Des Moines-Republican*, July 3, 17, 1928.

37. Hillsboro, Illinois, *Montgomery News*, October 22, 1945; Monticello, Wisconsin, *Monticello Messenger*, October 21, 1948; Clinton, Wisconsin, *Clinton Times Observer*, September 24, 1926, and October 1, 1936.

38. Algona, Iowa, *Upper Des Moines-Republican*, November 14, 1928; *Algona Upper Des Moines*, November 2, 1939, November 2,

16, 1948; Monticello, Wisconsin, *Monticello Messenger*, November 25, 1948; Rockville, Indiana, *Rockville Tribune*, November 4, 1948; Clinton, Wisconsin, *Clinton Times Observer*, September 24, October 22, 1926, and November 5, 1936.

39. Hillsboro, Illinois, *Montgomery News*, December 15, 29, 1905. For other examples of Christmas letters to Santa see *ibid.*, December 24, 1945, and Gallatin, Missouri, *North Missourian*, December 11, 1908. Missouri and Illinois papers were most addicted to publishing such letters. Monroe, Wisconsin, *Journal-Gazette*, December 7, 1906; Brookfield, Missouri, *Brookfield Gazette*, December 16, 1911; Ashville, Ohio, *Pickaway County News*, October 13 and December 8, 1916.

40. Ashville, Ohio, *Pickaway County News*, December 23, 1926; Algona, Iowa, *Algona Upper Des Moines*, October 12 and November 30, 1939; *Upper Des Moines-Republican*, December 5, 1928; Hillsboro, Illinois, *Montgomery News*, December 23, 1935; Rockville, Indiana, *Rockville Republican*, December 23, 1937; Clinton, Wisconsin, *Clinton Times Observer*, November 19, 1936.

41. Chatfield, Minnesota, *Chatfield News-Democrat*, December 30, 1926; Hillsboro, Illinois, *Montgomery News*, January 3, 1935; Gallatin, Missouri, *North Missourian*, December 26, 1935. See issue of May 23, 1935 for description of the Pattonsburg movie house.

42. Hillsboro, Illinois, *Montgomery News*, February 12, 1915, and December 30, 1935; Ashville, Ohio, *Pickaway County News*, January 14, 1926; Millington, Michigan, *Millington Herald*, April 10, 1936; Rockville, Indiana, *Rockville Tribune*, April 19, 1905; Gallatin, Missouri, *North Missourian*, February 26, 1925.

43. Chatfield, Minnesota, *Chatfield News-Democrat*, January 11, 1906, and March 4, 1926. The issue of January 4, 1906, also speaks of a winter indoor softball league. Indoor winter ball was also played in Michigan. See also Gallatin, Missouri, *North Missourian*, January 23, 1909; Clinton, Wisconsin, *Rock County Banner*, February 17, 1916.

44. Chatfield, Minnesota, *Chatfield News*, February 6, 1936.

45. Gallatin, Missouri, *North Missourian*, April 25, 1935; Rockville, Indiana, *Rockville Republican*, March 18, 1937; Chatfield, Minnesota, *Chatfield News*, April 18, 1946.

46. Rockville, Indiana, *Rockville Republican*, June 3, 1926, May 20, and 27, 1937; Gallatin, Missouri, *North Missourian*, May 28, 1925 and July 4, 1935; Millington, Michigan, *Millington Herald*, May 24, 1946 and May 29, 1936; Algona, Iowa, *Upper Des Moines-Republican*, May 23, 1928; *Algona Upper Des Moines*, May 25, 1948; Chatfield, Minnesota, *Chatfield News*, May 16, 1946.

47. The foregoing account of baseball is based on the Chatfield, Minnesota, *Chatfield News-Democrat*, January 11, March 1, 1906, and March 23, 1916; Gallatin, Missouri, *North Missourian*, September 2,

1898; April 9, 1909, July 4, 11, 18, and August 15, 1935; Clinton, Wisconsin, *Rock County Banner*, July 20, 1916; Hillsboro Illinois, *Montgomery News*, August 1, 1935; Rockville, Indiana, *Rockville Republican*, June 24, July 1, 8, and 15, 1937.

48. Clinton, Wisconsin, *Rock County Banner*, August 10 and 24, 1916; Ashville, Ohio, *Pickaway County News*, July 28, August 11, 1916, and July 29, 1926; Algona, Iowa, *Upper Des Moines-Republican*, April 22, 1908.

49. Ashville, Ohio, *Pickaway County News*, June 9, 1916; Rockville, Indiana, *Rockville Republican*, July 15, 1937.

50. Chatfield, Minnesota, *Chatfield News-Democrat*, April 1, July 1 and 8, 1926; Monticello, Wisconsin, *Monticello Messenger*, July 1, 1948; Hillsboro, Illinois, *Montgomery News*, July 5, 1945.

51. Hillsboro, Illinois, *Montgomery News*, May 4, 1915.

52. Monroe, Wisconsin, *Journal-Gazette*, April 10, May 18, June 8, 26, 29, July 3, 24, 31, 1906; Algona, Iowa, *Upper Des Moines-Republican*, July 10 and 24, 1918.

53. Gay MacLaren, *Morally We Roll Along* (Boston, 1938), 75, 78.

54. Clinton, Wisconsin, *Clinton Times Observer*, March 3 and April 2, 1926.

55. MacLaren, *Morally We Roll Along*, 151, 178–179, 164–165. Quotation on pages 164–165.

56. Thomas W. Duncan, *O, Chautauqua* (New York, 1935).

57. Hillsboro, Illinois, *Montgomery News*, August 17, 1915; Ashville, Ohio, *Pickaway County News*, September 1, 1916; Clinton, Wisconsin, *Rock County Banner*, June 29, 1916.

58. See, for example, James W. Conlin, "The Merom Bluff Chautauqua," *Indiana Magazine of History*, XXXVI (March, 1940), 23–29. Also, "Winona Woman's Club Book 1903–1907," Indiana State Library. This related to the Winona Lake Chautauqua Assembly. Most newspaper references before 1910 are concerned with independent Chautauquas.

59. MacLaren, *Morally We Roll Along*, 79.

60. Algona, Iowa, *Upper Des Moines-Republican*, April 10, 1918; Gallatin, Missouri, *North Missourian*, August 5, 12, 26, 1915; Rockville, Indiana, *Rockville Tribune*, August 7, 1917; Ashville, Ohio, *Pickaway County News*, June 23, 1916 and July 29, 1926.

61. MacLaren, *Morally We Roll Along*, 207.

62. Algona, Iowa, *Upper Des Moines-Republican*, July 8, 1908.

63. Duncan, *O, Chautauqua*, 133.

64. Rockville, Indiana, *Rockville Republican*, August 12 and 19, 1926; Clinton, Wisconsin, *Clinton Times Observer*, July 16 and 30, 1926.

65. MacLaren, *Morally We Roll Along*, 294–295.

66. Algona, Iowa, *Upper Des Moines-Republican,* July 11, 1928.

67. Hillsboro, Illinois, *Montgomery News,* April 9, 1945; Ashville, Ohio, *Pickaway County News,* July 29, 1926; Millington, Michigan, *Millington Herald,* July 26, 1946; "Some Small Communities at Play," *Recreation,* XXXVI (August, 1942), 291–295.

CHAPTER X.   PROGRESS—HOPES AND REALITIES

1. Booth Tarkington, *The Magnificent Ambersons* (New York, 1918), 388–389.

2. Brookfield, Missouri, *Brookfield Gazette,* February 18, 1886.

3. Gallatin, Missouri, *North Missourian,* May 14, 1909.

4. For example, Brookfield, Missouri, organized a Board of Trade in 1888; a Commercial Club in 1891 and again in 1900; a Retail Merchants' Association in 1903 which considered more than mercantile problems; Brookfield Improvement Association in 1905; Commercial Club in 1907; county Chamber of Commerce in 1919; Brookfield Chamber of Commerce in 1926. The names and dates are compiled from the *Brookfield Gazette.* Alma, Michigan, on the other hand, first organized a Business Man's Improvement Association in 1886; a Board of Trade 1901–1920; a Chamber of Commerce 1920–1929; and a Booster's Club in 1932. See Arthur Weimer, "Outline of the Economic History of Alma, Michigan Prior to 1900," *Michigan History Magazine,* XIX (Winter Number, 1935), 129–138 and "Determining Factors in the Economic Development of Alma," *ibid.* (Autumn Number), 1405–1410.

5. Brookfield, Missouri, *Brookfield Gazette,* December 2, 1871; May 29, September 4, 1873; May 26, 1875; April 26, July 5, 1877; September 6, 1888; August 12, 19, October 8, November 25, 1892; July 22, September 2, 1893. For other examples of early post-Civil War newspaper support of manufacturing see Algona, Iowa, *The Upper Des Moines,* January 10, 1867; Lacon, Illinois, *Lacon Gazette,* November 1, 1865; Greencastle, Indiana, *Putnam Republican Banner,* July 4, 1867; Tiffin, Ohio, *Tiffin Tribune,* May 13, 1869.

6. Russell S. McClure, "The Natural Gas Era in Northwestern Ohio," *Quarterly Bulletin* (Historical Society of Northwestern Ohio), XIV (1942), 83–105.

7. Brookfield, Missouri, *Brookfield Gazette,* July 21, August 11, November 3, 1887. For other examples of interest in local mineral resources see Centreville, Michigan, *St. Joseph County Republican,* March 24, 1888 and Hillsboro, Illinois, *Montgomery News,* April 14, 1905.

8. Centreville, Michigan, *St. Joseph County Republican,* July 24, 1869; Brookfield, Missouri, *Brookfield Gazette,* March 21, 1890;

Lacon, Illinois, *Lacon Home Journal,* November 22, 1894; Hillsboro, Ohio, *Hillsboro Gazette,* January 5, 1900.

9. Julius H. Ward, "The Revival of our Country Towns," *New England Magazine* (New Series), I (November, 1889), 243–248.

10. Henry J. Fletcher, "The Doom of the Small Town," *The Forum,* XIX (April, 1895), 214–223.

11. See Appendix II.

12. Brookfield, Missouri, *Linn County Budget-Gazette,* May 14, 1930; May 24, 1940.

13. Brookfield, Missouri, *Brookfield Gazette,* December 16, 23, 1905; January 13, June 9, 1906; April 13, 20, 27, June 1, 8, 15, 22, 29, July 6, 1907. Additional reports on the shoe factory and on other industrial promotions will be found in the *Brookfield Gazette* for August 17, October 5, 1907; March 14, 1908; November 20, 1909; October 28, November 11, 1911; October 10, 1914; May 13, 1916; January 27, September 29, 1917; August 24, 1918; December 6, 1919; and in the Brookfield, *Linn County Budget-Gazette,* December 9, 16, 1926; July 6, 1927; December 19, 1928; February 27, March 1, 1929; January 3, 5, 1940. For examples of industrial campaigns in other midwestern towns see Monroe, Wisconsin, *Journal-Gazette,* June 5, July 13, 1906; Algona, Iowa, *Upper Des Moines-Republican,* March 18, April 22, 1908; Hillsboro, Illinois, *Montgomery News,* July 11, 18, 1935; June 4, 25, November 8, 1945; Hastings, Michigan, *Hastings Banner,* January 12, February 2, 1910; Circleville, Ohio, *Pickaway County News,* January 14, 1916; Chatfield, Minnesota, *Chatfield News,* June 27, July 18, August 15, 1946.

14. Brookfield, Missouri, *Brookfield Gazette,* November 12, 1898.

15. Quoted in Dale Kramer, "Want a Factory?" *Survey Graphic,* XXIX (August, 1940), 438–441, 446–447.

16. Ed Howe, *The Story of a Country Town* (New York, 1917), 228–229.

17. *Sherwood Anderson's Memoirs* (New York, 1942), 87. See also his story, *Poor White* (New York, 1920) for a similar novel-length theme.

18. W. D. Knight, *Subsidization of Industry in Forty Selected Cities in Wisconsin 1930–1946,* Wisconsin Commerce Studies Vol. 1, No. 2, University of Wisconsin School of Commerce, Bureau of Business Research and Science, Madison, 1947.

19. Clinton, Wisconsin, *Times Observer,* series beginning November 21, 1935. The quotation is from the article which appeared in the issue of December 12, 1935.

20. Gustav P. Warber, *Social and Economic Survey of a Community in Northeastern Minnesota,* Bulletin of the University of Minnesota, Current Problems, No. 5, Minneapolis, March, 1915, 61; Perry P.

Denune, *The Social and Economic Relations of the Farmers with the Towns in Pickaway County, Ohio,* Bureau of Business Research, College of Agriculture, Columbus, Ohio, 1927, p. 60.

21. See Appendix III for a description of this movement.

22. Susan Fenimore Cooper, "Village Improvement Societies," *Putnam's Magazine,* IV (September, 1869), 359–366; "A Village Street— Before and After," *House Beautiful,* XXVII (April, 1910), 127–129. Articles commonly credited Stockbridge, Massachusetts, with starting village improvement. See, for example, Anonymous, "Village Improvement Associations," *Scribner's Monthly,* XIV (May, 1877), 97–107; Mary C. Robbins, "Village Improvement Societies," *The Atlantic Monthly,* LXXIX (February, 1897), 212–222; Roger Riordan, "Village Parks and Gardens," *Chautauquan,* VIII (May, 1888), 481–483; "Topics of the Hour," *Chautauquan,* XXXII (December, 1900), 317–319. For expressed interest in village improvement associations in the Middle West see Susan F. Stone, "The Town Beautiful," *Craftsman,* VI (May, 1904), 125–129.

23. "An Old Village on a New Model," *Survey,* XXXVII (March 24, 1917), 726.

24. Alfred H. Sinks, "The Old Home Town Fights to Live," *Collier's,* CXXIV (July 2, 1949), 28–29, 70–72.

25. M. T. Buckley, "The Linking of Village and Farm," *The American City* (Town and Country edition), XII (January, 1915), 19–22; Delbert Clark, "This Town Went Rural," *Rotarian,* LX (February, 1942), 41–42.

26. Innumerable articles telling how to build a better town or a better business have appeared throughout the course of the twentieth century. How to raise money for a community house; how to build up a great retail store in a small town; how the local chamber of commerce can be of service; how to operate a commercial club; how to meet mail-order competition; how to build a balanced program; how adult education can further home-town loyalty; how to increase recreational opportunities in the small town; how to build a community art center—these and other possibilities have been explained in article after article in periodicals ranging from those of limited circulation to others appealing to millions of Americans. See, for example, "How a Little Town Built a Community House by Getting 'Good and Mad,'" *The Literary Digest,* LXII (August 30, 1919), 98, 100; "A Community Center is the Hub of Town Progress," *The American City* (Town and Country edition), XIV (January, 1916), 10–11; Albert S. Gregg, "Three Young Men With Ideas," *The American Magazine,* LXXXII (October, 1916), 30–32; "What Your Association Can Do for You," *System,* XXXII (August, 1917), 256, 258, 260–263, and subsequent issues of the same periodical; Fred M. Hansen, "A Town Commercial

Club Which Gets Results," *The American City*, X (March, 1914), 259–261; W. C. Holman, "Keeping Retail Trade at Home," *System*, XXIII (January, 1913), 13–20; John A. Piquet, "Opportunity Faces Small Cities and Towns," *The American City*, XLII (May, 1930), 97–99; Grace M. Ellis, "Where Grownups Go to School," *Rotarian*, LX (March, 1942), 40–43; "Some Small Communities at Play," *Recreation*, XXXVI (August, 1942), 291–295; Bernard Ferguson, "Community Art Center Widely Used," *The American City*, LVI (August, 1941), 85.

27. See Appendix IV for a list of the detailed surveys on which the generalizations in this section are based.

28. See Appendix V for reports of detailed surveys of shopping habits.

29. See Denune study, trade area analysis bulletin of eleven southwest Iowa towns, and Jehlik and Wakeley bulletin, all cited in Appendix IV.

30. Edward O. Moe and Carl C. Taylor, *Culture of a Contemporary Rural Community: Irwin, Iowa*, U. S. Department of Agriculture, Bureau of Agricultural Economics, *Rural Life Studies* No. 5, December, 1942.

31. Edward Marshall, "The Scientific City of the Future, An Authorized Interview with Thomas A. Edison," *The Forum*, LXXVI (December, 1926), 823–829.

32. David C. Coyle, "Belonging," *The American City*, LVI (August, 1941), 71. Belief in this approach has led distinguished Americans like Arthur E. Morgan, former administrative head of the TVA, and a college president, to work ardently for the preservation of small communities. In 1940, Morgan took the lead in establishing "Community Service, Inc.," at Yellow Springs, Ohio, to provide information and help to small communities. In 1942, he published a book whose title indicates its theme: *The Small Community: Foundation of Democratic Life. What it is and How to Achieve It* (New York, 1942). For a well-reasoned statement of the values of community life see Baker Brownell, *The Human Community. Its Philosophy and Practice for a Time of Crisis* (New York, 1950).

33. "Rural Health: Vanishing Country M.D.'s," *Newsweek*, LVI (March 24, 1947), 58–60; Steven M. Spencer, "We Need More Country Doctors," *Saturday Evening Post*, CCXXI (October 9, 1948), 36–37, 54, 59, 61–62, 64; A. R. Mangus, *Hospitals for Rural People in Ohio*, Department of Rural Economics and Rural Sociology, Mimeograph Bulletin No. 184, Ohio State University and Ohio Agricultural Experiment Station, Columbus, Ohio, February, 1945; Robert L. McNamara, *Illness in the Farm Population of Two Homogeneous Areas of Missouri*, University of Missouri College of Agriculture, Agricultural

Experiment Station, Research Bulletin, 504, July, 1952; John H. Lane, Jr., *What Has Happened to the Country Doctor?*, University of Missouri College of Agriculture, Agricultural Experiment Station, Bulletin 594, February, 1953.

34. See studies and surveys listed in Appendix IV for the source of generalizations contained in this paragraph.

APPENDIXES

1. E. Brunner, G. S. Hughes, and M. Patten, *American Agricultural Villages* (New York, 1927).

2. Edmund Brunner and J. H. Kolb, *Rural Social Trends* (New York, 1933), 85.

3. See "Mr. Roosevelt's Commission on Farm Life," *The Independent*, LXV (August 13, 1908), 341–342; "The Commission on Country Life," *World's Work*, XVII (November, 1908), 10,860–10,861. Also, George F. Wells, "Is An Organized Country Life Movement Possible?" *Survey*, XXIX (January 4, 1913), 449–456; and Dwight Sanderson, "Country-Life Forces Mobilizing," *The American Review of Reviews*, LXIII (April, 1921), 421–425; Fred Eastman, "Country Life," *Survey*, XLI (February 8, 1919), 679–680.

4. Paul Walton Black, "Community Needs and the Community Institute," *The American City* (Town and Country edition), XII (May, 1915), 390–394. The University of Wisconsin perhaps has the best claim to having inaugurated studies intended to aid directly in the solution of problems experienced by midwestern country towns, although a number of other universities rapidly introduced similar programs. Departments of Rural Sociology or men whose interests ultimately placed them in that field took the lead. In 1919, when Harlan Paul Douglass published his book, *The Little Town: Especially in Its Rural Relationships* (New York, 1919), he called attention to the studies already completed by Professor Charles J. Galpin of the University of Wisconsin, in which Galpin explored the relationships between midwestern country towns and the surrounding countryside. A Minnesota study in 1928 freely admitted that Galpin's study of town and country relationships in Walworth County, Wisconsin, started in 1911, marked the first mapping of town trade areas, although the Minnesota study claimed to go further in its analysis of merchandising relationships. See H. Bruce Price and C. R. Hoffer, *Services of Rural Trade Centers in Distribution of Farm Supplies*, University of Minnesota Agricultural Experiment Station Bulletin No. 249, University Farm, St. Paul, 1928, 8–9. Other Wisconsin men like J. H. Kolb have continued and expanded the pioneer work of Galpin. See John H. Kolb and LeRoy J. Day, *Interdependence in Town and Country Relations in*

Rural Society, University of Wisconsin, Research Bulletin No. 172, Madison, December, 1950.

5. See *Operating Expenses of Retail Grocery Stores in Nebraska 1925,* Nebraska Studies in Business, No. 17, by the Committee on Business Research of the College of Business Administration, published by the Extension Division, University of Nebraska, Lincoln, 1926; *Influence of Automobiles and Good Roads on Retail Trade Centers,* No. 18, Lincoln, 1927. Also, *Retail Trade Area Analysis: 11 Southwest Iowa Towns,* prepared by Bureau of Business and Economic Research, State University of Iowa, July, 1950; *Retail Trading Area Analysis: Osage,* prepared by Bureau of Business and Economic Research, State University of Iowa, for Osage Chamber of Commerce, Osage, Iowa, January, 1951.

6. Roland S. Vaile, ed., *The Small City and Town: A Conference on Community Relations,* Minneapolis, 1930.

7. Paul J. Jehlik and Ray E. Wakeley, *Rural Organization in Process: A Case Study of Hamilton County, Iowa,* Agricultural Experiment Station, Ames, Iowa, and Sociology Subsection, Economics and Sociology Section, Division of Farm Population and Rural Life, Bureau of Agricultural Economics, United States Department of Agriculture Cooperating, Research Bulletin No. 365, Ames, Iowa, September, 1949.

8. Richard W. Poston, *Small Town Renaissance* (New York, 1950).

9. Tables from "Nebraska Studies in Business, No. 18," cited in Appendix IV.

10. See Price and Hoffer study listed in Appendix IV.

11. Edmund Brunner and J. H. Kolb, *Rural Social Trends,* 145–146.

Index